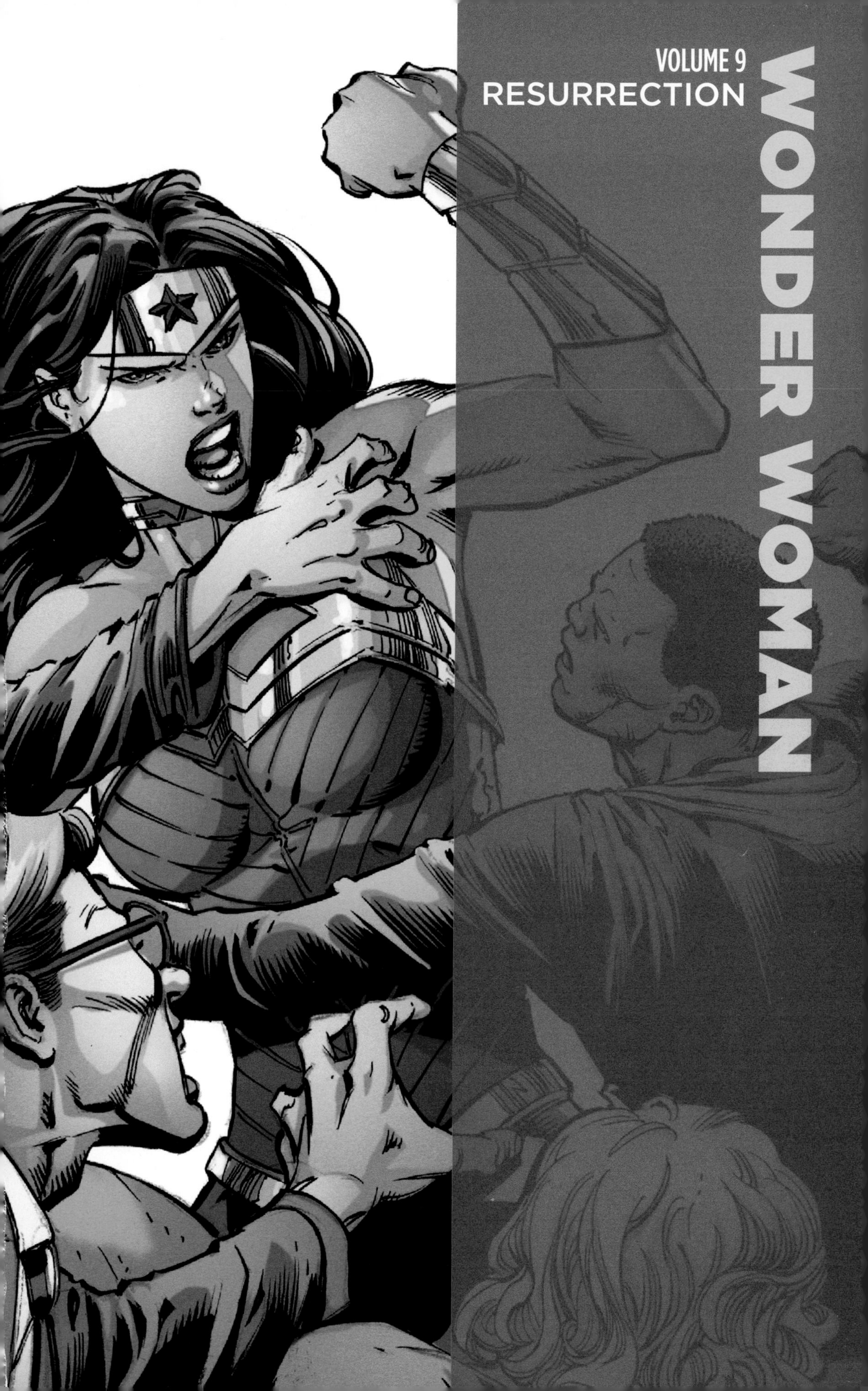
VOLUME 9
RESURRECTION
WONDER WOMAN

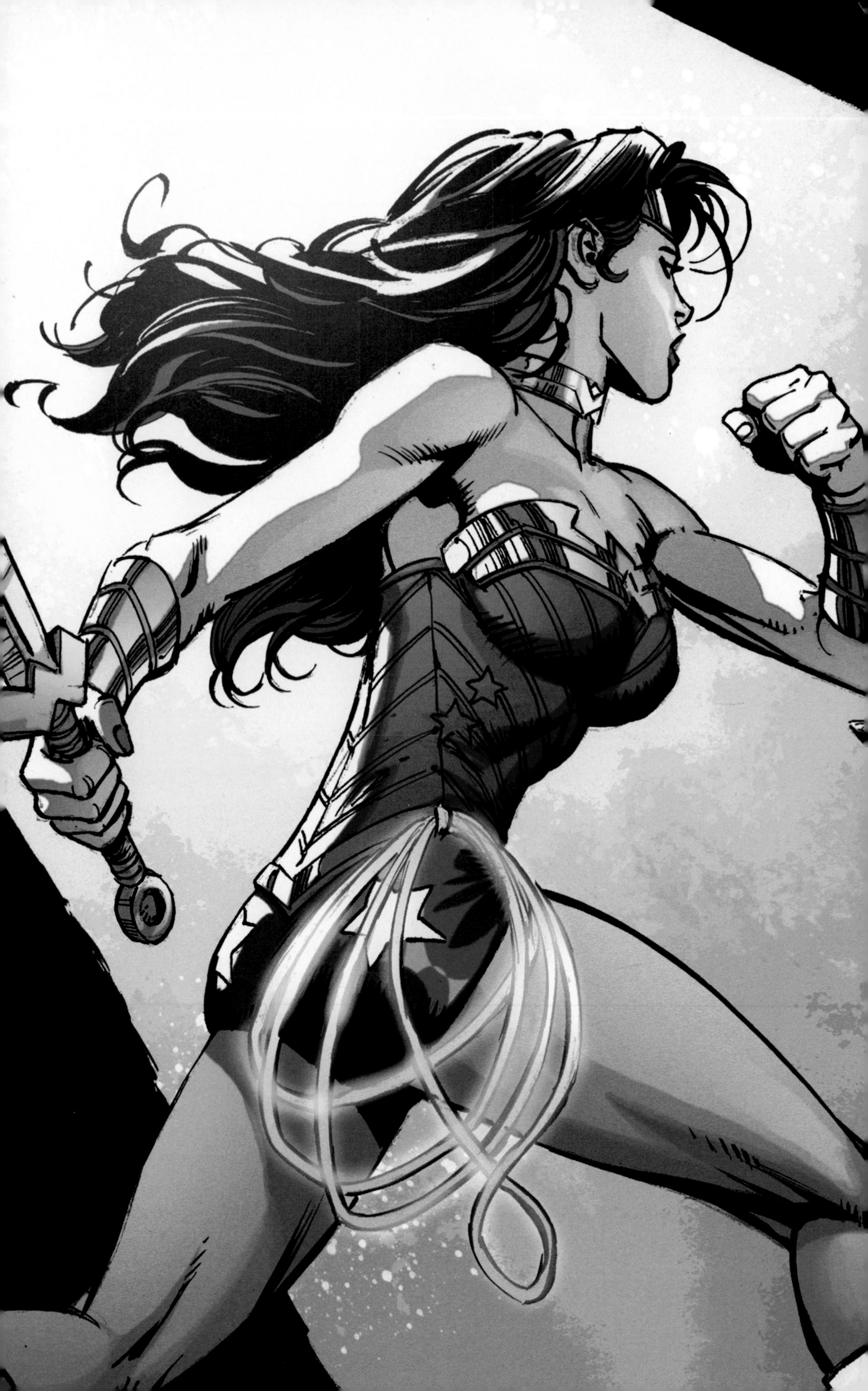

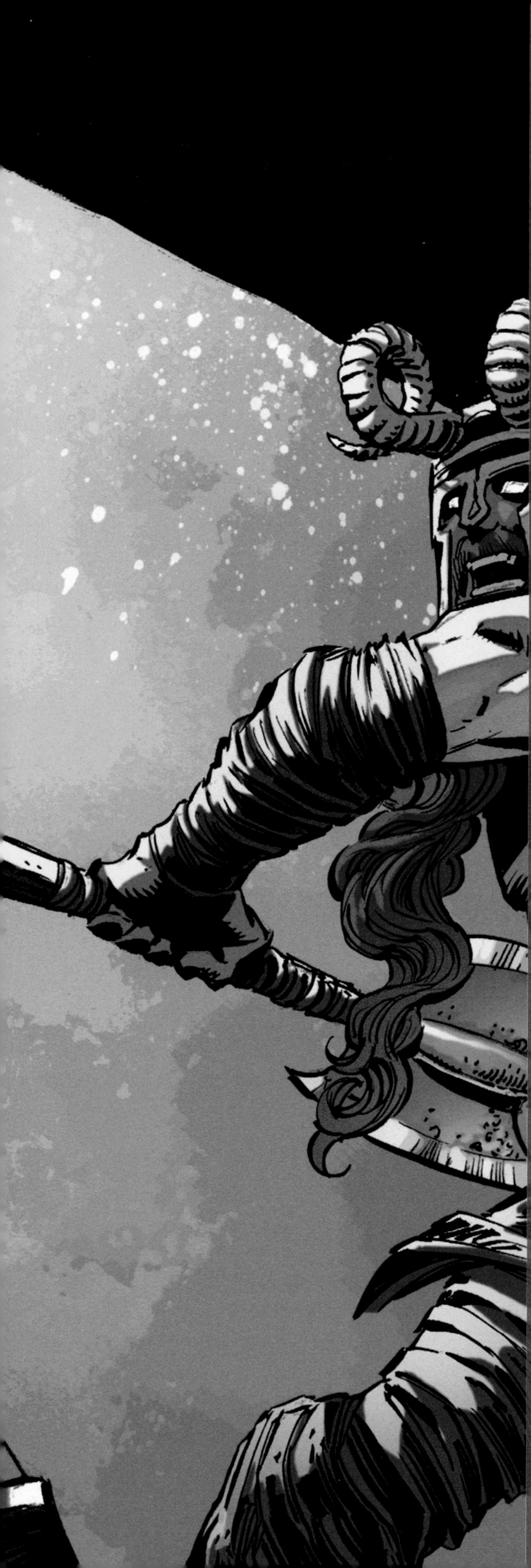

WONDER WOMAN

VOLUME 9
RESURRECTION

WRITTEN BY
MEREDITH FINCH

PENCILS BY
DAVID FINCH
JOHNNY DESJARDINS
MIGUEL MENDONÇA

INKS BY
SCOTT HANNA
DAVID FINCH
SANDU FLOREA
DEXTER VINES
DIANA EGEA
JUAN ALBARRAN

COLOR BY
BRAD ANDERSON
STEPHEN DOWNER
ULISES ARREOLA

LETTERS BY
ROB LEIGH

COLLECTION COVER ART BY
DAVID FINCH AND
BRAD ANDERSON

WONDER WOMAN CREATED BY
WILLIAM MOULTON MARSTON

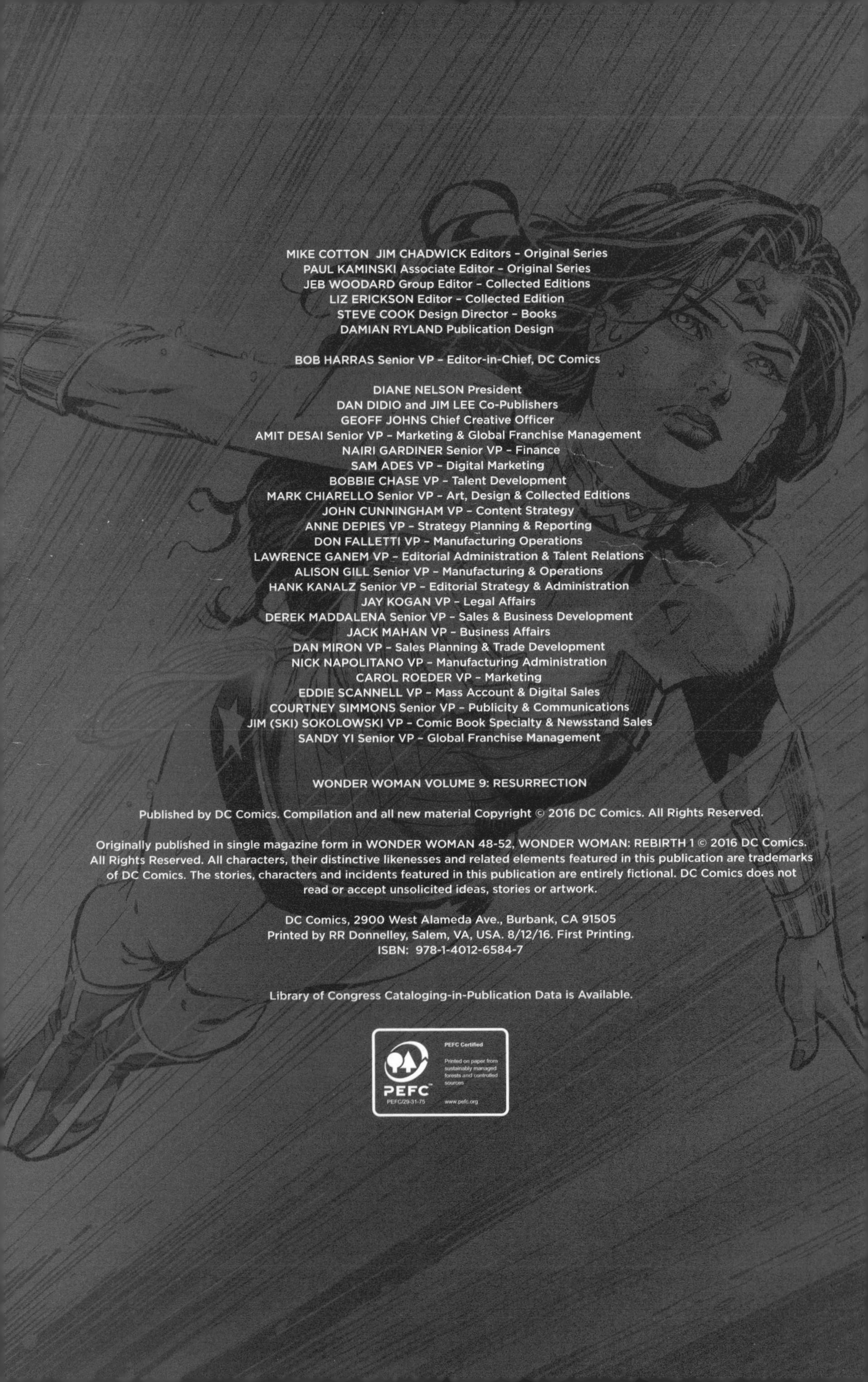

MIKE COTTON JIM CHADWICK Editors – Original Series
PAUL KAMINSKI Associate Editor – Original Series
JEB WOODARD Group Editor – Collected Editions
LIZ ERICKSON Editor – Collected Edition
STEVE COOK Design Director – Books
DAMIAN RYLAND Publication Design

BOB HARRAS Senior VP – Editor-in-Chief, DC Comics

DIANE NELSON President
DAN DIDIO and JIM LEE Co-Publishers
GEOFF JOHNS Chief Creative Officer
AMIT DESAI Senior VP – Marketing & Global Franchise Management
NAIRI GARDINER Senior VP – Finance
SAM ADES VP – Digital Marketing
BOBBIE CHASE VP – Talent Development
MARK CHIARELLO Senior VP – Art, Design & Collected Editions
JOHN CUNNINGHAM VP – Content Strategy
ANNE DEPIES VP – Strategy Planning & Reporting
DON FALLETTI VP – Manufacturing Operations
LAWRENCE GANEM VP – Editorial Administration & Talent Relations
ALISON GILL Senior VP – Manufacturing & Operations
HANK KANALZ Senior VP – Editorial Strategy & Administration
JAY KOGAN VP – Legal Affairs
DEREK MADDALENA Senior VP – Sales & Business Development
JACK MAHAN VP – Business Affairs
DAN MIRON VP – Sales Planning & Trade Development
NICK NAPOLITANO VP – Manufacturing Administration
CAROL ROEDER VP – Marketing
EDDIE SCANNELL VP – Mass Account & Digital Sales
COURTNEY SIMMONS Senior VP – Publicity & Communications
JIM (SKI) SOKOLOWSKI VP – Comic Book Specialty & Newsstand Sales
SANDY YI Senior VP – Global Franchise Management

WONDER WOMAN VOLUME 9: RESURRECTION

DC Comics, 2900 West Alameda Ave., Burbank, CA 91505
Printed by RR Donnelley, Salem, VA, USA. 8/12/16. First Printing.
ISBN: 978-1-4012-6584-7

Library of Congress Cataloging-in-Publication Data is Available.

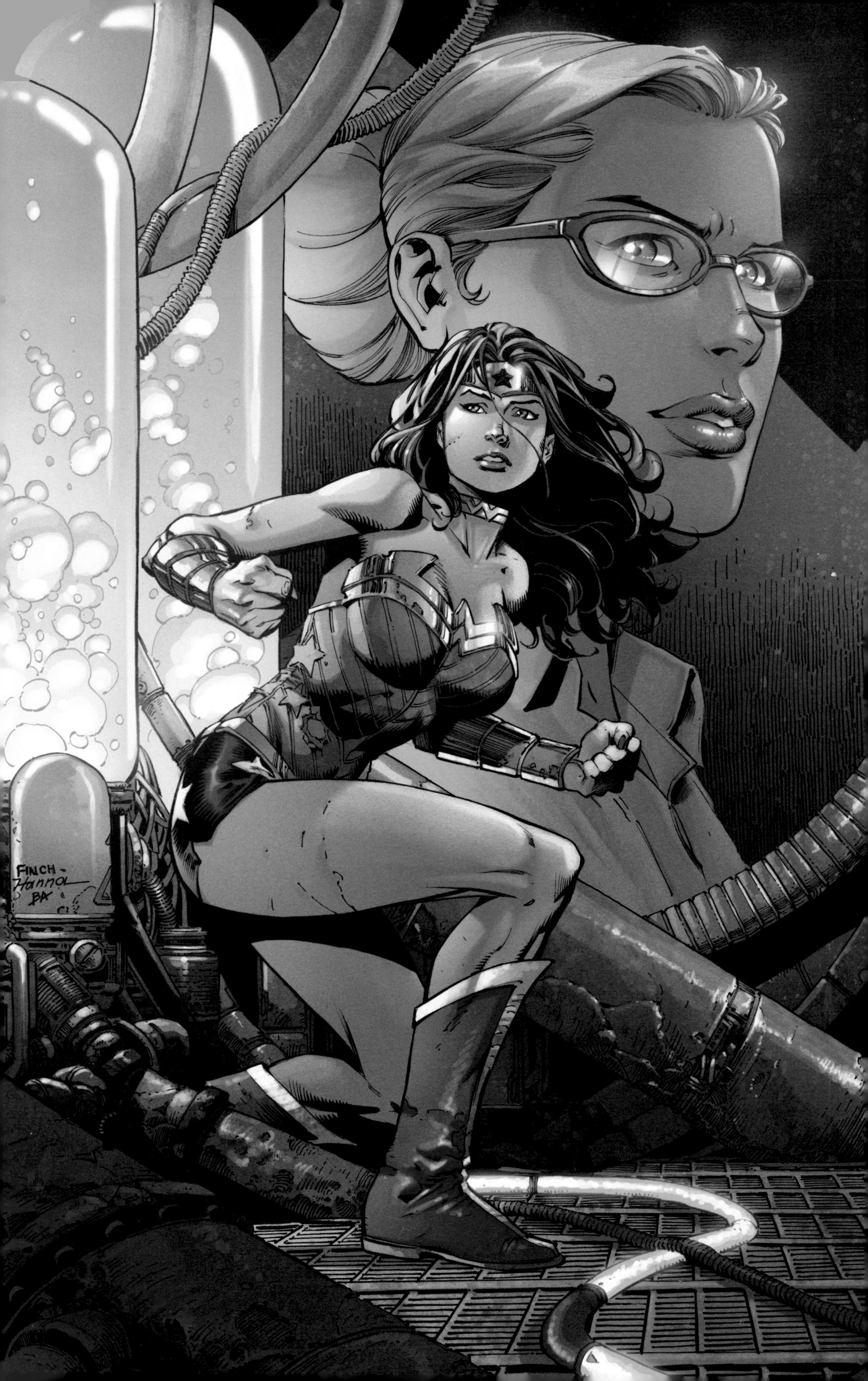
FINCH-
Hanna
BA

THE PRICE OF POISON

MEREDITH FINCH writer DAVID FINCH penciller SCOTT HANNA inker BRAD ANDERSON colorist ROB LEIGH letterer
cover art by DAVID FINCH, SCOTT HANNA & BRAD ANDERSON

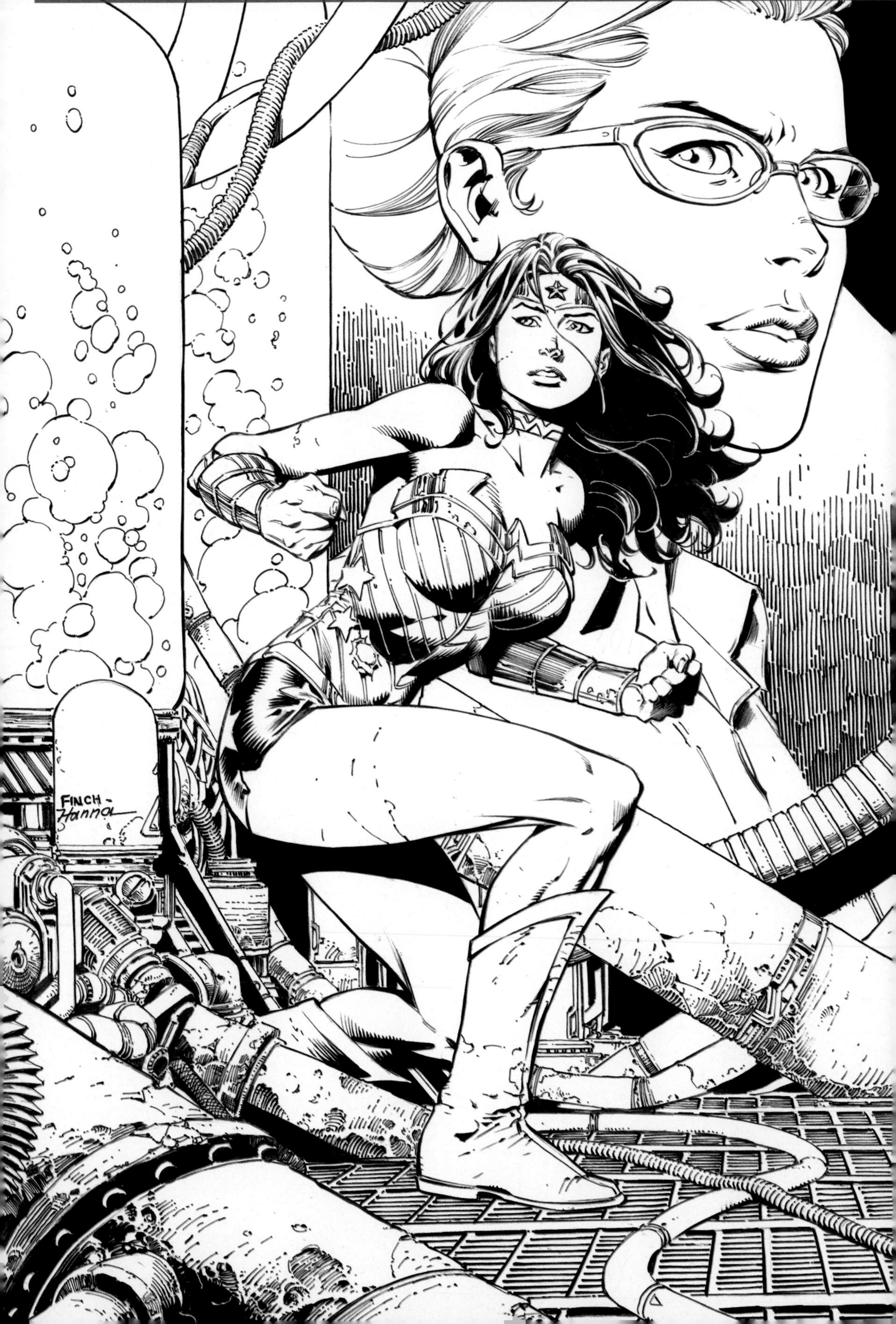
FINCH-
Hanna

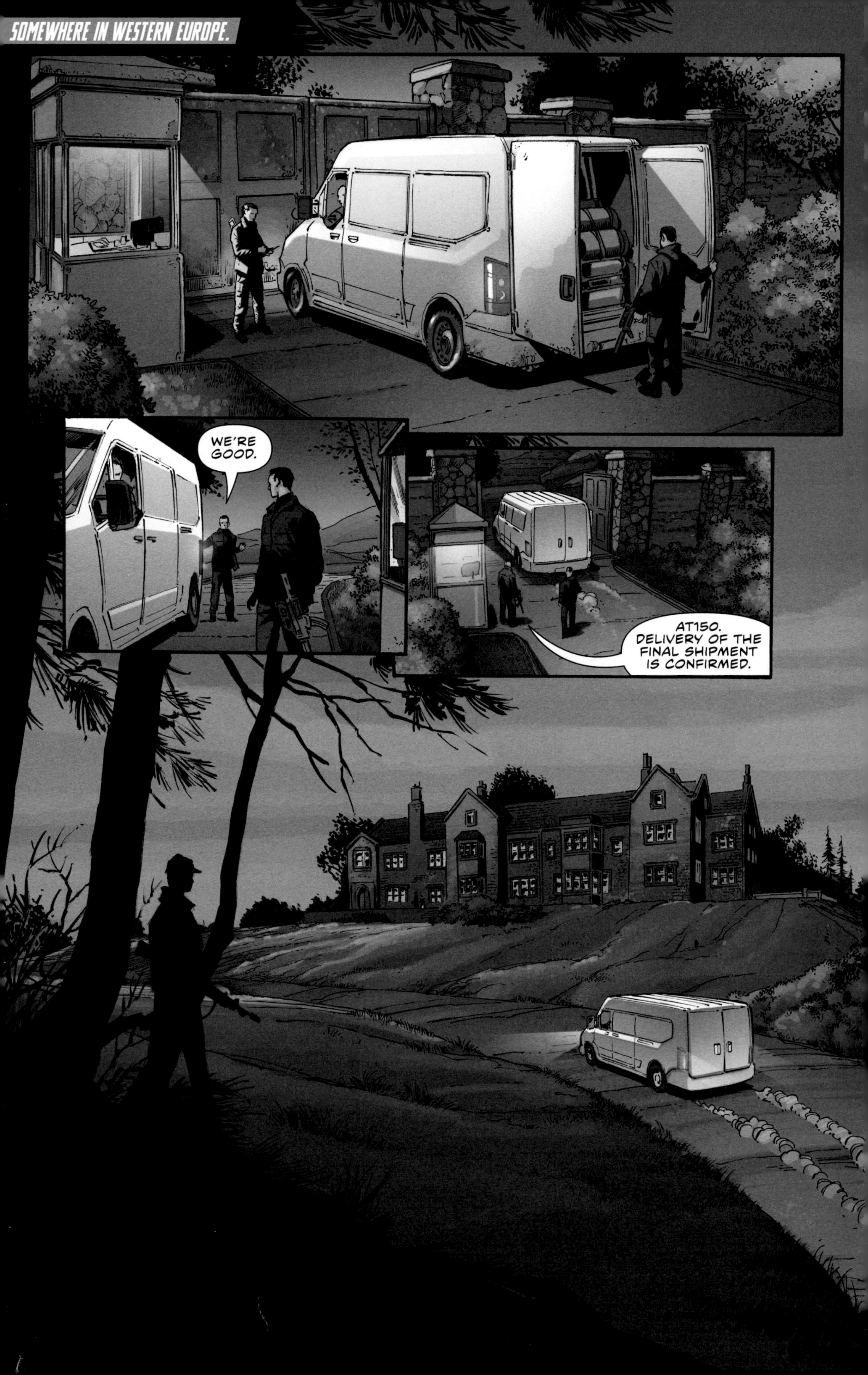
SOMEWHERE IN WESTERN EUROPE.
WE'RE GOOD.
AT150. DELIVERY OF THE FINAL SHIPMENT IS CONFIRMED.

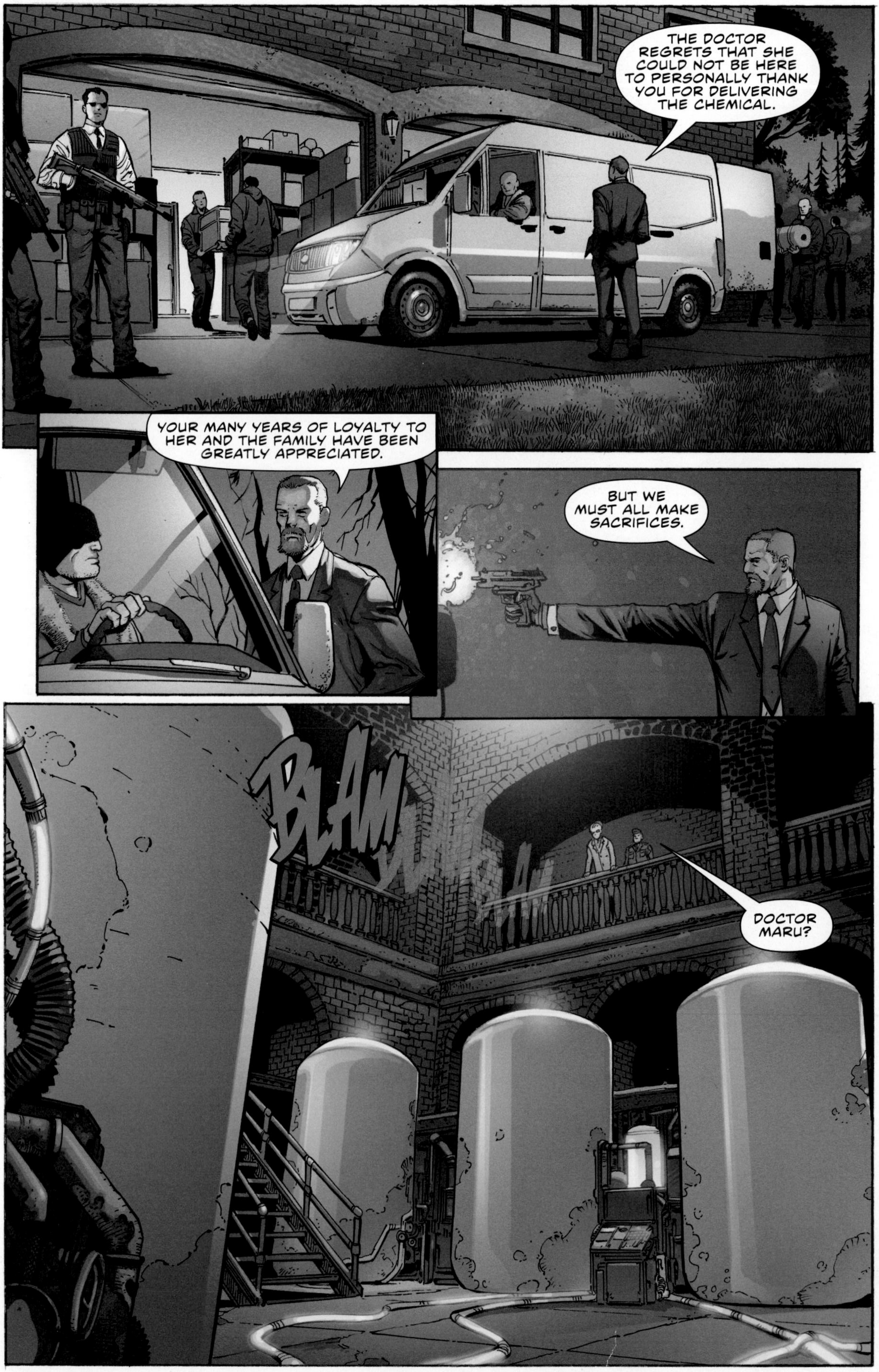
THE DOCTOR REGRETS THAT SHE COULD NOT BE HERE TO PERSONALLY THANK YOU FOR DELIVERING THE CHEMICAL.
YOUR MANY YEARS OF LOYALTY TO HER AND THE FAMILY HAVE BEEN GREATLY APPRECIATED.
BUT WE MUST ALL MAKE SACRIFICES.
BLAM
DOCTOR MARU?

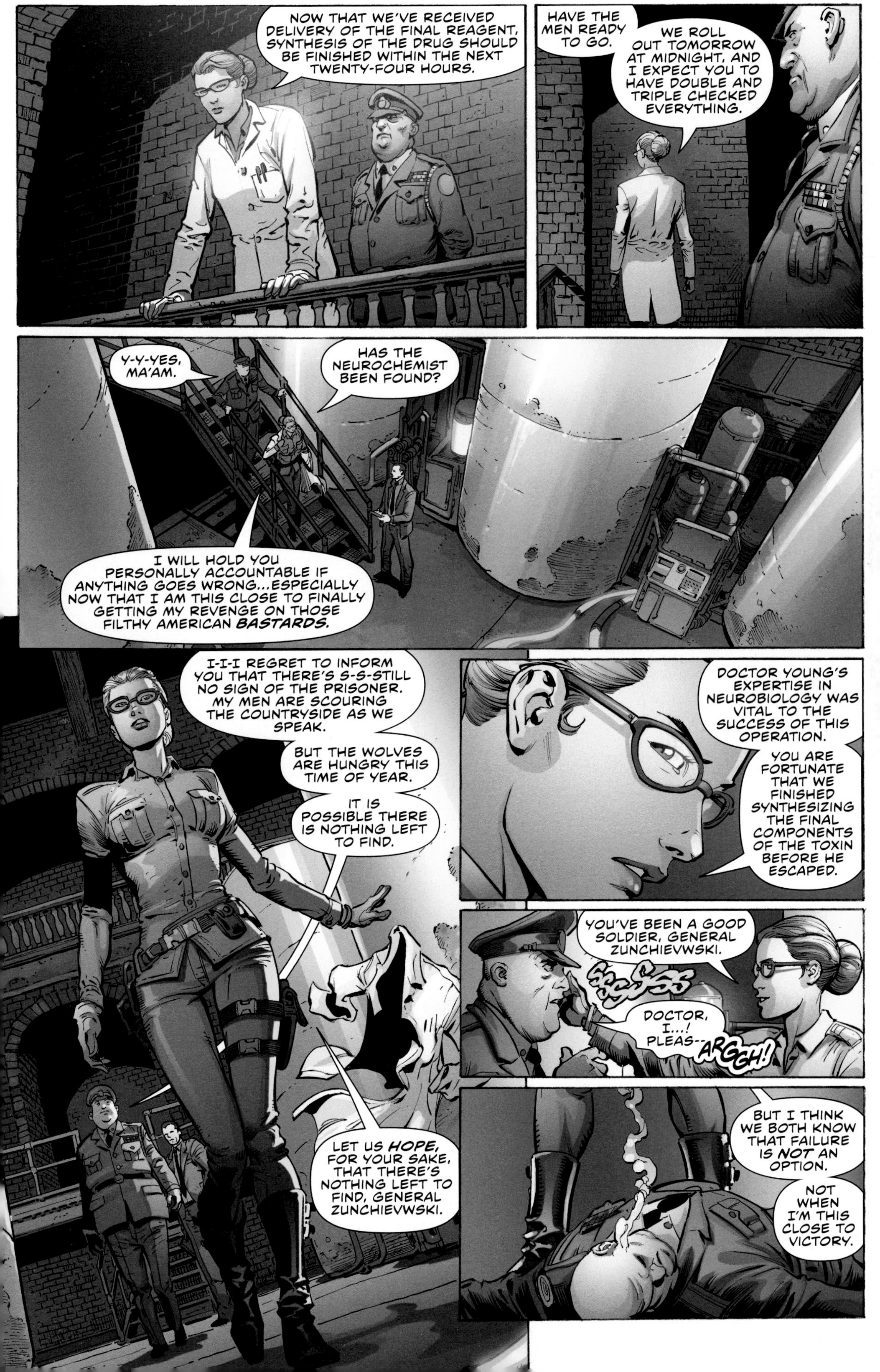
NOW THAT WE'VE RECEIVED DELIVERY OF THE FINAL REAGENT, SYNTHESIS OF THE DRUG SHOULD BE FINISHED WITHIN THE NEXT TWENTY-FOUR HOURS.
HAVE THE MEN READY TO GO.
WE ROLL OUT TOMORROW AT MIDNIGHT, AND I EXPECT YOU TO HAVE DOUBLE AND TRIPLE CHECKED EVERYTHING.
Y-Y-YES, MA'AM.
HAS THE NEUROCHEMIST BEEN FOUND?
I WILL HOLD YOU PERSONALLY ACCOUNTABLE IF ANYTHING GOES WRONG...ESPECIALLY NOW THAT I AM THIS CLOSE TO FINALLY GETTING MY REVENGE ON THOSE FILTHY AMERICAN BASTARDS.
I-I-I REGRET TO INFORM YOU THAT THERE'S S-S-STILL NO SIGN OF THE PRISONER. MY MEN ARE SCOURING THE COUNTRYSIDE AS WE SPEAK.
BUT THE WOLVES ARE HUNGRY THIS TIME OF YEAR.
IT IS POSSIBLE THERE IS NOTHING LEFT TO FIND.
LET US HOPE, FOR YOUR SAKE, THAT THERE'S NOTHING LEFT TO FIND, GENERAL ZUNCHIEVWSKI.
DOCTOR YOUNG'S EXPERTISE IN NEUROBIOLOGY WAS VITAL TO THE SUCCESS OF THIS OPERATION.
YOU ARE FORTUNATE THAT WE FINISHED SYNTHESIZING THE FINAL COMPONENTS OF THE TOXIN BEFORE HE ESCAPED.
YOU'VE BEEN A GOOD SOLDIER, GENERAL ZUNCHIEVWSKI.
SSSSSSS
DOCTOR, I...! PLEAS--
ARGGH!
BUT I THINK WE BOTH KNOW THAT FAILURE IS NOT AN OPTION.
NOT WHEN I'M THIS CLOSE TO VICTORY.

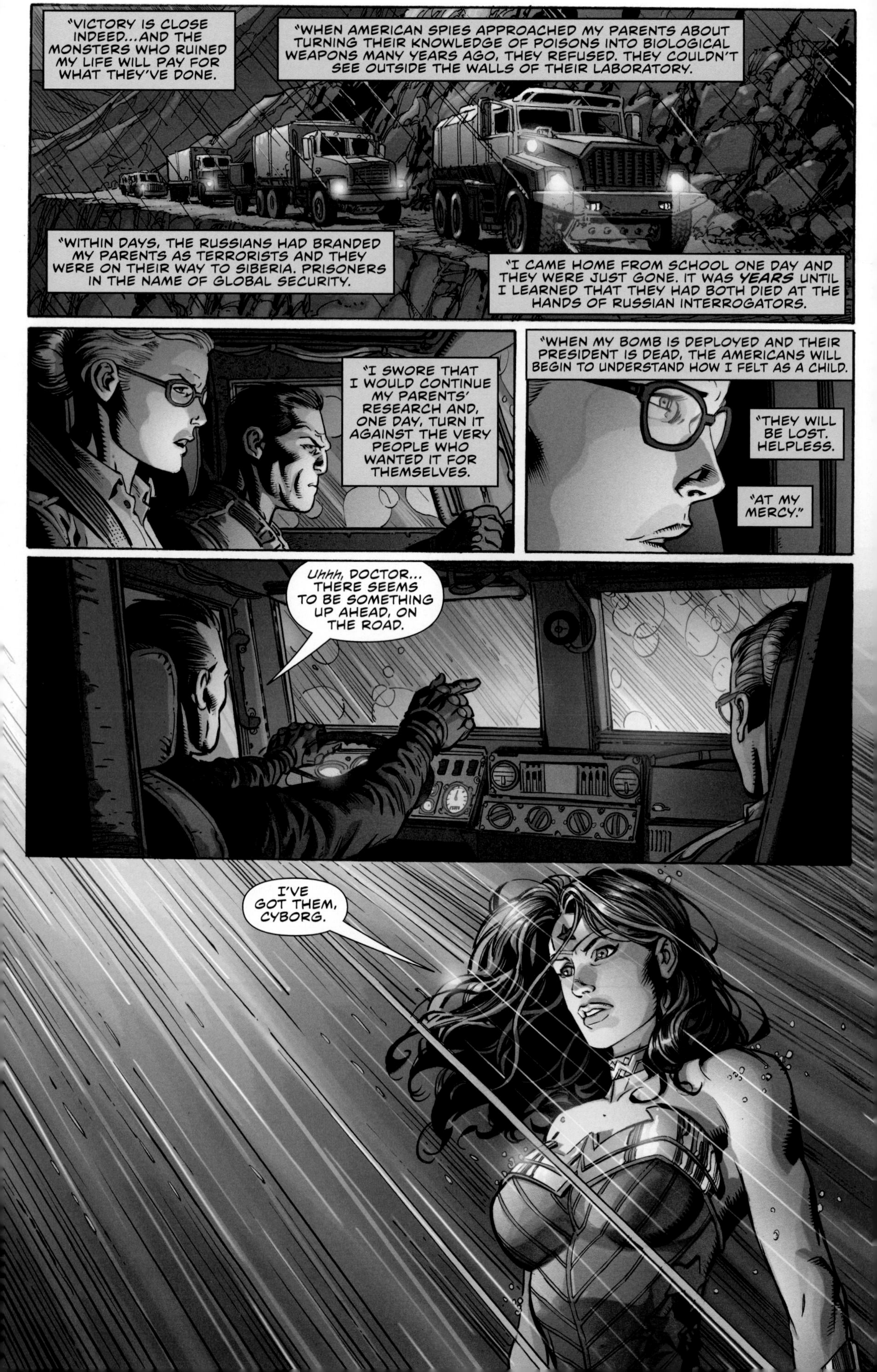
"VICTORY IS CLOSE INDEED...AND THE MONSTERS WHO RUINED MY LIFE WILL PAY FOR WHAT THEY'VE DONE.
"WHEN AMERICAN SPIES APPROACHED MY PARENTS ABOUT TURNING THEIR KNOWLEDGE OF POISONS INTO BIOLOGICAL WEAPONS MANY YEARS AGO, THEY REFUSED. THEY COULDN'T SEE OUTSIDE THE WALLS OF THEIR LABORATORY.
"WITHIN DAYS, THE RUSSIANS HAD BRANDED MY PARENTS AS TERRORISTS AND THEY WERE ON THEIR WAY TO SIBERIA. PRISONERS IN THE NAME OF GLOBAL SECURITY.
"I CAME HOME FROM SCHOOL ONE DAY AND THEY WERE JUST GONE. IT WAS *YEARS* UNTIL I LEARNED THAT THEY HAD BOTH DIED AT THE HANDS OF RUSSIAN INTERROGATORS.
"I SWORE THAT I WOULD CONTINUE MY PARENTS' RESEARCH AND, ONE DAY, TURN IT AGAINST THE VERY PEOPLE WHO WANTED IT FOR THEMSELVES.
"WHEN MY BOMB IS DEPLOYED AND THEIR PRESIDENT IS DEAD, THE AMERICANS WILL BEGIN TO UNDERSTAND HOW I FELT AS A CHILD.
"THEY WILL BE LOST. HELPLESS.
"AT MY MERCY."
Uhhh, DOCTOR... THERE SEEMS TO BE SOMETHING UP AHEAD, ON THE ROAD.
I'VE GOT THEM, CYBORG.

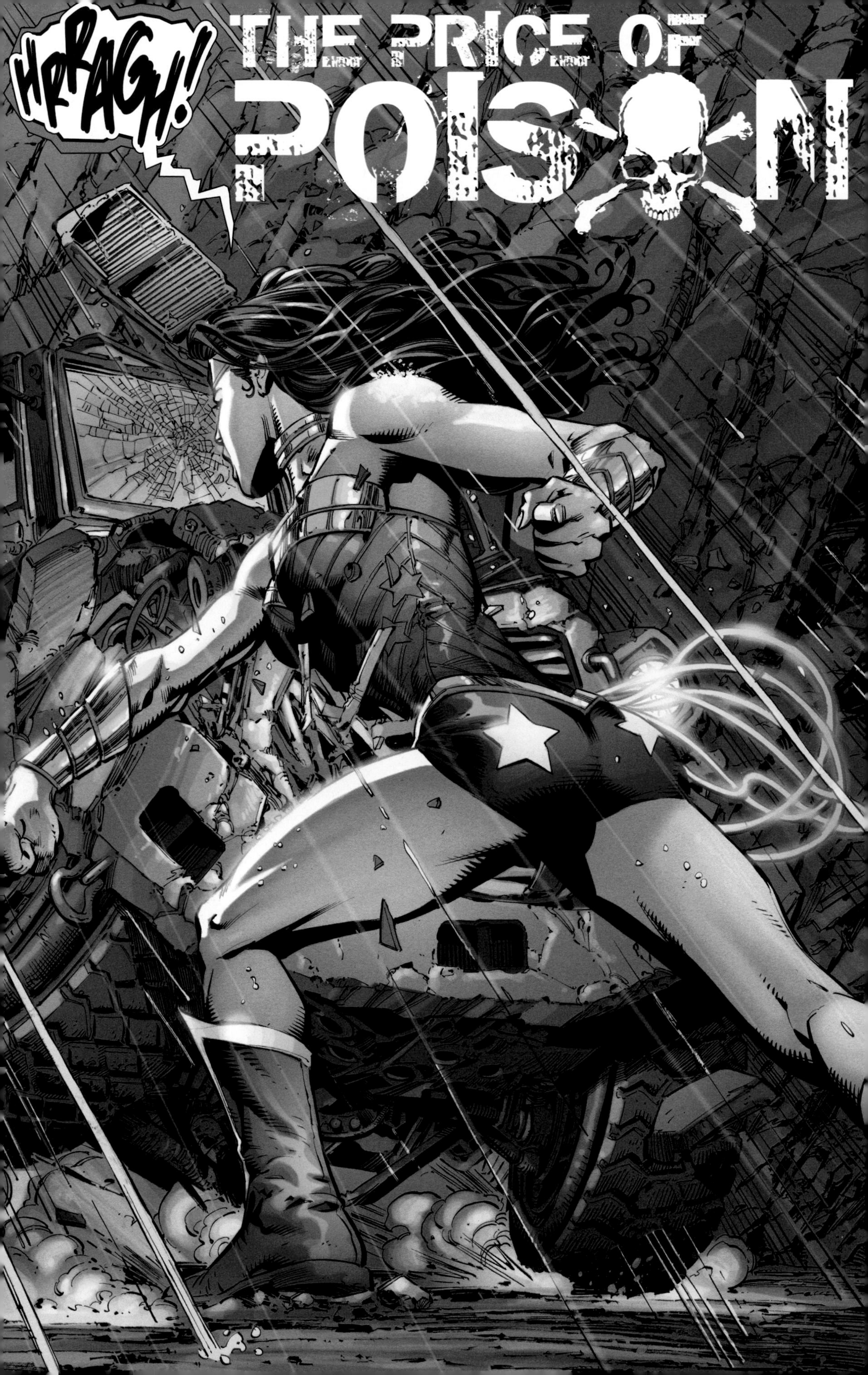
HRRAGH!
THE PRICE OF POISON

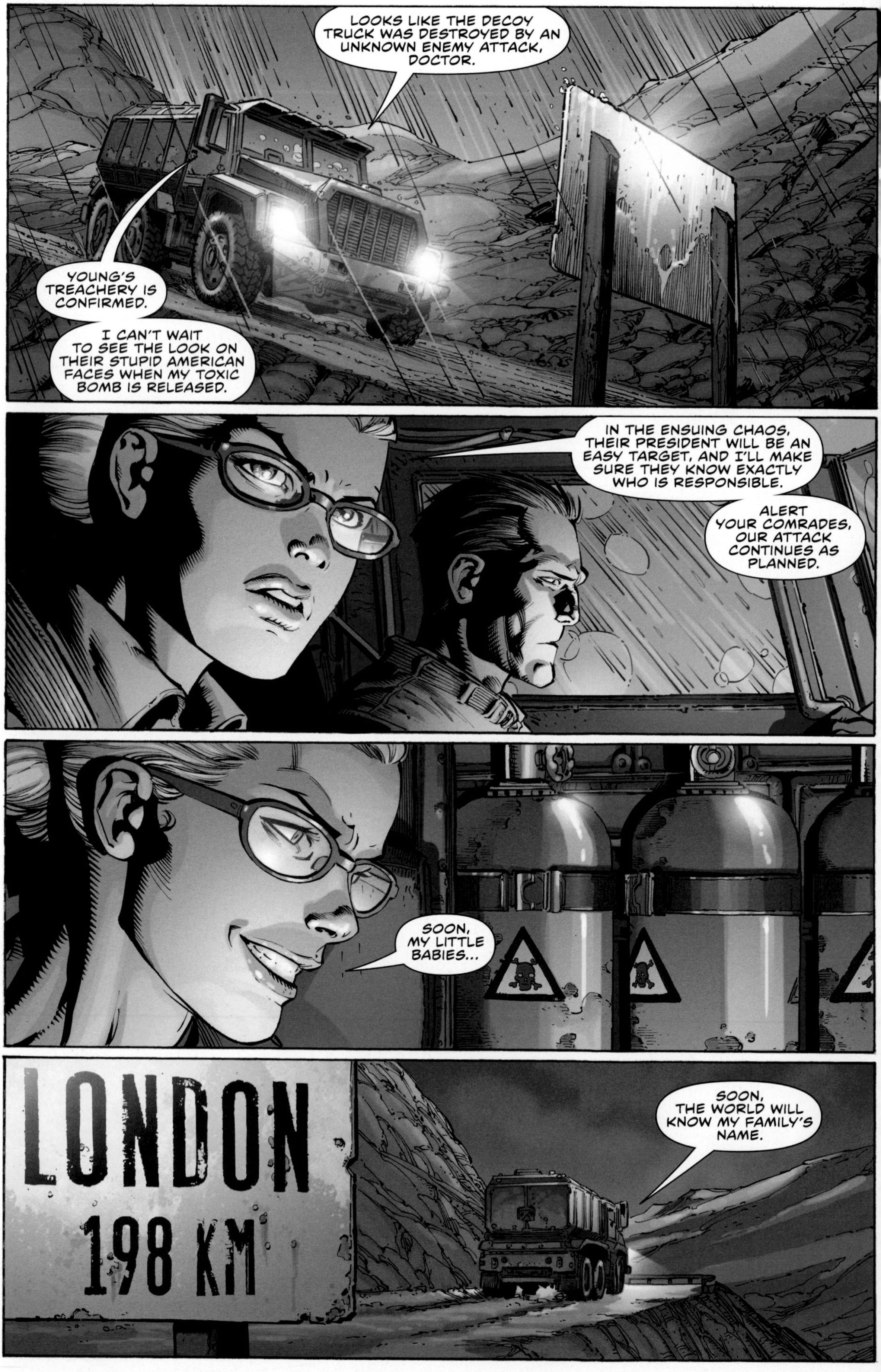
LOOKS LIKE THE DECOY TRUCK WAS DESTROYED BY AN UNKNOWN ENEMY ATTACK, DOCTOR.
YOUNG'S TREACHERY IS CONFIRMED.
I CAN'T WAIT TO SEE THE LOOK ON THEIR STUPID AMERICAN FACES WHEN MY TOXIC BOMB IS RELEASED.
IN THE ENSUING CHAOS, THEIR PRESIDENT WILL BE AN EASY TARGET, AND I'LL MAKE SURE THEY KNOW EXACTLY WHO IS RESPONSIBLE.
ALERT YOUR COMRADES, OUR ATTACK CONTINUES AS PLANNED.
SOON, MY LITTLE BABIES...
LONDON
198 KM
SOON, THE WORLD WILL KNOW MY FAMILY'S NAME.

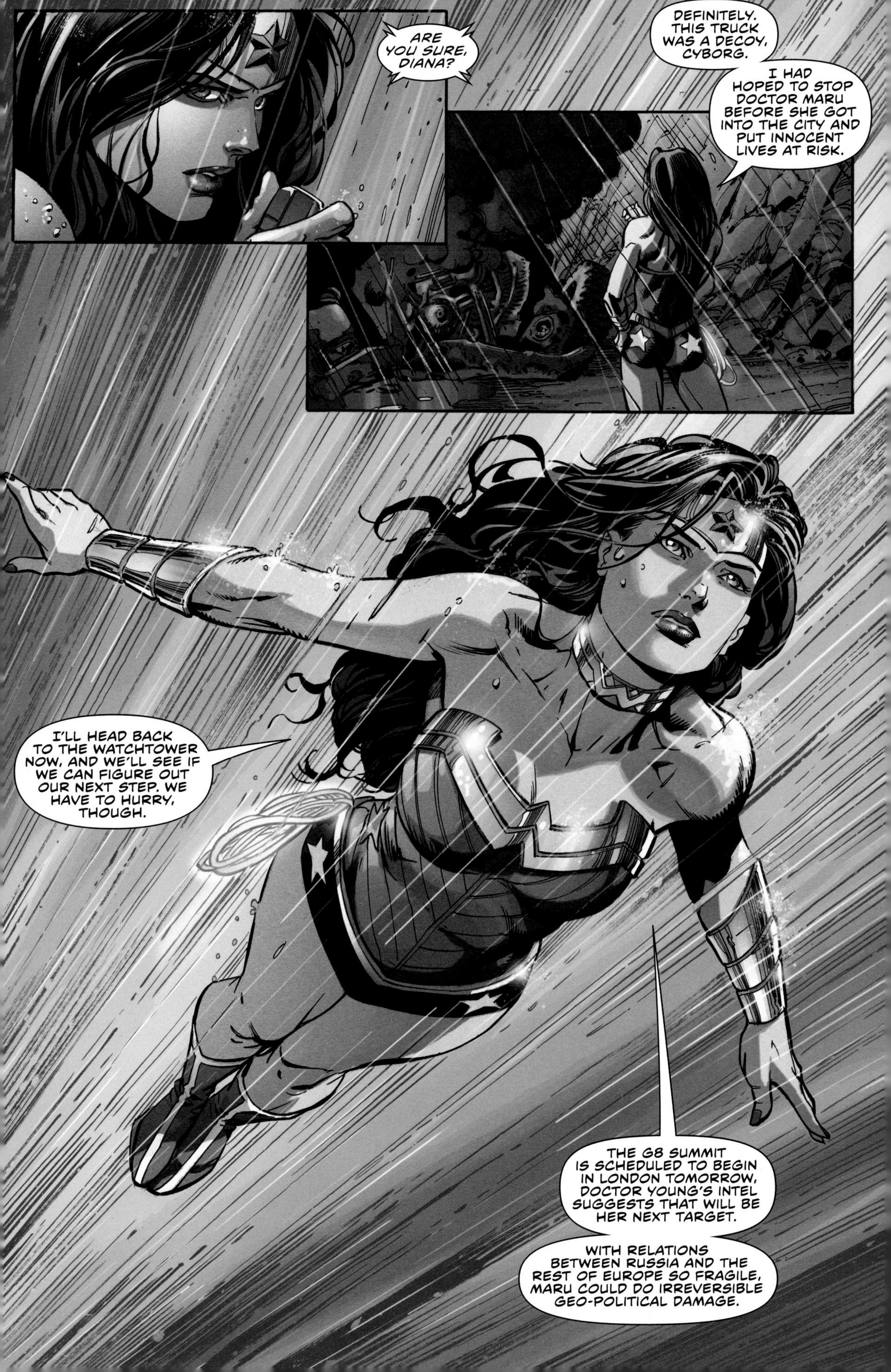
ARE YOU SURE, DIANA?
DEFINITELY. THIS TRUCK WAS A DECOY, CYBORG.
I HAD HOPED TO STOP DOCTOR MARU BEFORE SHE GOT INTO THE CITY AND PUT INNOCENT LIVES AT RISK.
I'LL HEAD BACK TO THE WATCHTOWER NOW, AND WE'LL SEE IF WE CAN FIGURE OUT OUR NEXT STEP. WE HAVE TO HURRY, THOUGH.
THE G8 SUMMIT IS SCHEDULED TO BEGIN IN LONDON TOMORROW, DOCTOR YOUNG'S INTEL SUGGESTS THAT WILL BE HER NEXT TARGET.
WITH RELATIONS BETWEEN RUSSIA AND THE REST OF EUROPE SO FRAGILE, MARU COULD DO IRREVERSIBLE GEO-POLITICAL DAMAGE.

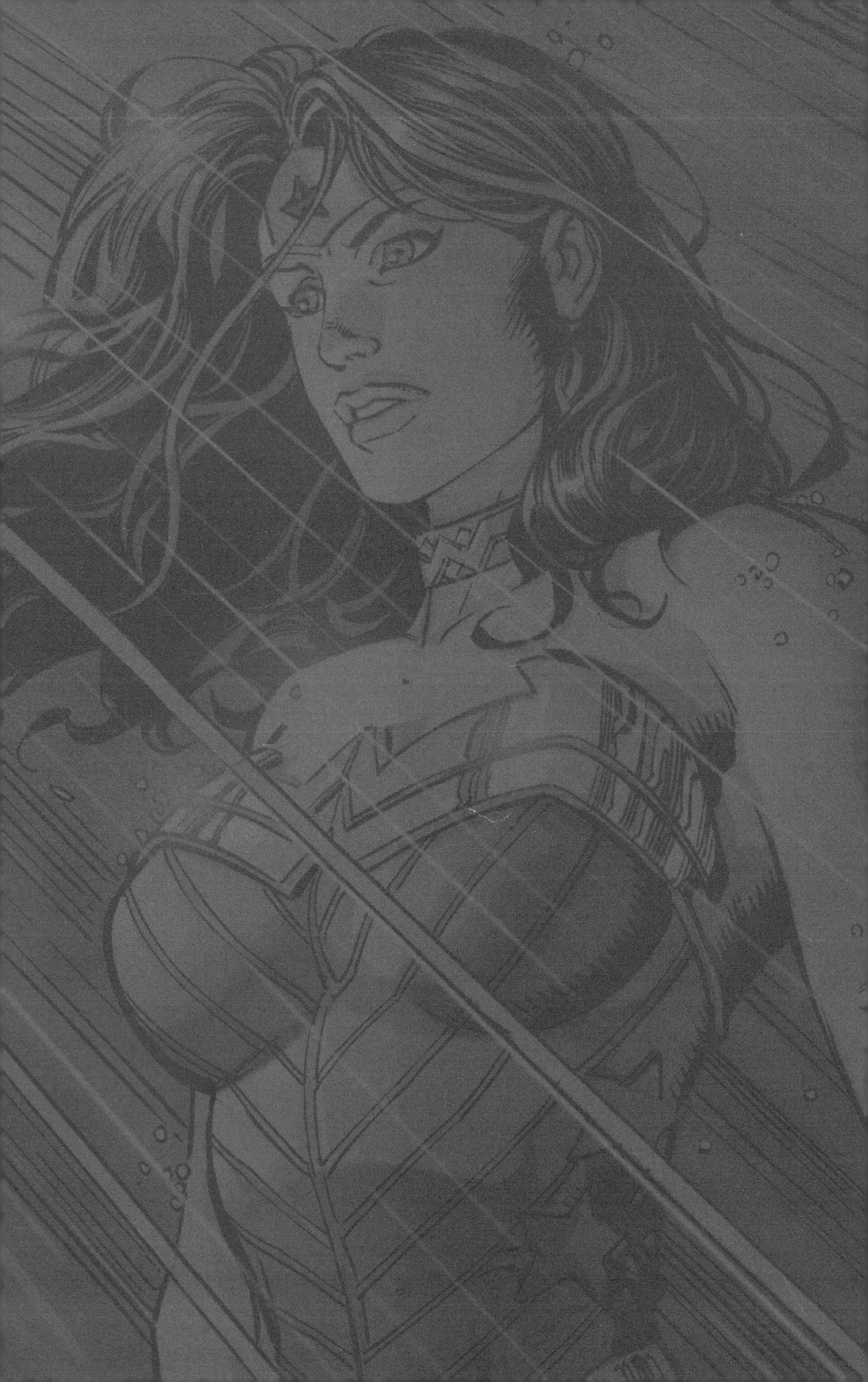

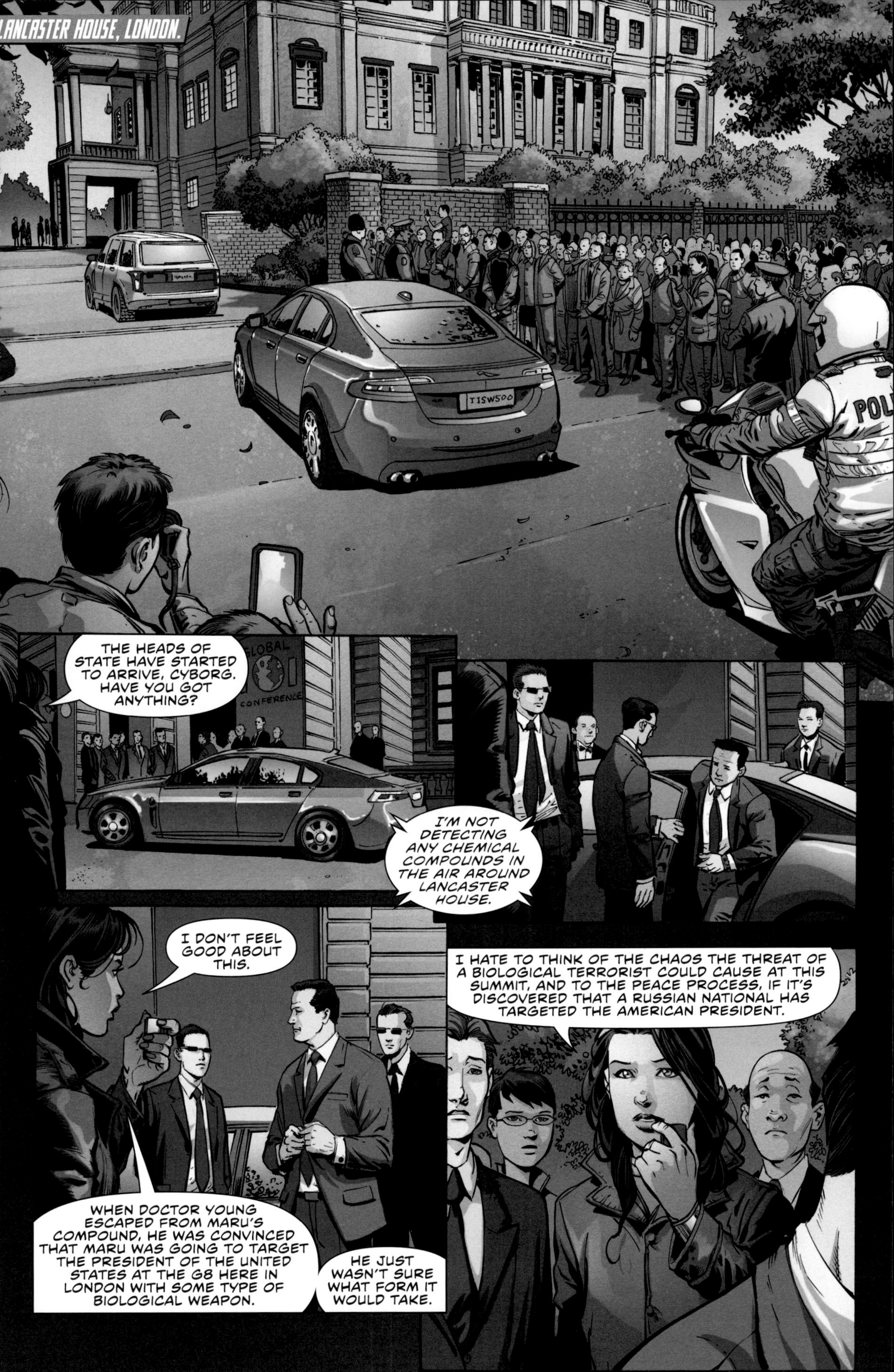
LANCASTER HOUSE, LONDON.
POLI
THE HEADS OF STATE HAVE STARTED TO ARRIVE, CYBORG. HAVE YOU GOT ANYTHING?
GLOBAL CONFERENCE
I'M NOT DETECTING ANY CHEMICAL COMPOUNDS IN THE AIR AROUND LANCASTER HOUSE.
I DON'T FEEL GOOD ABOUT THIS.
WHEN DOCTOR YOUNG ESCAPED FROM MARU'S COMPOUND, HE WAS CONVINCED THAT MARU WAS GOING TO TARGET THE PRESIDENT OF THE UNITED STATES AT THE G8 HERE IN LONDON WITH SOME TYPE OF BIOLOGICAL WEAPON.
HE JUST WASN'T SURE WHAT FORM IT WOULD TAKE.
I HATE TO THINK OF THE CHAOS THE THREAT OF A BIOLOGICAL TERRORIST COULD CAUSE AT THIS SUMMIT, AND TO THE PEACE PROCESS, IF IT'S DISCOVERED THAT A RUSSIAN NATIONAL HAS TARGETED THE AMERICAN PRESIDENT.

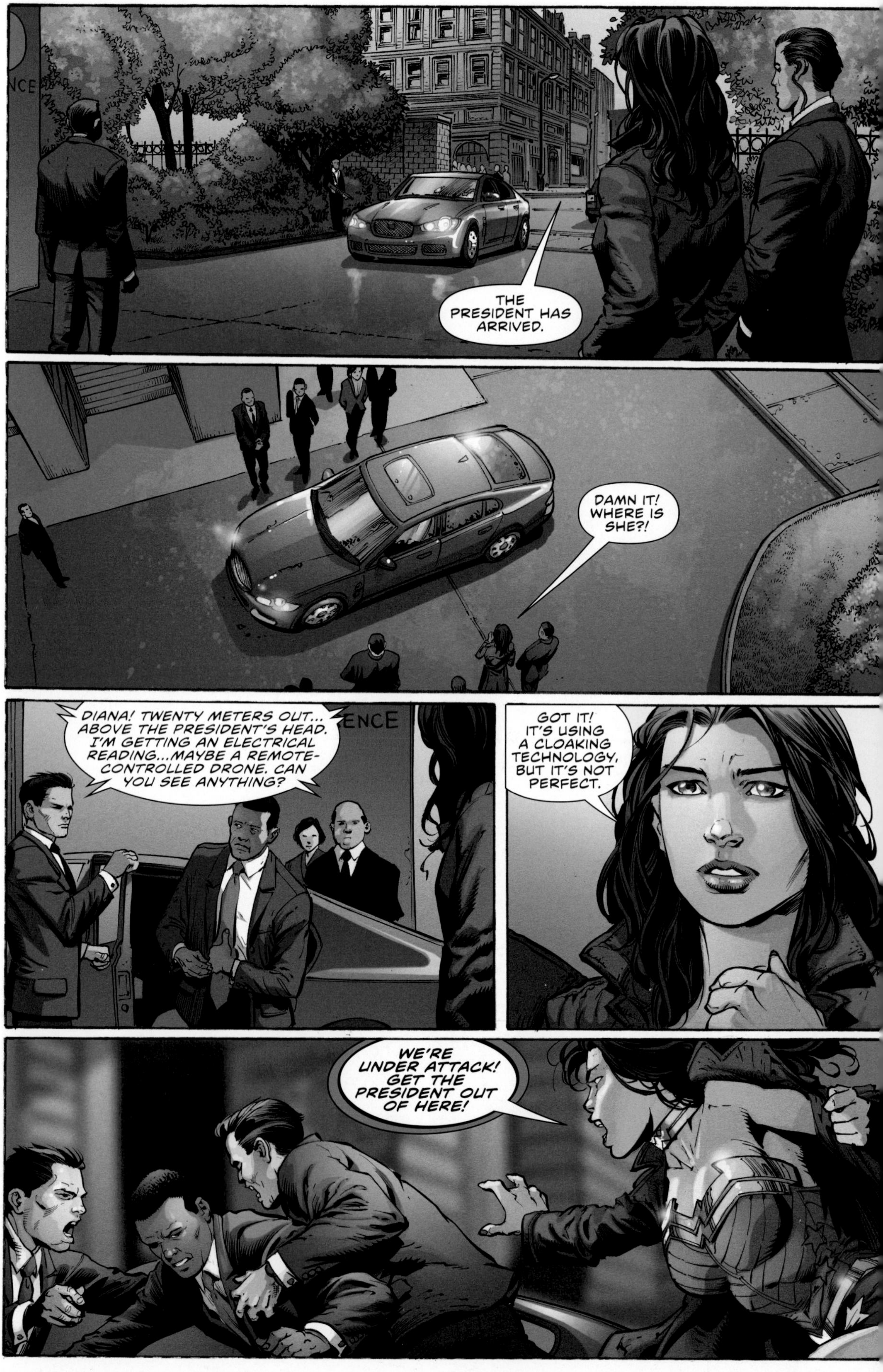
ENCE
THE PRESIDENT HAS ARRIVED.
DAMN IT! WHERE IS SHE?!
DIANA! TWENTY METERS OUT... ABOVE THE PRESIDENT'S HEAD. I'M GETTING AN ELECTRICAL READING...MAYBE A REMOTE-CONTROLLED DRONE. CAN YOU SEE ANYTHING?
ENCE
GOT IT! IT'S USING A CLOAKING TECHNOLOGY, BUT IT'S NOT PERFECT.
WE'RE UNDER ATTACK! GET THE PRESIDENT OUT OF HERE!

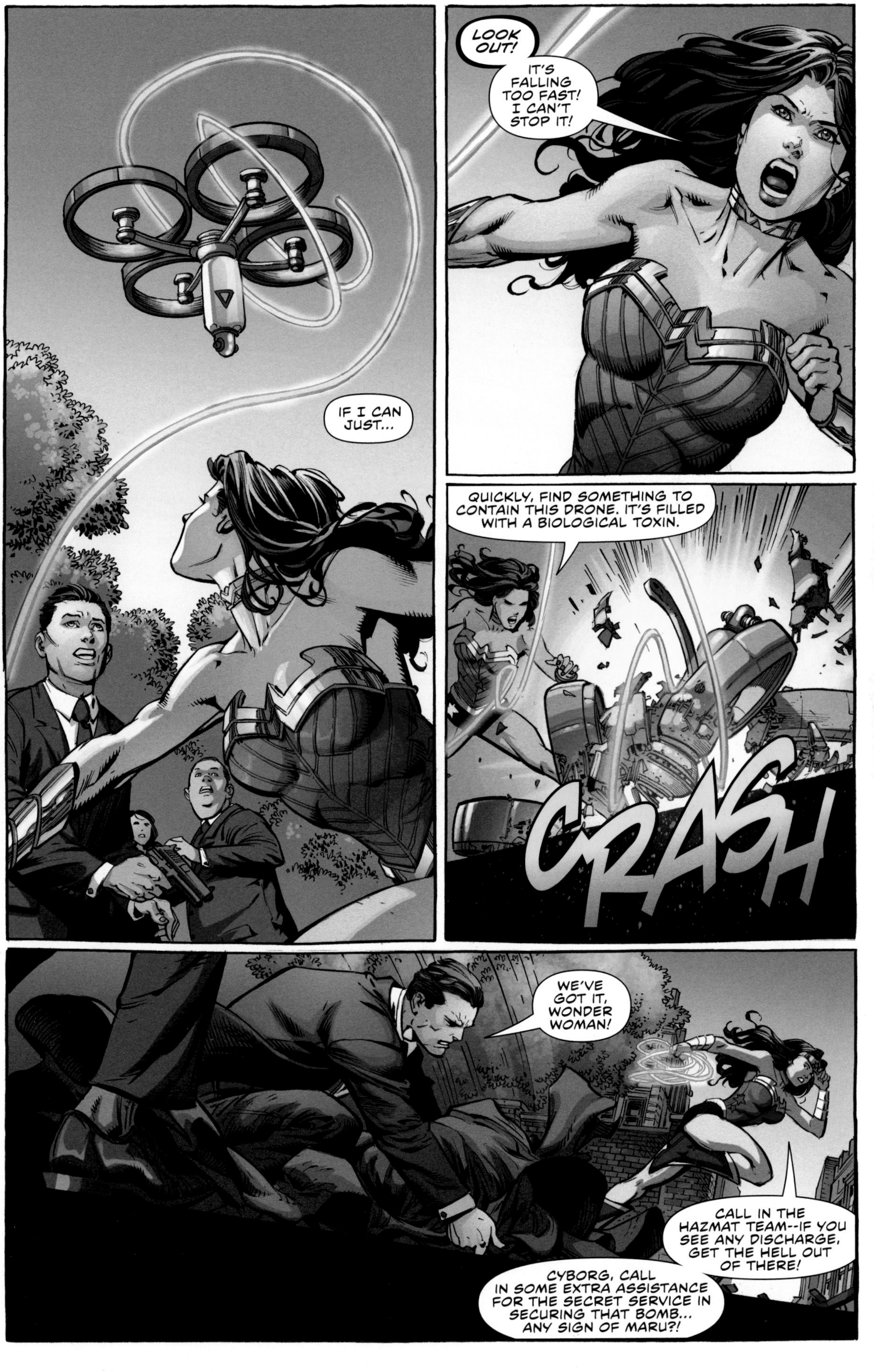
IF I CAN JUST...
LOOK OUT!
IT'S FALLING TOO FAST! I CAN'T STOP IT!
QUICKLY, FIND SOMETHING TO CONTAIN THIS DRONE. IT'S FILLED WITH A BIOLOGICAL TOXIN.
CRASH
WE'VE GOT IT, WONDER WOMAN!
CALL IN THE HAZMAT TEAM--IF YOU SEE ANY DISCHARGE, GET THE HELL OUT OF THERE!
CYBORG, CALL IN SOME EXTRA ASSISTANCE FOR THE SECRET SERVICE IN SECURING THAT BOMB... ANY SIGN OF MARU?!

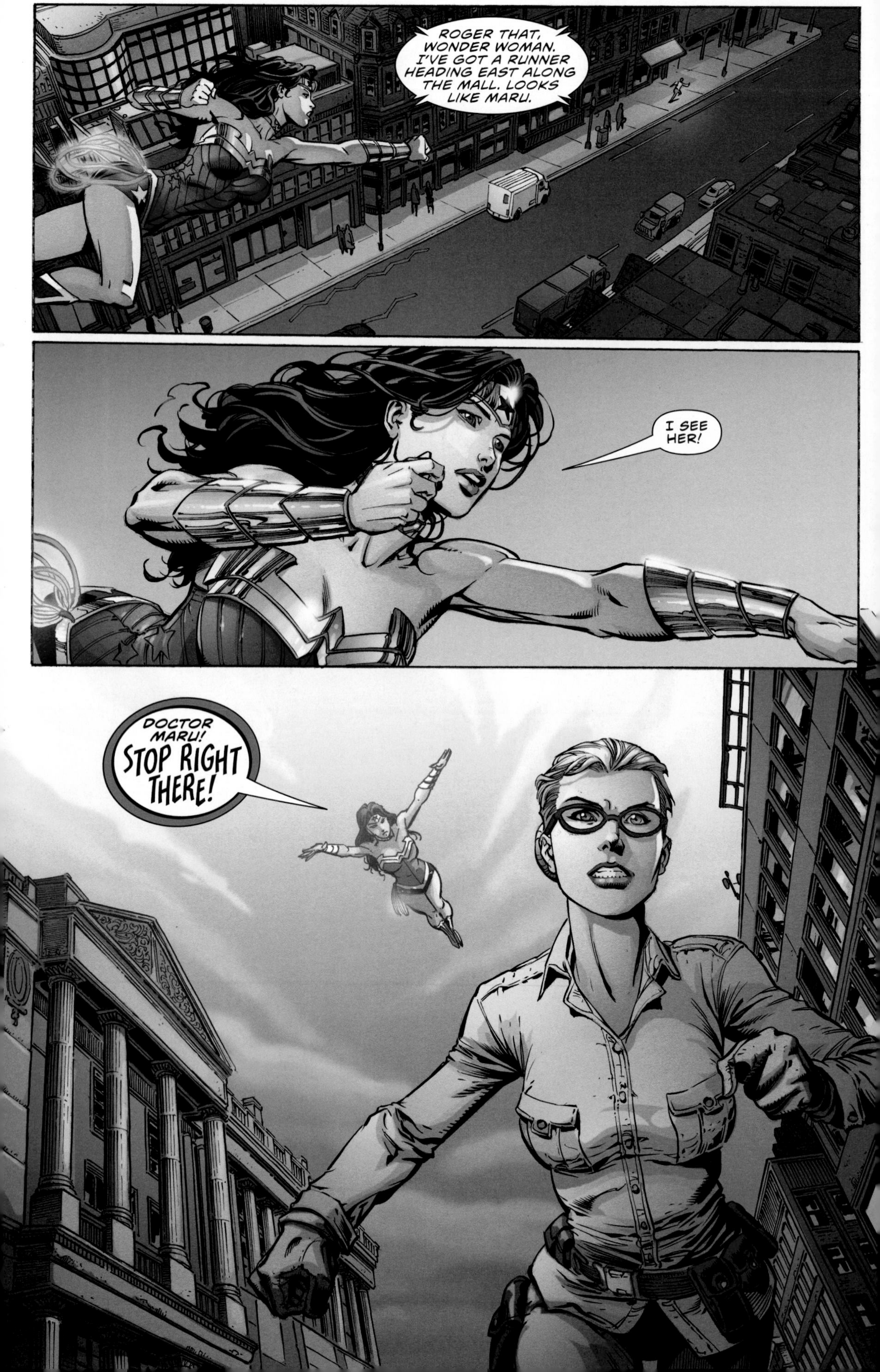
ROGER THAT, WONDER WOMAN. I'VE GOT A RUNNER HEADING EAST ALONG THE MALL. LOOKS LIKE MARU.
I SEE HER!
DOCTOR MARU! STOP RIGHT THERE!

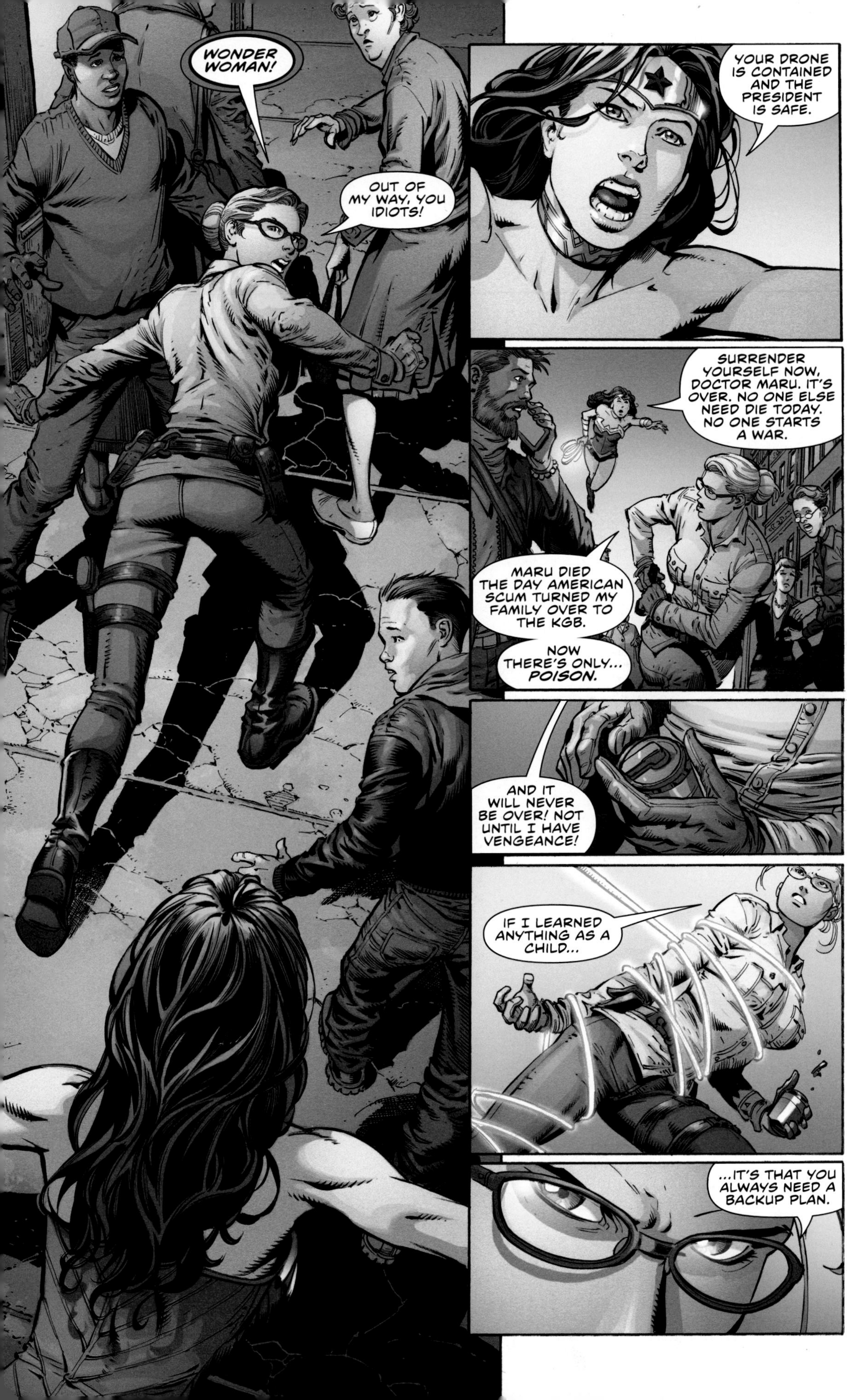
WONDER WOMAN!
OUT OF MY WAY, YOU IDIOTS!
YOUR DRONE IS CONTAINED AND THE PRESIDENT IS SAFE.
SURRENDER YOURSELF NOW, DOCTOR MARU. IT'S OVER. NO ONE ELSE NEED DIE TODAY. NO ONE STARTS A WAR.
MARU DIED THE DAY AMERICAN SCUM TURNED MY FAMILY OVER TO THE KGB.
NOW THERE'S ONLY... POISON.
AND IT WILL NEVER BE OVER! NOT UNTIL I HAVE VENGEANCE!
IF I LEARNED ANYTHING AS A CHILD...
...IT'S THAT YOU ALWAYS NEED A BACKUP PLAN.

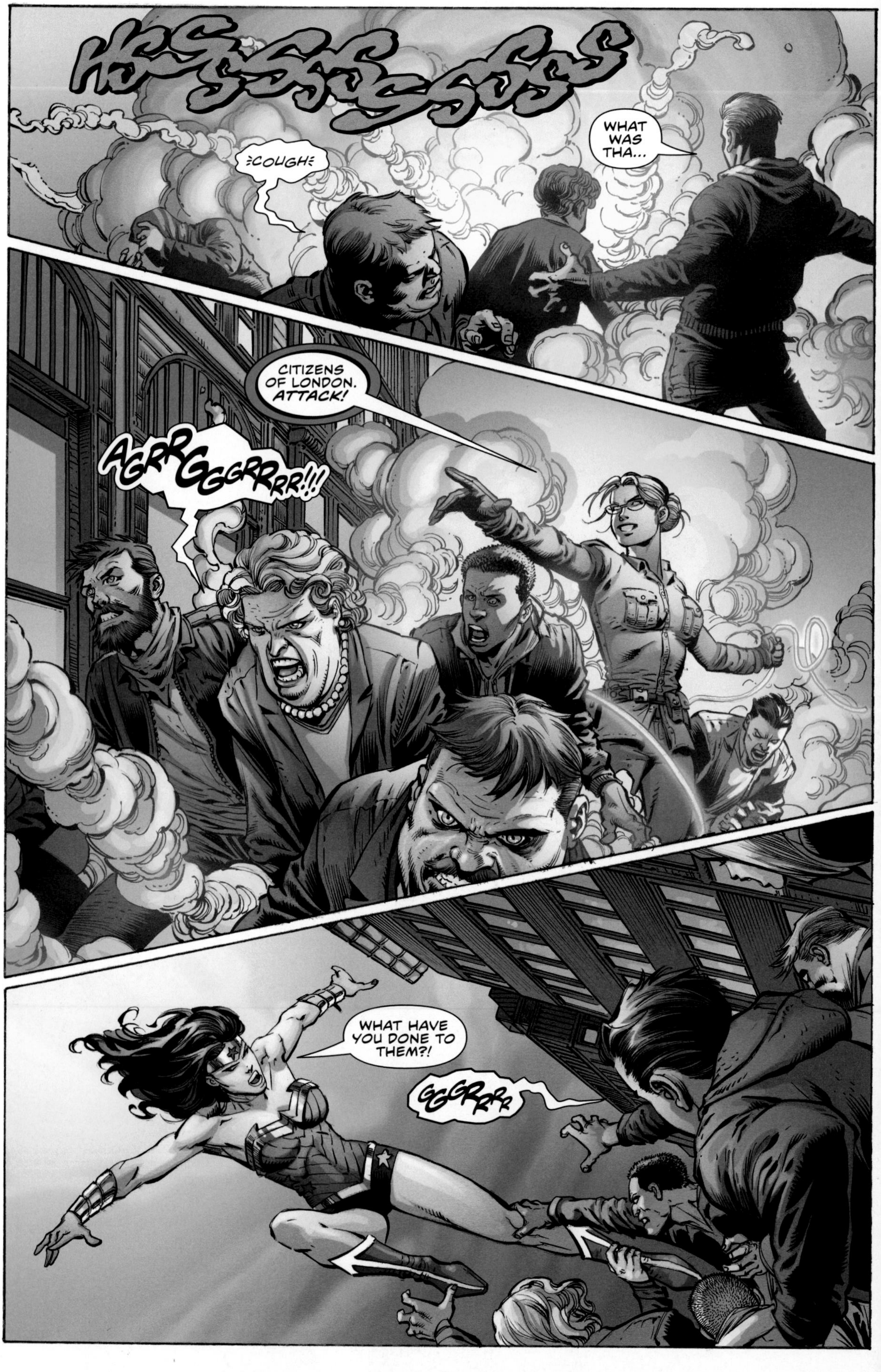
HSSSSSSSSSS
COUGH
WHAT WAS THA...
CITIZENS OF LONDON. ATTACK!
AGRRGGGRRRR!!!
WHAT HAVE YOU DONE TO THEM?!
GGGRRRR

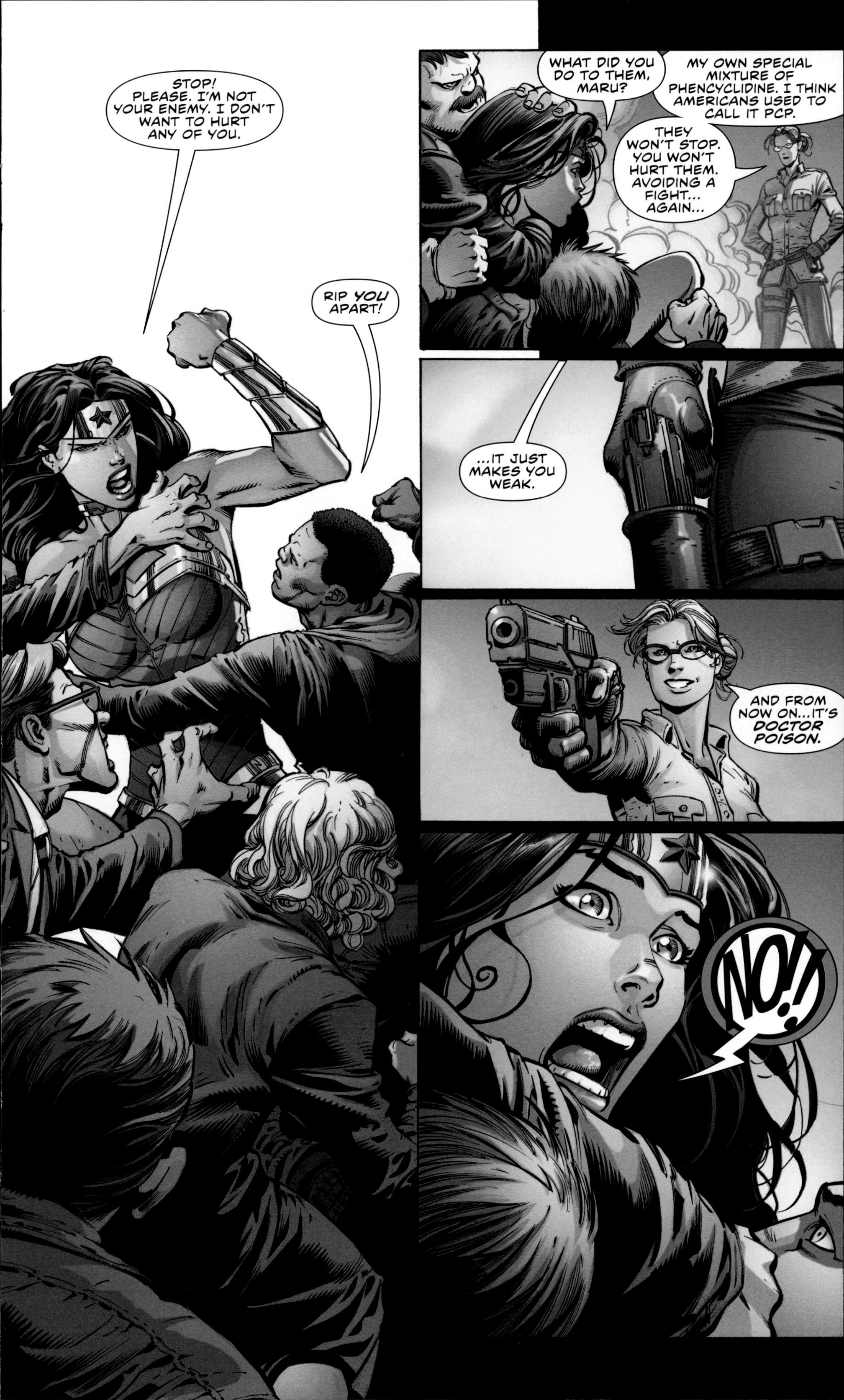
STOP! PLEASE. I'M NOT YOUR ENEMY. I DON'T WANT TO HURT ANY OF YOU.
RIP YOU APART!
WHAT DID YOU DO TO THEM, MARU?
MY OWN SPECIAL MIXTURE OF PHENCYCLIDINE. I THINK AMERICANS USED TO CALL IT PCP.
THEY WON'T STOP. YOU WON'T HURT THEM. AVOIDING A FIGHT... AGAIN...
...IT JUST MAKES YOU WEAK.
AND FROM NOW ON...IT'S DOCTOR POISON.
NO!!

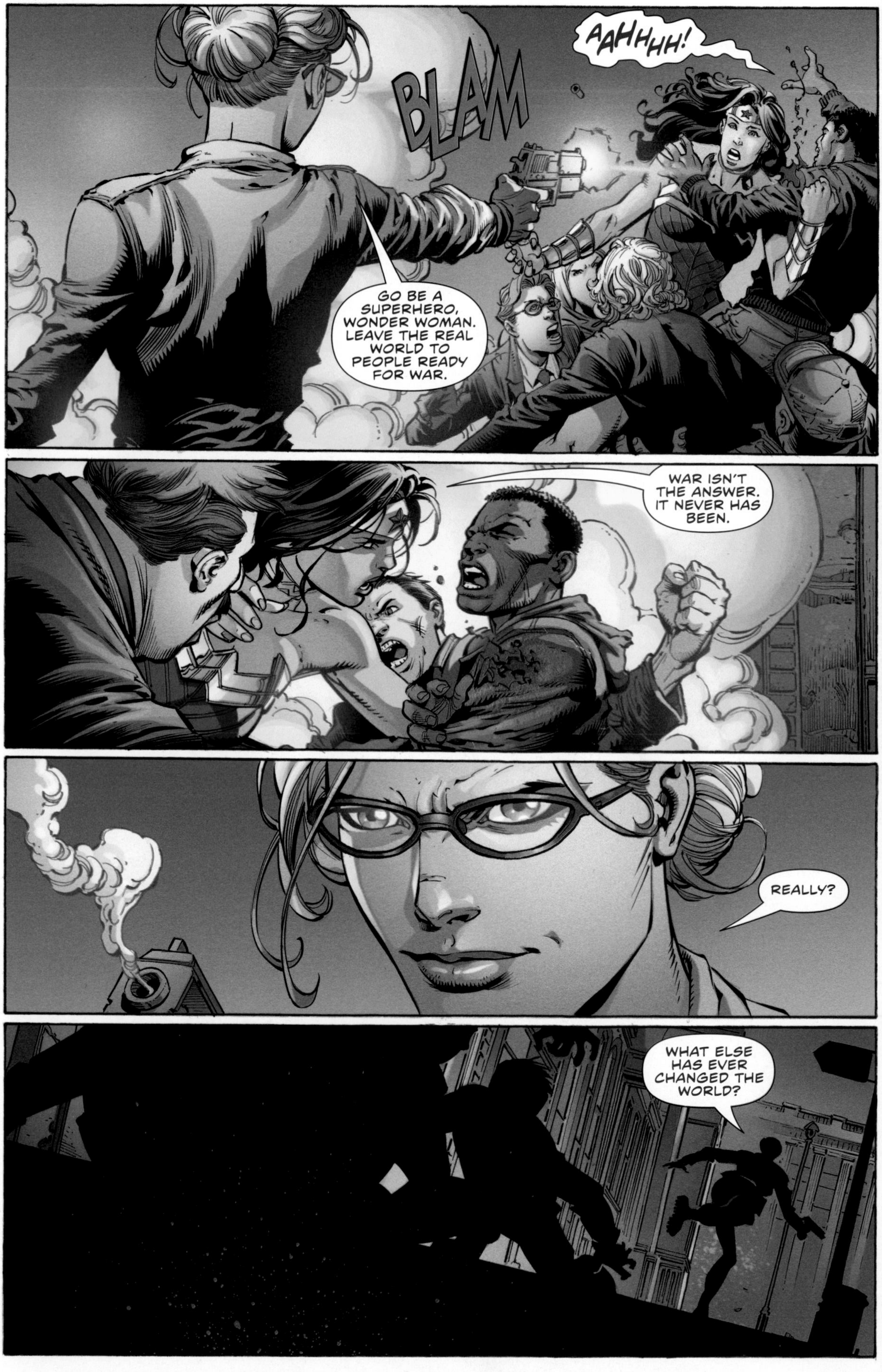
BLAM
AAHHHH!
GO BE A SUPERHERO, WONDER WOMAN. LEAVE THE REAL WORLD TO PEOPLE READY FOR WAR.
WAR ISN'T THE ANSWER. IT NEVER HAS BEEN.
REALLY?
WHAT ELSE HAS EVER CHANGED THE WORLD?

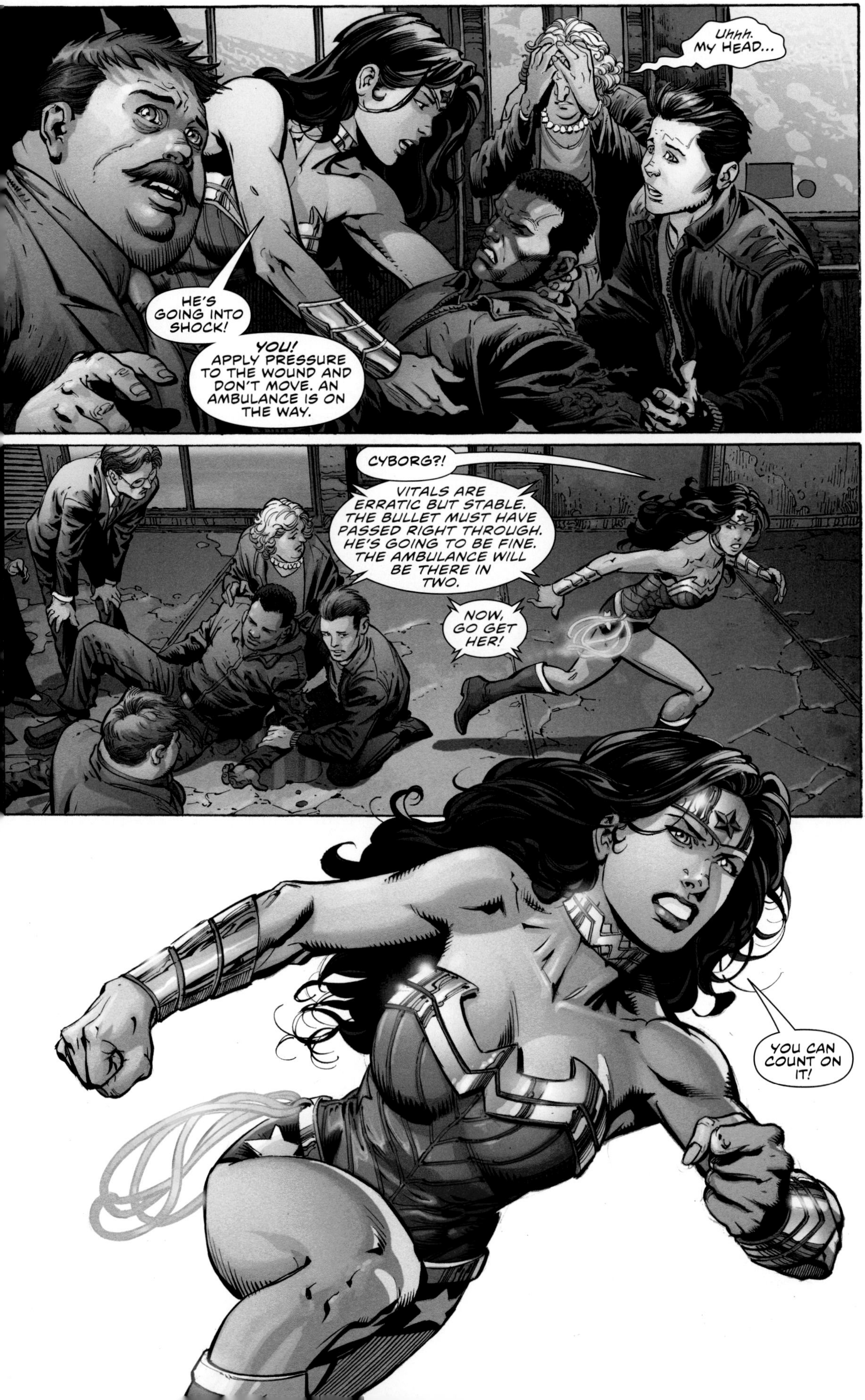
Uhhh. MY HEAD...
HE'S GOING INTO SHOCK!
YOU! APPLY PRESSURE TO THE WOUND AND DON'T MOVE. AN AMBULANCE IS ON THE WAY.
CYBORG?!
VITALS ARE ERRATIC BUT STABLE. THE BULLET MUST HAVE PASSED RIGHT THROUGH. HE'S GOING TO BE FINE. THE AMBULANCE WILL BE THERE IN TWO.
NOW, GO GET HER!
YOU CAN COUNT ON IT!

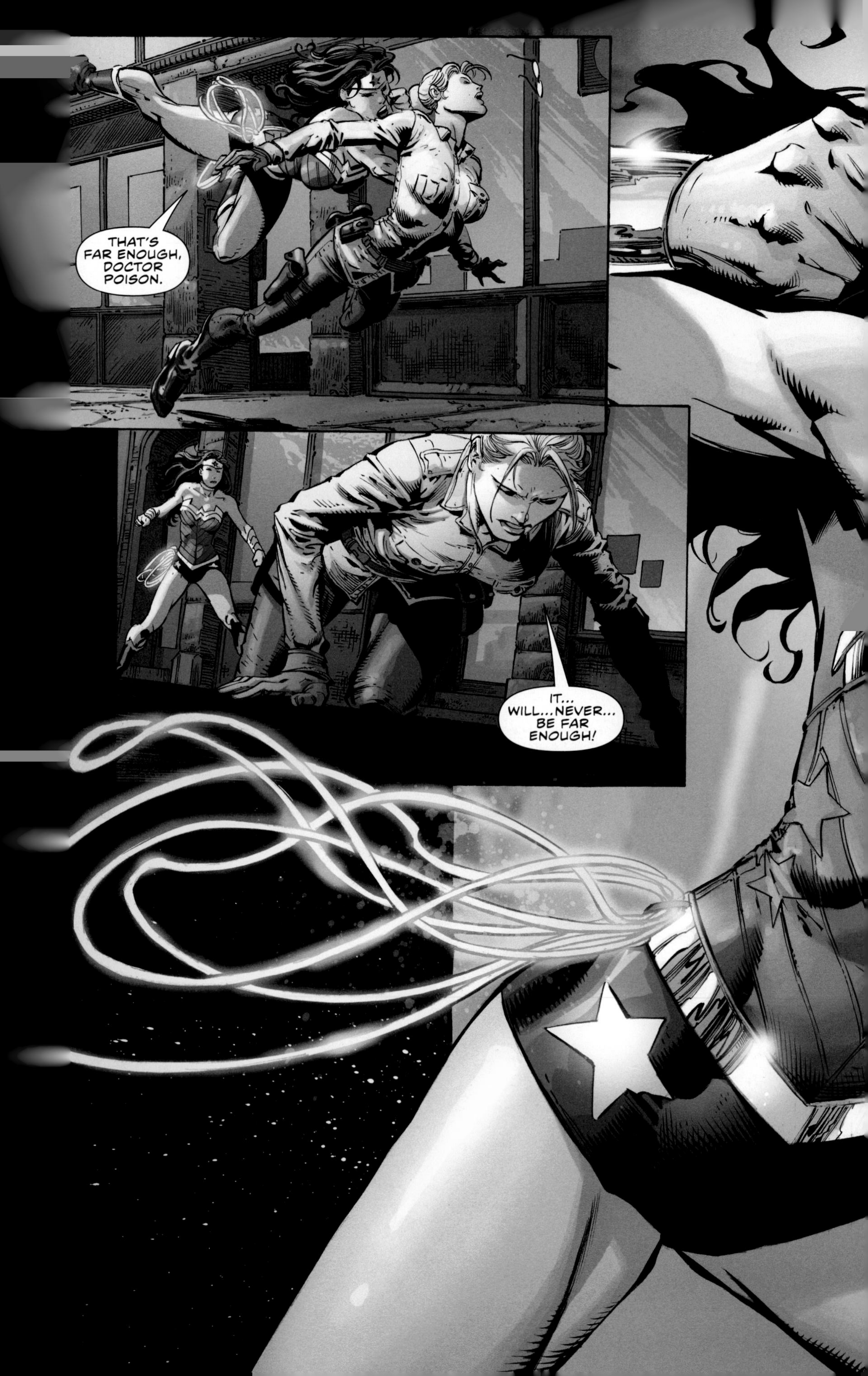
THAT'S FAR ENOUGH, DOCTOR POISON.
IT... WILL...NEVER... BE FAR ENOUGH!

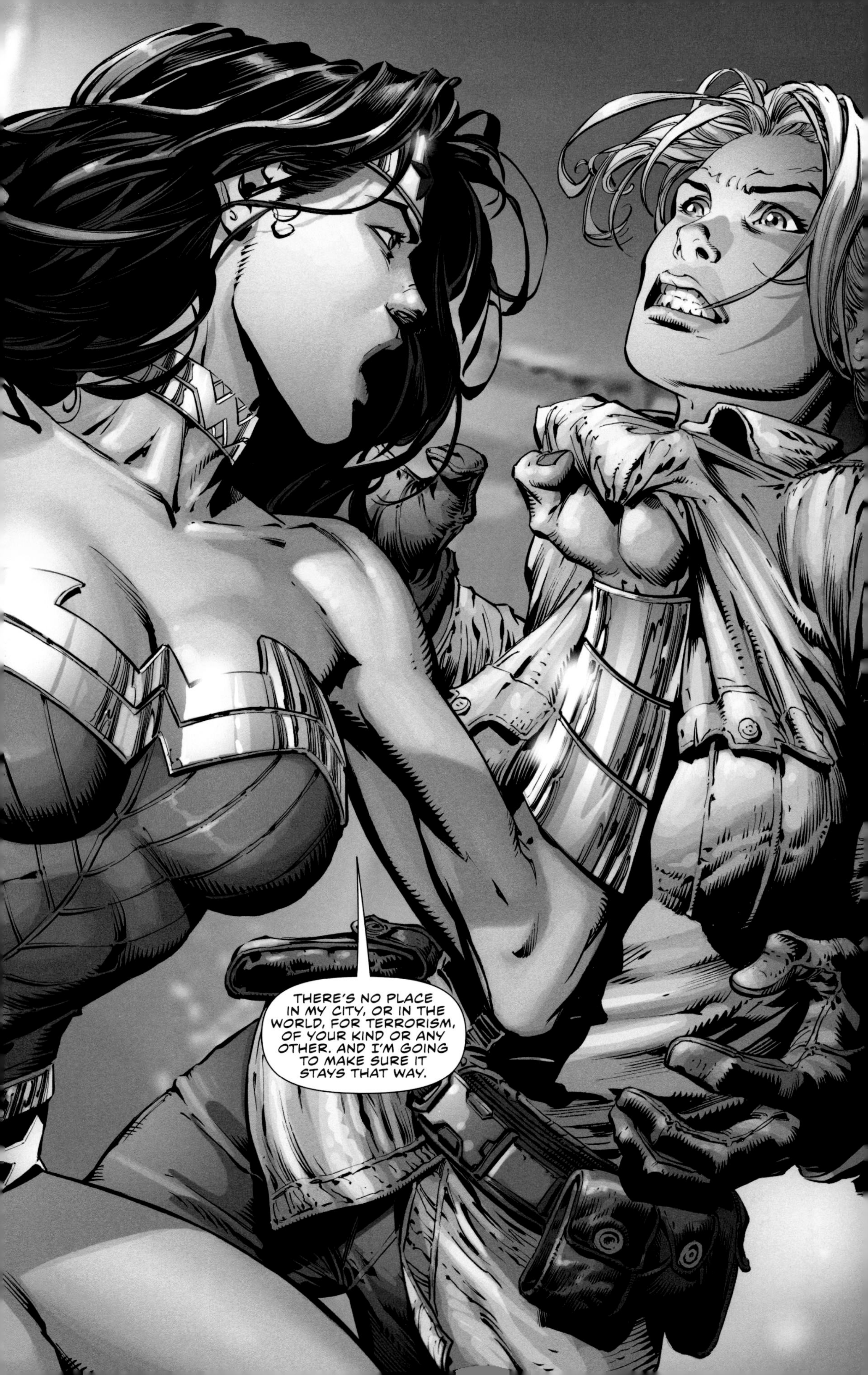
THERE'S NO PLACE IN MY CITY, OR IN THE WORLD, FOR TERRORISM, OF YOUR KIND OR ANY OTHER. AND I'M GOING TO MAKE SURE IT STAYS THAT WAY.

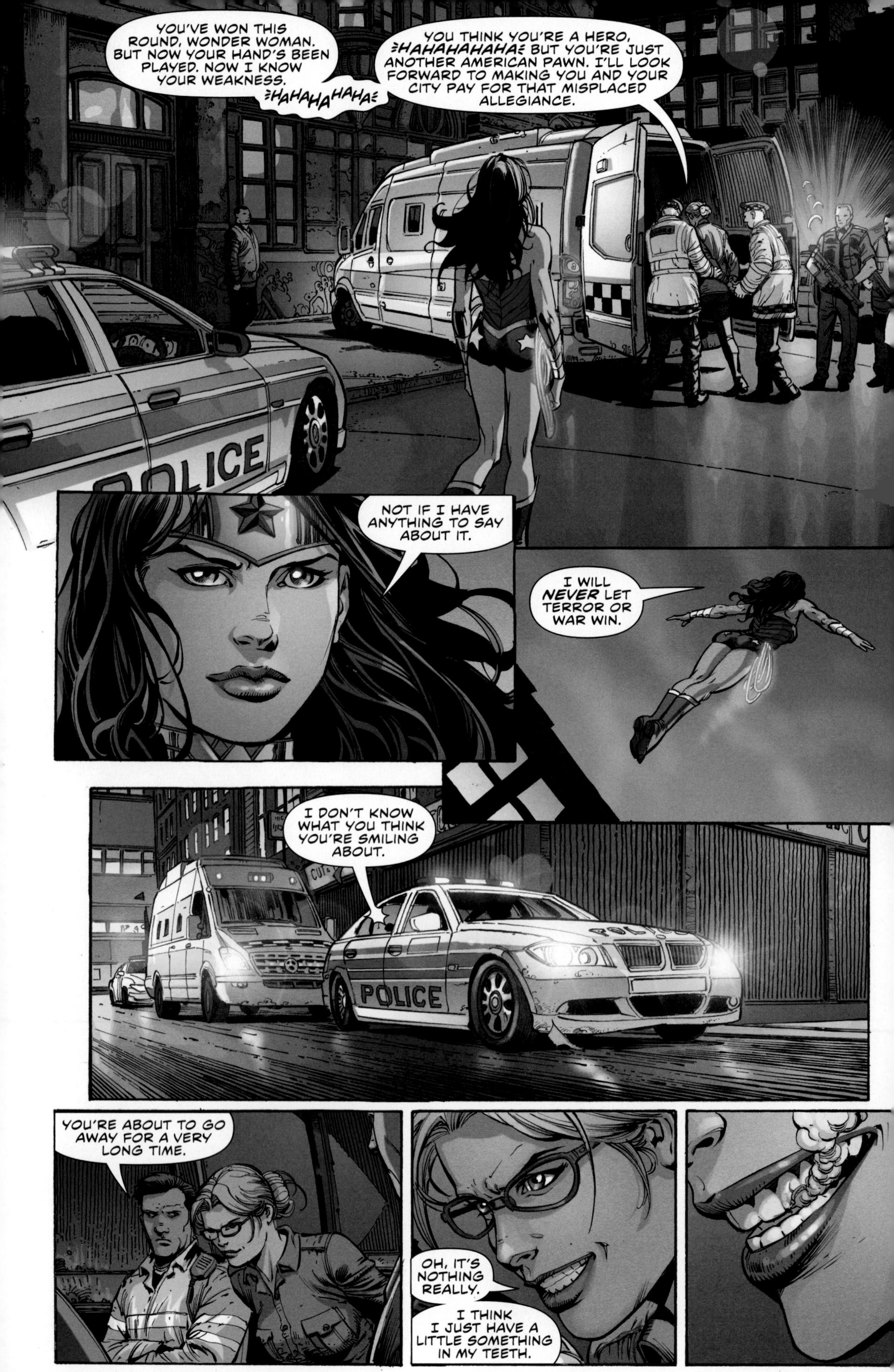
YOU'VE WON THIS ROUND, WONDER WOMAN. BUT NOW YOUR HAND'S BEEN PLAYED. NOW I KNOW YOUR WEAKNESS.
HAHAHAHAHAHA
YOU THINK YOU'RE A HERO, HAHAHAHAHA! BUT YOU'RE JUST ANOTHER AMERICAN PAWN. I'LL LOOK FORWARD TO MAKING YOU AND YOUR CITY PAY FOR THAT MISPLACED ALLEGIANCE.
POLICE
NOT IF I HAVE ANYTHING TO SAY ABOUT IT.
I WILL NEVER LET TERROR OR WAR WIN.
I DON'T KNOW WHAT YOU THINK YOU'RE SMILING ABOUT.
POLICE
YOU'RE ABOUT TO GO AWAY FOR A VERY LONG TIME.
OH, IT'S NOTHING REALLY.
I THINK I JUST HAVE A LITTLE SOMETHING IN MY TEETH.

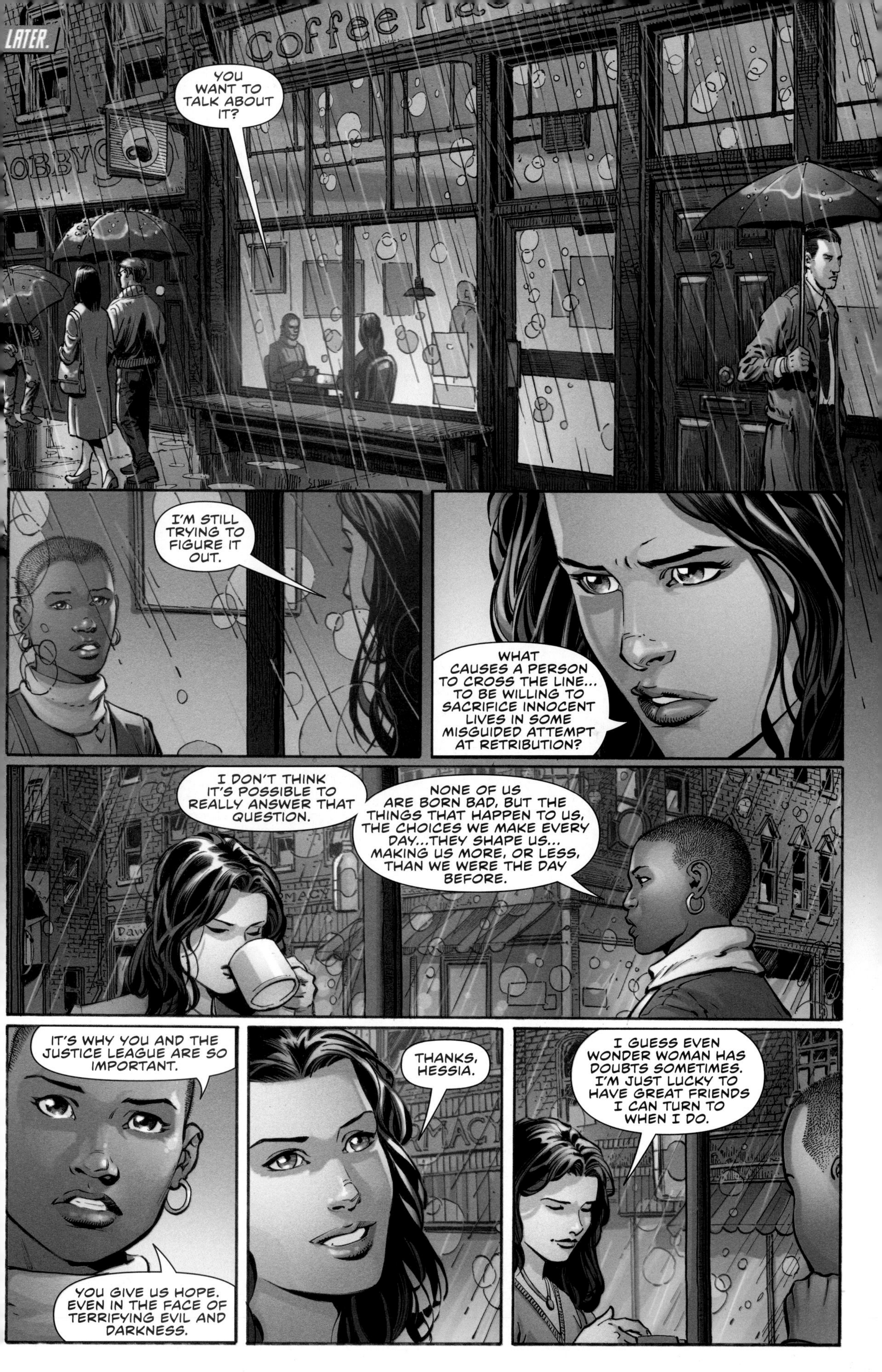
LATER.
Coffee
HOBBY
21
YOU WANT TO TALK ABOUT IT?
I'M STILL TRYING TO FIGURE IT OUT.
WHAT CAUSES A PERSON TO CROSS THE LINE... TO BE WILLING TO SACRIFICE INNOCENT LIVES IN SOME MISGUIDED ATTEMPT AT RETRIBUTION?
I DON'T THINK IT'S POSSIBLE TO REALLY ANSWER THAT QUESTION.
NONE OF US ARE BORN BAD, BUT THE THINGS THAT HAPPEN TO US, THE CHOICES WE MAKE EVERY DAY...THEY SHAPE US... MAKING US MORE, OR LESS, THAN WE WERE THE DAY BEFORE.
IT'S WHY YOU AND THE JUSTICE LEAGUE ARE SO IMPORTANT.
YOU GIVE US HOPE. EVEN IN THE FACE OF TERRIFYING EVIL AND DARKNESS.
THANKS, HESSIA.
I GUESS EVEN WONDER WOMAN HAS DOUBTS SOMETIMES. I'M JUST LUCKY TO HAVE GREAT FRIENDS I CAN TURN TO WHEN I DO.

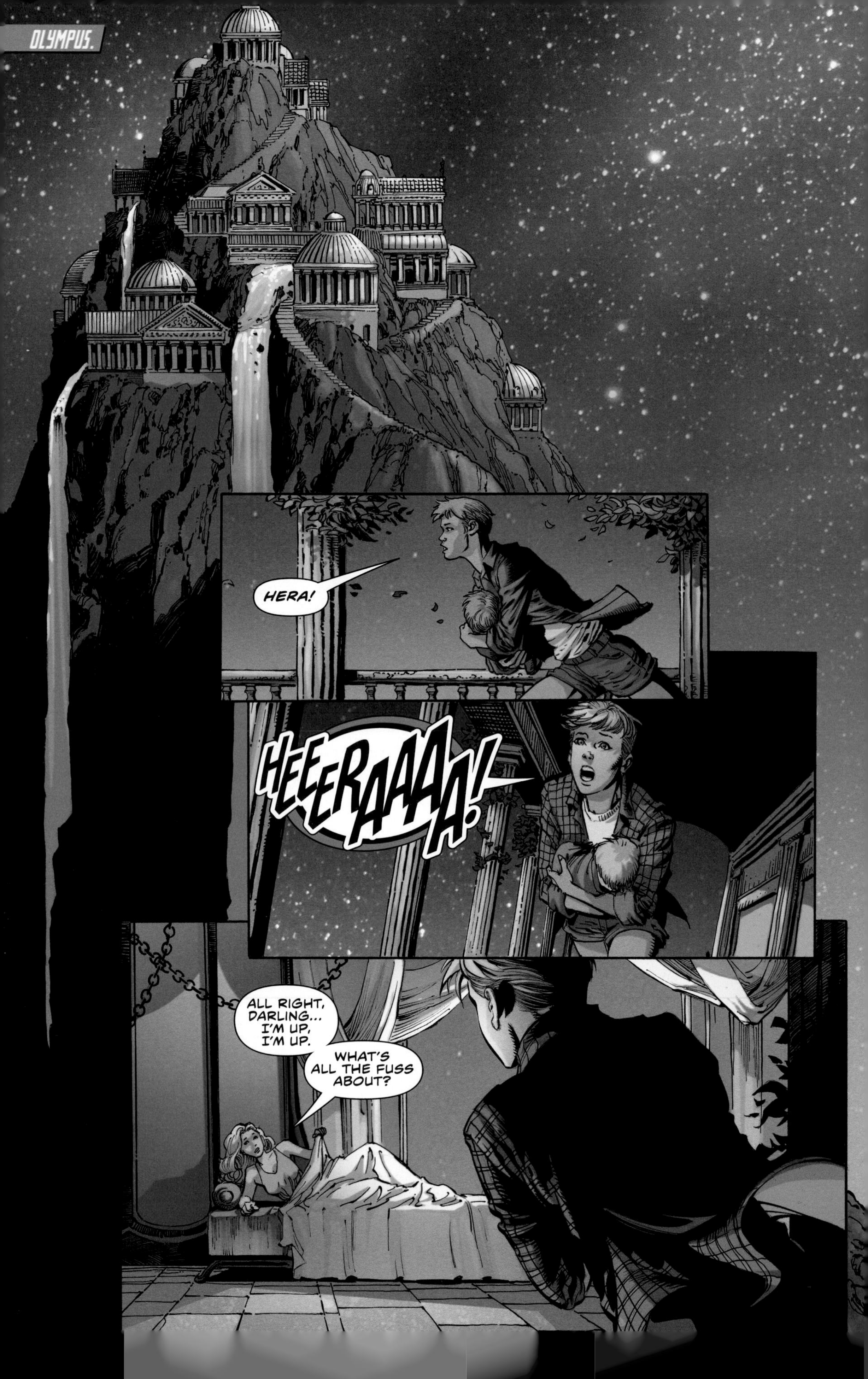
OLYMPUS.
HERA!
HEEERAAAA!
ALL RIGHT, DARLING... I'M UP, I'M UP.
WHAT'S ALL THE FUSS ABOUT?

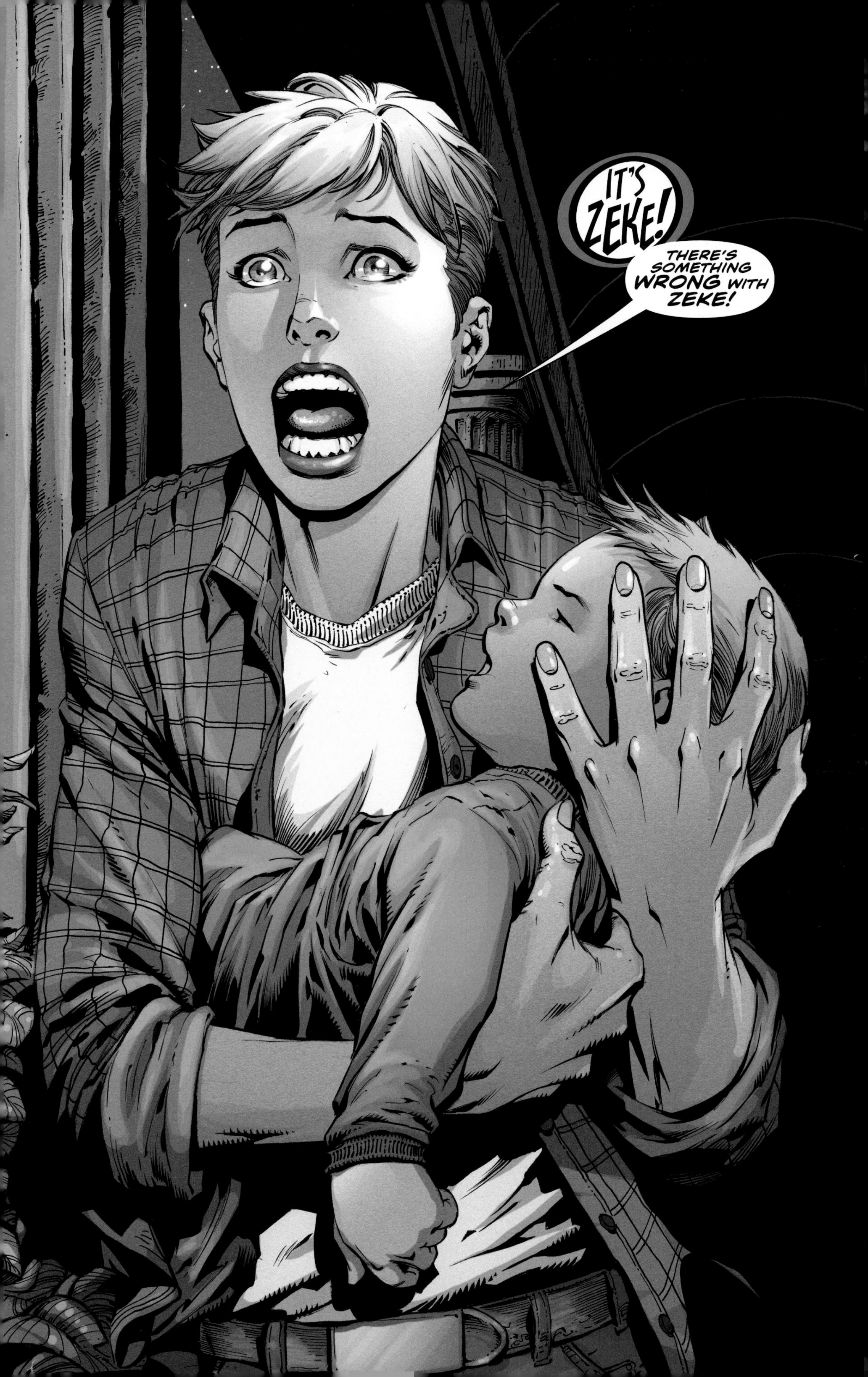
IT'S ZEKE!
THERE'S SOMETHING WRONG WITH ZEKE!

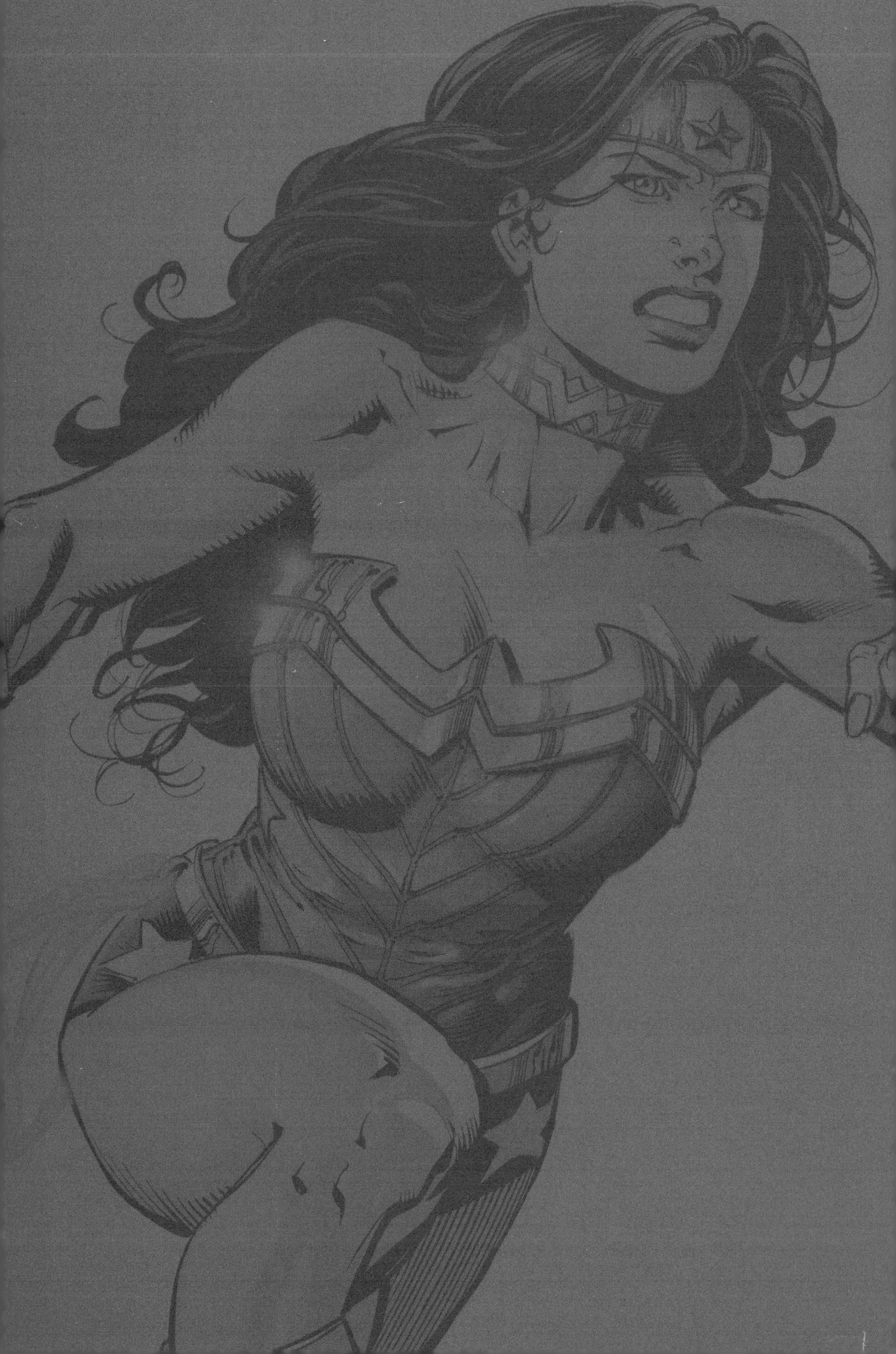

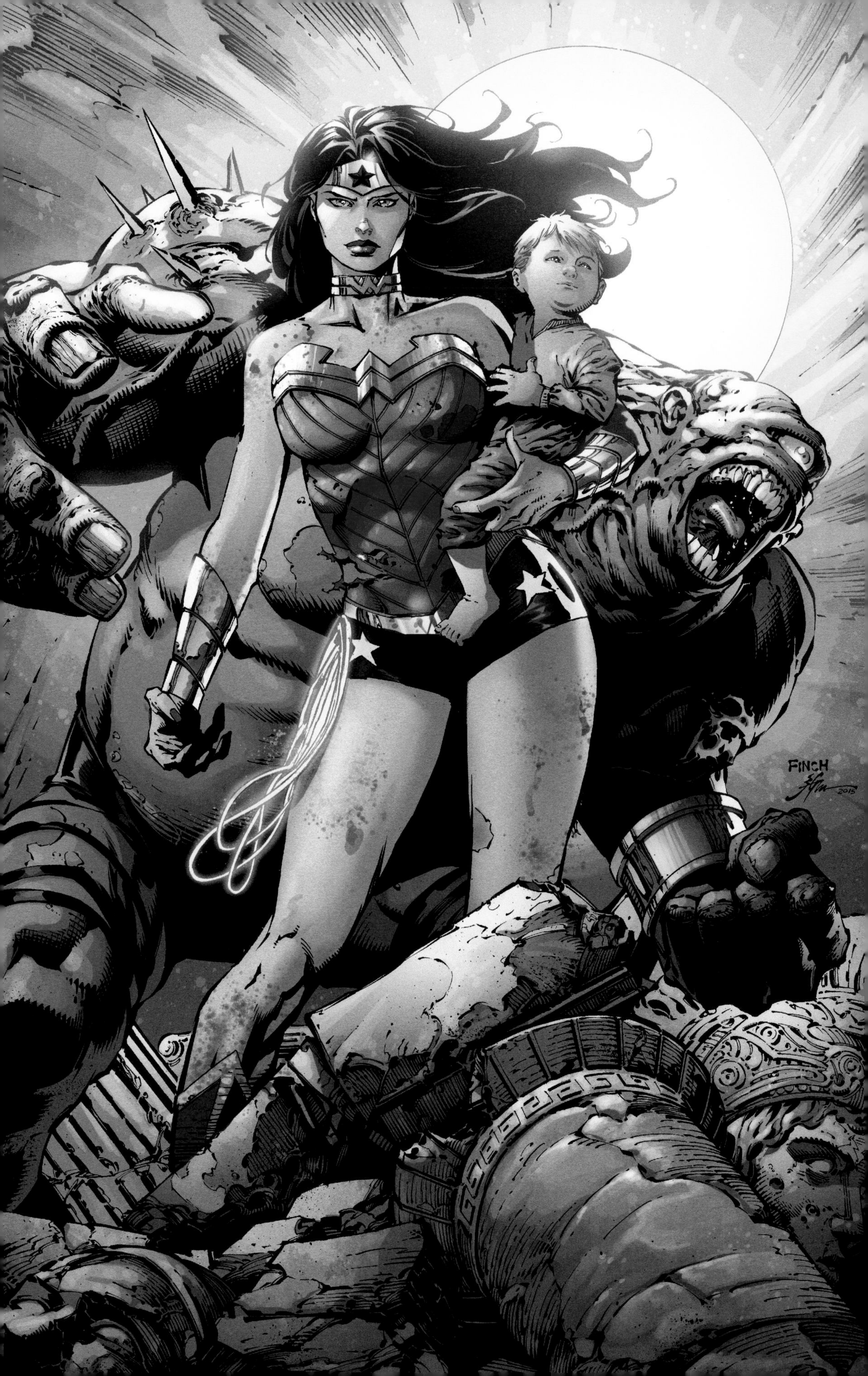
FINCH

WHAT LIES BENEATH

MEREDITH FINCH writer DAVID FINCH penciller SCOTT HANNA DAVID FINCH inkers BRAD ANDERSON colorist ROB LEIGH letterer
cover art by DAVID FINCH, JONATHAN GLAPION & BRAD ANDERSON

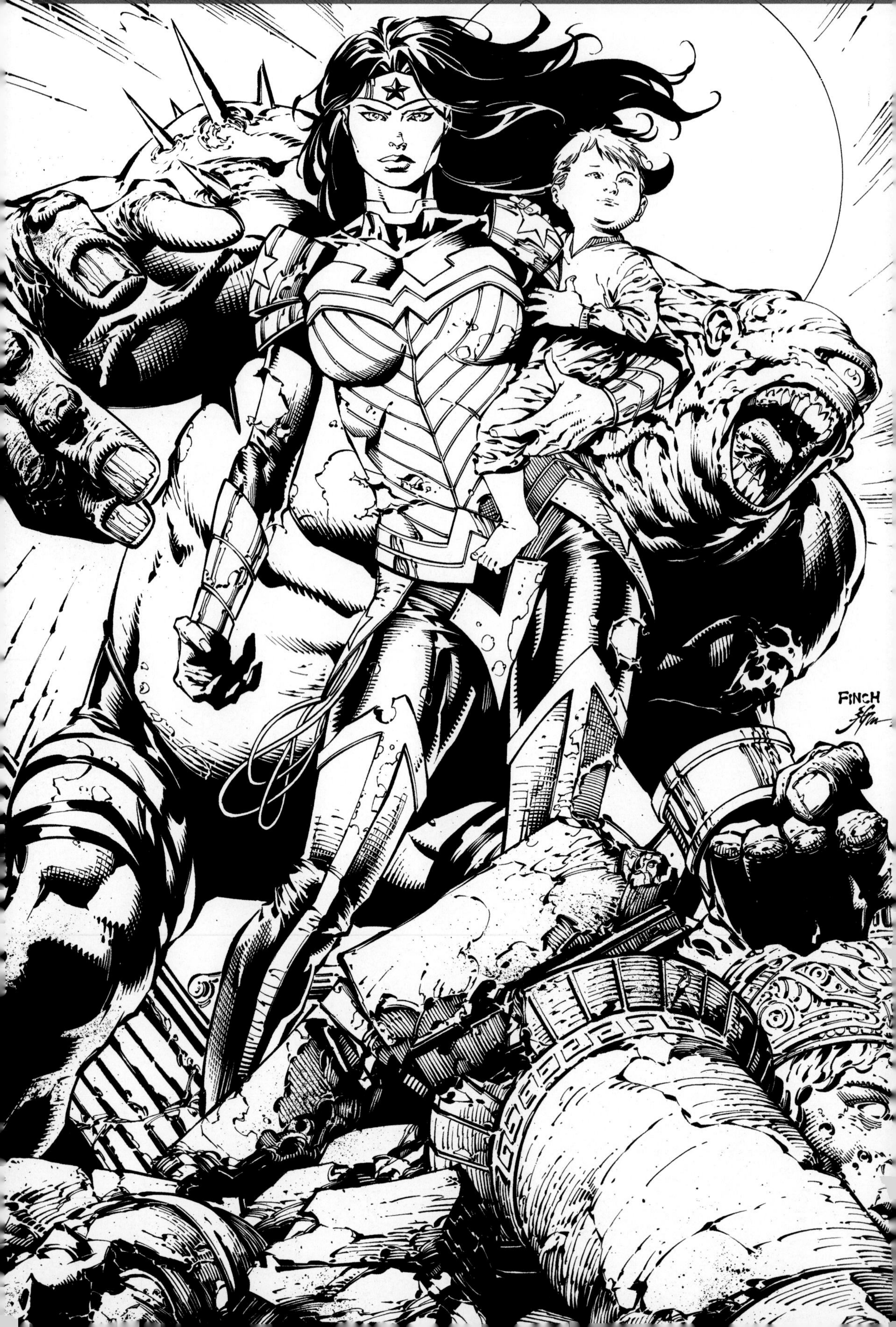
FINCH

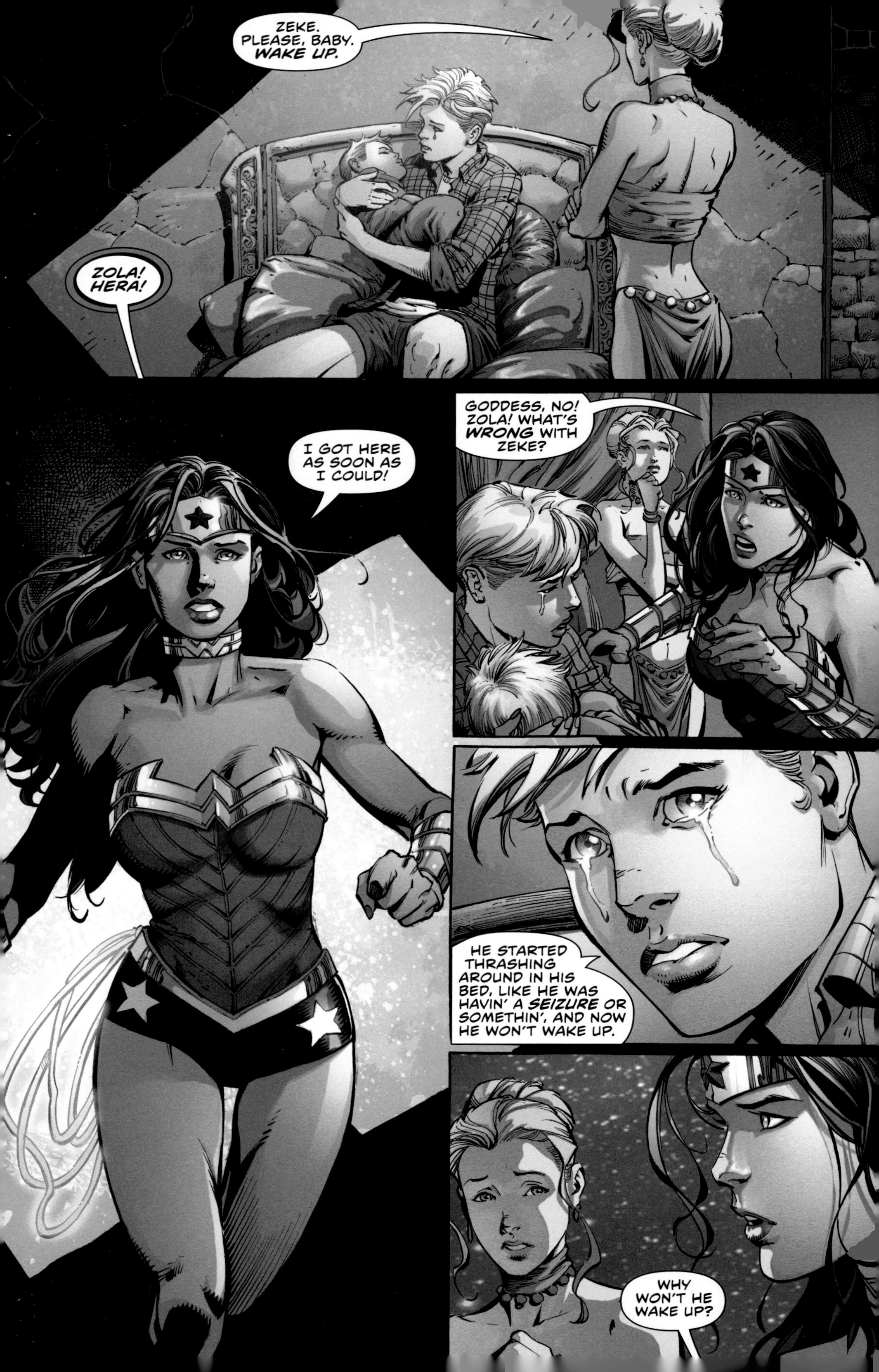
ZEKE. PLEASE, BABY. WAKE UP.
ZOLA! HERA!
I GOT HERE AS SOON AS I COULD!
GODDESS, NO! ZOLA! WHAT'S WRONG WITH ZEKE?
HE STARTED THRASHING AROUND IN HIS BED, LIKE HE WAS HAVIN' A SEIZURE OR SOMETHIN', AND NOW HE WON'T WAKE UP.
WHY WON'T HE WAKE UP?

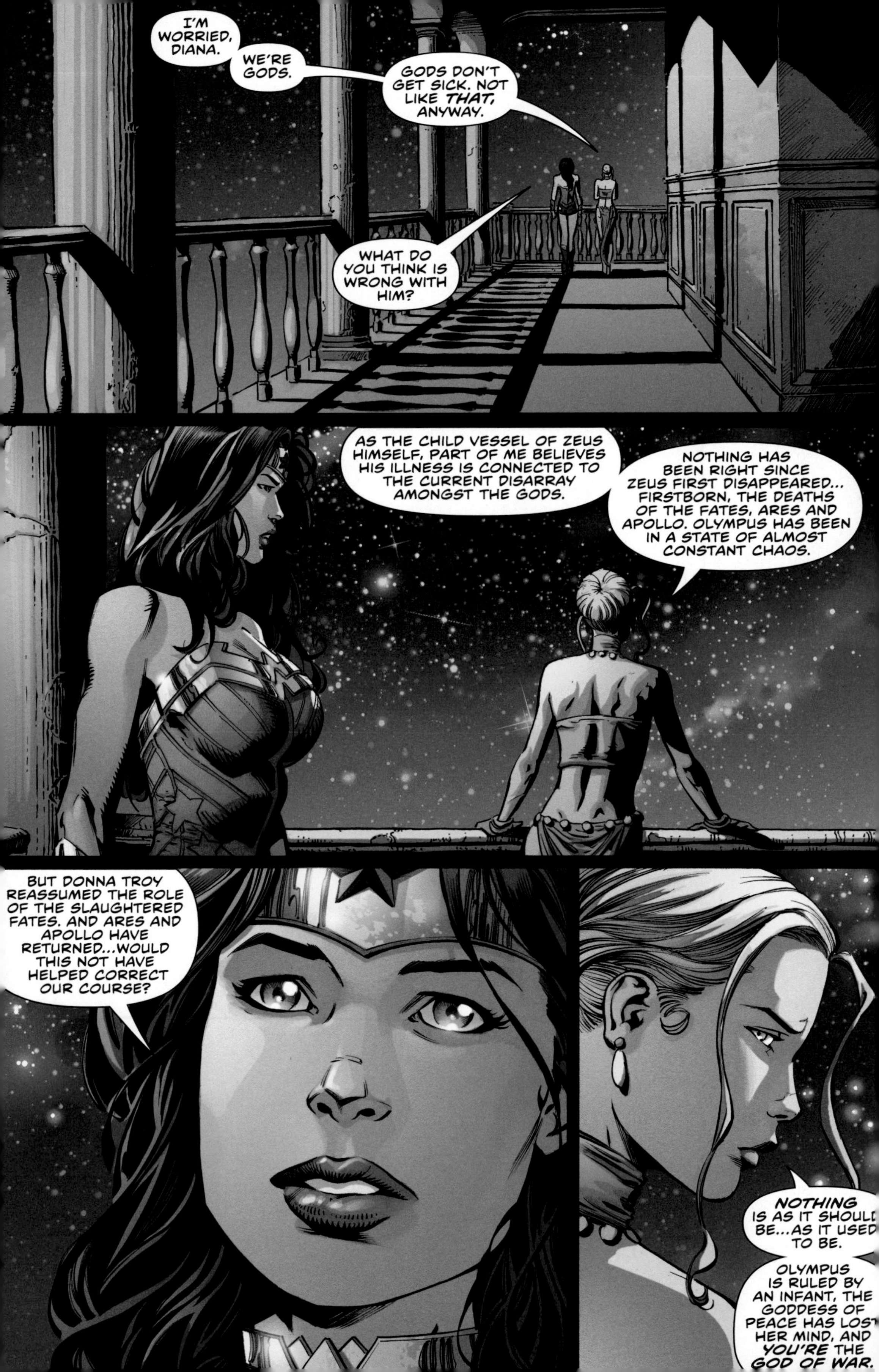
I'M WORRIED, DIANA.
WE'RE GODS.
GODS DON'T GET SICK. NOT LIKE *THAT,* ANYWAY.
WHAT DO YOU THINK IS WRONG WITH HIM?
AS THE CHILD VESSEL OF ZEUS HIMSELF, PART OF ME BELIEVES HIS ILLNESS IS CONNECTED TO THE CURRENT DISARRAY AMONGST THE GODS.
NOTHING HAS BEEN RIGHT SINCE ZEUS FIRST DISAPPEARED... FIRSTBORN, THE DEATHS OF THE FATES, ARES AND APOLLO. OLYMPUS HAS BEEN IN A STATE OF ALMOST CONSTANT CHAOS.
BUT DONNA TROY REASSUMED THE ROLE OF THE SLAUGHTERED FATES. AND ARES AND APOLLO HAVE RETURNED...WOULD THIS NOT HAVE HELPED CORRECT OUR COURSE?
NOTHING IS AS IT SHOULD BE...AS IT USED TO BE.
OLYMPUS IS RULED BY AN INFANT, THE GODDESS OF PEACE HAS LOST HER MIND, AND *YOU'RE* THE *GOD OF WAR.*

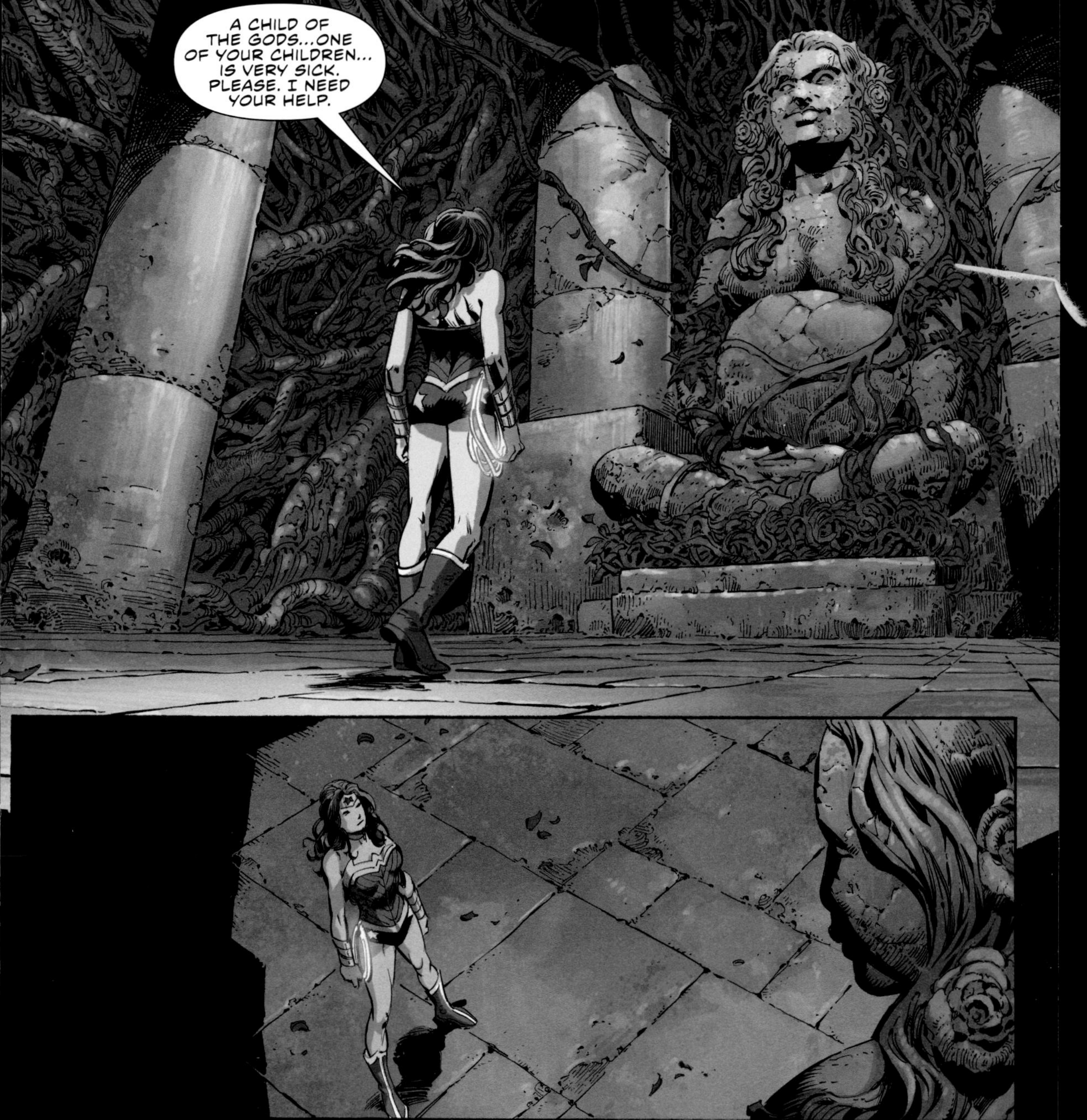
A CHILD OF THE GODS...ONE OF YOUR CHILDREN... IS VERY SICK. PLEASE. I NEED YOUR HELP.

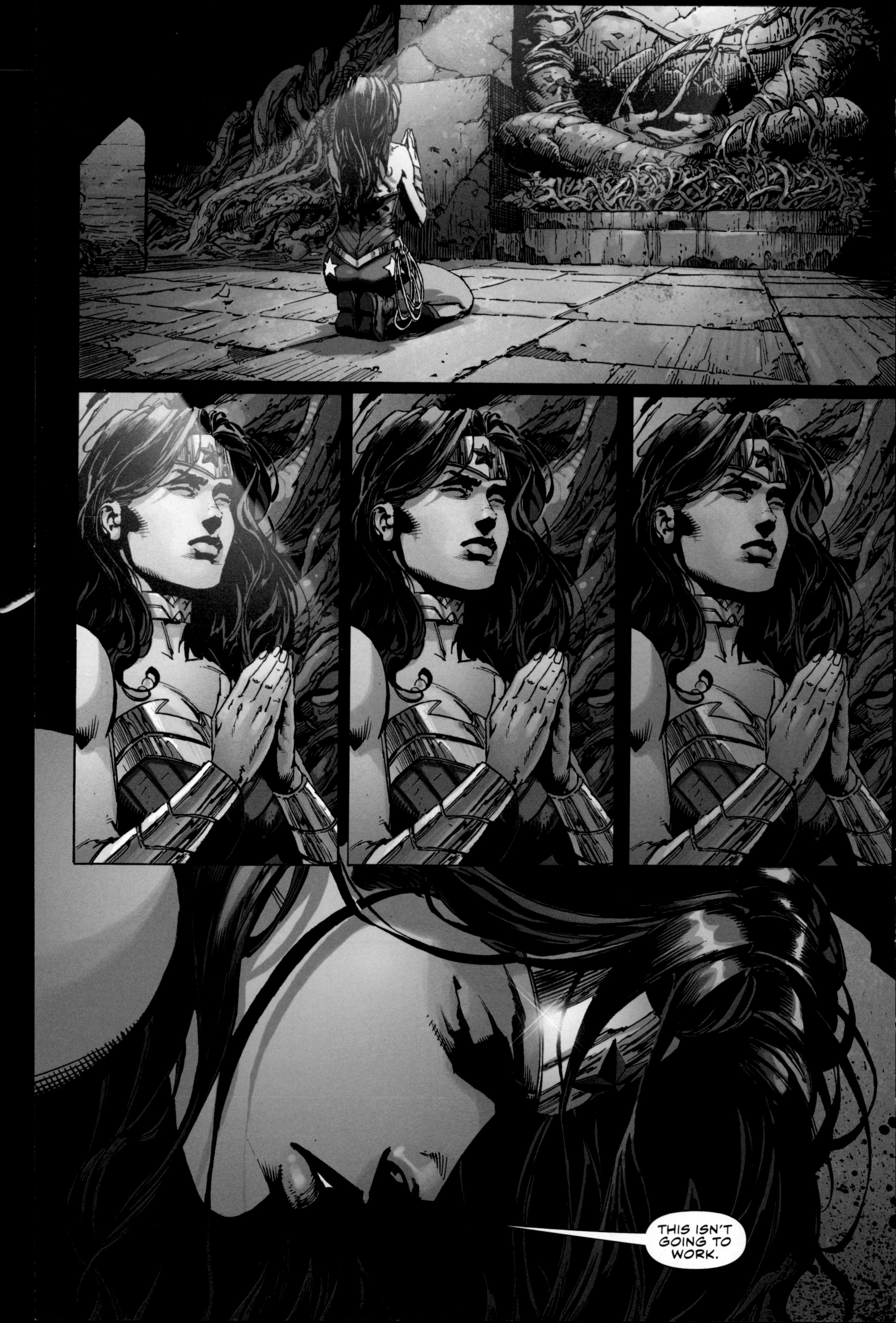
THIS ISN'T GOING TO WORK.

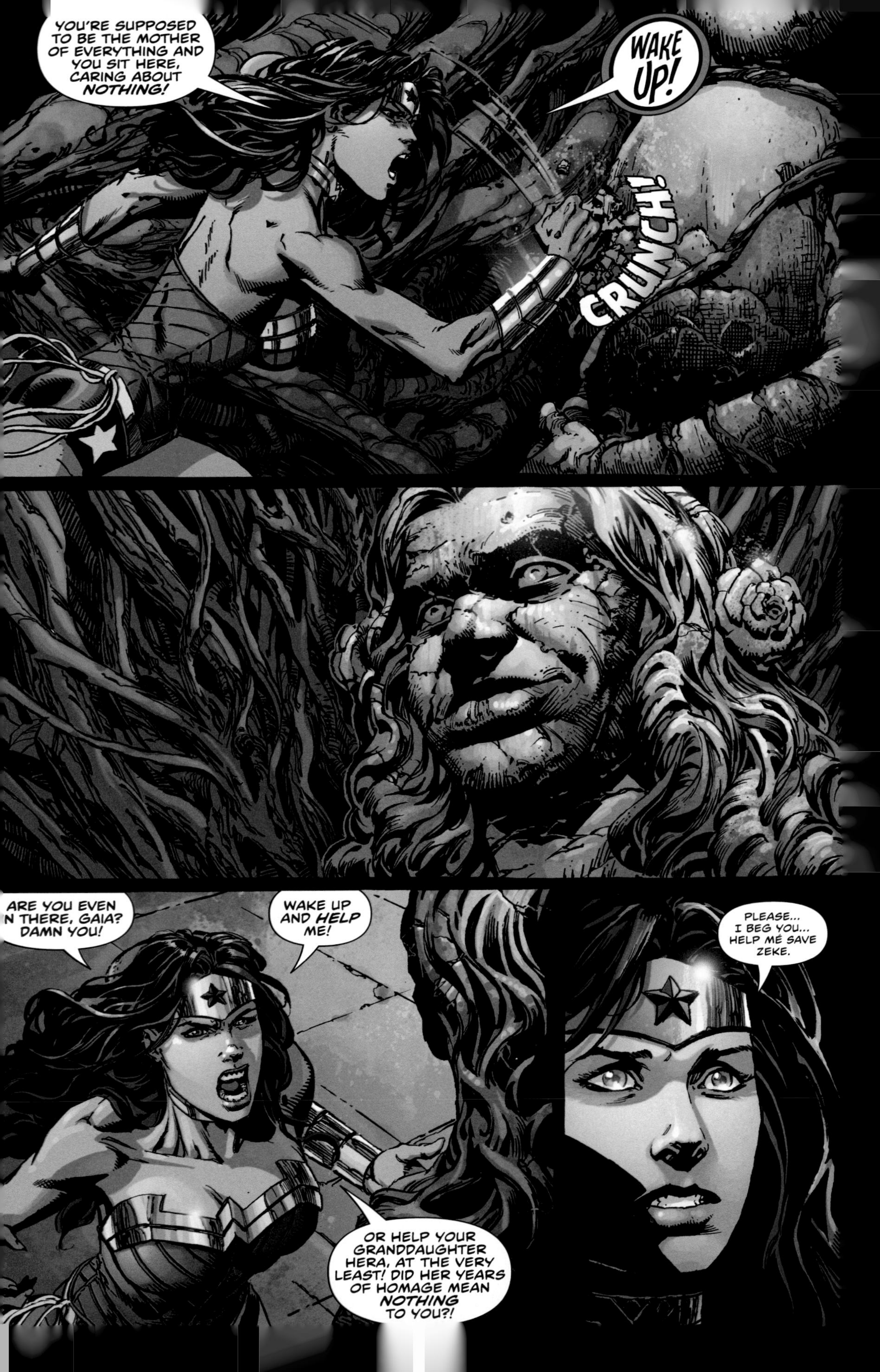

YOU'RE SUPPOSED TO BE THE MOTHER OF EVERYTHING AND YOU SIT HERE, CARING ABOUT NOTHING!
WAKE UP!
CRUNCH!
ARE YOU EVEN N THERE, GAIA? DAMN YOU!
WAKE UP AND HELP ME!
OR HELP YOUR GRANDDAUGHTER HERA, AT THE VERY LEAST! DID HER YEARS OF HOMAGE MEAN NOTHING TO YOU?!
PLEASE... I BEG YOU... HELP ME SAVE ZEKE.

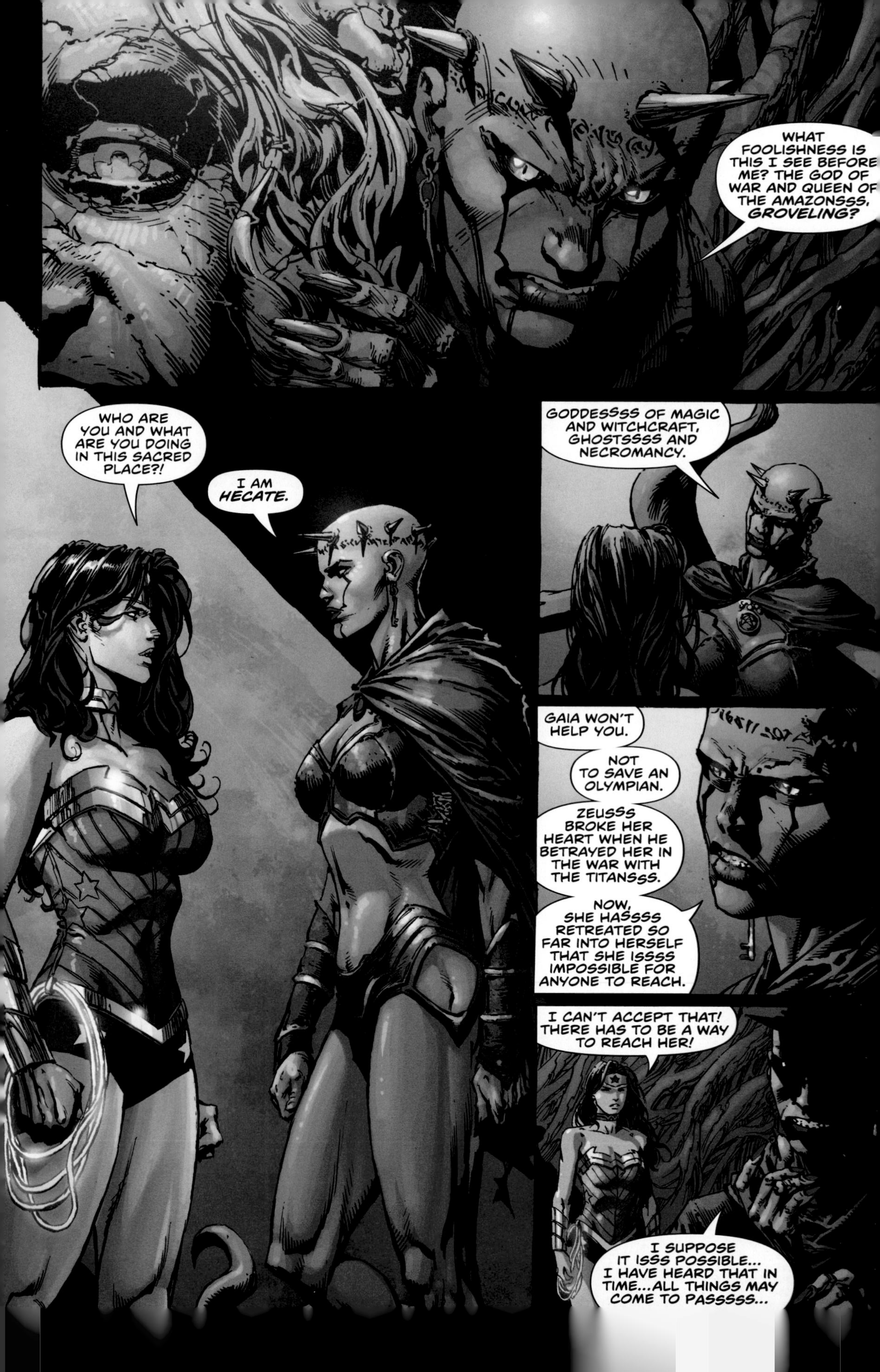
WHAT FOOLISHNESS IS THIS I SEE BEFORE ME? THE GOD OF WAR AND QUEEN OF THE AMAZONSSS, GROVELING?
WHO ARE YOU AND WHAT ARE YOU DOING IN THIS SACRED PLACE?!
I AM HECATE.
GODDESSSS OF MAGIC AND WITCHCRAFT, GHOSTSSSS AND NECROMANCY.
GAIA WON'T HELP YOU.
NOT TO SAVE AN OLYMPIAN.
ZEUSSS BROKE HER HEART WHEN HE BETRAYED HER IN THE WAR WITH THE TITANSSS.
NOW, SHE HASSSS RETREATED SO FAR INTO HERSELF THAT SHE ISSSS IMPOSSIBLE FOR ANYONE TO REACH.
I CAN'T ACCEPT THAT! THERE HAS TO BE A WAY TO REACH HER!
I SUPPOSE IT ISSS POSSIBLE... I HAVE HEARD THAT IN TIME...ALL THINGS MAY COME TO PASSSSS...

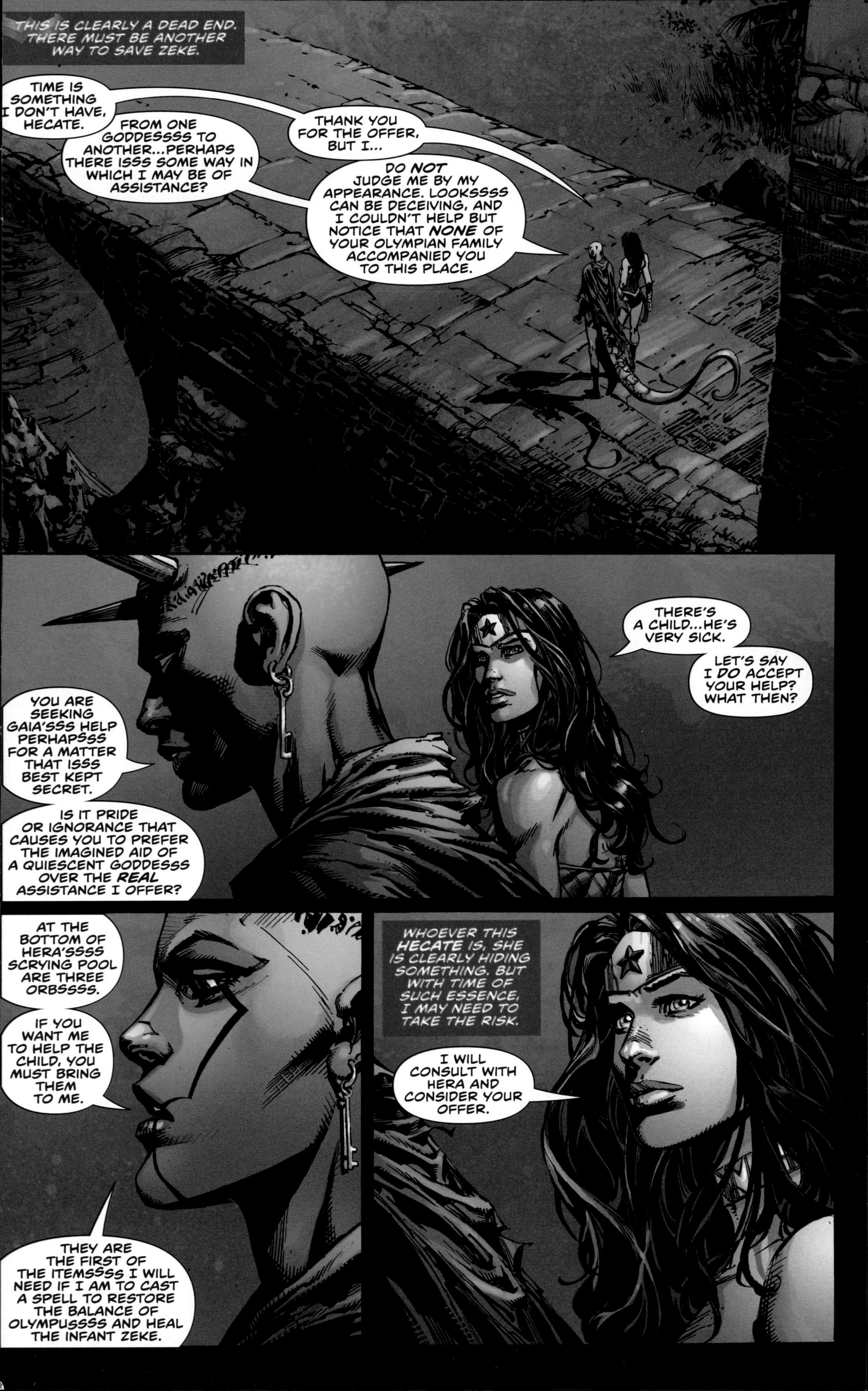
THIS IS CLEARLY A DEAD END. THERE MUST BE ANOTHER WAY TO SAVE ZEKE.
TIME IS SOMETHING I DON'T HAVE, HECATE.
THANK YOU FOR THE OFFER, BUT I...
FROM ONE GODDESSSS TO ANOTHER...PERHAPS THERE ISSS SOME WAY IN WHICH I MAY BE OF ASSISTANCE?
DO NOT JUDGE ME BY MY APPEARANCE. LOOKSSSS CAN BE DECEIVING, AND I COULDN'T HELP BUT NOTICE THAT NONE OF YOUR OLYMPIAN FAMILY ACCOMPANIED YOU TO THIS PLACE.
THERE'S A CHILD...HE'S VERY SICK.
LET'S SAY I DO ACCEPT YOUR HELP? WHAT THEN?
YOU ARE SEEKING GAIA'SSS HELP PERHAPSSS FOR A MATTER THAT ISSS BEST KEPT SECRET.
IS IT PRIDE OR IGNORANCE THAT CAUSES YOU TO PREFER THE IMAGINED AID OF A QUIESCENT GODDESSS OVER THE REAL ASSISTANCE I OFFER?
AT THE BOTTOM OF HERA'SSSS SCRYING POOL ARE THREE ORBSSSS.
IF YOU WANT ME TO HELP THE CHILD, YOU MUST BRING THEM TO ME.
THEY ARE THE FIRST OF THE ITEMSSSS I WILL NEED IF I AM TO CAST A SPELL TO RESTORE THE BALANCE OF OLYMPUSSSS AND HEAL THE INFANT ZEKE.
WHOEVER THIS HECATE IS, SHE IS CLEARLY HIDING SOMETHING. BUT WITH TIME OF SUCH ESSENCE, I MAY NEED TO TAKE THE RISK.
I WILL CONSULT WITH HERA AND CONSIDER YOUR OFFER.

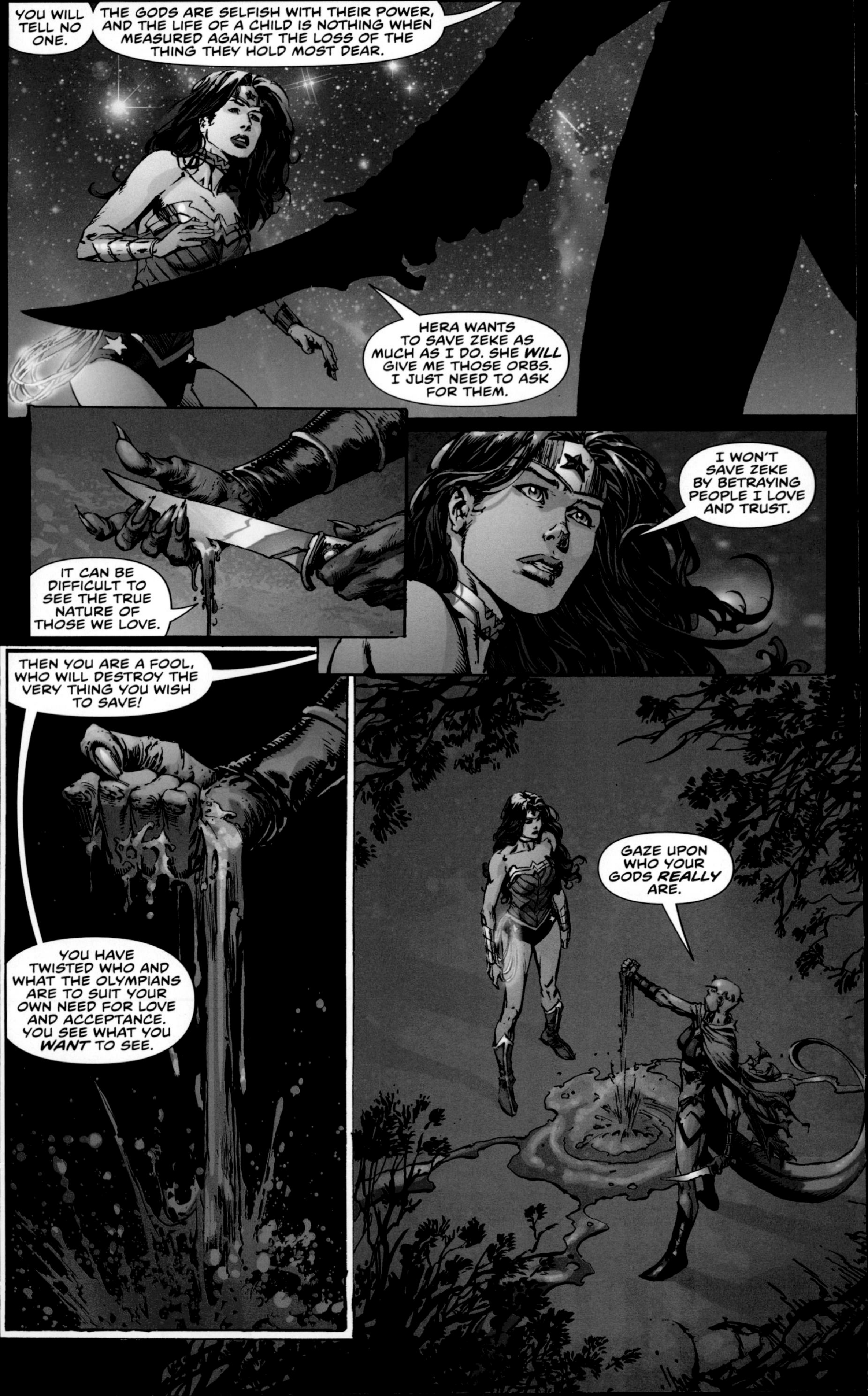
YOU WILL TELL NO ONE.
THE GODS ARE SELFISH WITH THEIR POWER, AND THE LIFE OF A CHILD IS NOTHING WHEN MEASURED AGAINST THE LOSS OF THE THING THEY HOLD MOST DEAR.
HERA WANTS TO SAVE ZEKE AS MUCH AS I DO. SHE *WILL* GIVE ME THOSE ORBS. I JUST NEED TO ASK FOR THEM.
IT CAN BE DIFFICULT TO SEE THE TRUE NATURE OF THOSE WE LOVE.
I WON'T SAVE ZEKE BY BETRAYING PEOPLE I LOVE AND TRUST.
THEN YOU ARE A FOOL, WHO WILL DESTROY THE VERY THING YOU WISH TO SAVE!
YOU HAVE TWISTED WHO AND WHAT THE OLYMPIANS ARE TO SUIT YOUR OWN NEED FOR LOVE AND ACCEPTANCE. YOU SEE WHAT YOU *WANT* TO SEE.
GAZE UPON WHO YOUR GODS *REALLY* ARE.

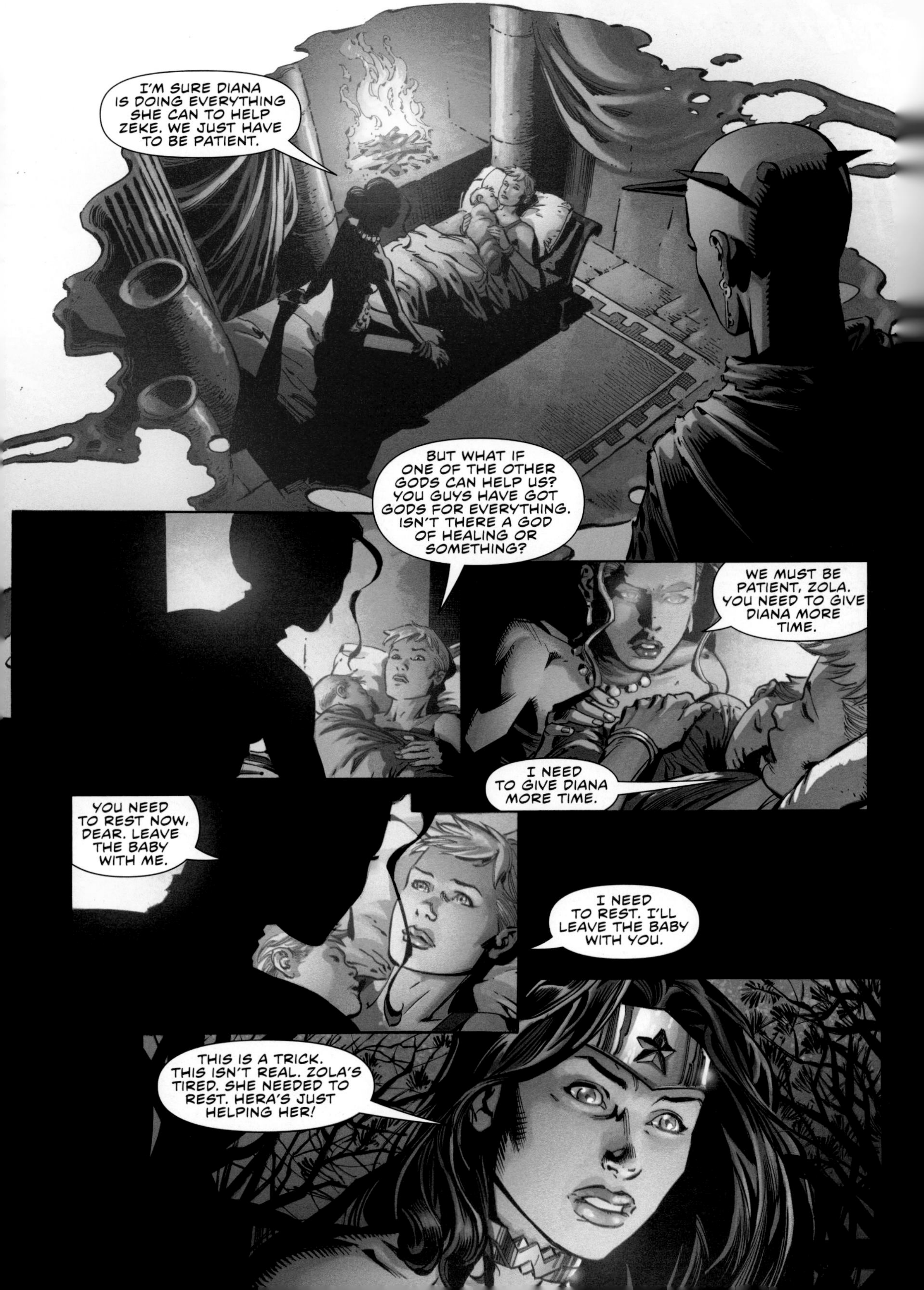
I'M SURE DIANA IS DOING EVERYTHING SHE CAN TO HELP ZEKE. WE JUST HAVE TO BE PATIENT.
BUT WHAT IF ONE OF THE OTHER GODS CAN HELP US? YOU GUYS HAVE GOT GODS FOR EVERYTHING. ISN'T THERE A GOD OF HEALING OR SOMETHING?
WE MUST BE PATIENT, ZOLA. YOU NEED TO GIVE DIANA MORE TIME.
I NEED TO GIVE DIANA MORE TIME.
YOU NEED TO REST NOW, DEAR. LEAVE THE BABY WITH ME.
I NEED TO REST. I'LL LEAVE THE BABY WITH YOU.
THIS IS A TRICK. THIS ISN'T REAL. ZOLA'S TIRED. SHE NEEDED TO REST. HERA'S JUST HELPING HER!

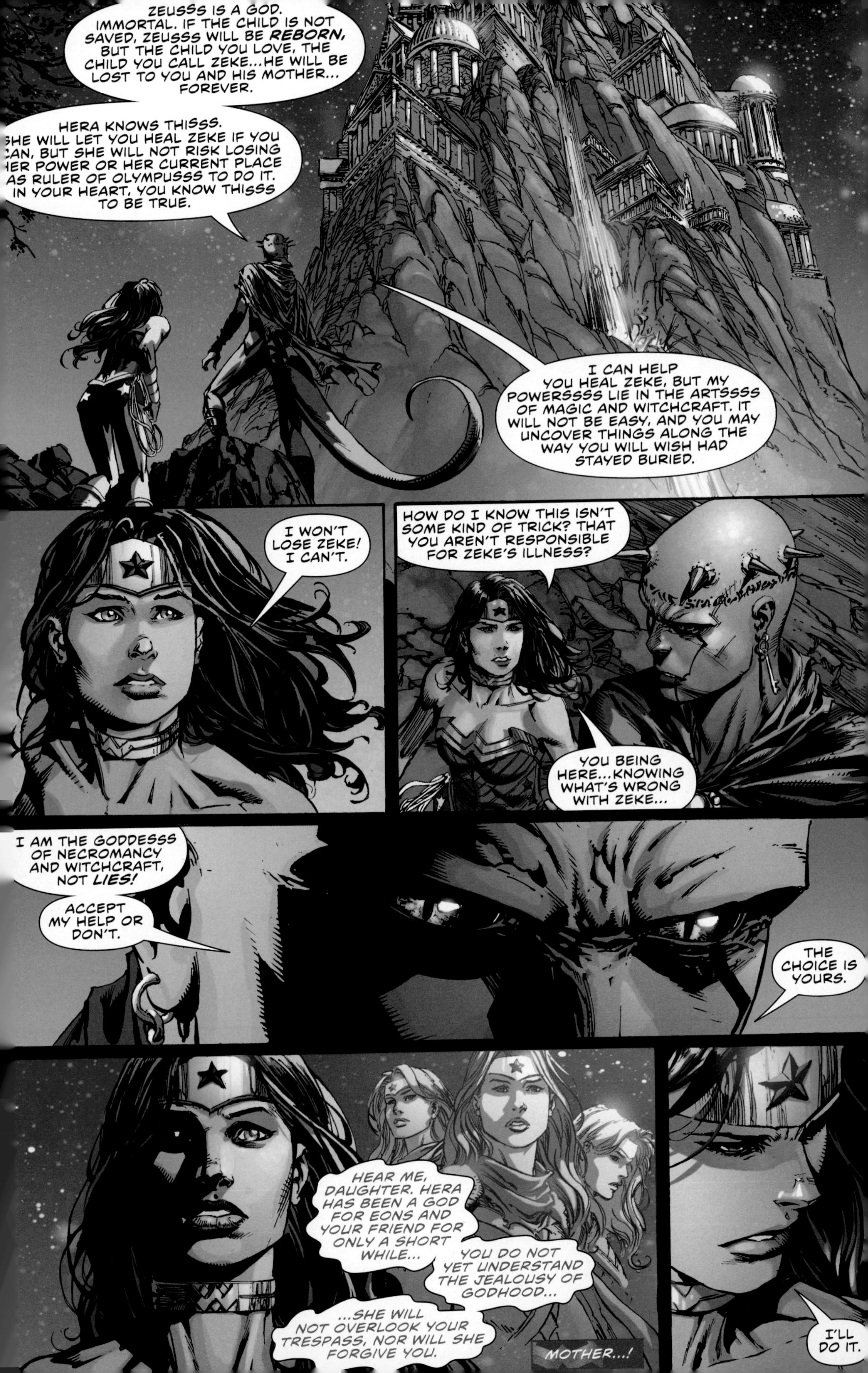
ZEUSSS IS A GOD. IMMORTAL. IF THE CHILD IS NOT SAVED, ZEUSSS WILL BE REBORN, BUT THE CHILD YOU LOVE, THE CHILD YOU CALL ZEKE...HE WILL BE LOST TO YOU AND HIS MOTHER... FOREVER.
HERA KNOWS THISSS. SHE WILL LET YOU HEAL ZEKE IF YOU CAN, BUT SHE WILL NOT RISK LOSING HER POWER OR HER CURRENT PLACE AS RULER OF OLYMPUSSS TO DO IT. IN YOUR HEART, YOU KNOW THISSS TO BE TRUE.
I CAN HELP YOU HEAL ZEKE, BUT MY POWERSSSS LIE IN THE ARTSSSS OF MAGIC AND WITCHCRAFT. IT WILL NOT BE EASY, AND YOU MAY UNCOVER THINGS ALONG THE WAY YOU WILL WISH HAD STAYED BURIED.
I WON'T LOSE ZEKE! I CAN'T.
HOW DO I KNOW THIS ISN'T SOME KIND OF TRICK? THAT YOU AREN'T RESPONSIBLE FOR ZEKE'S ILLNESS?
YOU BEING HERE...KNOWING WHAT'S WRONG WITH ZEKE...
I AM THE GODDESSS OF NECROMANCY AND WITCHCRAFT, NOT LIES!
ACCEPT MY HELP OR DON'T.
THE CHOICE IS YOURS.
HEAR ME, DAUGHTER. HERA HAS BEEN A GOD FOR EONS AND YOUR FRIEND FOR ONLY A SHORT WHILE...
YOU DO NOT YET UNDERSTAND THE JEALOUSY OF GODHOOD...
...SHE WILL NOT OVERLOOK YOUR TRESPASS, NOR WILL SHE FORGIVE YOU.
MOTHER...!
I'LL DO IT.

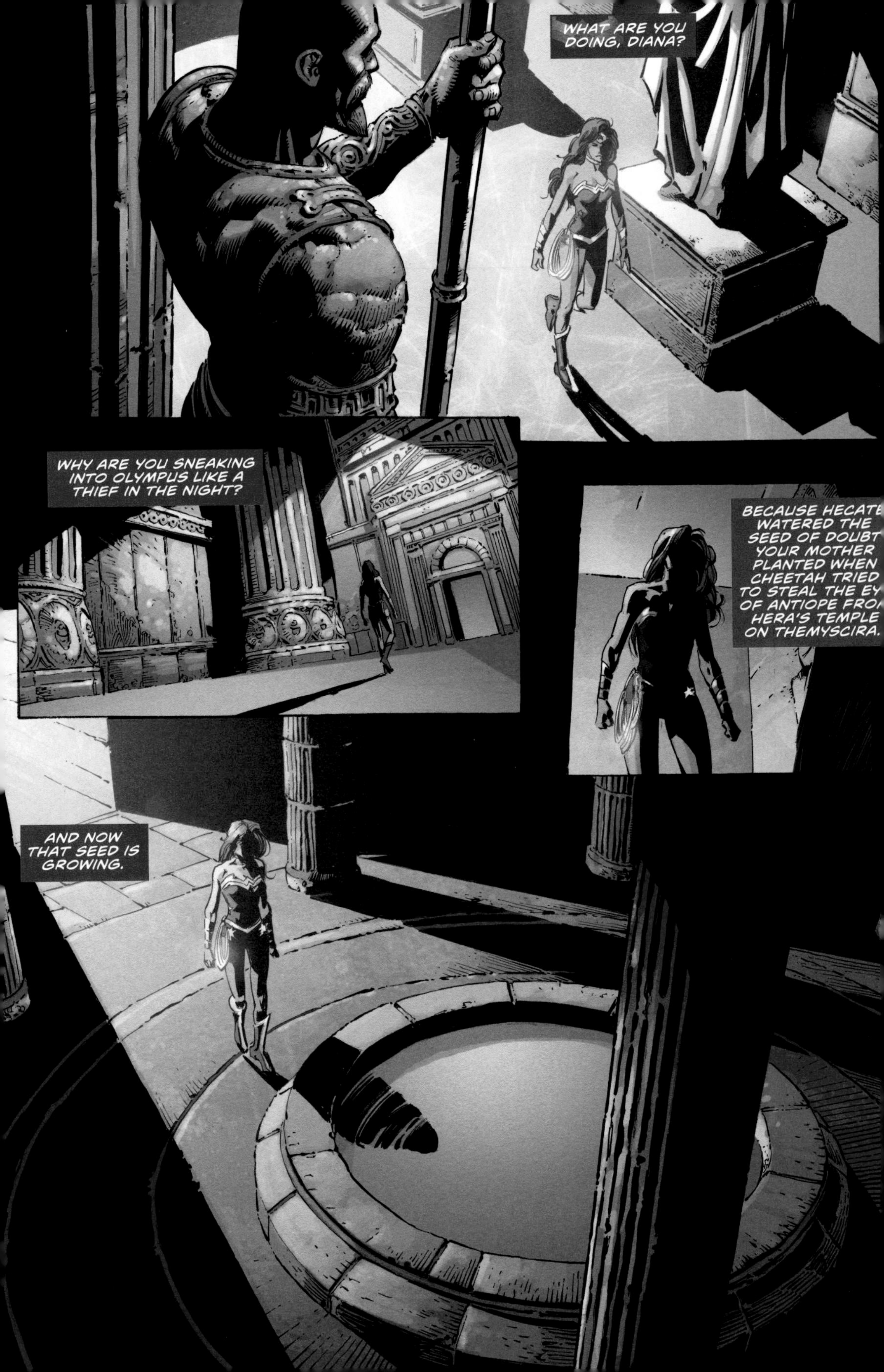
WHAT ARE YOU DOING, DIANA?
WHY ARE YOU SNEAKING INTO OLYMPUS LIKE A THIEF IN THE NIGHT?
BECAUSE HECATE WATERED THE SEED OF DOUBT YOUR MOTHER PLANTED WHEN CHEETAH TRIED TO STEAL THE EY OF ANTIOPE FRO HERA'S TEMPLE ON THEMYSCIRA.
AND NOW THAT SEED IS GROWING.

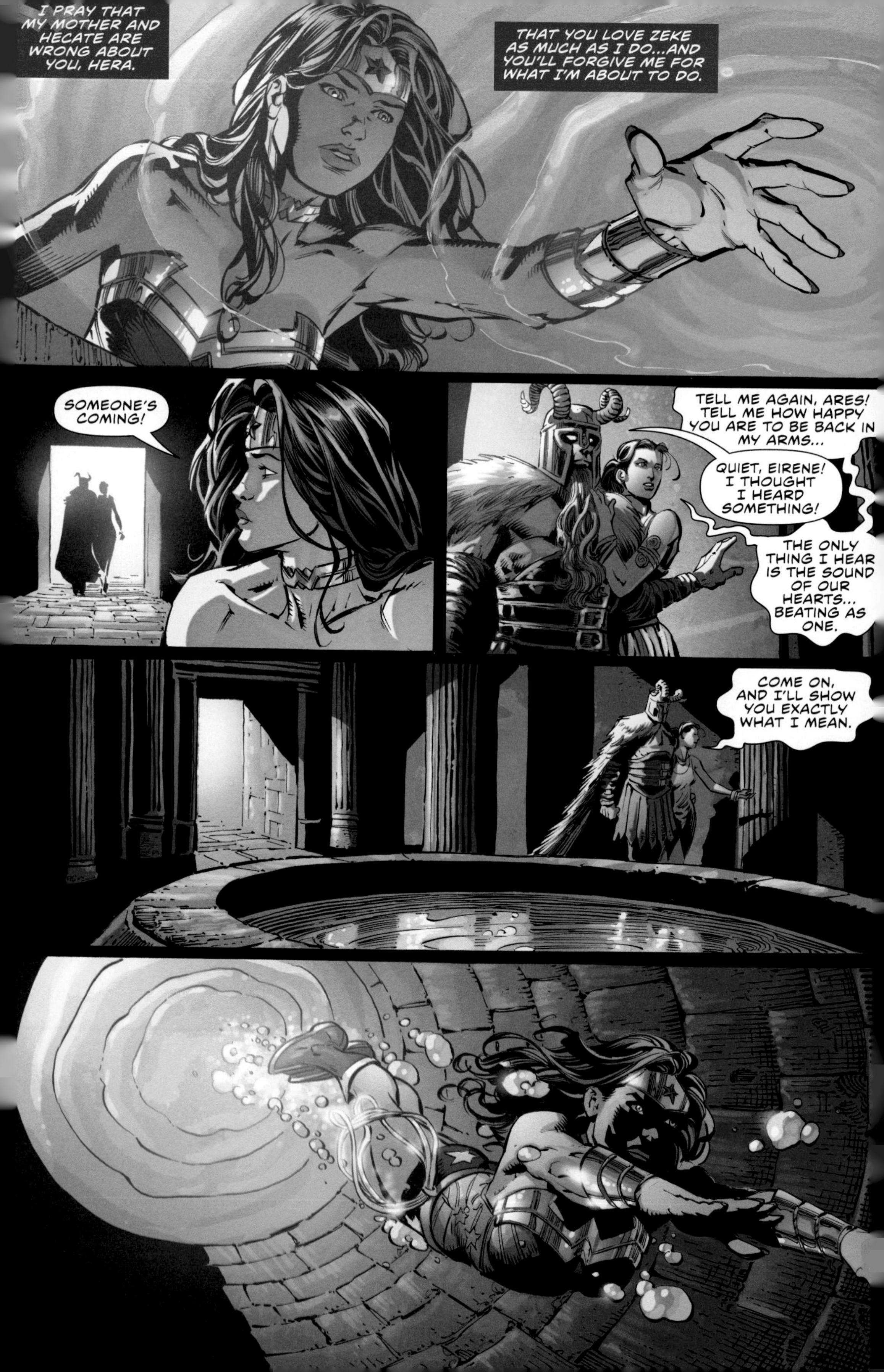
I PRAY THAT MY MOTHER AND HECATE ARE WRONG ABOUT YOU, HERA.
THAT YOU LOVE ZEKE AS MUCH AS I DO...AND YOU'LL FORGIVE ME FOR WHAT I'M ABOUT TO DO.
SOMEONE'S COMING!
TELL ME AGAIN, ARES! TELL ME HOW HAPPY YOU ARE TO BE BACK IN MY ARMS...
QUIET, EIRENE! I THOUGHT I HEARD SOMETHING!
THE ONLY THING I HEAR IS THE SOUND OF OUR HEARTS... BEATING AS ONE.
COME ON, AND I'LL SHOW YOU EXACTLY WHAT I MEAN.

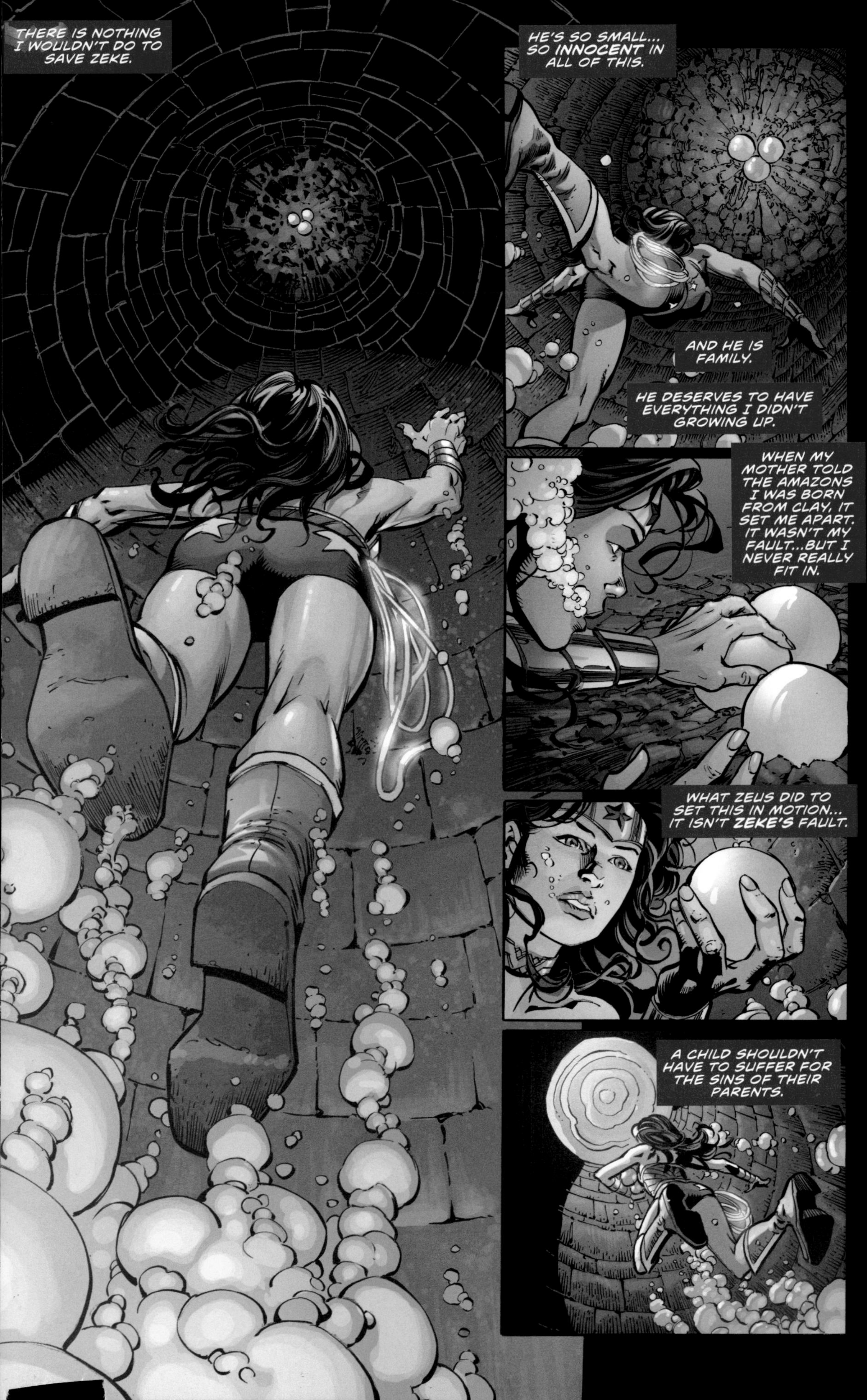
THERE IS NOTHING I WOULDN'T DO TO SAVE ZEKE.
HE'S SO SMALL... SO INNOCENT IN ALL OF THIS.
AND HE IS FAMILY.
HE DESERVES TO HAVE EVERYTHING I DIDN'T GROWING UP.
WHEN MY MOTHER TOLD THE AMAZONS I WAS BORN FROM CLAY, IT SET ME APART. IT WASN'T MY FAULT...BUT I NEVER REALLY FIT IN.
WHAT ZEUS DID TO SET THIS IN MOTION... IT ISN'T ZEKE'S FAULT.
A CHILD SHOULDN'T HAVE TO SUFFER FOR THE SINS OF THEIR PARENTS.

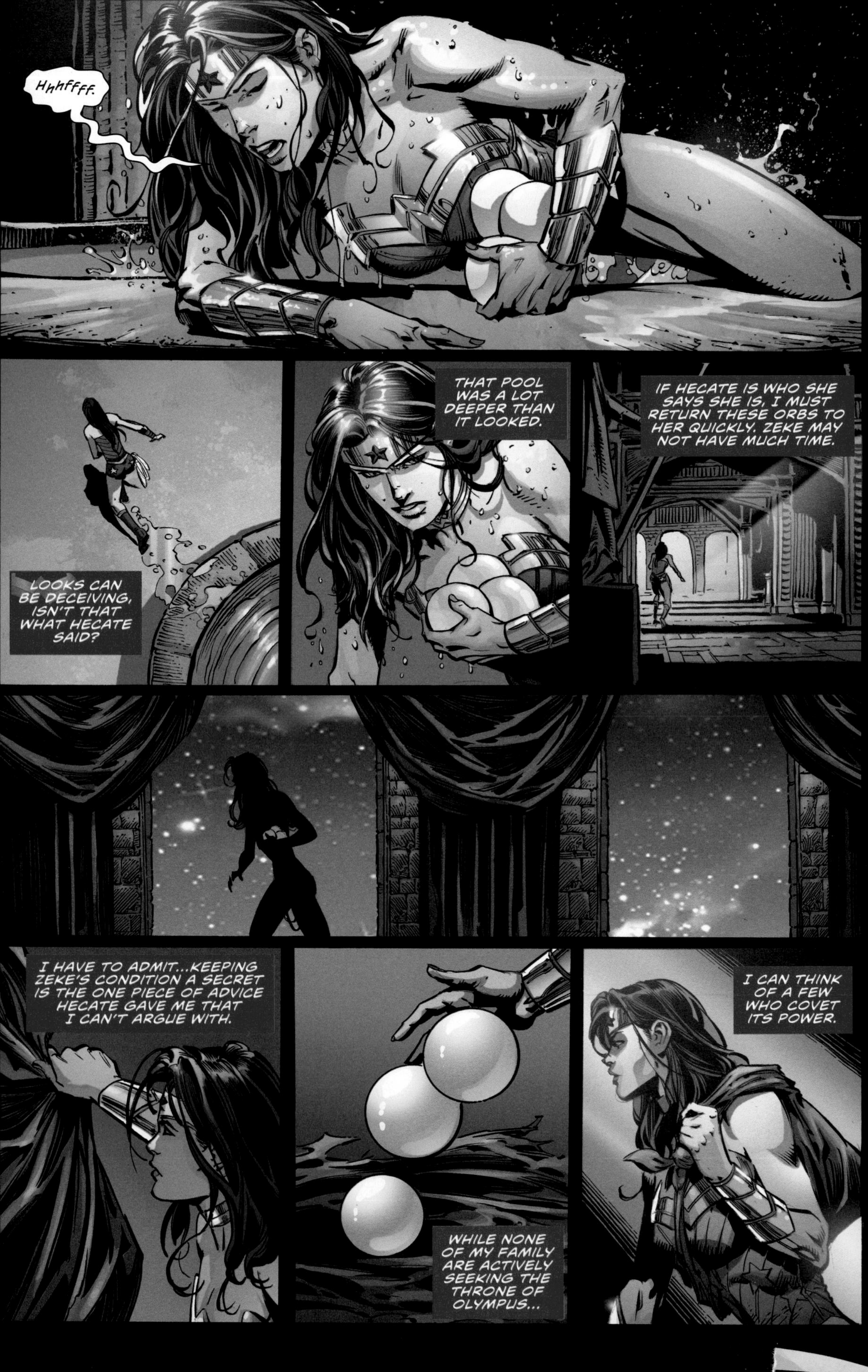
Hnhffff.
LOOKS CAN BE DECEIVING, ISN'T THAT WHAT HECATE SAID?
THAT POOL WAS A LOT DEEPER THAN IT LOOKED.
IF HECATE IS WHO SHE SAYS SHE IS, I MUST RETURN THESE ORBS TO HER QUICKLY. ZEKE MAY NOT HAVE MUCH TIME.
I HAVE TO ADMIT...KEEPING ZEKE'S CONDITION A SECRET IS THE ONE PIECE OF ADVICE HECATE GAVE ME THAT I CAN'T ARGUE WITH.
WHILE NONE OF MY FAMILY ARE ACTIVELY SEEKING THE THRONE OF OLYMPUS...
I CAN THINK OF A FEW WHO COVET ITS POWER.

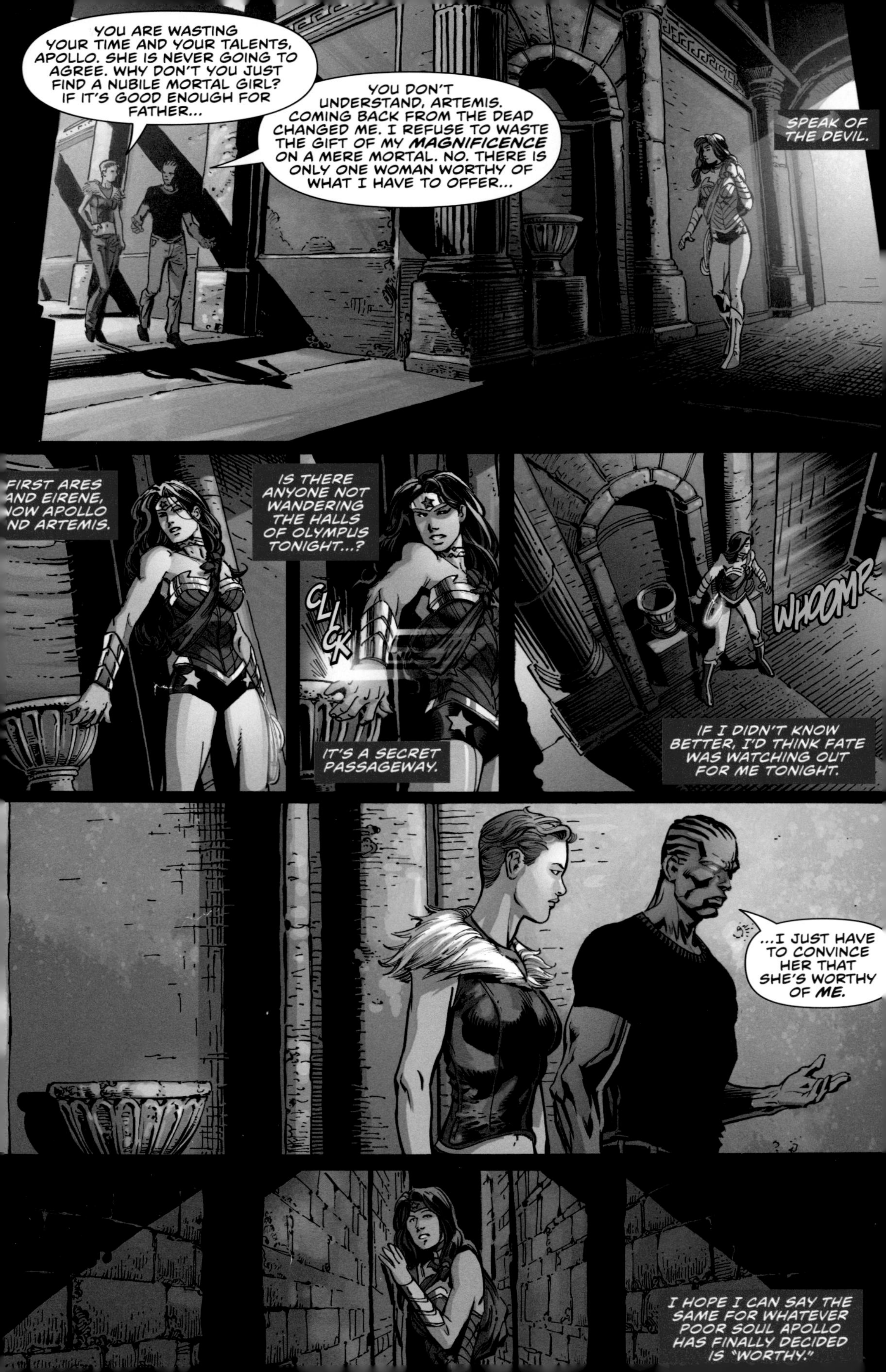
YOU ARE WASTING YOUR TIME AND YOUR TALENTS, APOLLO. SHE IS NEVER GOING TO AGREE. WHY DON'T YOU JUST FIND A NUBILE MORTAL GIRL? IF IT'S GOOD ENOUGH FOR FATHER...
YOU DON'T UNDERSTAND, ARTEMIS. COMING BACK FROM THE DEAD CHANGED ME. I REFUSE TO WASTE THE GIFT OF MY MAGNIFICENCE ON A MERE MORTAL. NO. THERE IS ONLY ONE WOMAN WORTHY OF WHAT I HAVE TO OFFER...
SPEAK OF THE DEVIL.
FIRST ARES AND EIRENE, NOW APOLLO AND ARTEMIS.
IS THERE ANYONE NOT WANDERING THE HALLS OF OLYMPUS TONIGHT...?
CLICK
IT'S A SECRET PASSAGEWAY.
WHOOMP
IF I DIDN'T KNOW BETTER, I'D THINK FATE WAS WATCHING OUT FOR ME TONIGHT.
...I JUST HAVE TO CONVINCE HER THAT SHE'S WORTHY OF ME.
I HOPE I CAN SAY THE SAME FOR WHATEVER POOR SOUL APOLLO HAS FINALLY DECIDED IS "WORTHY."

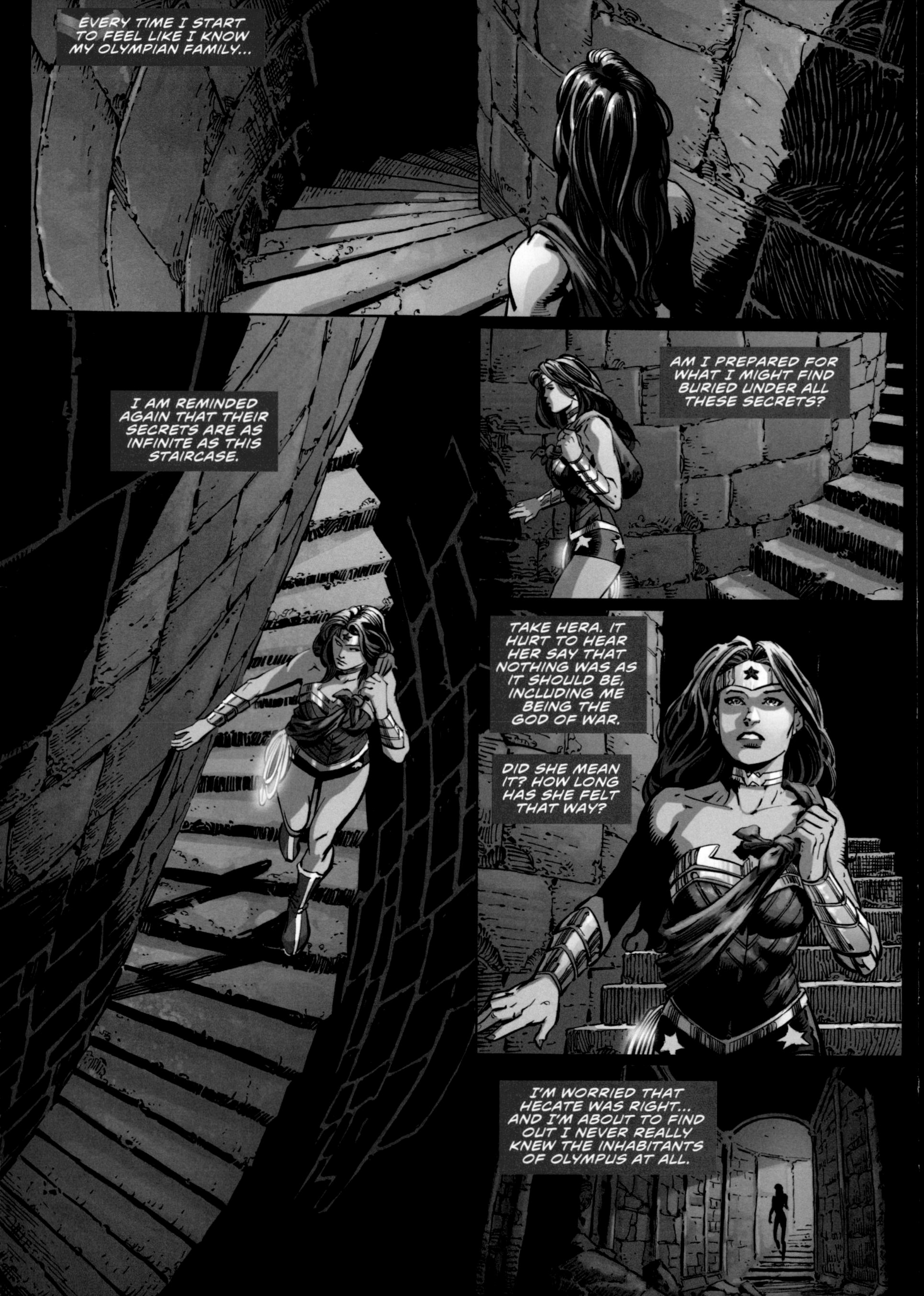
EVERY TIME I START TO FEEL LIKE I KNOW MY OLYMPIAN FAMILY...
I AM REMINDED AGAIN THAT THEIR SECRETS ARE AS INFINITE AS THIS STAIRCASE.
AM I PREPARED FOR WHAT I MIGHT FIND BURIED UNDER ALL THESE SECRETS?
TAKE HERA. IT HURT TO HEAR HER SAY THAT NOTHING WAS AS IT SHOULD BE, INCLUDING ME BEING THE GOD OF WAR.
DID SHE MEAN IT? HOW LONG HAS SHE FELT THAT WAY?
I'M WORRIED THAT HECATE WAS RIGHT... AND I'M ABOUT TO FIND OUT I NEVER REALLY KNEW THE INHABITANTS OF OLYMPUS AT ALL.

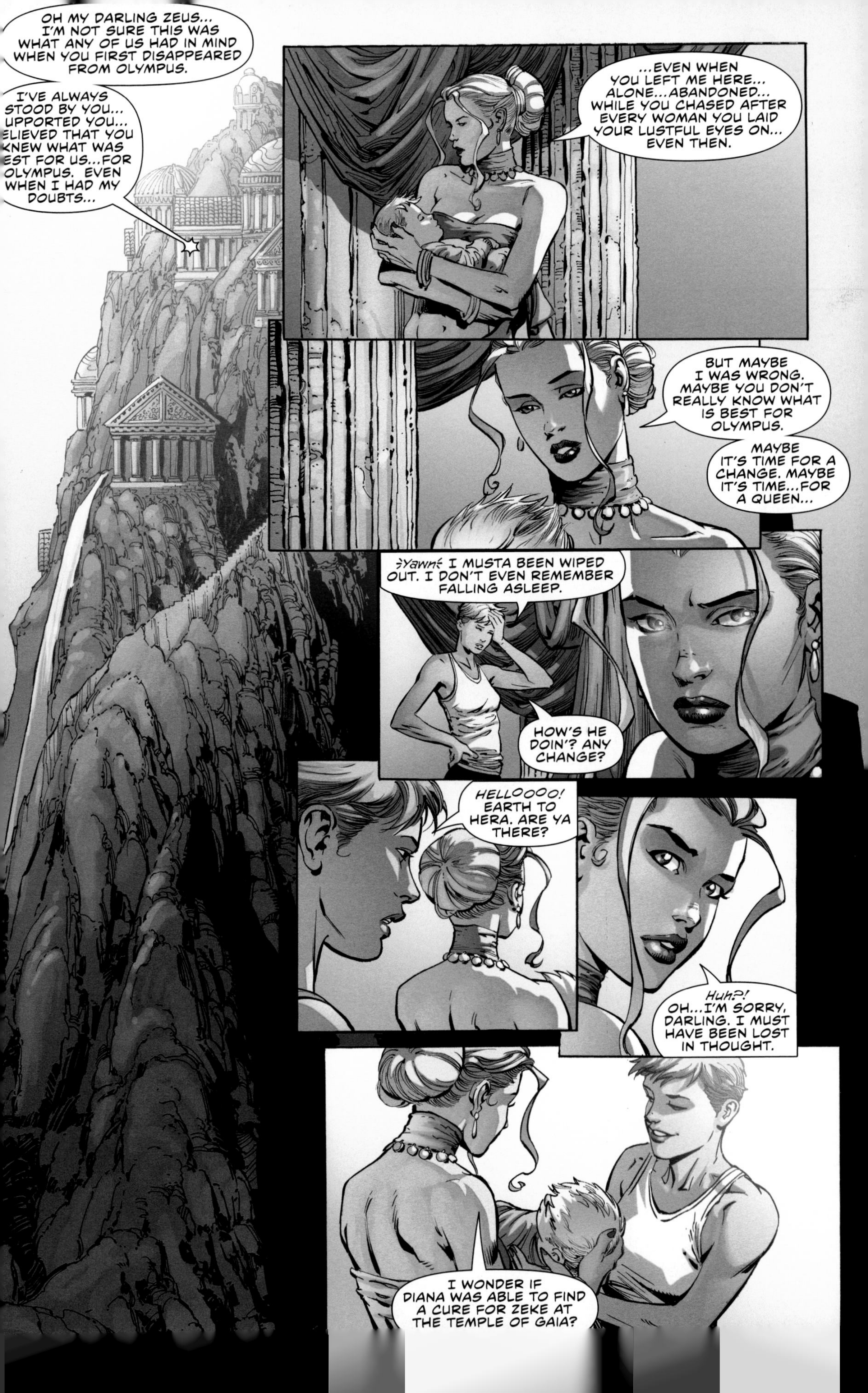
OH MY DARLING ZEUS... I'M NOT SURE THIS WAS WHAT ANY OF US HAD IN MIND WHEN YOU FIRST DISAPPEARED FROM OLYMPUS.
I'VE ALWAYS STOOD BY YOU... UPPORTED YOU... ELIEVED THAT YOU KNEW WHAT WAS EST FOR US...FOR OLYMPUS. EVEN WHEN I HAD MY DOUBTS...
...EVEN WHEN YOU LEFT ME HERE... ALONE...ABANDONED... WHILE YOU CHASED AFTER EVERY WOMAN YOU LAID YOUR LUSTFUL EYES ON... EVEN THEN.
BUT MAYBE I WAS WRONG. MAYBE YOU DON'T REALLY KNOW WHAT IS BEST FOR OLYMPUS.
MAYBE IT'S TIME FOR A CHANGE. MAYBE IT'S TIME...FOR A QUEEN...
⪢Yawn⪡ I MUSTA BEEN WIPED OUT. I DON'T EVEN REMEMBER FALLING ASLEEP.
HOW'S HE DOIN'? ANY CHANGE?
HELLOOOO! EARTH TO HERA. ARE YA THERE?
Huh?! OH...I'M SORRY, DARLING. I MUST HAVE BEEN LOST IN THOUGHT.
I WONDER IF DIANA WAS ABLE TO FIND A CURE FOR ZEKE AT THE TEMPLE OF GAIA?

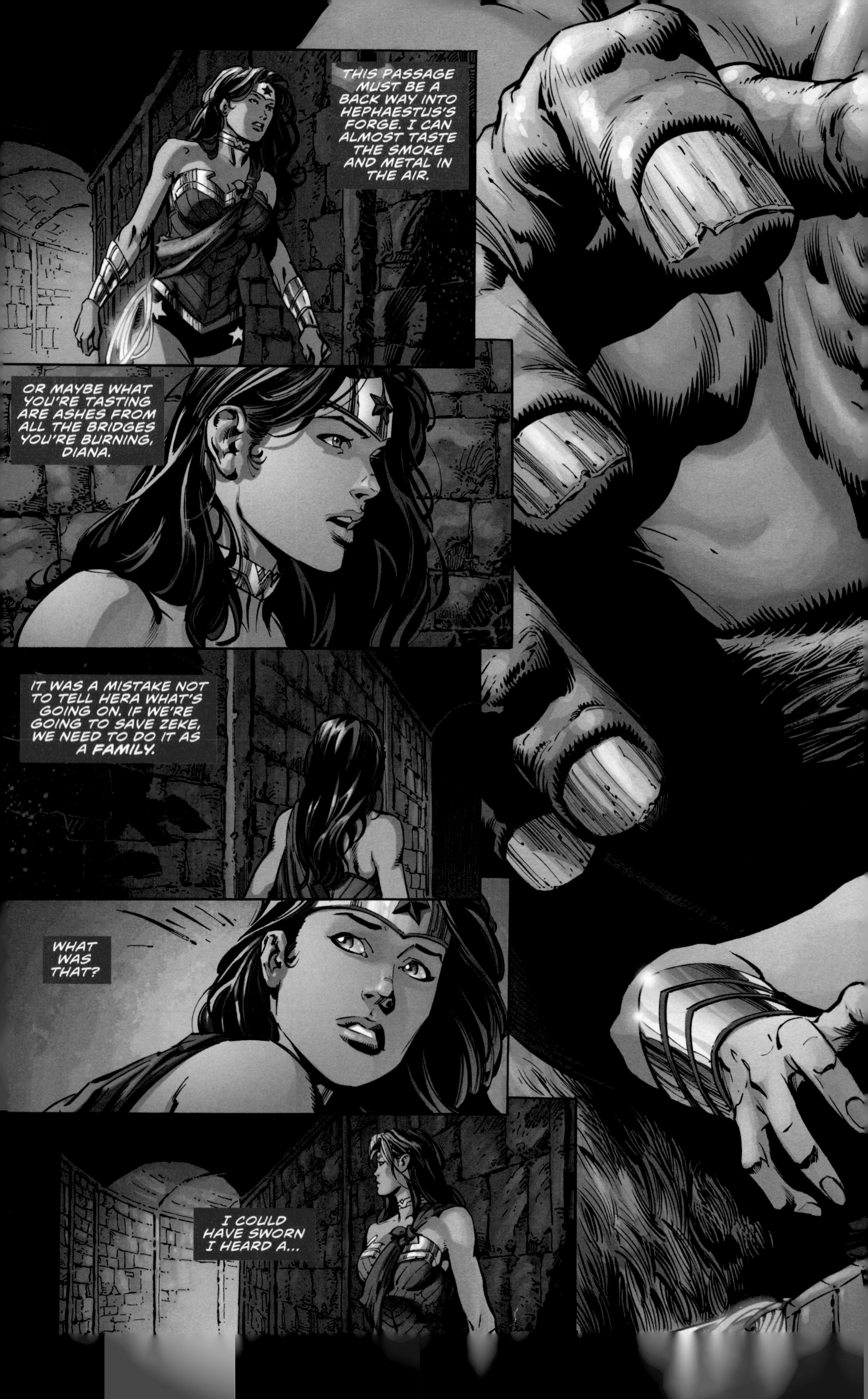
THIS PASSAGE MUST BE A BACK WAY INTO HEPHAESTUS'S FORGE. I CAN ALMOST TASTE THE SMOKE AND METAL IN THE AIR.
OR MAYBE WHAT YOU'RE TASTING ARE ASHES FROM ALL THE BRIDGES YOU'RE BURNING, DIANA.
IT WAS A MISTAKE NOT TO TELL HERA WHAT'S GOING ON. IF WE'RE GOING TO SAVE ZEKE, WE NEED TO DO IT AS A FAMILY.
WHAT WAS THAT?
I COULD HAVE SWORN I HEARD A...

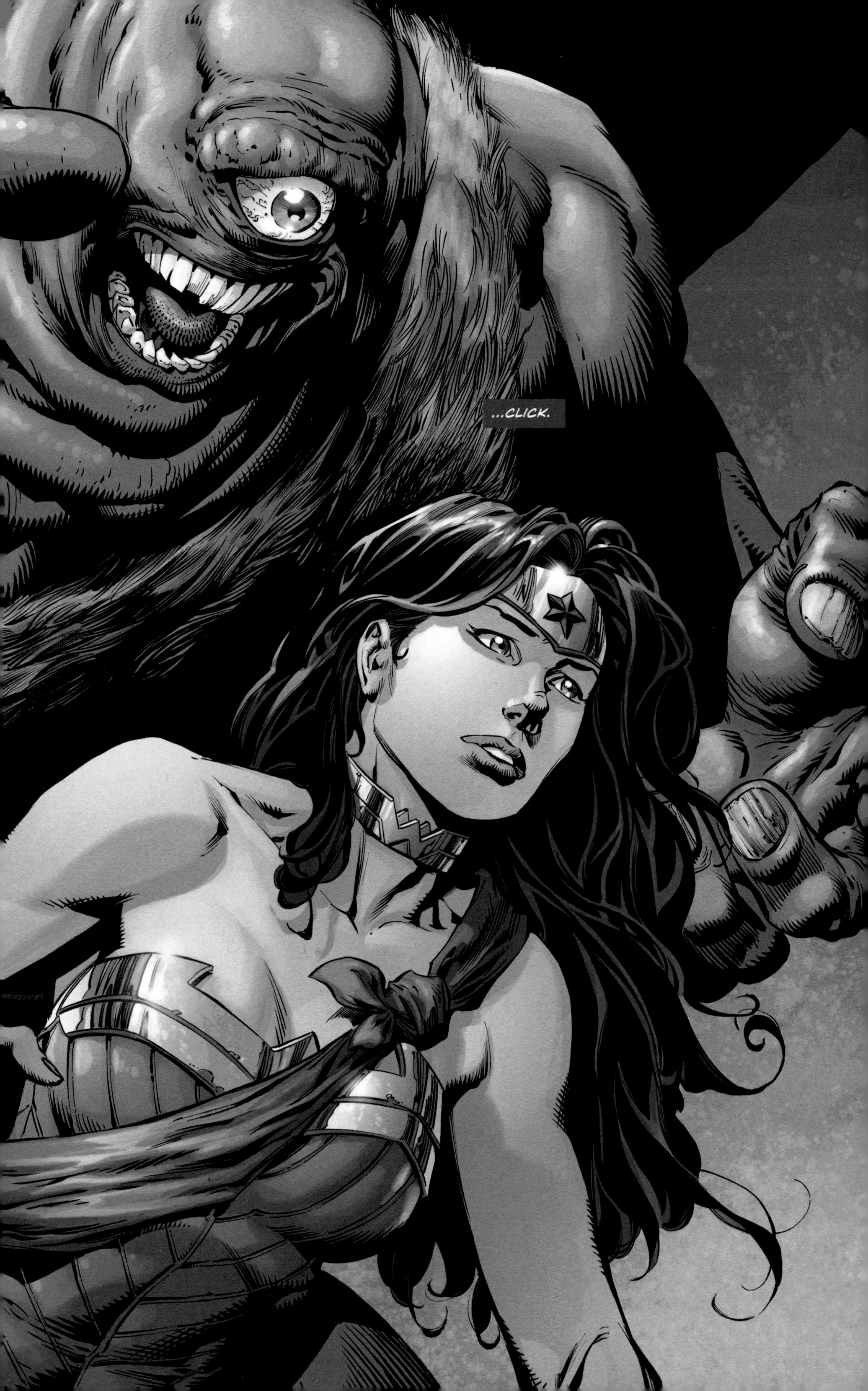
...CLICK.

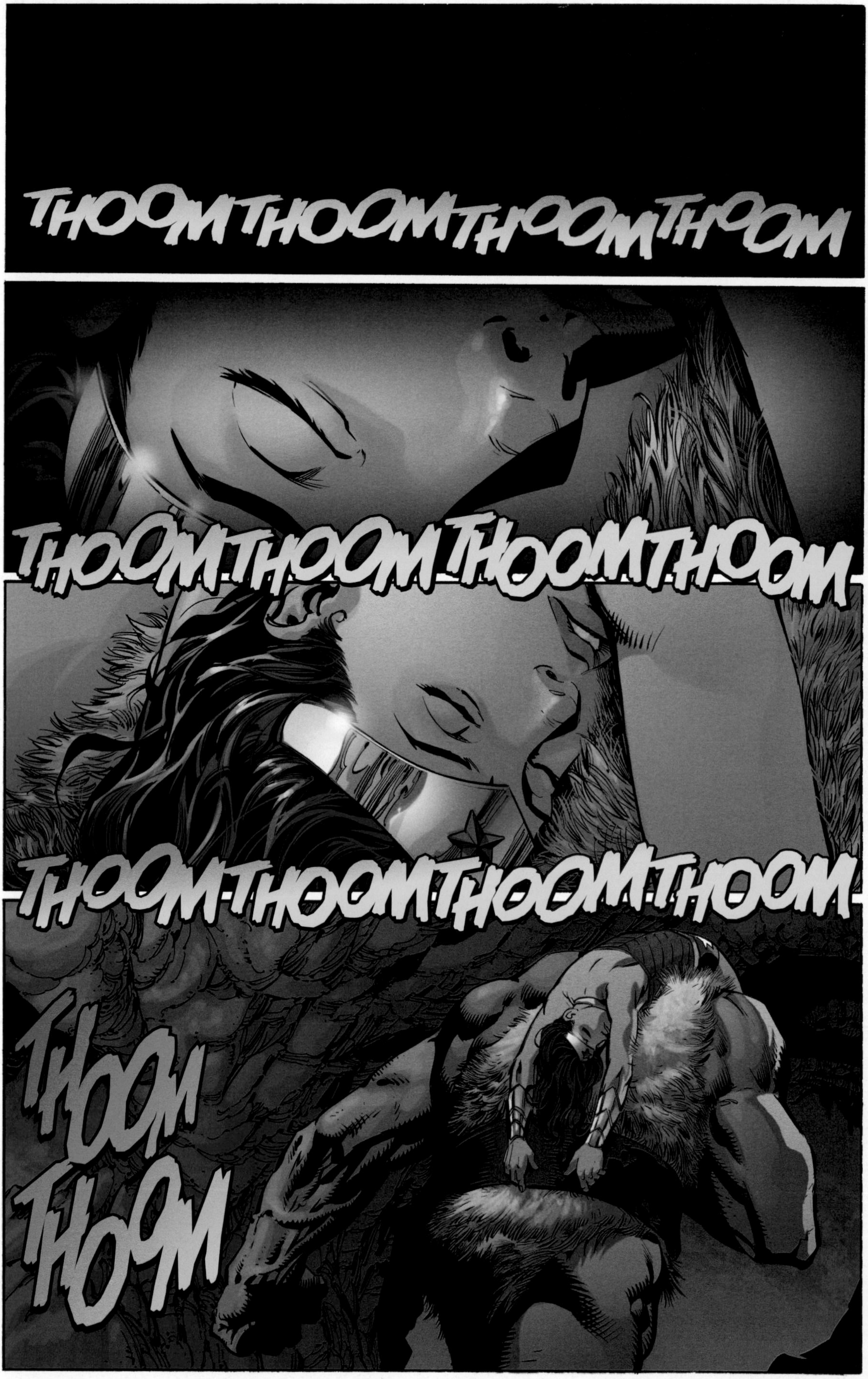
THOOM THOOM THOOM THOOM
THOOM THOOM THOOM THOOM
THOOM THOOM THOOM THOOM
THOOM
THOOM

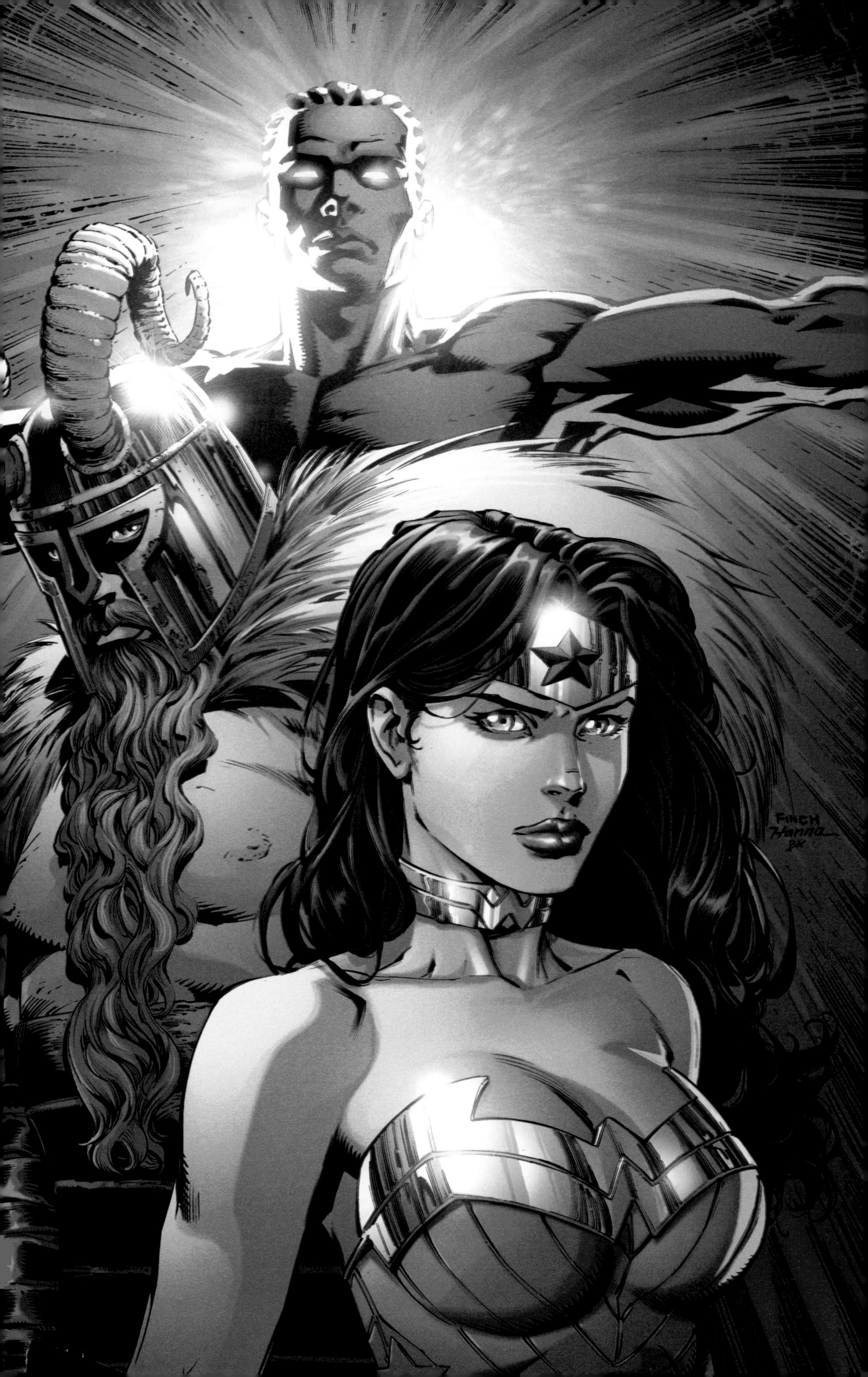
FINCH
Hanna
BK

SECRETS AND LIES

MEREDITH FINCH writer DAVID FINCH JOHNNY DESJARDINS pencillers SCOTT HANNA inker BRAD ANDERSON colorist ROB LEIGH letterer

YOU CAN'T CHANGE FATE

MIGUEL MENDONÇA penciller SANDU FLOREA inker STEPHEN DOWNER colorist ROB LEIGH letterer

cover art by DAVID FINCH, SCOTT HANNA & BRAD ANDERSON

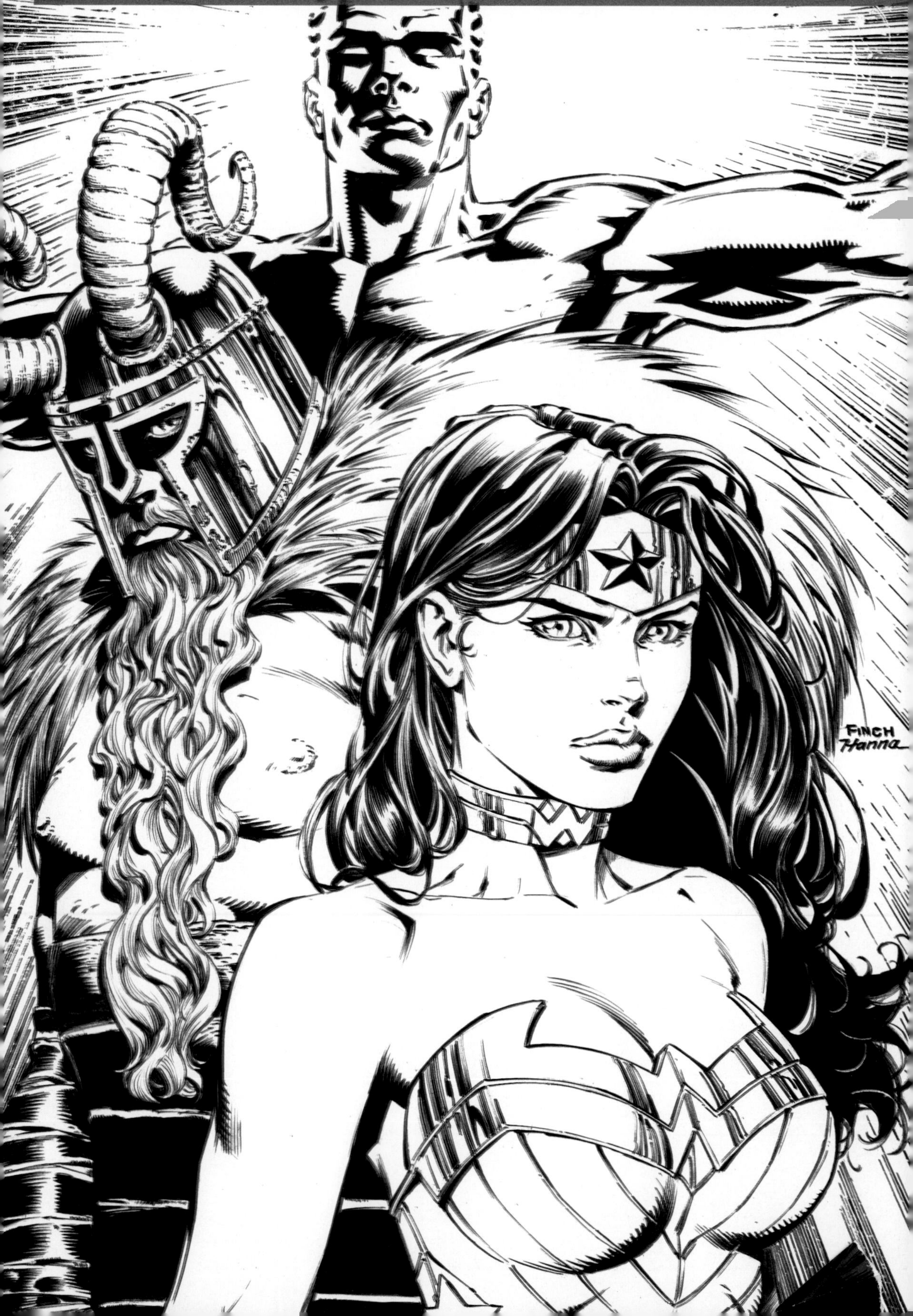
FINCH
Hanna

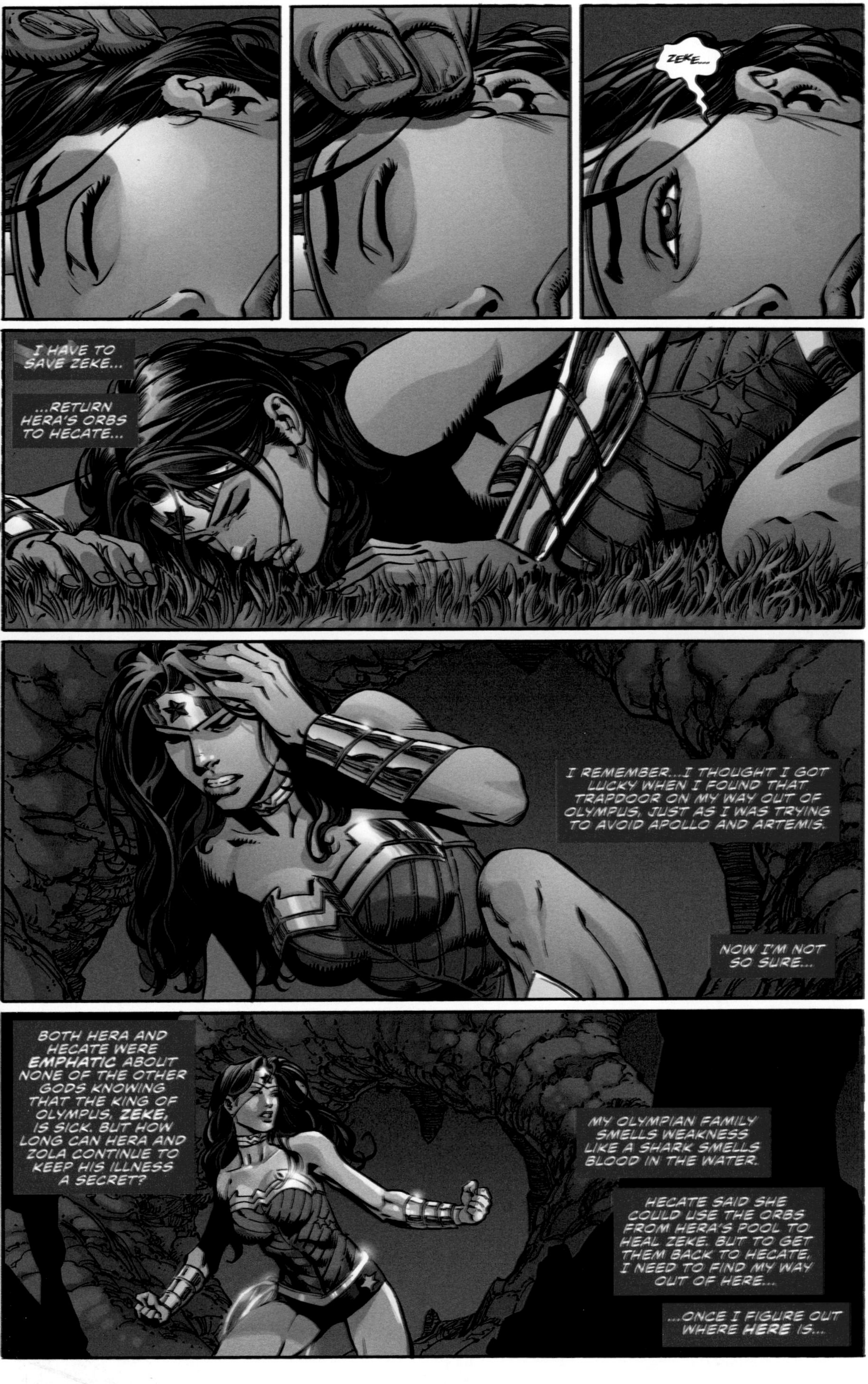
ZEKE...
I HAVE TO SAVE ZEKE...
...RETURN HERA'S ORBS TO HECATE...
I REMEMBER...I THOUGHT I GOT LUCKY WHEN I FOUND THAT TRAPDOOR ON MY WAY OUT OF OLYMPUS, JUST AS I WAS TRYING TO AVOID APOLLO AND ARTEMIS.
NOW I'M NOT SO SURE...
BOTH HERA AND HECATE WERE EMPHATIC ABOUT NONE OF THE OTHER GODS KNOWING THAT THE KING OF OLYMPUS, ZEKE, IS SICK. BUT HOW LONG CAN HERA AND ZOLA CONTINUE TO KEEP HIS ILLNESS A SECRET?
MY OLYMPIAN FAMILY SMELLS WEAKNESS LIKE A SHARK SMELLS BLOOD IN THE WATER.
HECATE SAID SHE COULD USE THE ORBS FROM HERA'S POOL TO HEAL ZEKE. BUT TO GET THEM BACK TO HECATE, I NEED TO FIND MY WAY OUT OF HERE...
...ONCE I FIGURE OUT WHERE HERE IS...

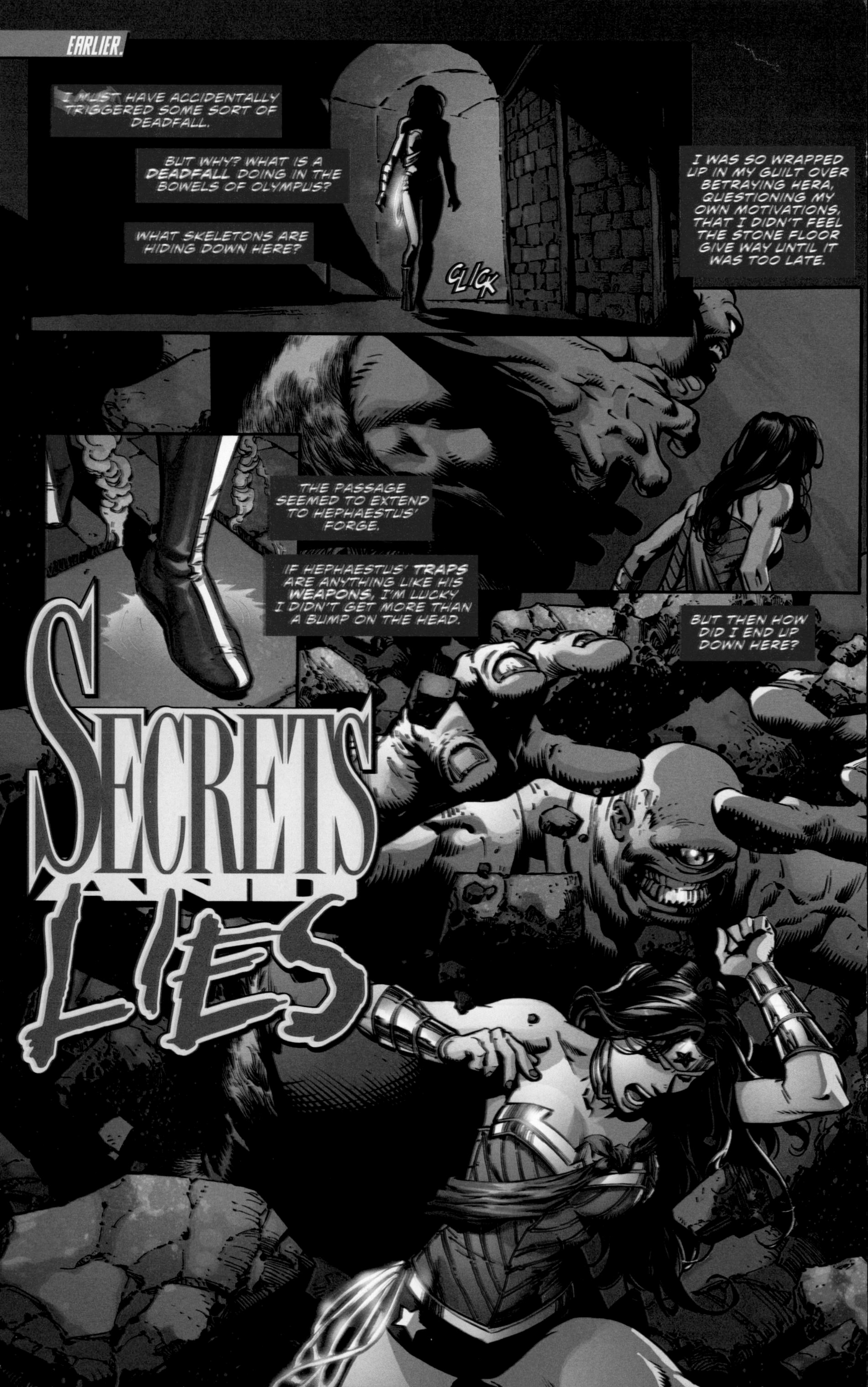
EARLIER.
I MUST HAVE ACCIDENTALLY TRIGGERED SOME SORT OF DEADFALL.
BUT WHY? WHAT IS A DEADFALL DOING IN THE BOWELS OF OLYMPUS?
WHAT SKELETONS ARE HIDING DOWN HERE?
CLICK
I WAS SO WRAPPED UP IN MY GUILT OVER BETRAYING HERA, QUESTIONING MY OWN MOTIVATIONS, THAT I DIDN'T FEEL THE STONE FLOOR GIVE WAY UNTIL IT WAS TOO LATE.
THE PASSAGE SEEMED TO EXTEND TO HEPHAESTUS' FORGE.
IF HEPHAESTUS' TRAPS ARE ANYTHING LIKE HIS WEAPONS, I'M LUCKY I DIDN'T GET MORE THAN A BUMP ON THE HEAD.
BUT THEN HOW DID I END UP DOWN HERE?
SECRETS AND LIES

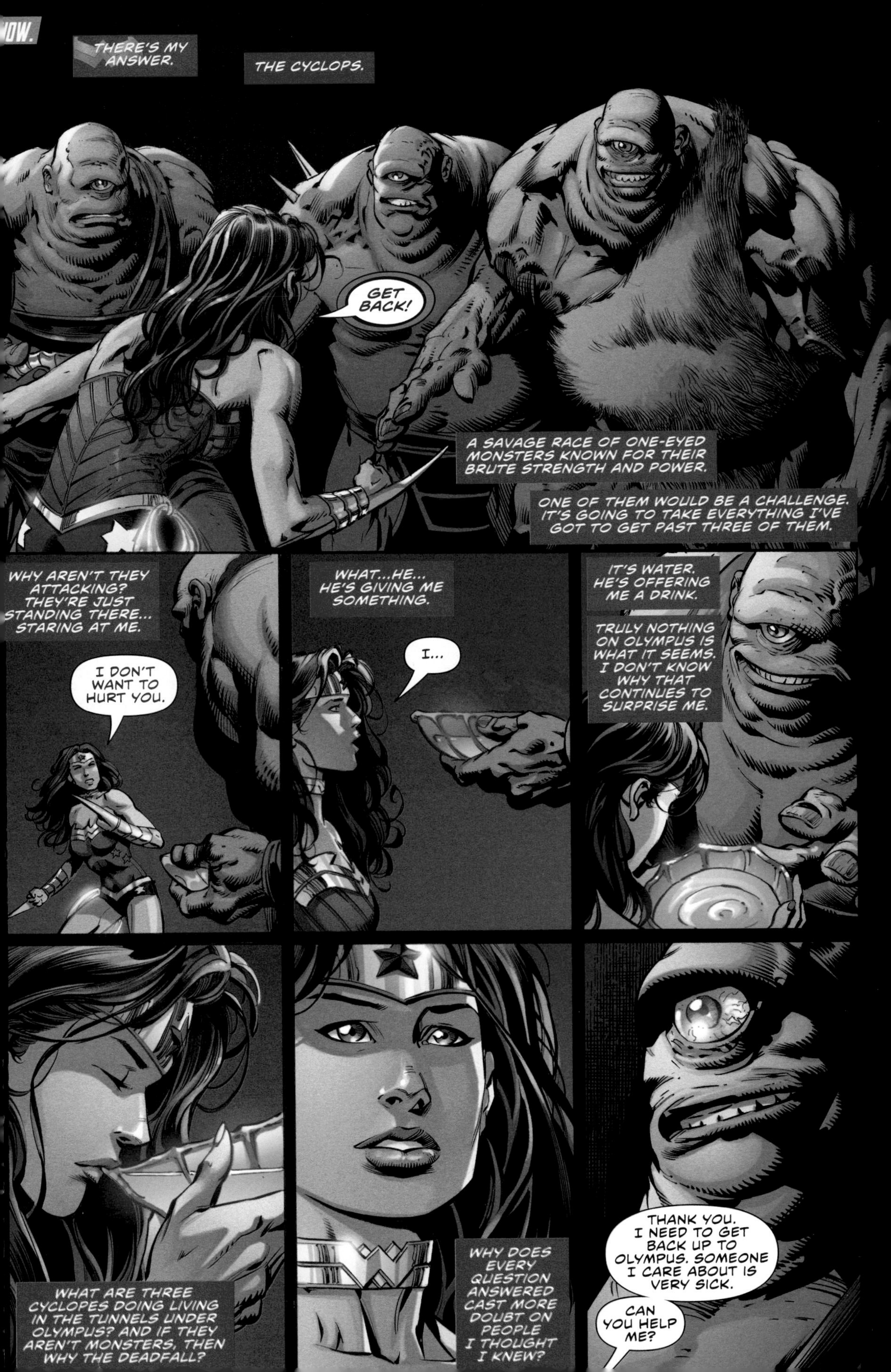
NOW.
THERE'S MY ANSWER.
THE CYCLOPS.
GET BACK!
A SAVAGE RACE OF ONE-EYED MONSTERS KNOWN FOR THEIR BRUTE STRENGTH AND POWER.
ONE OF THEM WOULD BE A CHALLENGE. IT'S GOING TO TAKE EVERYTHING I'VE GOT TO GET PAST THREE OF THEM.
WHY AREN'T THEY ATTACKING? THEY'RE JUST STANDING THERE... STARING AT ME.
I DON'T WANT TO HURT YOU.
WHAT...HE... HE'S GIVING ME SOMETHING.
I...
IT'S WATER. HE'S OFFERING ME A DRINK.
TRULY NOTHING ON OLYMPUS IS WHAT IT SEEMS. I DON'T KNOW WHY THAT CONTINUES TO SURPRISE ME.
WHAT ARE THREE CYCLOPES DOING LIVING IN THE TUNNELS UNDER OLYMPUS? AND IF THEY AREN'T MONSTERS, THEN WHY THE DEADFALL?
WHY DOES EVERY QUESTION ANSWERED CAST MORE DOUBT ON PEOPLE I THOUGHT I KNEW?
THANK YOU. I NEED TO GET BACK UP TO OLYMPUS. SOMEONE I CARE ABOUT IS VERY SICK.
CAN YOU HELP ME?

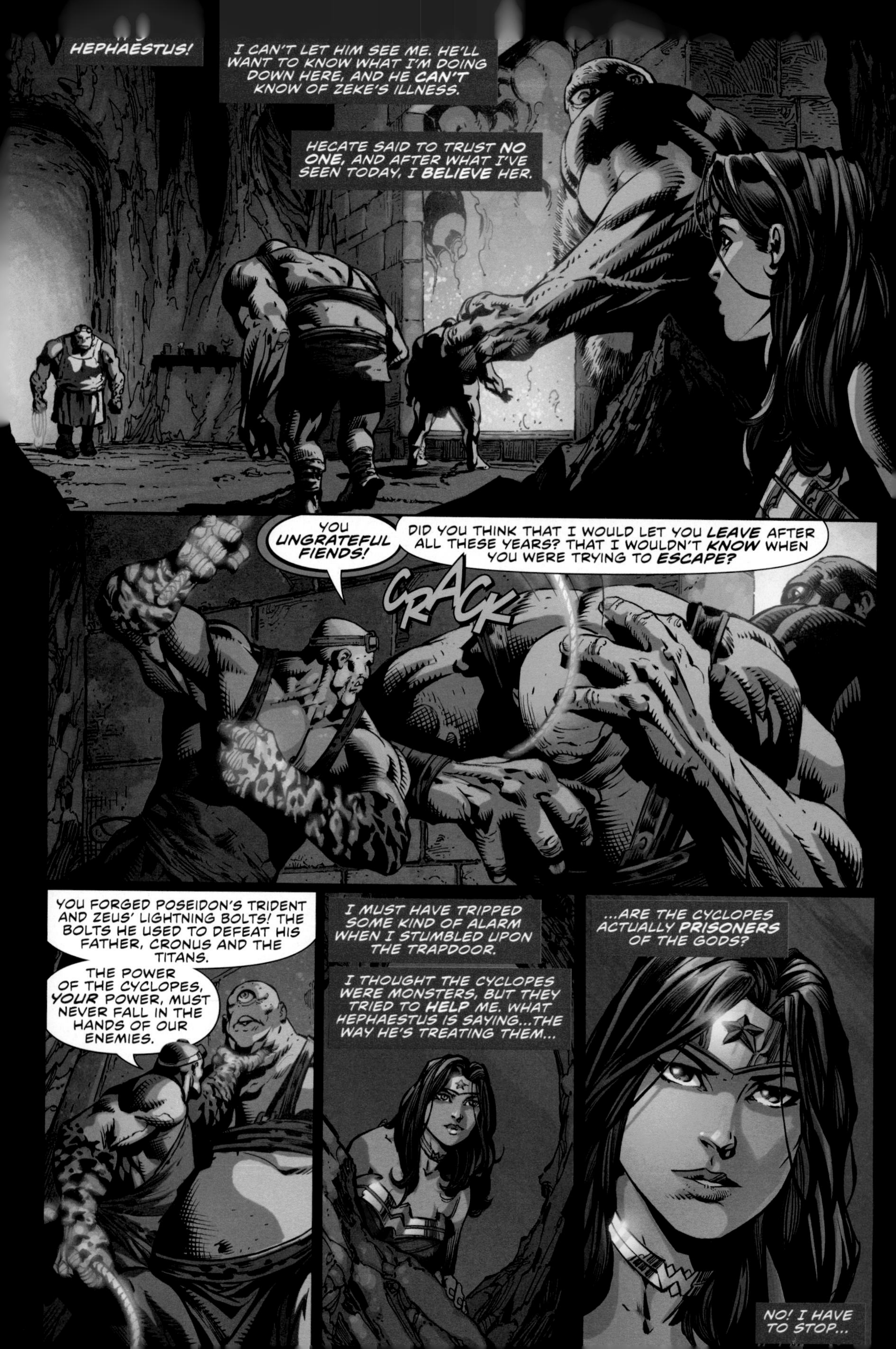
HEPHAESTUS!
I CAN'T LET HIM SEE ME. HE'LL WANT TO KNOW WHAT I'M DOING DOWN HERE, AND HE CAN'T KNOW OF ZEKE'S ILLNESS.
HECATE SAID TO TRUST NO ONE, AND AFTER WHAT I'VE SEEN TODAY, I BELIEVE HER.
YOU UNGRATEFUL FIENDS!
DID YOU THINK THAT I WOULD LET YOU LEAVE AFTER ALL THESE YEARS? THAT I WOULDN'T KNOW WHEN YOU WERE TRYING TO ESCAPE?
CRACK
YOU FORGED POSEIDON'S TRIDENT AND ZEUS' LIGHTNING BOLTS! THE BOLTS HE USED TO DEFEAT HIS FATHER, CRONUS AND THE TITANS.
THE POWER OF THE CYCLOPES, YOUR POWER, MUST NEVER FALL IN THE HANDS OF OUR ENEMIES.
I MUST HAVE TRIPPED SOME KIND OF ALARM WHEN I STUMBLED UPON THE TRAPDOOR.
I THOUGHT THE CYCLOPES WERE MONSTERS, BUT THEY TRIED TO HELP ME. WHAT HEPHAESTUS IS SAYING...THE WAY HE'S TREATING THEM...
...ARE THE CYCLOPES ACTUALLY PRISONERS OF THE GODS?
NO! I HAVE TO STOP...

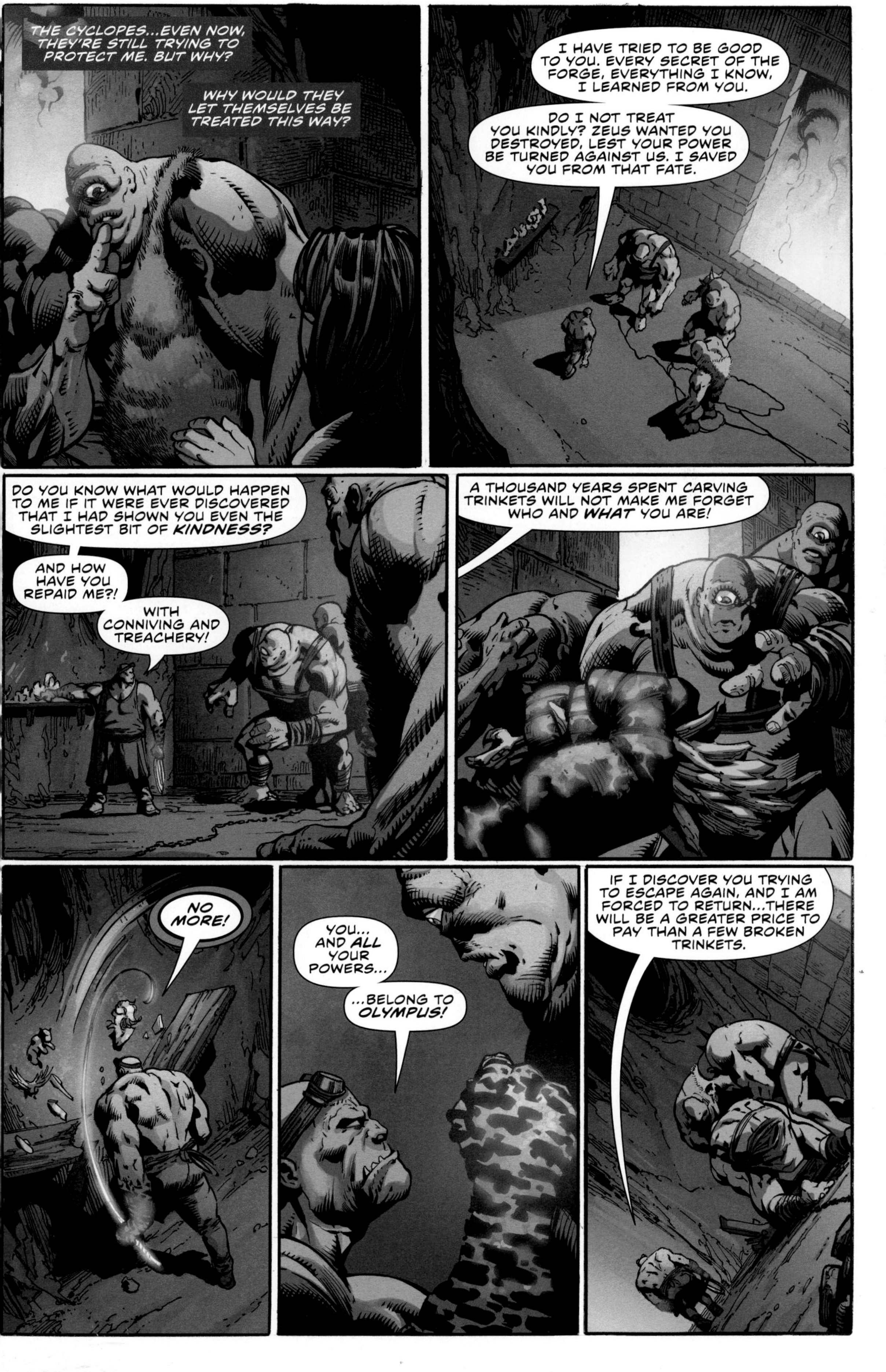
THE CYCLOPES...EVEN NOW, THEY'RE STILL TRYING TO PROTECT ME. BUT WHY?
WHY WOULD THEY LET THEMSELVES BE TREATED THIS WAY?
I HAVE TRIED TO BE GOOD TO YOU. EVERY SECRET OF THE FORGE, EVERYTHING I KNOW, I LEARNED FROM YOU.
DO I NOT TREAT YOU KINDLY? ZEUS WANTED YOU DESTROYED, LEST YOUR POWER BE TURNED AGAINST US. I SAVED YOU FROM THAT FATE.
DO YOU KNOW WHAT WOULD HAPPEN TO ME IF IT WERE EVER DISCOVERED THAT I HAD SHOWN YOU EVEN THE SLIGHTEST BIT OF KINDNESS?
AND HOW HAVE YOU REPAID ME?!
WITH CONNIVING AND TREACHERY!
A THOUSAND YEARS SPENT CARVING TRINKETS WILL NOT MAKE ME FORGET WHO AND WHAT YOU ARE!
NO MORE!
YOU... AND ALL YOUR POWERS...
...BELONG TO OLYMPUS!
IF I DISCOVER YOU TRYING TO ESCAPE AGAIN, AND I AM FORCED TO RETURN...THERE WILL BE A GREATER PRICE TO PAY THAN A FEW BROKEN TRINKETS.

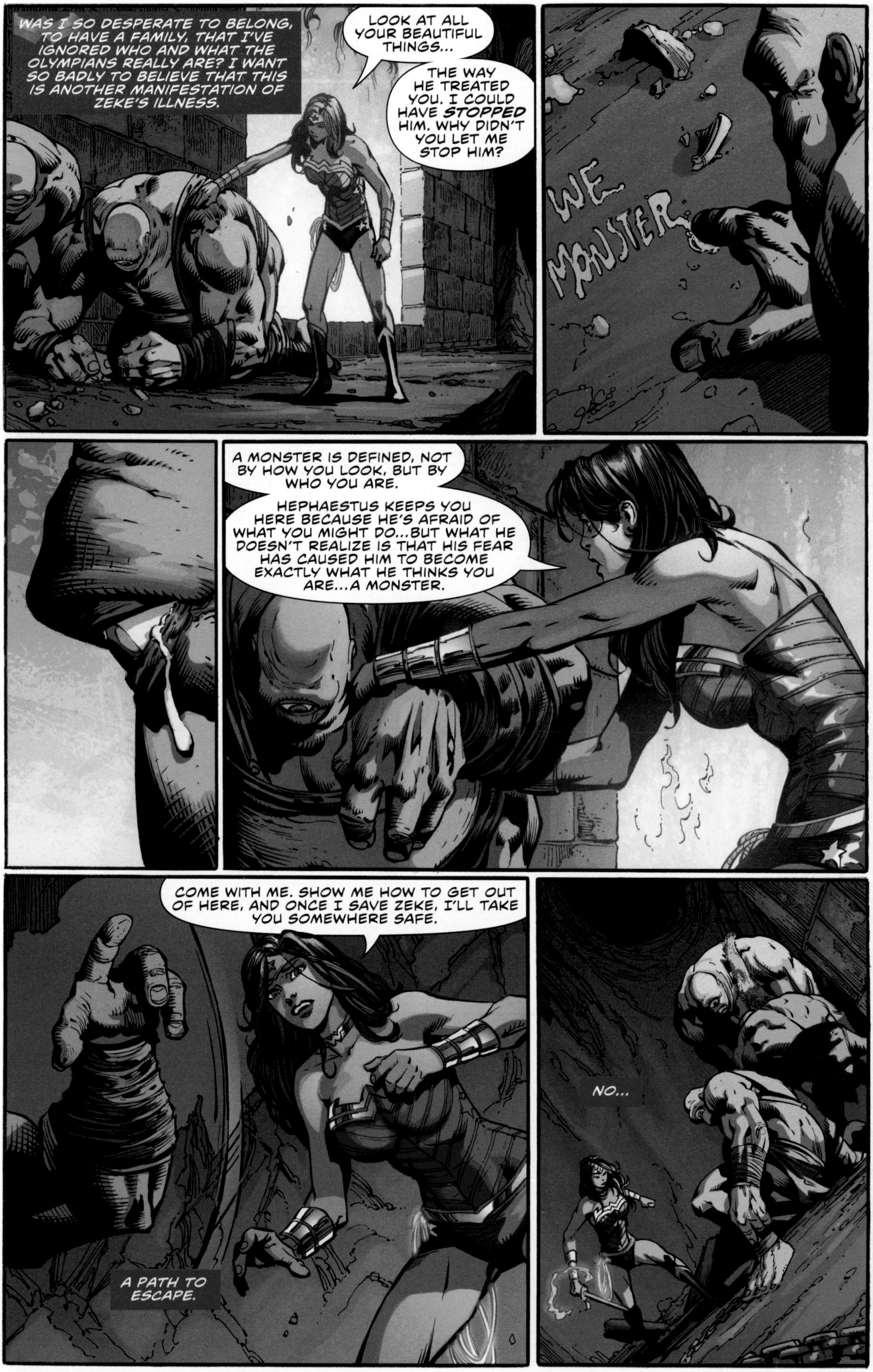
WAS I SO DESPERATE TO BELONG, TO HAVE A FAMILY, THAT I'VE IGNORED WHO AND WHAT THE OLYMPIANS REALLY ARE? I WANT SO BADLY TO BELIEVE THAT THIS IS ANOTHER MANIFESTATION OF ZEKE'S ILLNESS.
LOOK AT ALL YOUR BEAUTIFUL THINGS...
THE WAY HE TREATED YOU. I COULD HAVE STOPPED HIM. WHY DIDN'T YOU LET ME STOP HIM?
WE MONSTER
A MONSTER IS DEFINED, NOT BY HOW YOU LOOK, BUT BY WHO YOU ARE.
HEPHAESTUS KEEPS YOU HERE BECAUSE HE'S AFRAID OF WHAT YOU MIGHT DO...BUT WHAT HE DOESN'T REALIZE IS THAT HIS FEAR HAS CAUSED HIM TO BECOME EXACTLY WHAT HE THINKS YOU ARE...A MONSTER.
COME WITH ME. SHOW ME HOW TO GET OUT OF HERE, AND ONCE I SAVE ZEKE, I'LL TAKE YOU SOMEWHERE SAFE.
A PATH TO ESCAPE.
NO...

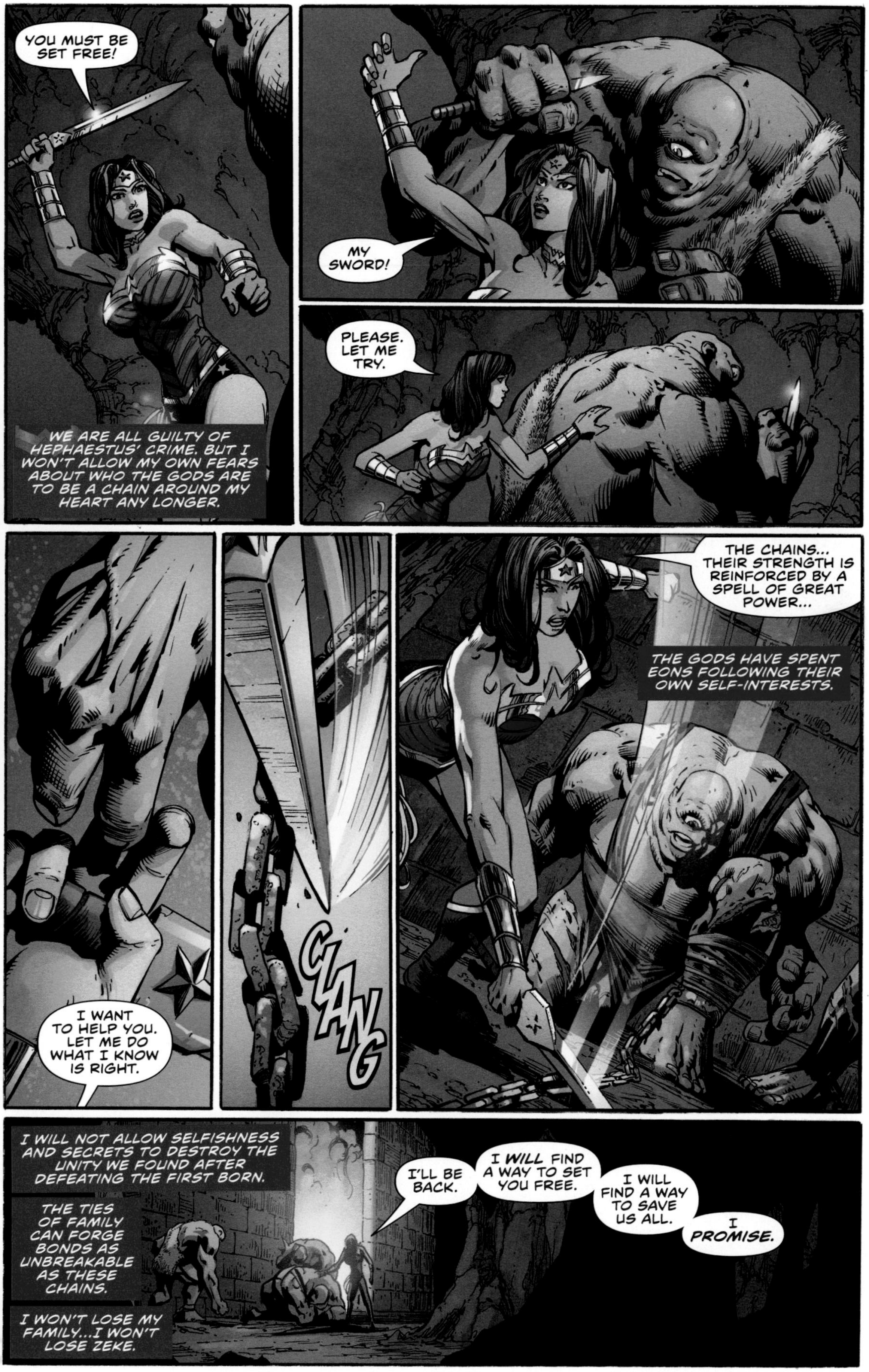

YOU MUST BE SET FREE!
MY SWORD!
PLEASE. LET ME TRY.
WE ARE ALL GUILTY OF HEPHAESTUS' CRIME. BUT I WON'T ALLOW MY OWN FEARS ABOUT WHO THE GODS ARE TO BE A CHAIN AROUND MY HEART ANY LONGER.
I WANT TO HELP YOU. LET ME DO WHAT I KNOW IS RIGHT.
CLANG
THE CHAINS... THEIR STRENGTH IS REINFORCED BY A SPELL OF GREAT POWER...
THE GODS HAVE SPENT EONS FOLLOWING THEIR OWN SELF-INTERESTS.
I WILL NOT ALLOW SELFISHNESS AND SECRETS TO DESTROY THE UNITY WE FOUND AFTER DEFEATING THE FIRST BORN.
THE TIES OF FAMILY CAN FORGE BONDS AS UNBREAKABLE AS THESE CHAINS.
I WON'T LOSE MY FAMILY...I WON'T LOSE ZEKE.
I'LL BE BACK.
I WILL FIND A WAY TO SET YOU FREE.
I WILL FIND A WAY TO SAVE US ALL.
I PROMISE.

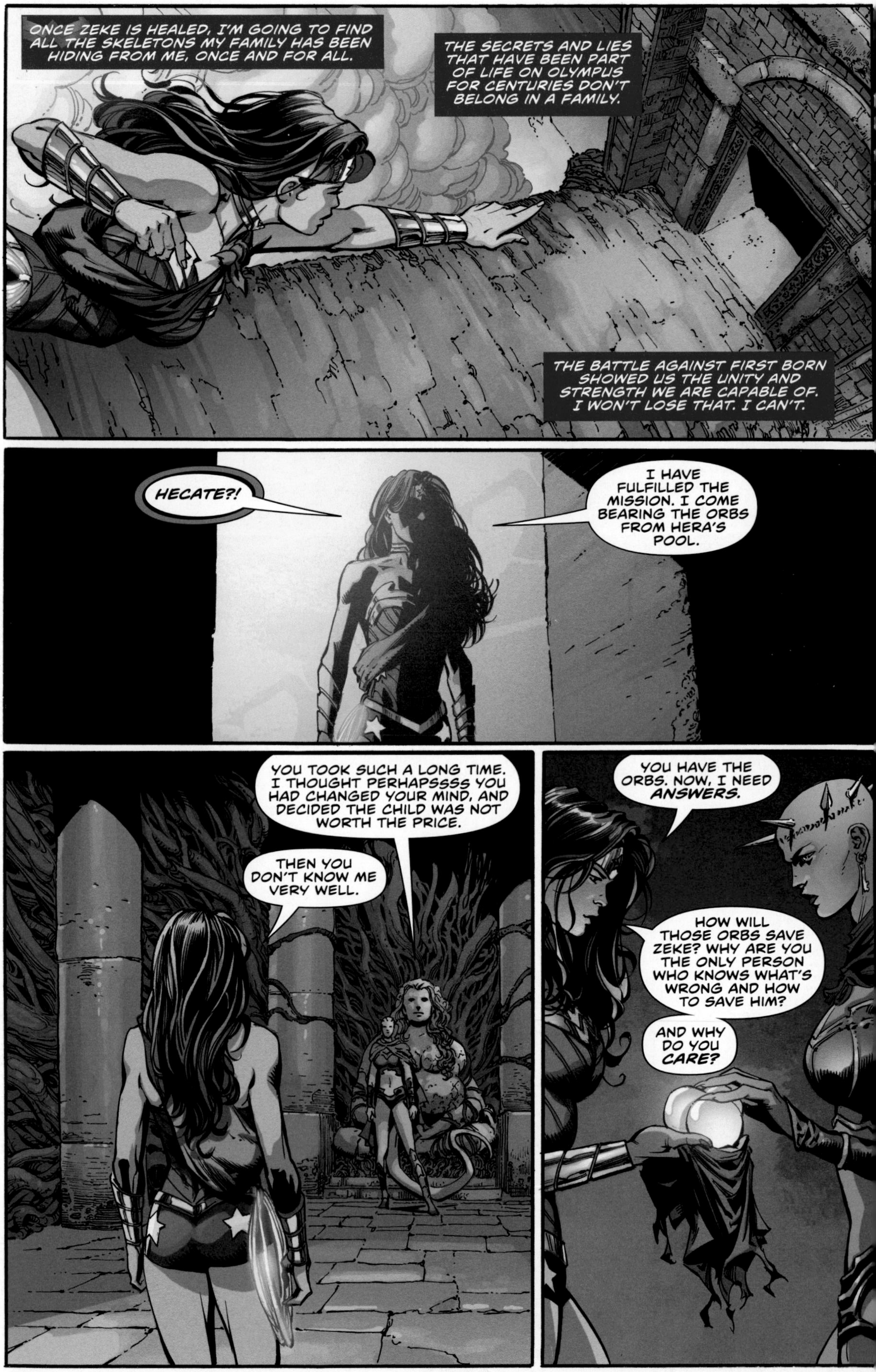
ONCE ZEKE IS HEALED, I'M GOING TO FIND ALL THE SKELETONS MY FAMILY HAS BEEN HIDING FROM ME, ONCE AND FOR ALL.
THE SECRETS AND LIES THAT HAVE BEEN PART OF LIFE ON OLYMPUS FOR CENTURIES DON'T BELONG IN A FAMILY.
THE BATTLE AGAINST FIRST BORN SHOWED US THE UNITY AND STRENGTH WE ARE CAPABLE OF. I WON'T LOSE THAT. I CAN'T.
HECATE?!
I HAVE FULFILLED THE MISSION. I COME BEARING THE ORBS FROM HERA'S POOL.
YOU TOOK SUCH A LONG TIME. I THOUGHT PERHAPSSSS YOU HAD CHANGED YOUR MIND, AND DECIDED THE CHILD WAS NOT WORTH THE PRICE.
THEN YOU DON'T KNOW ME VERY WELL.
YOU HAVE THE ORBS. NOW, I NEED ANSWERS.
HOW WILL THOSE ORBS SAVE ZEKE? WHY ARE YOU THE ONLY PERSON WHO KNOWS WHAT'S WRONG AND HOW TO SAVE HIM?
AND WHY DO YOU CARE?

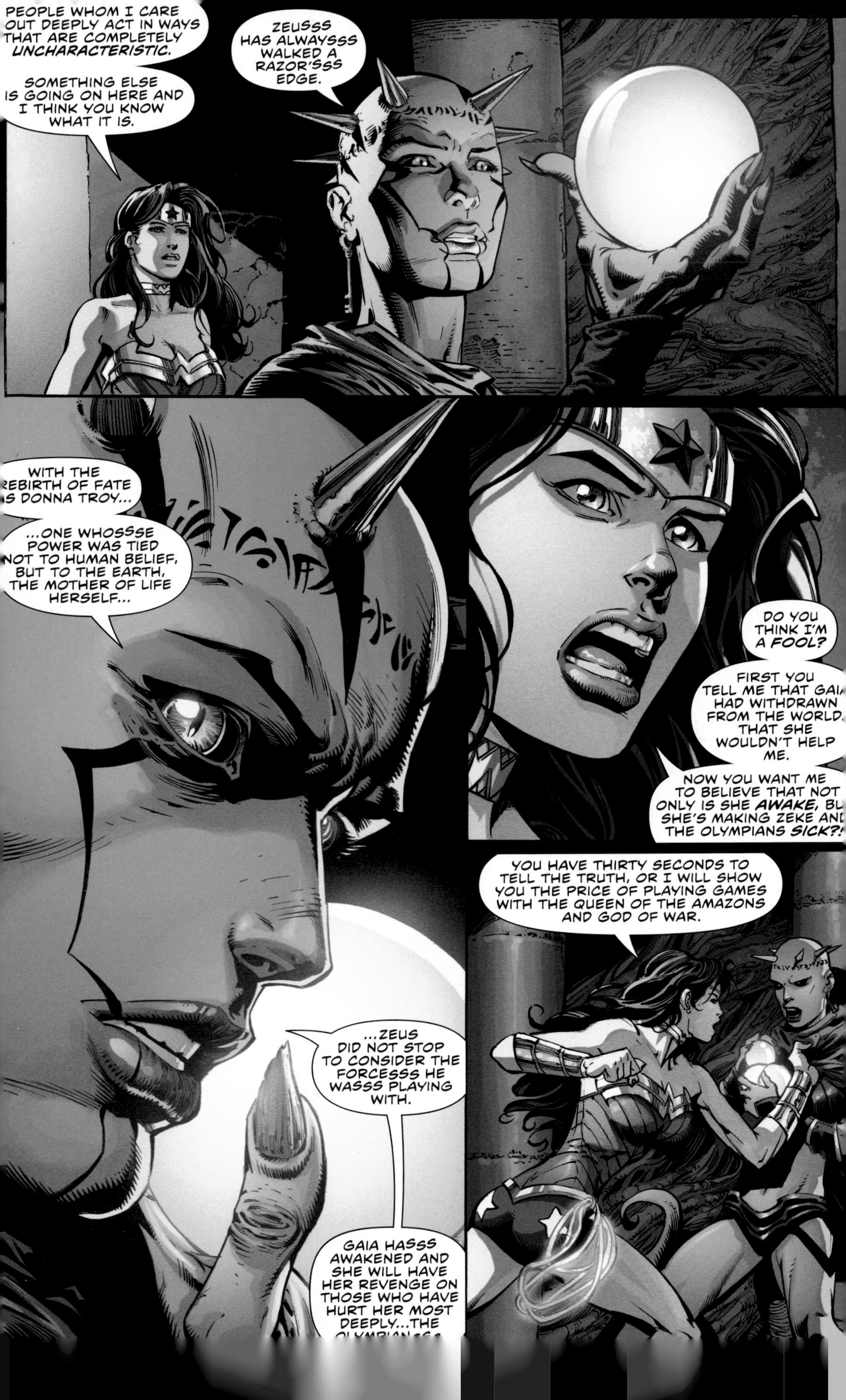
PEOPLE WHOM I CARE OUT DEEPLY ACT IN WAYS THAT ARE COMPLETELY *UNCHARACTERISTIC.*
SOMETHING ELSE IS GOING ON HERE AND I THINK YOU KNOW WHAT IT IS.
ZEUSSS HAS ALWAYSSS WALKED A RAZOR'SSS EDGE.
WITH THE REBIRTH OF FATE S DONNA TROY...
...ONE WHOSSSE POWER WAS TIED NOT TO HUMAN BELIEF, BUT TO THE EARTH, THE MOTHER OF LIFE HERSELF...
DO YOU THINK I'M A *FOOL?*
FIRST YOU TELL ME THAT GAI HAD WITHDRAWN FROM THE WORLD. THAT SHE WOULDN'T HELP ME.
NOW YOU WANT ME TO BELIEVE THAT NOT ONLY IS SHE *AWAKE,* BU SHE'S MAKING ZEKE AN THE OLYMPIANS *SICK?!*
YOU HAVE THIRTY SECONDS TO TELL THE TRUTH, OR I WILL SHOW YOU THE PRICE OF PLAYING GAMES WITH THE QUEEN OF THE AMAZONS AND GOD OF WAR.
...ZEUS DID NOT STOP TO CONSIDER THE FORCESSS HE WASSS PLAYING WITH.
GAIA HASSS AWAKENED AND SHE WILL HAVE HER REVENGE ON THOSE WHO HAVE HURT HER MOST DEEPLY...THE

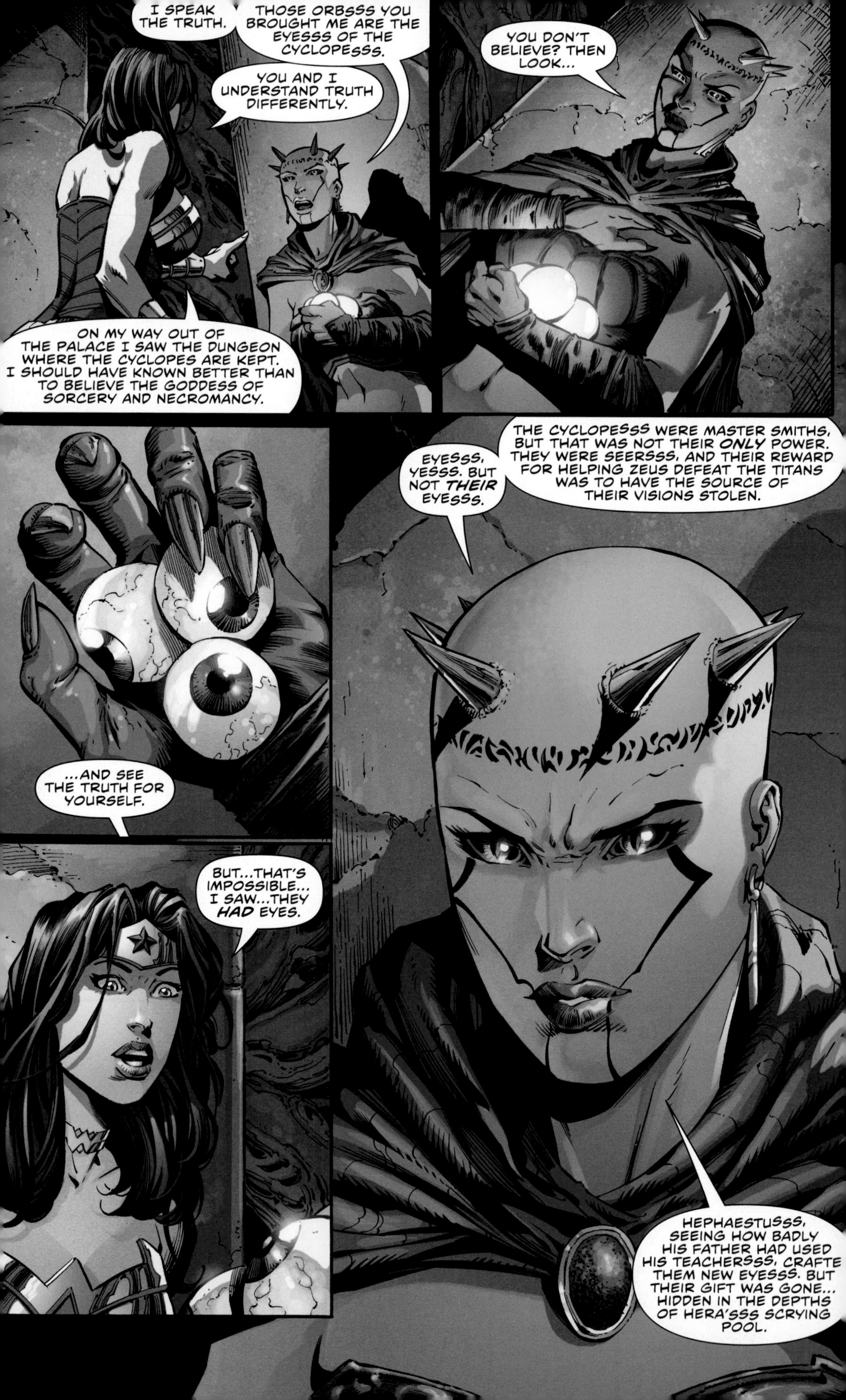
I SPEAK THE TRUTH.
THOSE ORBSSS YOU BROUGHT ME ARE THE EYESSS OF THE CYCLOPESSS.
YOU AND I UNDERSTAND TRUTH DIFFERENTLY.
ON MY WAY OUT OF THE PALACE I SAW THE DUNGEON WHERE THE CYCLOPES ARE KEPT. I SHOULD HAVE KNOWN BETTER THAN TO BELIEVE THE GODDESS OF SORCERY AND NECROMANCY.
YOU DON'T BELIEVE? THEN LOOK...
...AND SEE THE TRUTH FOR YOURSELF.
BUT...THAT'S IMPOSSIBLE... I SAW...THEY *HAD* EYES.
EYESSS, YESSS. BUT NOT *THEIR* EYESSS.
THE CYCLOPESSS WERE MASTER SMITHS, BUT THAT WAS NOT THEIR *ONLY* POWER. THEY WERE SEERSSS, AND THEIR REWARD FOR HELPING ZEUS DEFEAT THE TITANS WAS TO HAVE THE SOURCE OF THEIR VISIONS STOLEN.
HEPHAESTUSSS, SEEING HOW BADLY HIS FATHER HAD USED HIS TEACHERSSS, CRAFTE THEM NEW EYESSS. BUT THEIR GIFT WAS GONE... HIDDEN IN THE DEPTHS OF HERA'SSS SCRYING POOL.

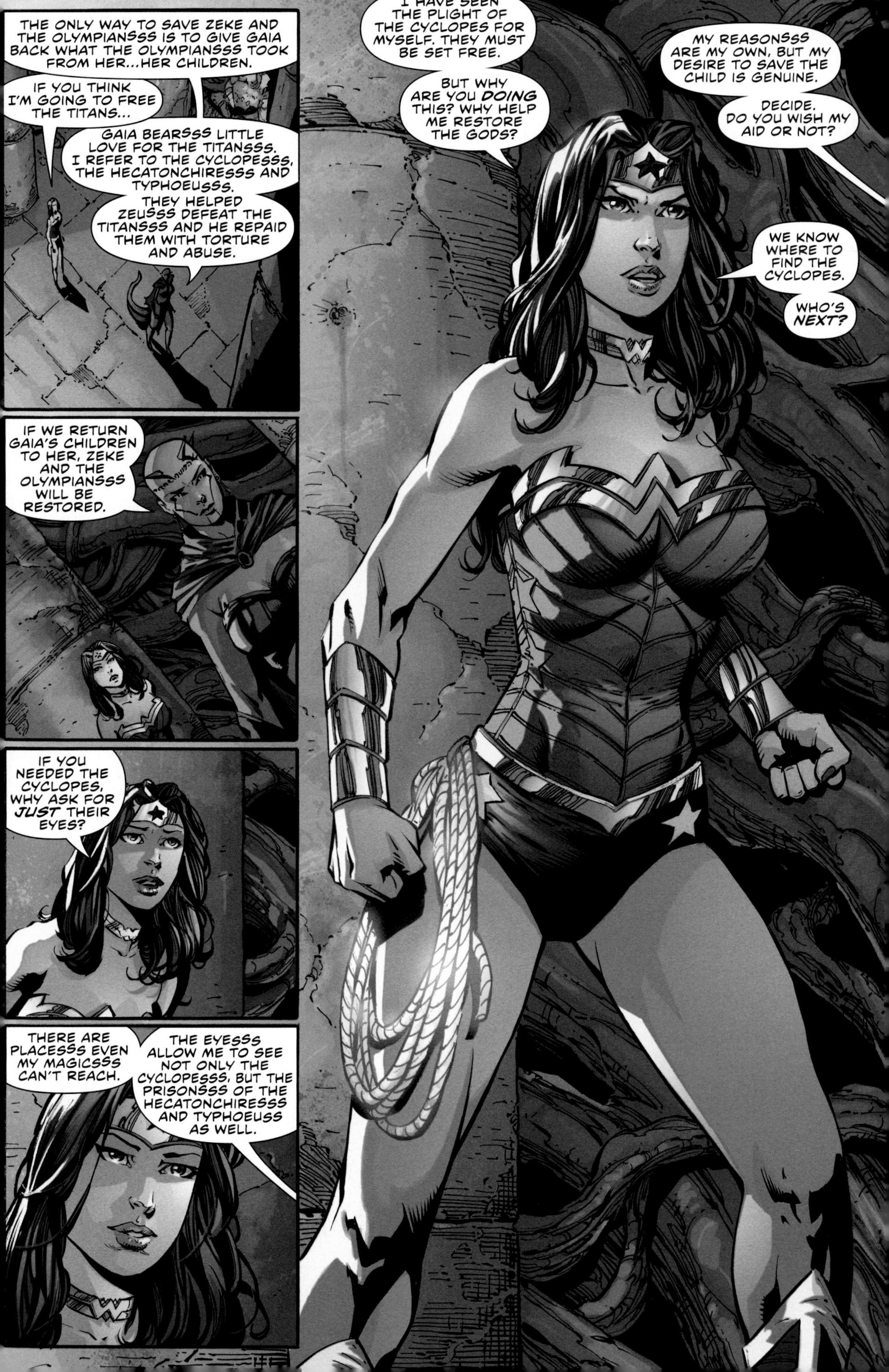
THE ONLY WAY TO SAVE ZEKE AND THE OLYMPIANSSS IS TO GIVE GAIA BACK WHAT THE OLYMPIANSSS TOOK FROM HER...HER CHILDREN.
IF YOU THINK I'M GOING TO FREE THE TITANS...
GAIA BEARSSS LITTLE LOVE FOR THE TITANSSS. I REFER TO THE CYCLOPESSS, THE HECATONCHIRESSS AND TYPHOEUSSS.
THEY HELPED ZEUSSS DEFEAT THE TITANSSS AND HE REPAID THEM WITH TORTURE AND ABUSE.
IF WE RETURN GAIA'S CHILDREN TO HER, ZEKE AND THE OLYMPIANSSS WILL BE RESTORED.
IF YOU NEEDED THE CYCLOPES, WHY ASK FOR JUST THEIR EYES?
THERE ARE PLACESSS EVEN MY MAGICSSS CAN'T REACH.
THE EYESSS ALLOW ME TO SEE NOT ONLY THE CYCLOPESSS, BUT THE PRISONSSS OF THE HECATONCHIRESSS AND TYPHOEUSS AS WELL.
I HAVE SEEN THE PLIGHT OF THE CYCLOPES FOR MYSELF. THEY MUST BE SET FREE.
BUT WHY ARE YOU DOING THIS? WHY HELP ME RESTORE THE GODS?
MY REASONSSS ARE MY OWN, BUT MY DESIRE TO SAVE THE CHILD IS GENUINE.
DECIDE. DO YOU WISH MY AID OR NOT?
WE KNOW WHERE TO FIND THE CYCLOPES.
WHO'S NEXT?

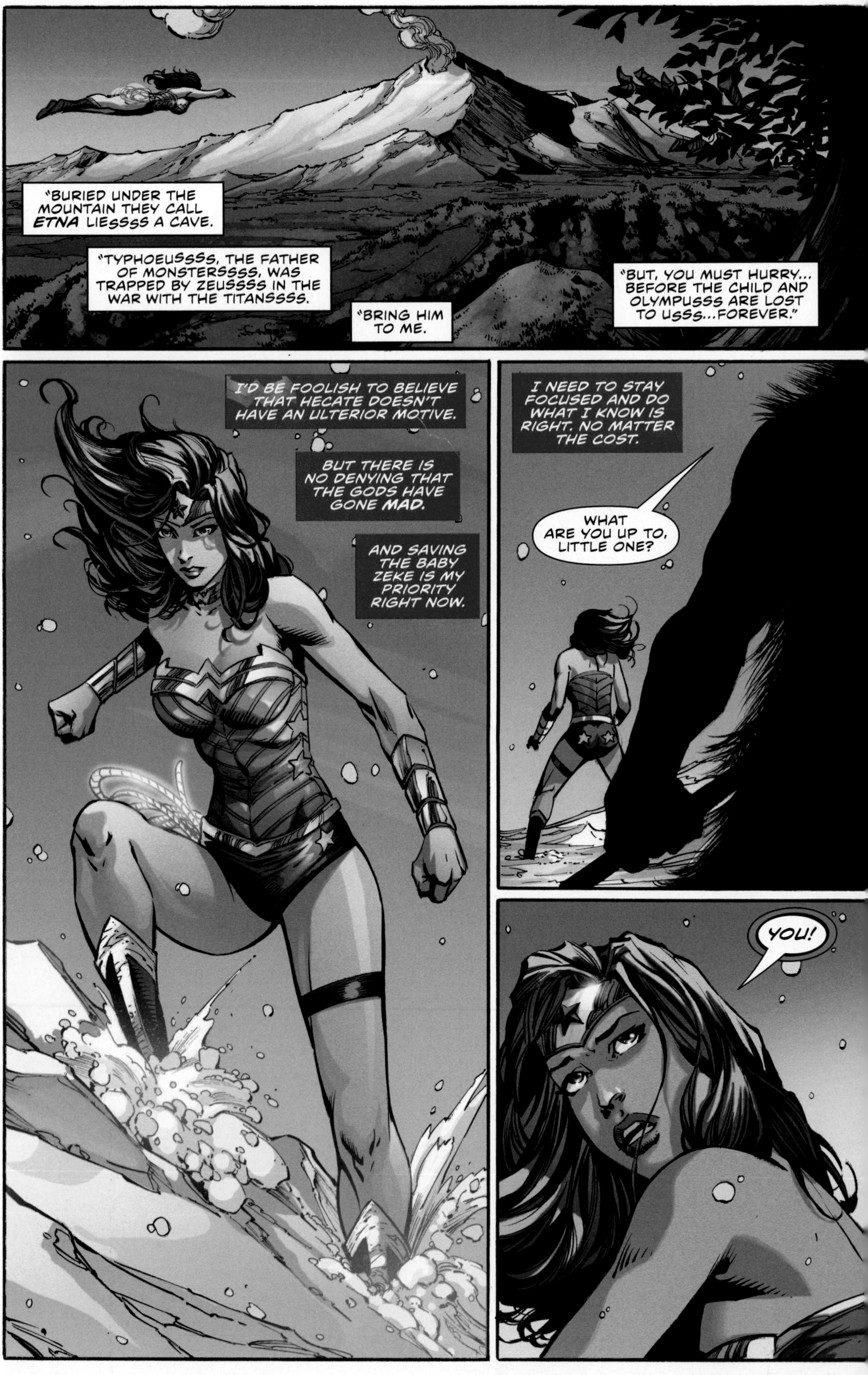

"BURIED UNDER THE MOUNTAIN THEY CALL ETNA LIESSSS A CAVE.
"TYPHOEUSSSS, THE FATHER OF MONSTERSSSS, WAS TRAPPED BY ZEUSSSS IN THE WAR WITH THE TITANSSSS.
"BRING HIM TO ME.
"BUT, YOU MUST HURRY... BEFORE THE CHILD AND OLYMPUSSS ARE LOST TO USSS...FOREVER."
I'D BE FOOLISH TO BELIEVE THAT HECATE DOESN'T HAVE AN ULTERIOR MOTIVE.
BUT THERE IS NO DENYING THAT THE GODS HAVE GONE MAD.
AND SAVING THE BABY ZEKE IS MY PRIORITY RIGHT NOW.
I NEED TO STAY FOCUSED AND DO WHAT I KNOW IS RIGHT. NO MATTER THE COST.
WHAT ARE YOU UP TO, LITTLE ONE?
YOU!

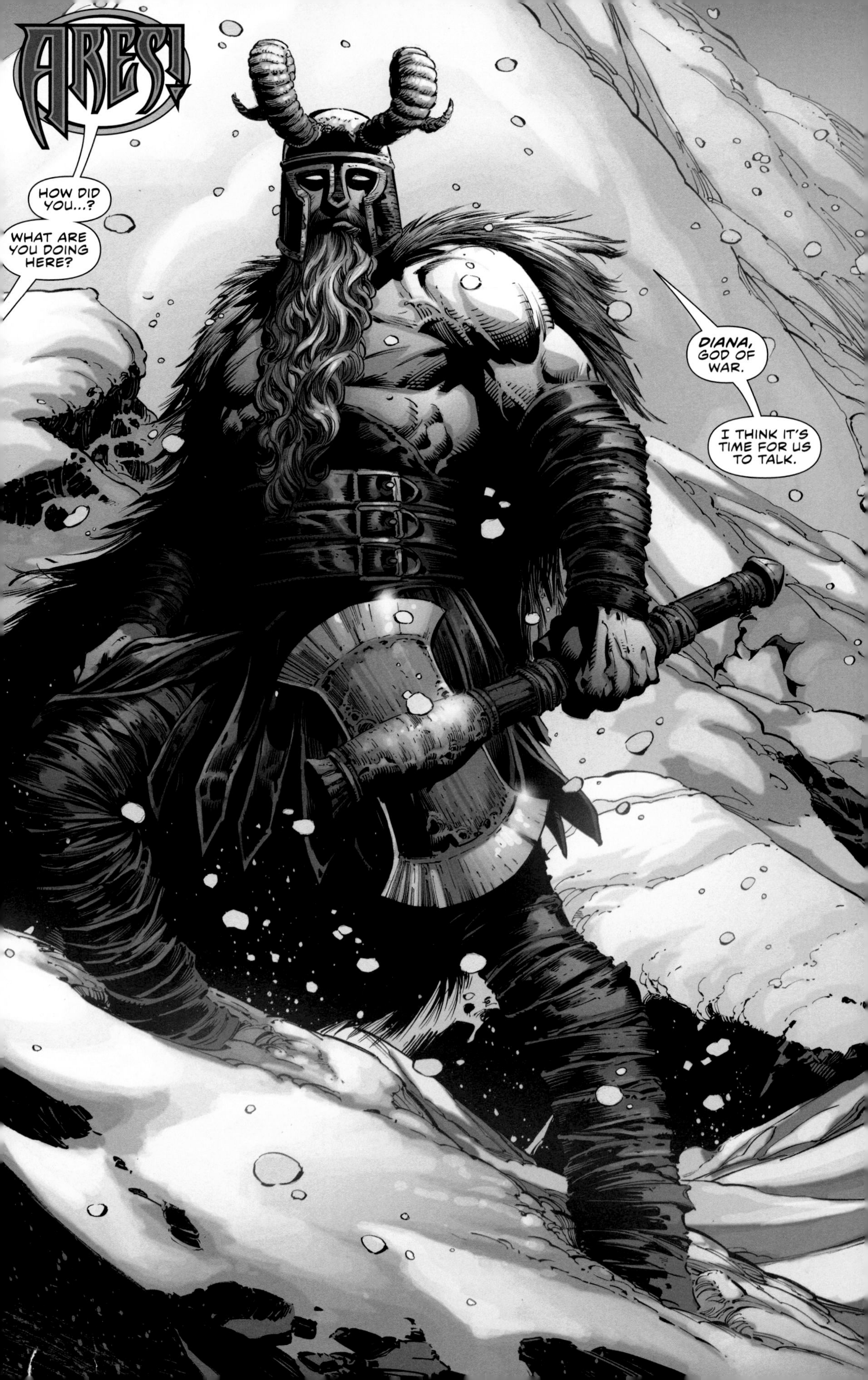
ARES!
HOW DID YOU...?
WHAT ARE YOU DOING HERE?
DIANA, GOD OF WAR.
I THINK IT'S TIME FOR US TO TALK.

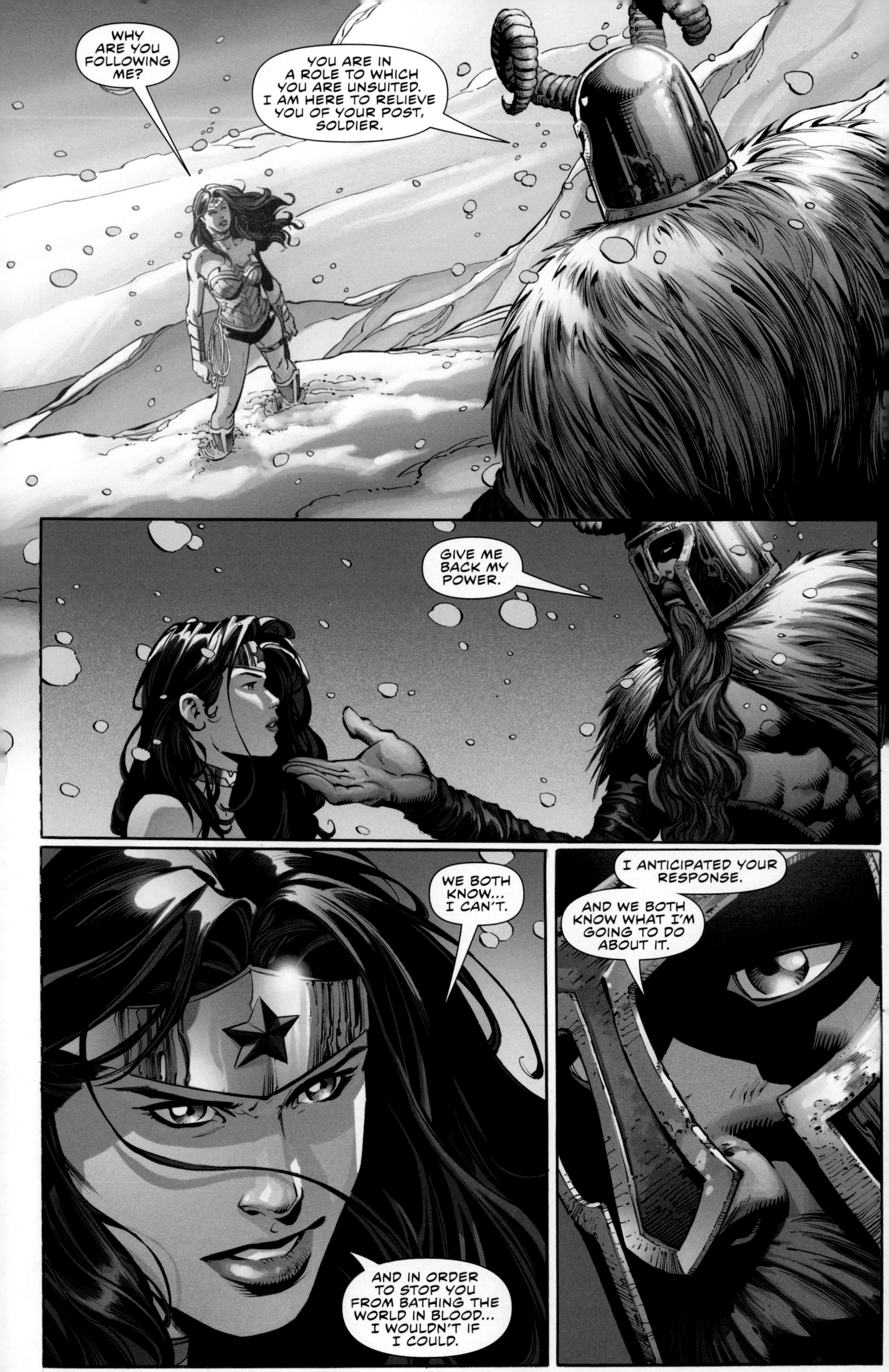
WHY ARE YOU FOLLOWING ME?
YOU ARE IN A ROLE TO WHICH YOU ARE UNSUITED. I AM HERE TO RELIEVE YOU OF YOUR POST, SOLDIER.
GIVE ME BACK MY POWER.
WE BOTH KNOW... I CAN'T.
AND IN ORDER TO STOP YOU FROM BATHING THE WORLD IN BLOOD... I WOULDN'T IF I COULD.
I ANTICIPATED YOUR RESPONSE.
AND WE BOTH KNOW WHAT I'M GOING TO DO ABOUT IT.

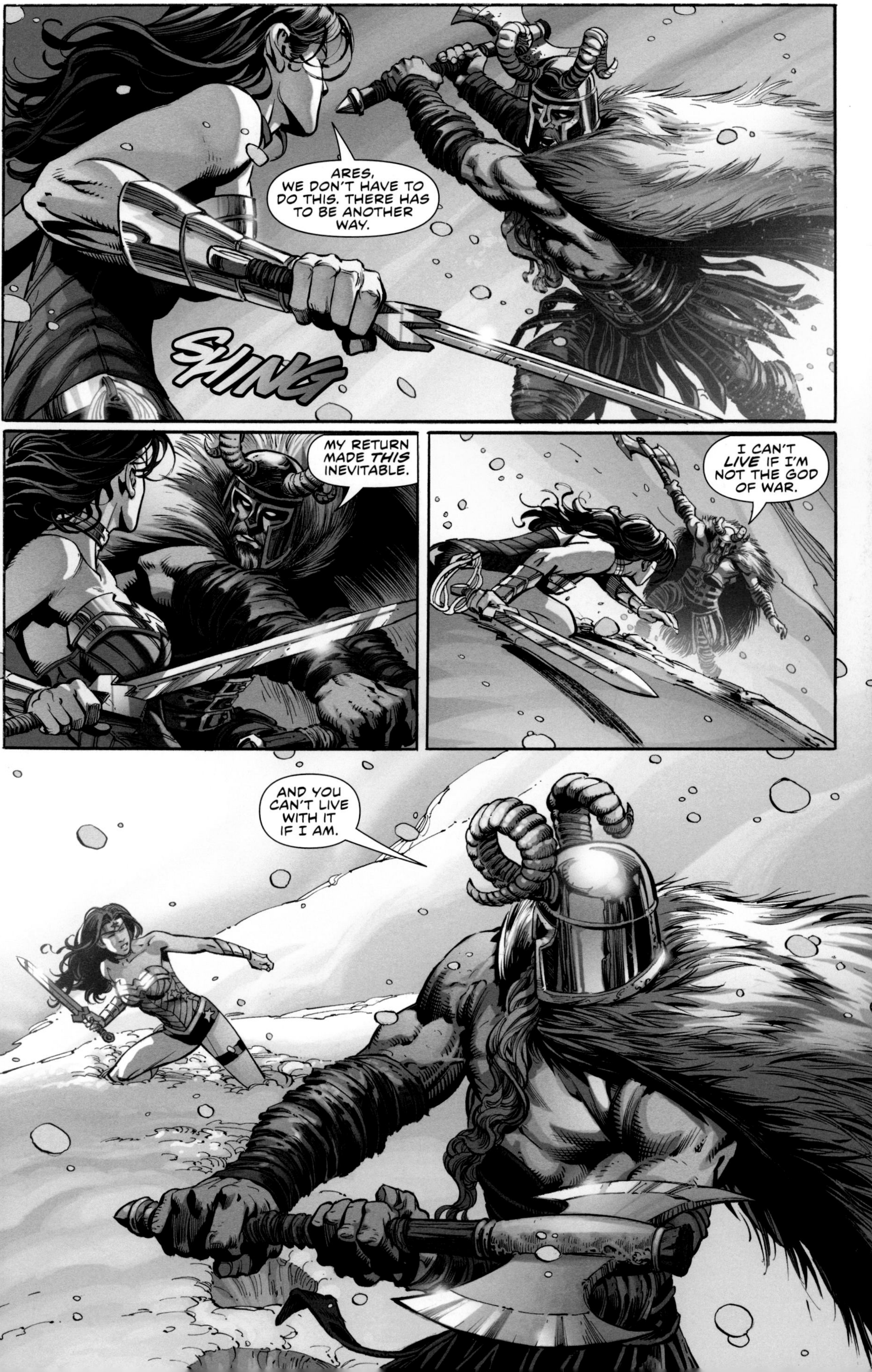
ARES, WE DON'T HAVE TO DO THIS. THERE HAS TO BE ANOTHER WAY.
SHING
MY RETURN MADE *THIS* INEVITABLE.
I CAN'T *LIVE* IF I'M NOT THE GOD OF WAR.
AND YOU CAN'T LIVE WITH IT IF I AM.

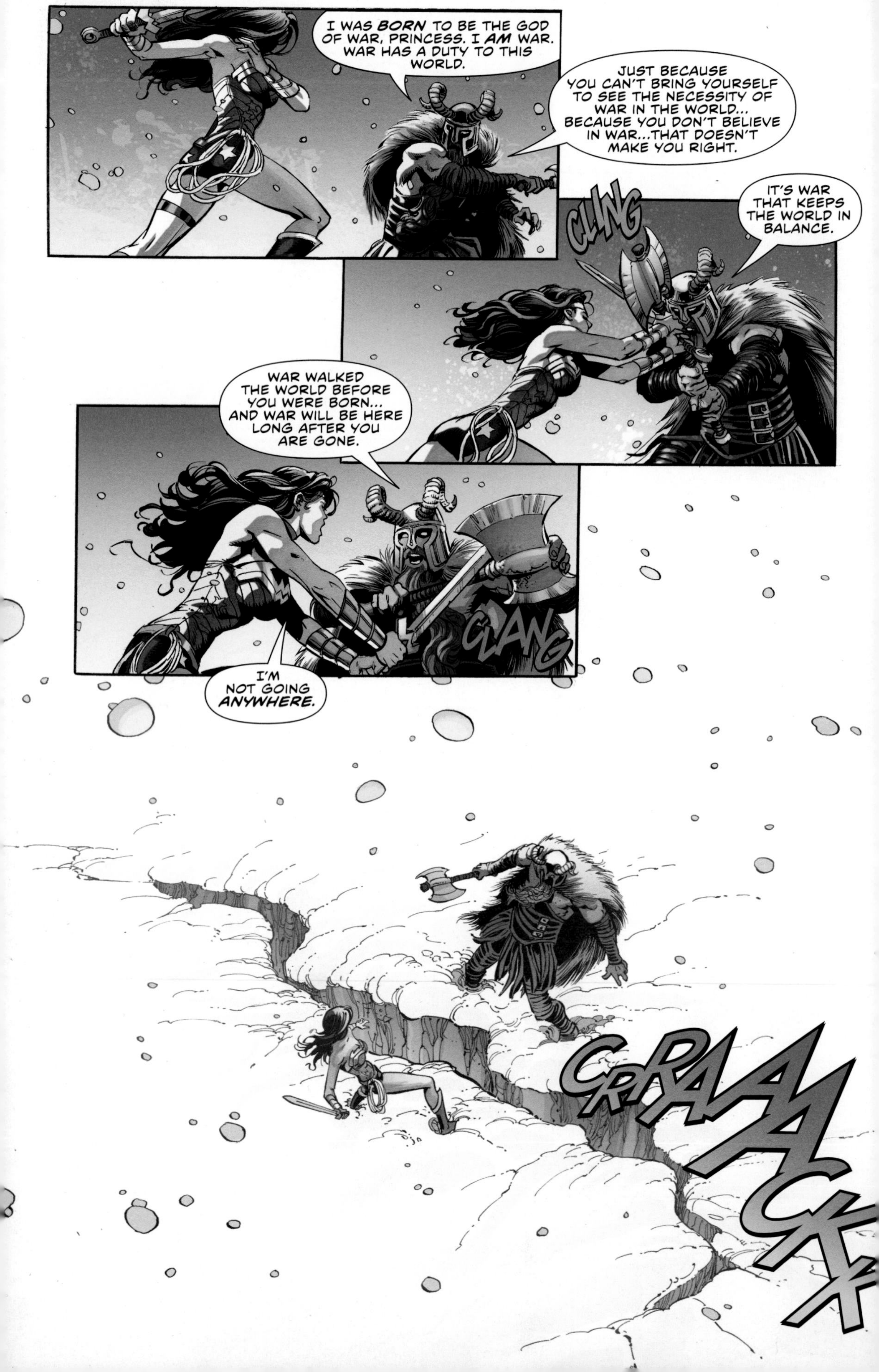

I WAS BORN TO BE THE GOD OF WAR, PRINCESS. I AM WAR. WAR HAS A DUTY TO THIS WORLD.
JUST BECAUSE YOU CAN'T BRING YOURSELF TO SEE THE NECESSITY OF WAR IN THE WORLD... BECAUSE YOU DON'T BELIEVE IN WAR...THAT DOESN'T MAKE YOU RIGHT.
CLING
IT'S WAR THAT KEEPS THE WORLD IN BALANCE.
WAR WALKED THE WORLD BEFORE YOU WERE BORN... AND WAR WILL BE HERE LONG AFTER YOU ARE GONE.
CLANG
I'M NOT GOING ANYWHERE.
CRRAAACKK

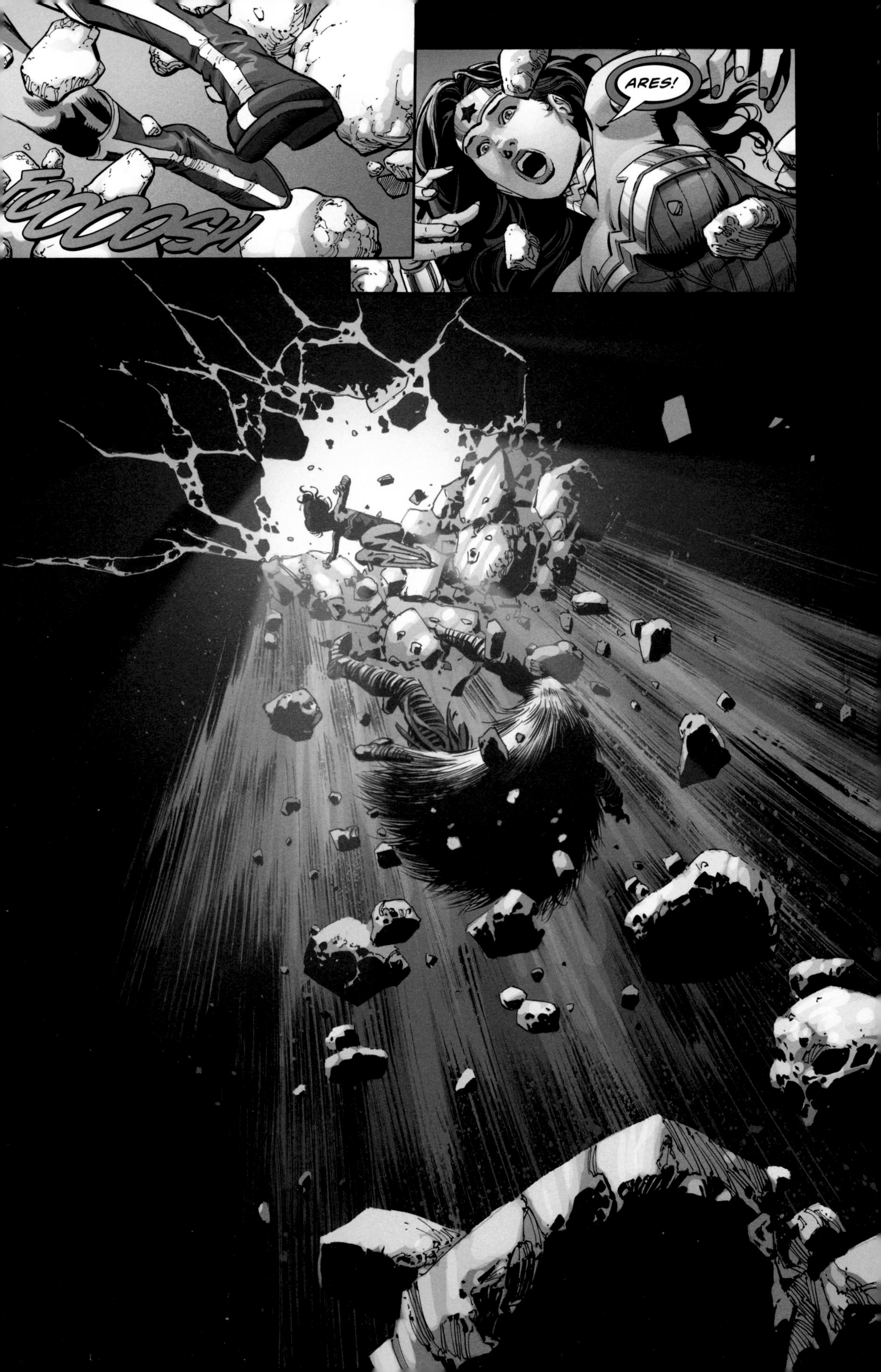

FOOOOSH
ARES!

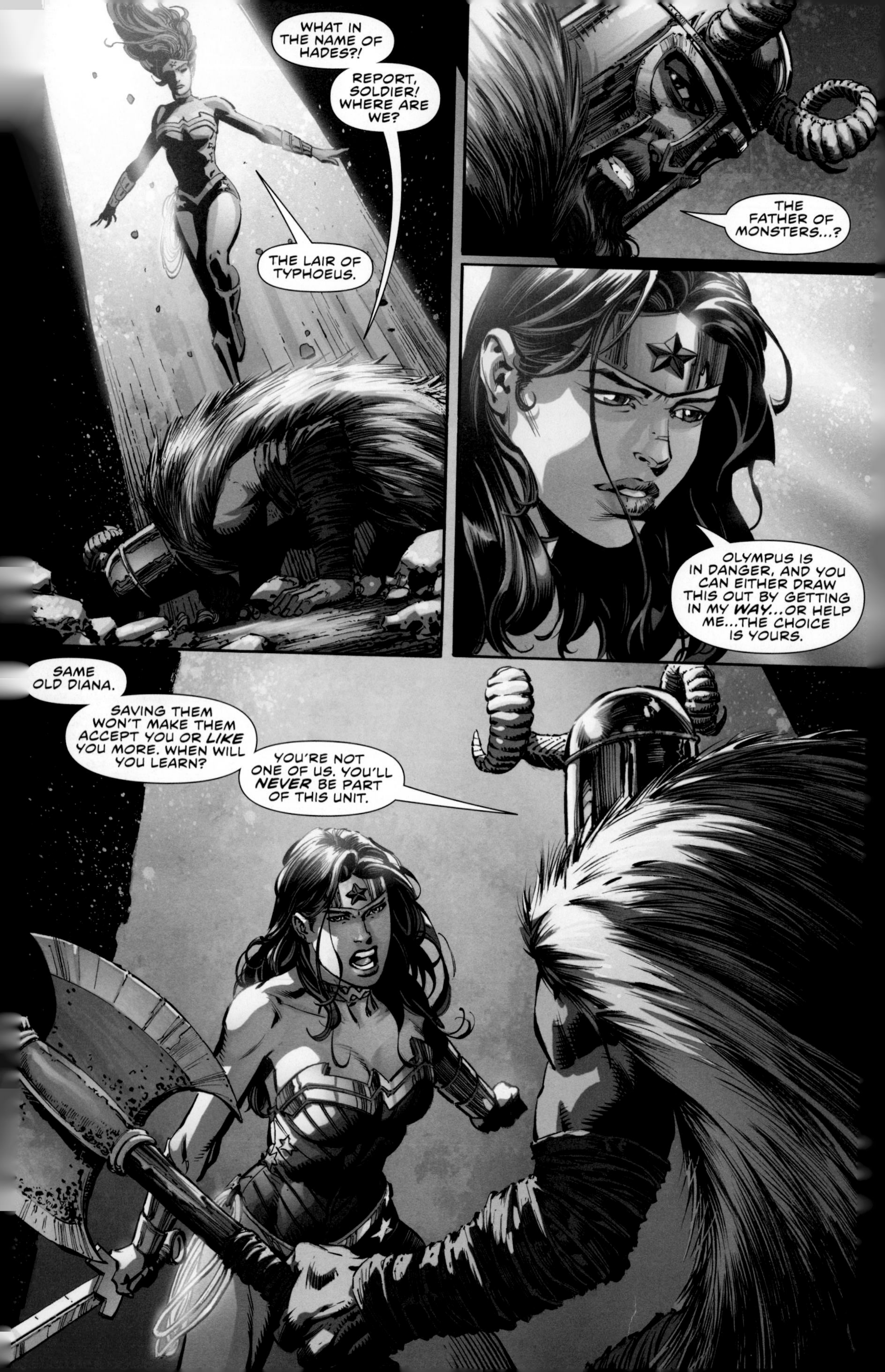
WHAT IN THE NAME OF HADES?!
REPORT, SOLDIER! WHERE ARE WE?
THE LAIR OF TYPHOEUS.
THE FATHER OF MONSTERS...?
OLYMPUS IS IN DANGER, AND YOU CAN EITHER DRAW THIS OUT BY GETTING IN MY WAY...OR HELP ME...THE CHOICE IS YOURS.
SAME OLD DIANA.
SAVING THEM WON'T MAKE THEM ACCEPT YOU OR LIKE YOU MORE. WHEN WILL YOU LEARN?
YOU'RE NOT ONE OF US. YOU'LL NEVER BE PART OF THIS UNIT.

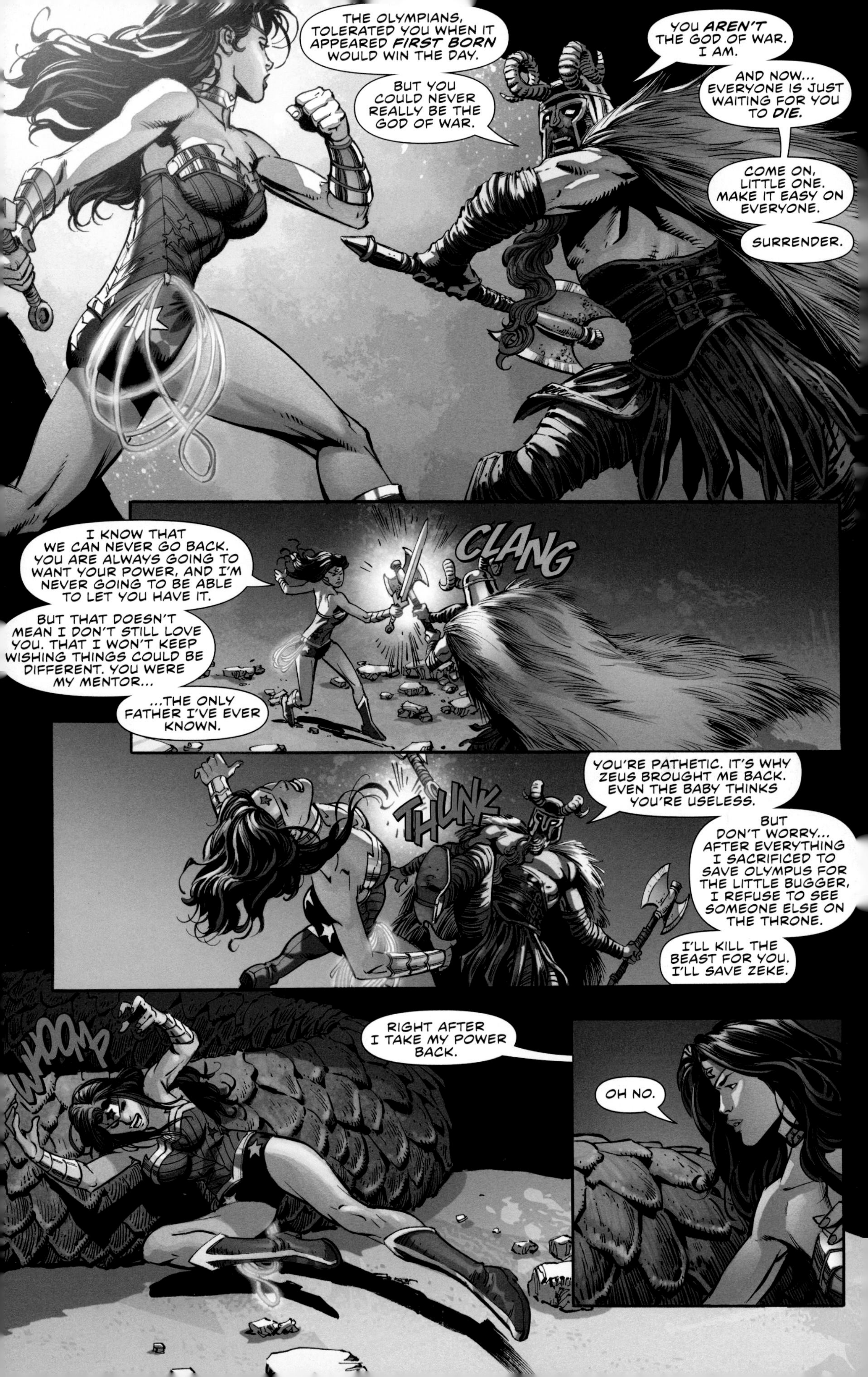
THE OLYMPIANS, TOLERATED YOU WHEN IT APPEARED FIRST BORN WOULD WIN THE DAY.
BUT YOU COULD NEVER REALLY BE THE GOD OF WAR.
YOU AREN'T THE GOD OF WAR. I AM.
AND NOW... EVERYONE IS JUST WAITING FOR YOU TO DIE.
COME ON, LITTLE ONE. MAKE IT EASY ON EVERYONE.
SURRENDER.
I KNOW THAT WE CAN NEVER GO BACK. YOU ARE ALWAYS GOING TO WANT YOUR POWER, AND I'M NEVER GOING TO BE ABLE TO LET YOU HAVE IT.
BUT THAT DOESN'T MEAN I DON'T STILL LOVE YOU. THAT I WON'T KEEP WISHING THINGS COULD BE DIFFERENT. YOU WERE MY MENTOR...
...THE ONLY FATHER I'VE EVER KNOWN.
CLANG
THUNK
YOU'RE PATHETIC. IT'S WHY ZEUS BROUGHT ME BACK. EVEN THE BABY THINKS YOU'RE USELESS.
BUT DON'T WORRY... AFTER EVERYTHING I SACRIFICED TO SAVE OLYMPUS FOR THE LITTLE BUGGER, I REFUSE TO SEE SOMEONE ELSE ON THE THRONE.
I'LL KILL THE BEAST FOR YOU. I'LL SAVE ZEKE.
WHOOMP
RIGHT AFTER I TAKE MY POWER BACK.
OH NO.

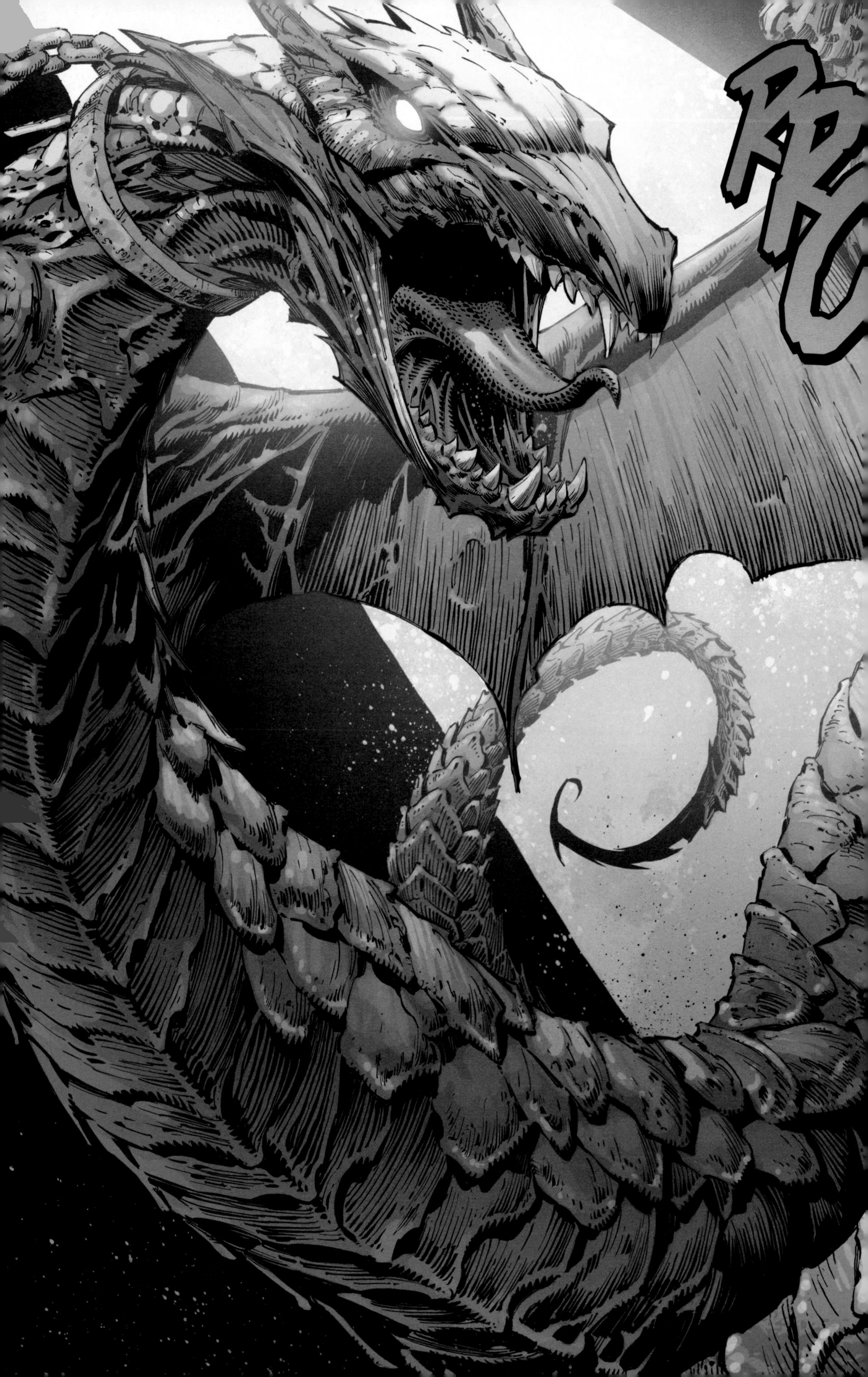

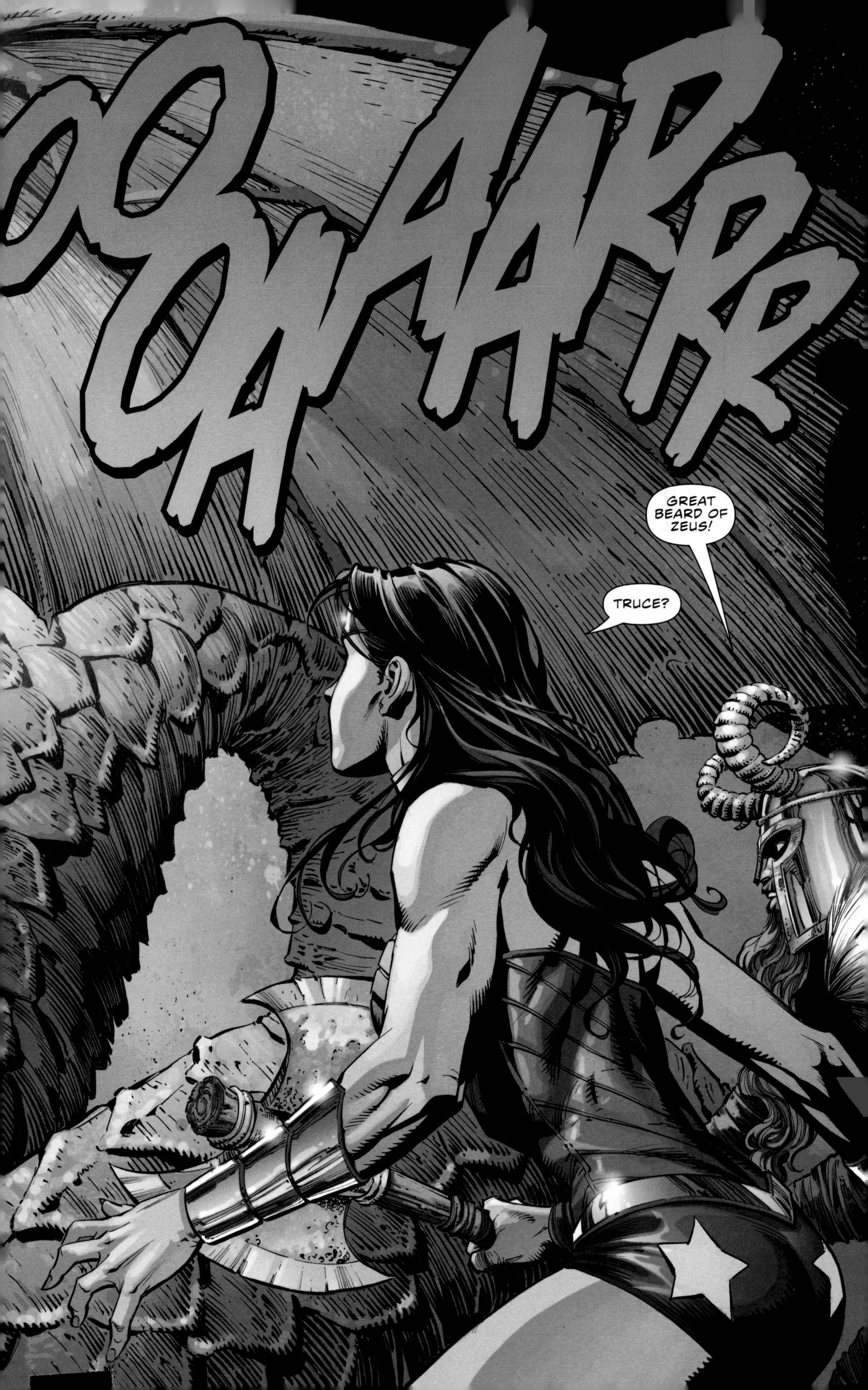
GREAT BEARD OF ZEUS!
TRUCE?

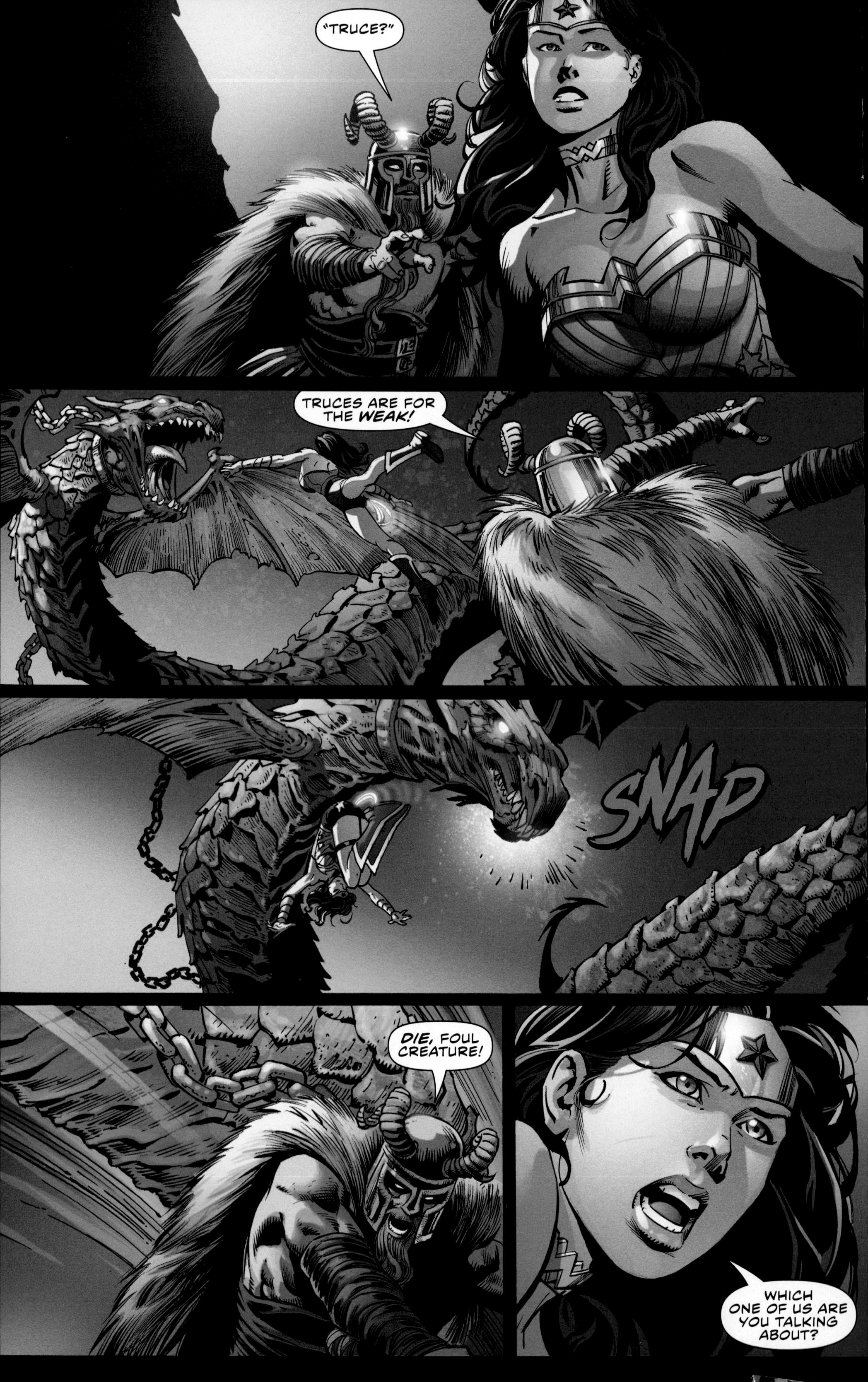
"TRUCE?"
TRUCES ARE FOR THE WEAK!
SNAP
DIE, FOUL CREATURE!
WHICH ONE OF US ARE YOU TALKING ABOUT?

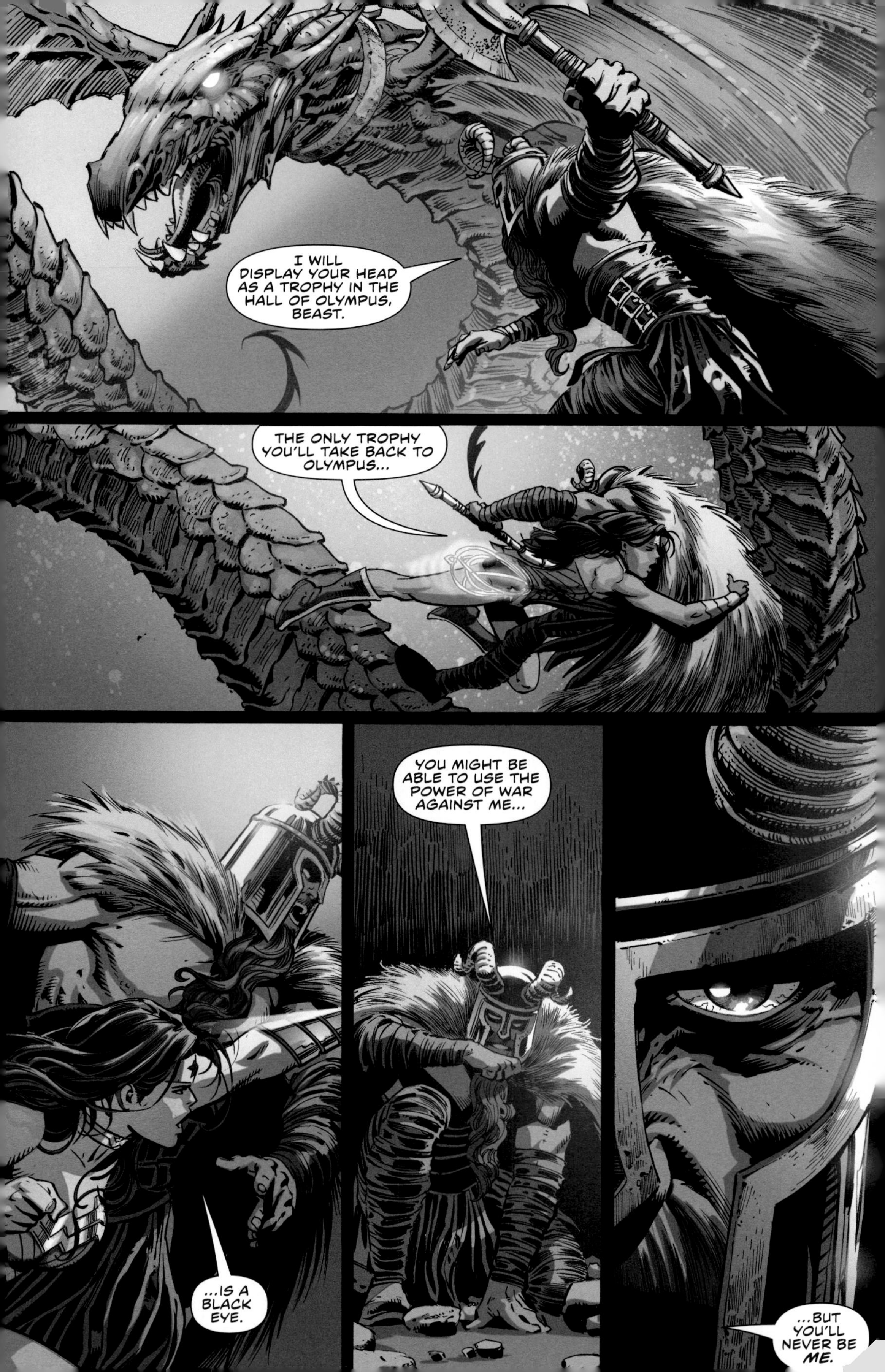
I WILL DISPLAY YOUR HEAD AS A TROPHY IN THE HALL OF OLYMPUS, BEAST.
THE ONLY TROPHY YOU'LL TAKE BACK TO OLYMPUS...
...IS A BLACK EYE.
YOU MIGHT BE ABLE TO USE THE POWER OF WAR AGAINST ME...
...BUT YOU'LL NEVER BE *ME*.

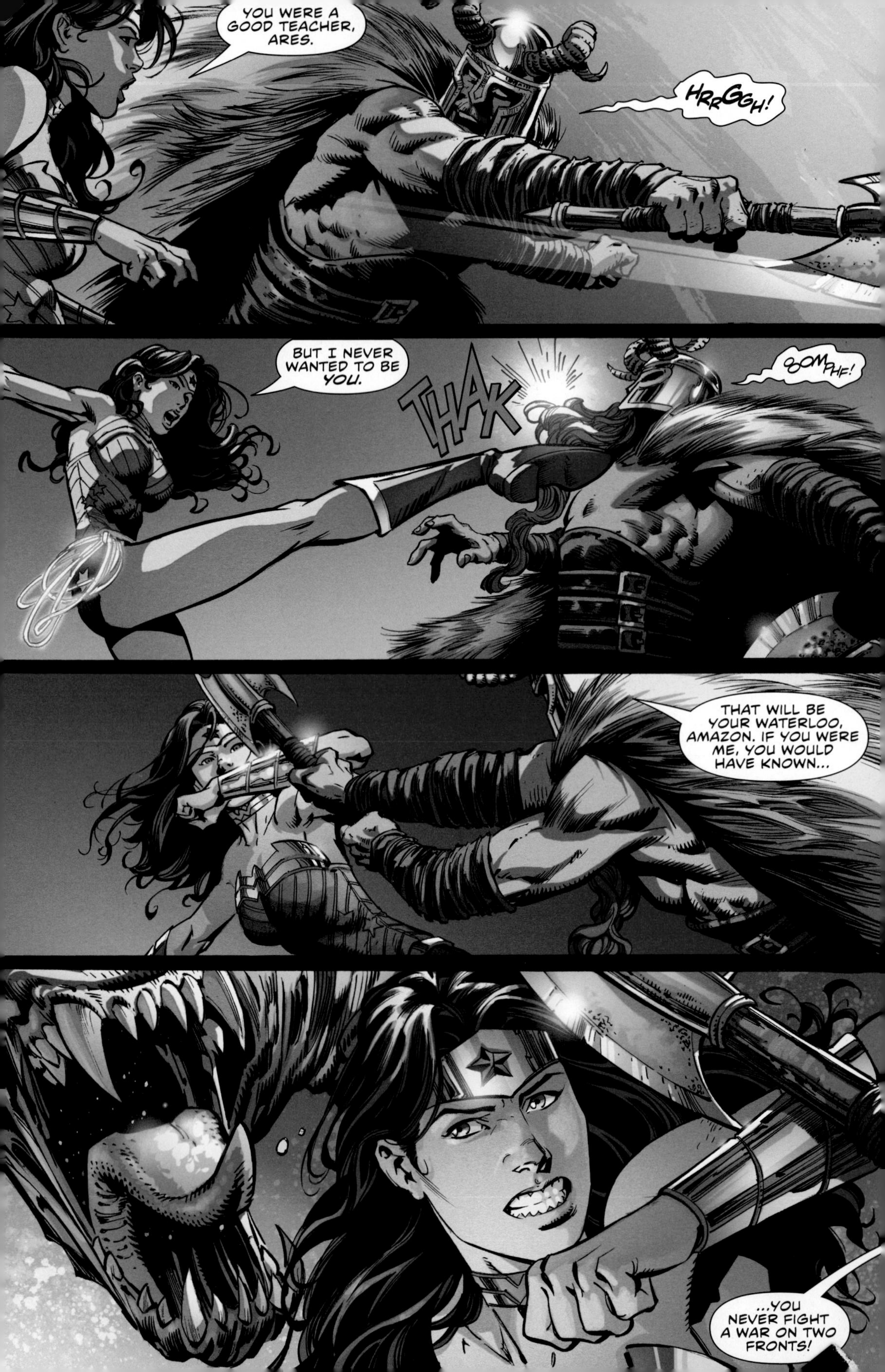
YOU WERE A GOOD TEACHER, ARES.
HRRGGH!
BUT I NEVER WANTED TO BE YOU.
THAK
OOMPHF!
THAT WILL BE YOUR WATERLOO, AMAZON. IF YOU WERE ME, YOU WOULD HAVE KNOWN...
...YOU NEVER FIGHT A WAR ON TWO FRONTS!

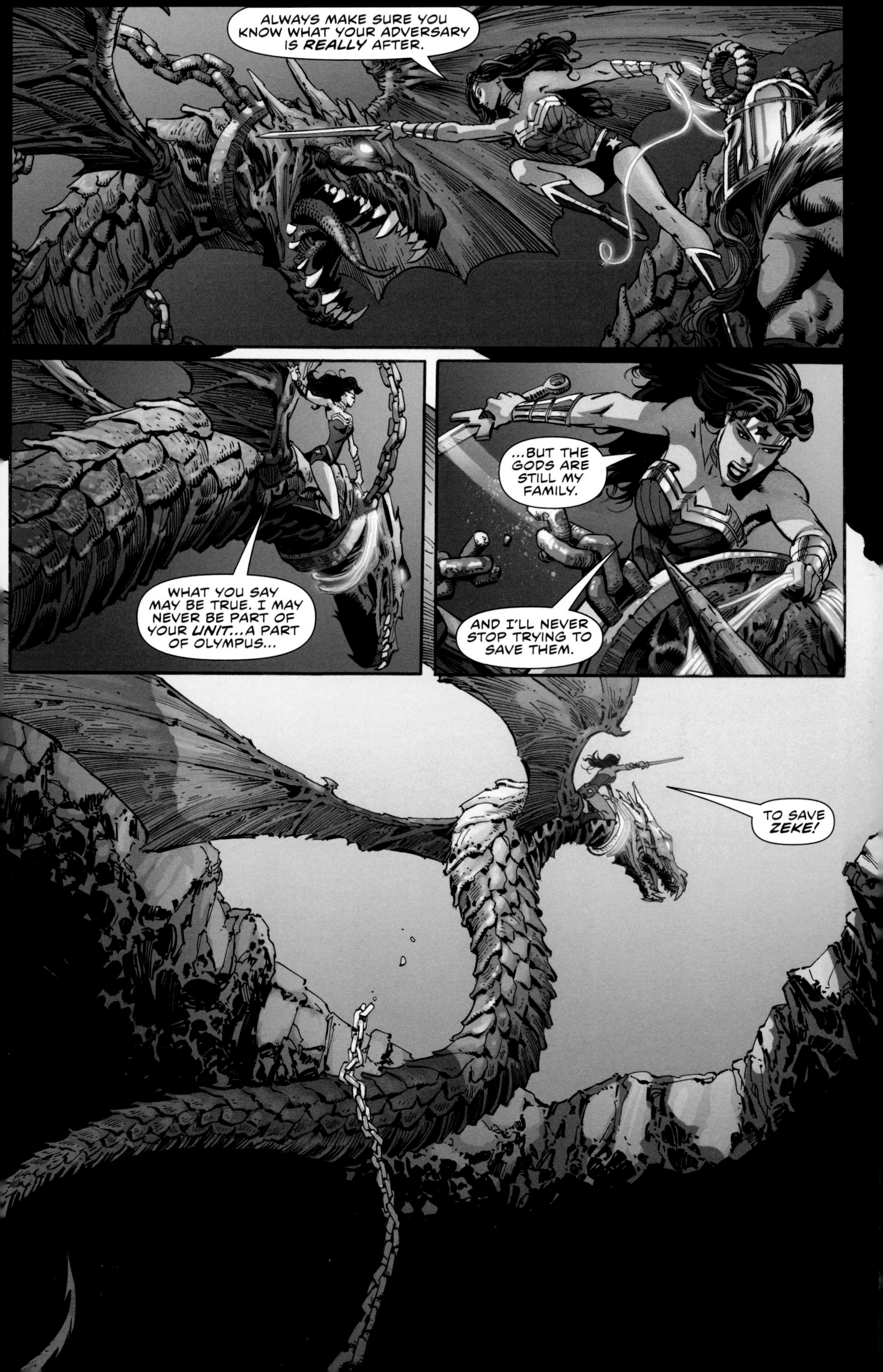
ALWAYS MAKE SURE YOU KNOW WHAT YOUR ADVERSARY IS REALLY AFTER.
WHAT YOU SAY MAY BE TRUE. I MAY NEVER BE PART OF YOUR UNIT...A PART OF OLYMPUS...
...BUT THE GODS ARE STILL MY FAMILY.
AND I'LL NEVER STOP TRYING TO SAVE THEM.
TO SAVE ZEKE!

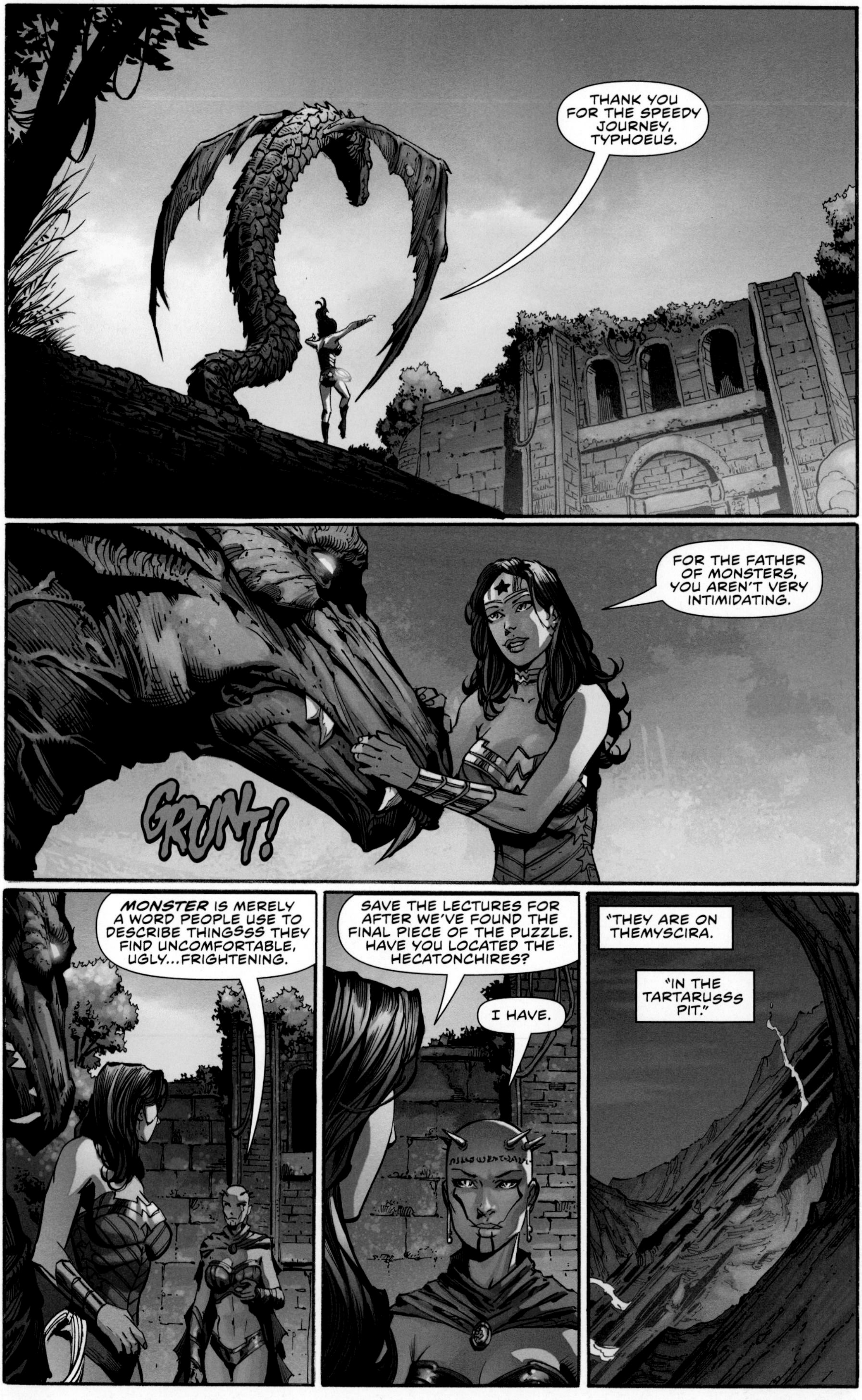
THANK YOU FOR THE SPEEDY JOURNEY, TYPHOEUS.
FOR THE FATHER OF MONSTERS, YOU AREN'T VERY INTIMIDATING.
GRUNT!
MONSTER IS MERELY A WORD PEOPLE USE TO DESCRIBE THINGSSS THEY FIND UNCOMFORTABLE, UGLY...FRIGHTENING.
SAVE THE LECTURES FOR AFTER WE'VE FOUND THE FINAL PIECE OF THE PUZZLE. HAVE YOU LOCATED THE HECATONCHIRES?
I HAVE.
"THEY ARE ON THEMYSCIRA.
"IN THE TARTARUSSS PIT."

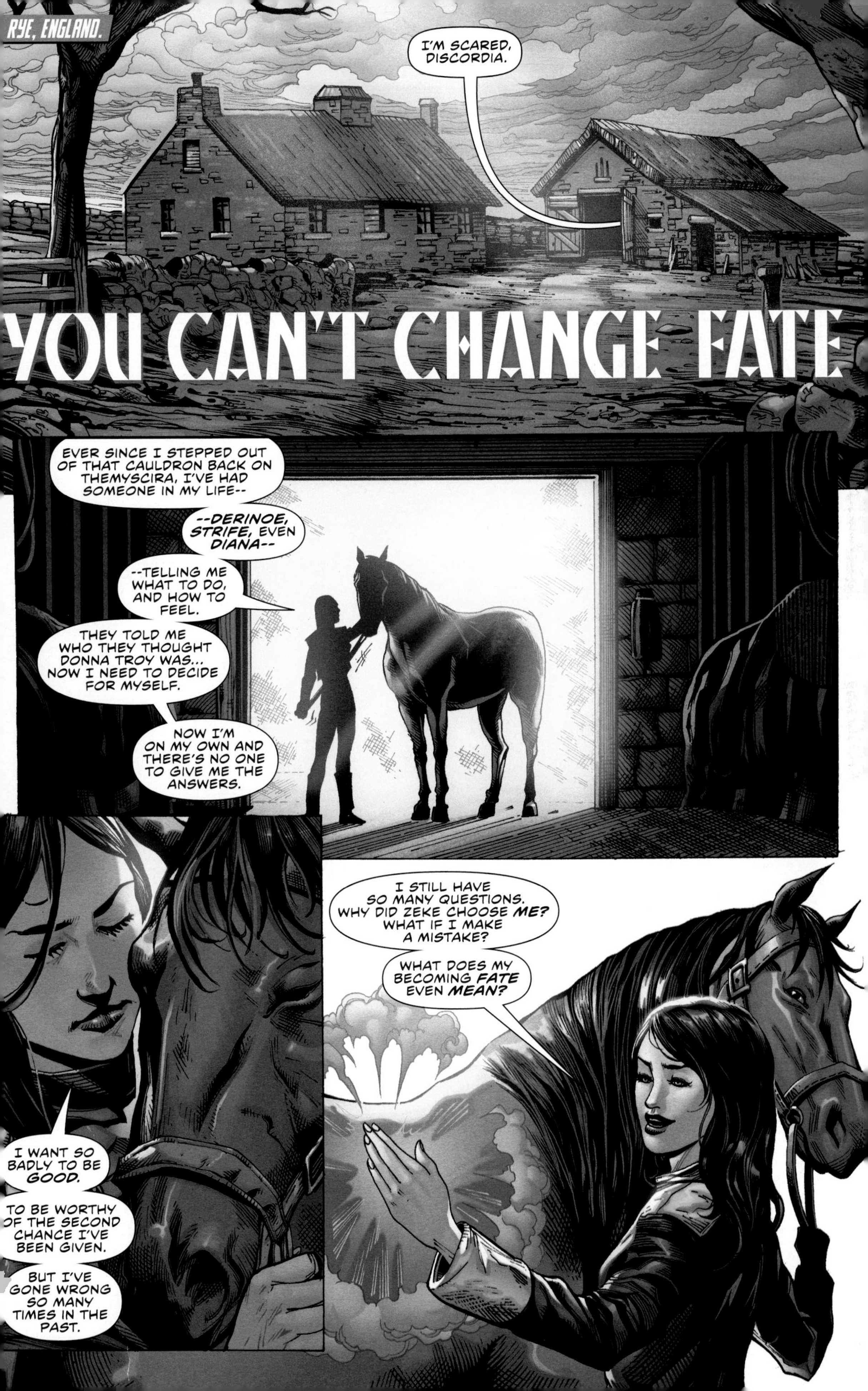
RYE, ENGLAND.
I'M SCARED, DISCORDIA.
YOU CAN'T CHANGE FATE
EVER SINCE I STEPPED OUT OF THAT CAULDRON BACK ON THEMYSCIRA, I'VE HAD SOMEONE IN MY LIFE--
--DERINOE, STRIFE, EVEN DIANA--
--TELLING ME WHAT TO DO, AND HOW TO FEEL.
THEY TOLD ME WHO THEY THOUGHT DONNA TROY WAS... NOW I NEED TO DECIDE FOR MYSELF.
NOW I'M ON MY OWN AND THERE'S NO ONE TO GIVE ME THE ANSWERS.
I WANT SO BADLY TO BE GOOD.
TO BE WORTHY OF THE SECOND CHANCE I'VE BEEN GIVEN.
BUT I'VE GONE WRONG SO MANY TIMES IN THE PAST.
I STILL HAVE SO MANY QUESTIONS. WHY DID ZEKE CHOOSE ME? WHAT IF I MAKE A MISTAKE?
WHAT DOES MY BECOMING FATE EVEN MEAN?

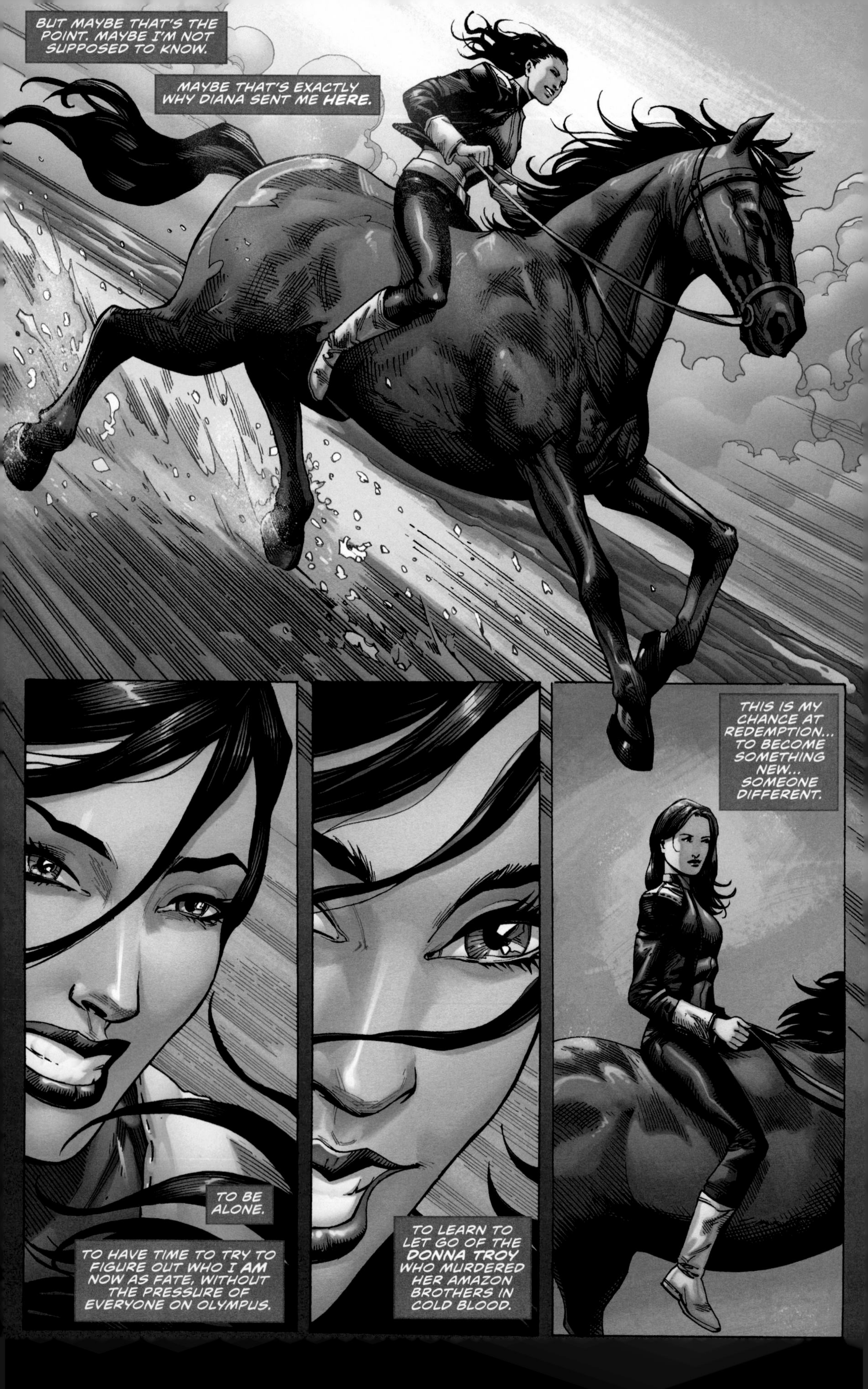
BUT MAYBE THAT'S THE POINT. MAYBE I'M NOT SUPPOSED TO KNOW.
MAYBE THAT'S EXACTLY WHY DIANA SENT ME HERE.
TO BE ALONE.
TO HAVE TIME TO TRY TO FIGURE OUT WHO I AM NOW AS FATE, WITHOUT THE PRESSURE OF EVERYONE ON OLYMPUS.
TO LEARN TO LET GO OF THE DONNA TROY WHO MURDERED HER AMAZON BROTHERS IN COLD BLOOD.
THIS IS MY CHANCE AT REDEMPTION... TO BECOME SOMETHING NEW... SOMEONE DIFFERENT.

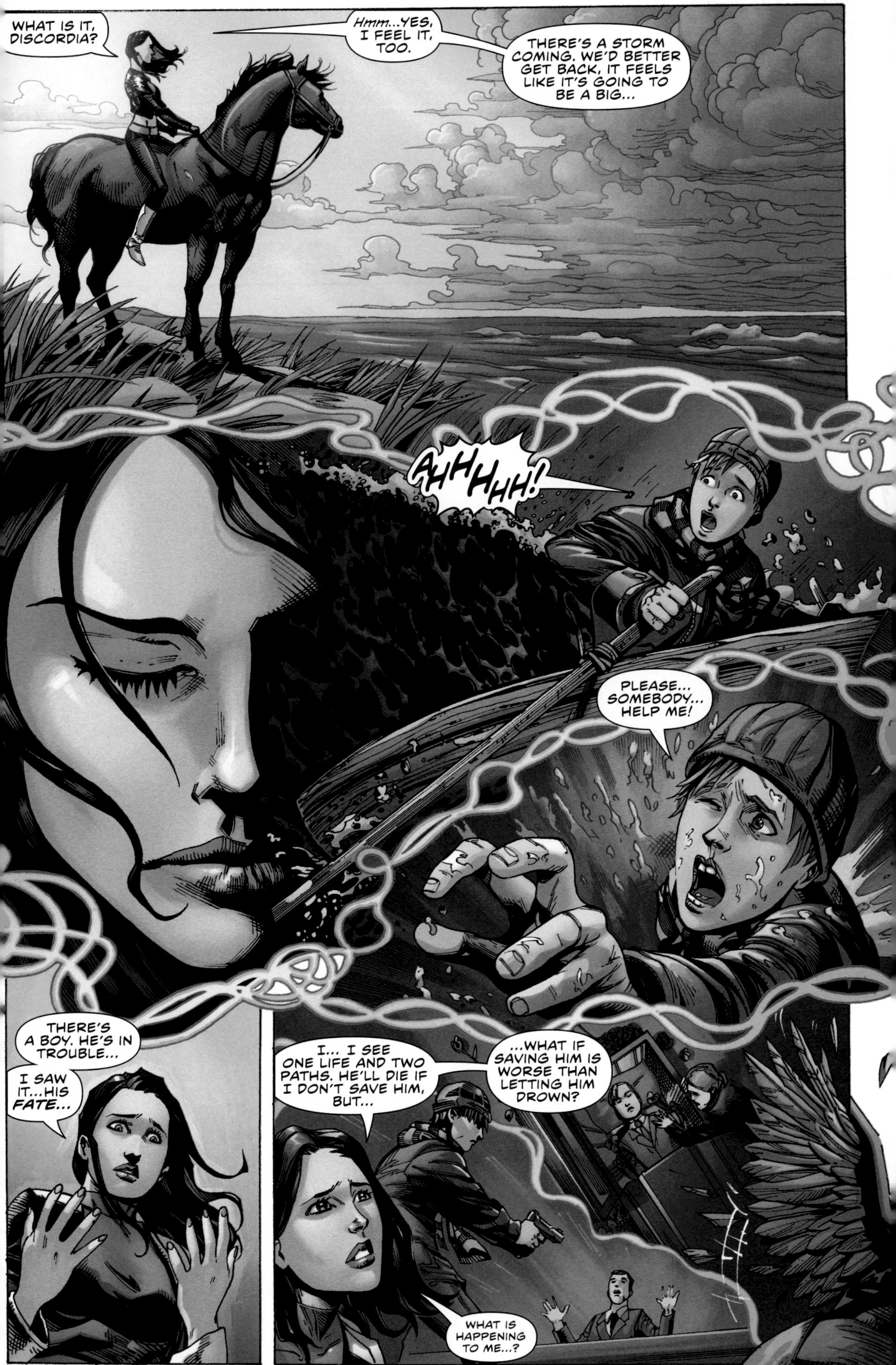
WHAT IS IT, DISCORDIA?
Hmm...YES, I FEEL IT, TOO.
THERE'S A STORM COMING. WE'D BETTER GET BACK, IT FEELS LIKE IT'S GOING TO BE A BIG...
AHHHHH!
PLEASE... SOMEBODY... HELP ME!
THERE'S A BOY. HE'S IN TROUBLE...
I SAW IT...HIS FATE...
I... I SEE ONE LIFE AND TWO PATHS. HE'LL DIE IF I DON'T SAVE HIM, BUT...
...WHAT IF SAVING HIM IS WORSE THAN LETTING HIM DROWN?
WHAT IS HAPPENING TO ME...?

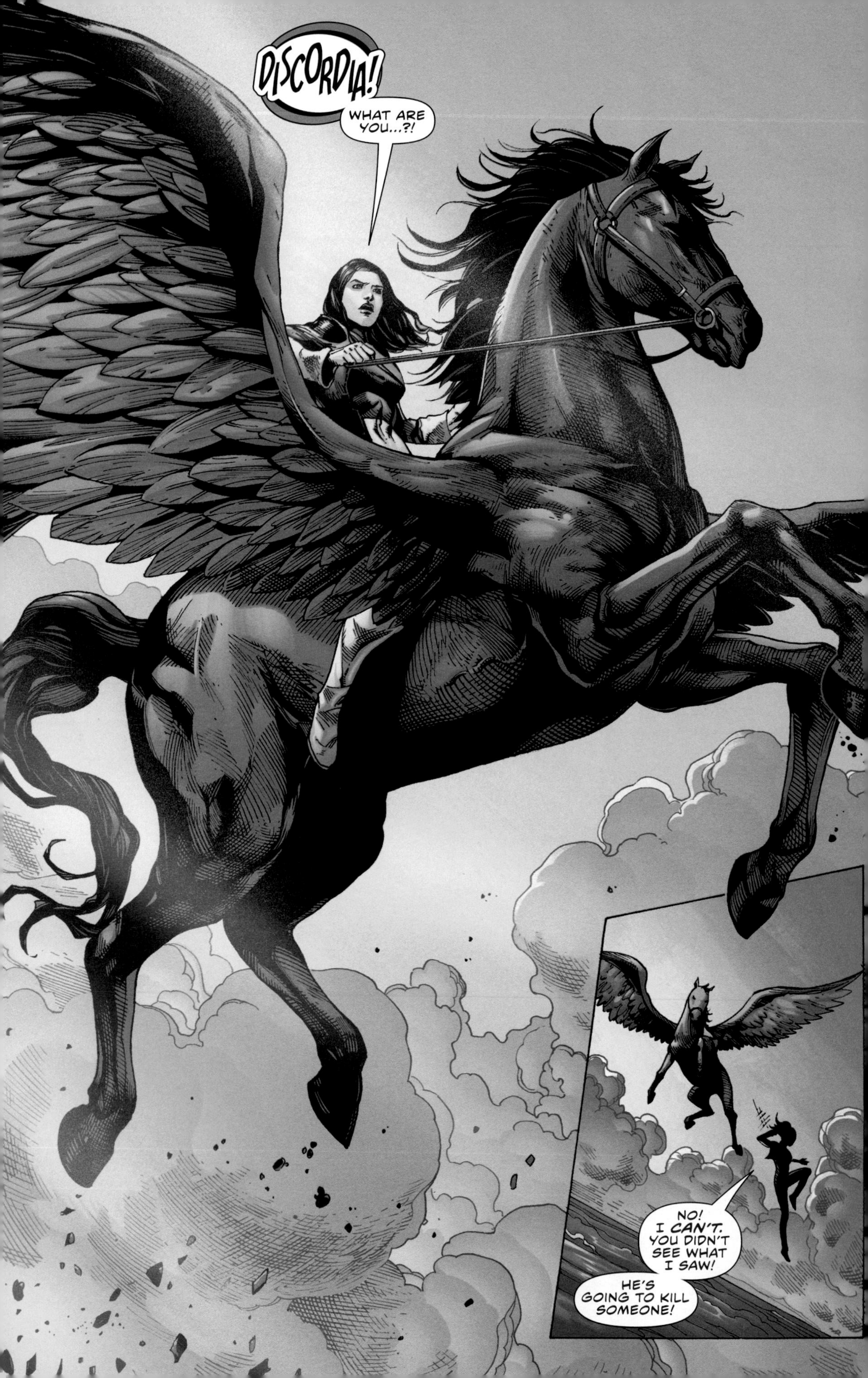
DISCORDIA!
WHAT ARE YOU...?!
NO! I CAN'T. YOU DIDN'T SEE WHAT I SAW!
HE'S GOING TO KILL SOMEONE!

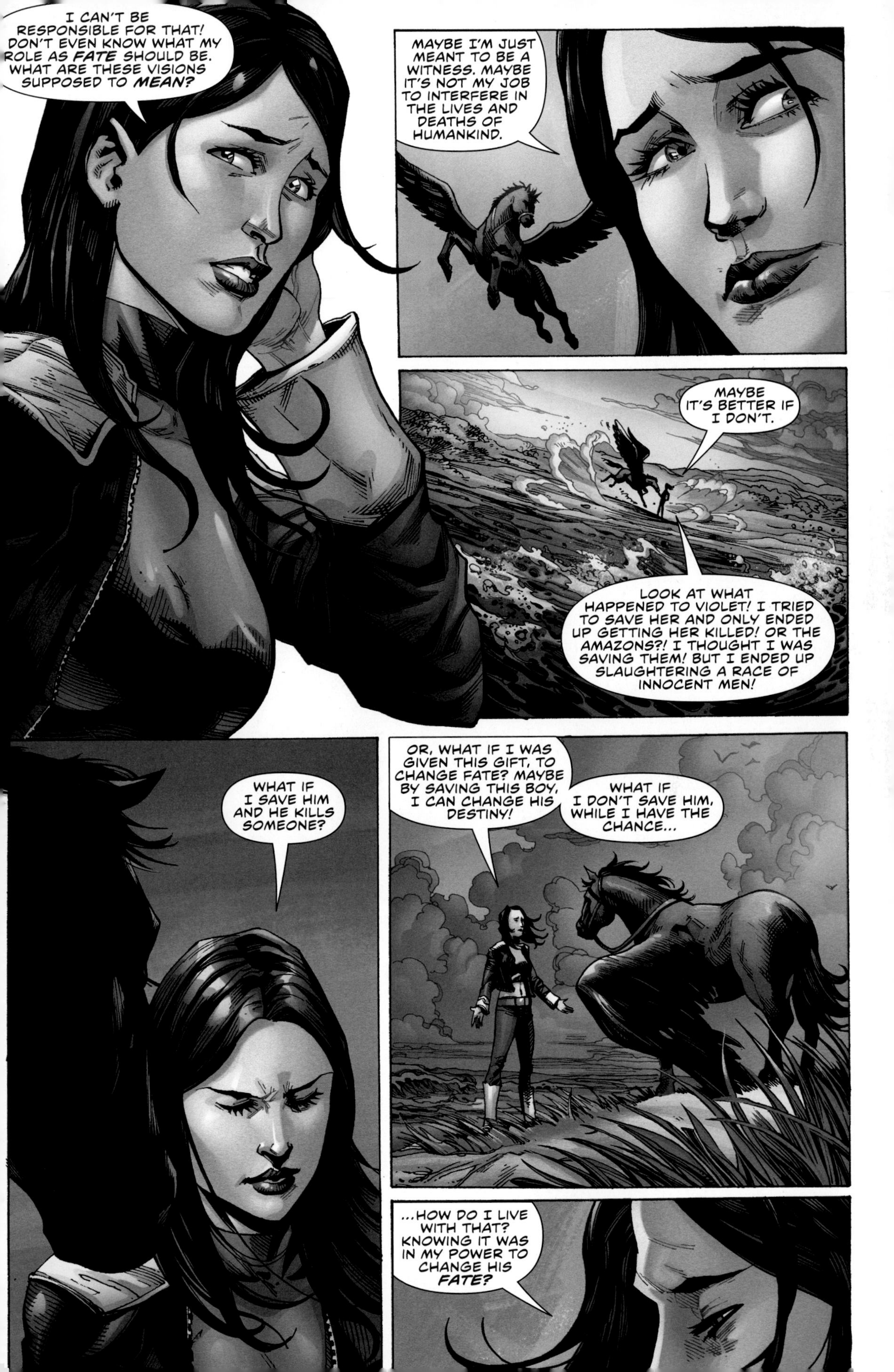
I CAN'T BE RESPONSIBLE FOR THAT! DON'T EVEN KNOW WHAT MY ROLE AS *FATE* SHOULD BE. WHAT ARE THESE VISIONS SUPPOSED TO *MEAN?*
MAYBE I'M JUST MEANT TO BE A WITNESS. MAYBE IT'S NOT MY JOB TO INTERFERE IN THE LIVES AND DEATHS OF HUMANKIND.
MAYBE IT'S BETTER IF I DON'T.
LOOK AT WHAT HAPPENED TO VIOLET! I TRIED TO SAVE HER AND ONLY ENDED UP GETTING HER KILLED! OR THE AMAZONS?! I THOUGHT I WAS SAVING THEM! BUT I ENDED UP SLAUGHTERING A RACE OF INNOCENT MEN!
WHAT IF I SAVE HIM AND HE KILLS SOMEONE?
OR, WHAT IF I WAS GIVEN THIS GIFT, TO CHANGE FATE? MAYBE BY SAVING THIS BOY, I CAN CHANGE HIS DESTINY!
WHAT IF I DON'T SAVE HIM, WHILE I HAVE THE CHANCE...
...HOW DO I LIVE WITH THAT? KNOWING IT WAS IN MY POWER TO CHANGE HIS *FATE?*

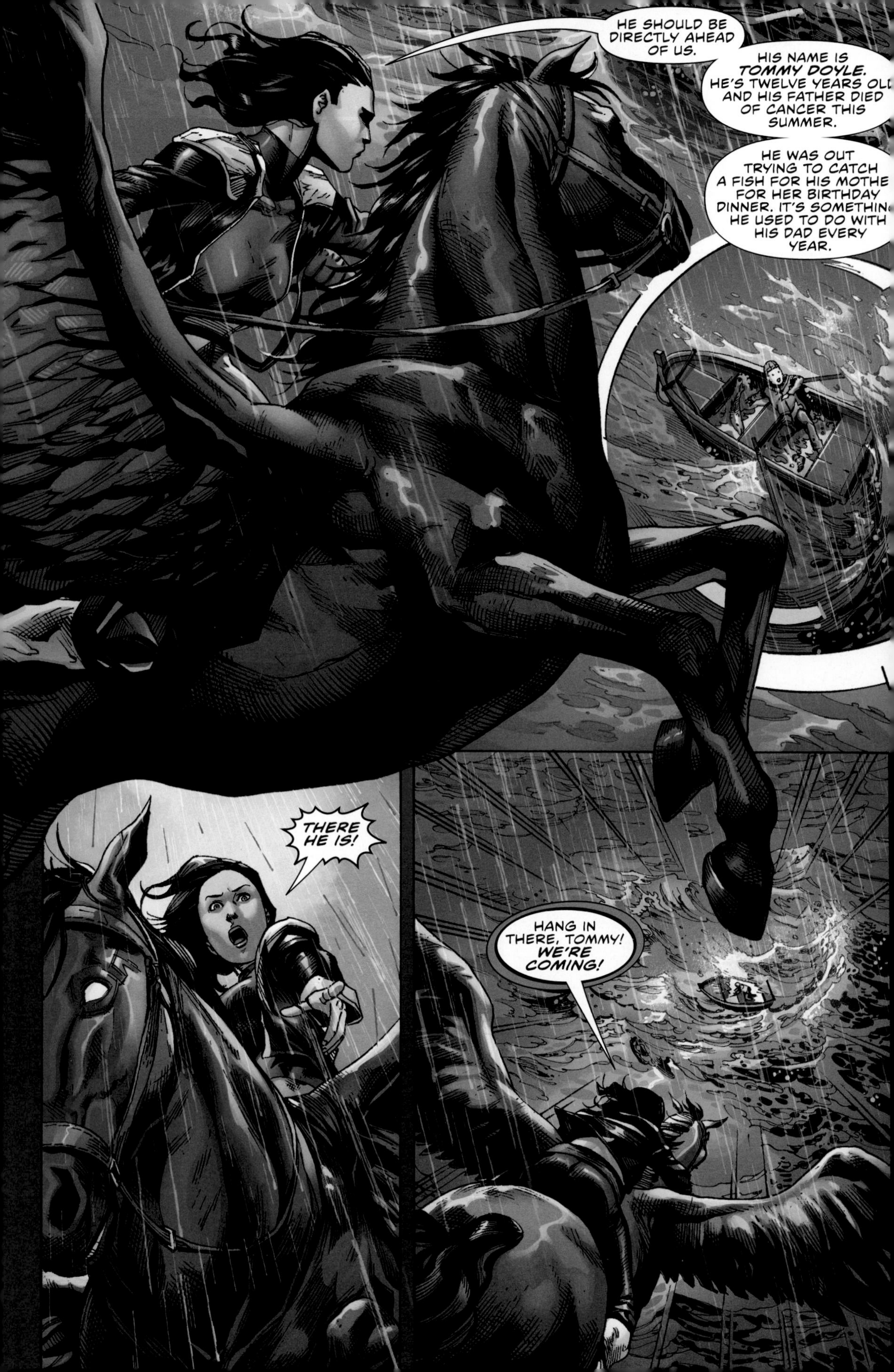
HE SHOULD BE DIRECTLY AHEAD OF US.
HIS NAME IS *TOMMY DOYLE.* HE'S TWELVE YEARS OLD AND HIS FATHER DIED OF CANCER THIS SUMMER.
HE WAS OUT TRYING TO CATCH A FISH FOR HIS MOTHER FOR HER BIRTHDAY DINNER. IT'S SOMETHING HE USED TO DO WITH HIS DAD EVERY YEAR.
THERE HE IS!
HANG IN THERE, TOMMY! *WE'RE COMING!*

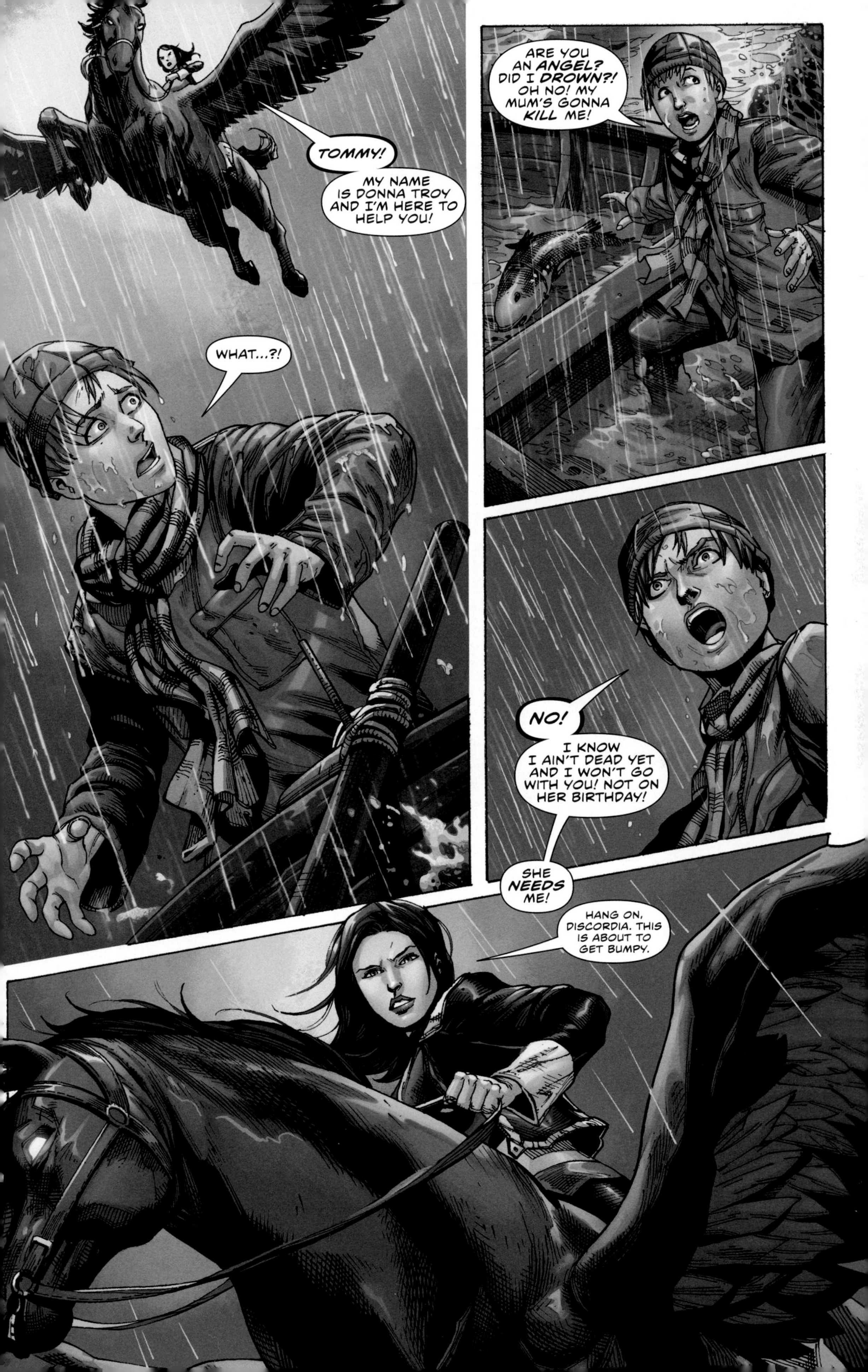
TOMMY!
MY NAME IS DONNA TROY AND I'M HERE TO HELP YOU!
WHAT...?!
ARE YOU AN ANGEL? DID I DROWN?! OH NO! MY MUM'S GONNA KILL ME!
NO!
I KNOW I AIN'T DEAD YET AND I WON'T GO WITH YOU! NOT ON HER BIRTHDAY!
SHE NEEDS ME!
HANG ON, DISCORDIA. THIS IS ABOUT TO GET BUMPY.

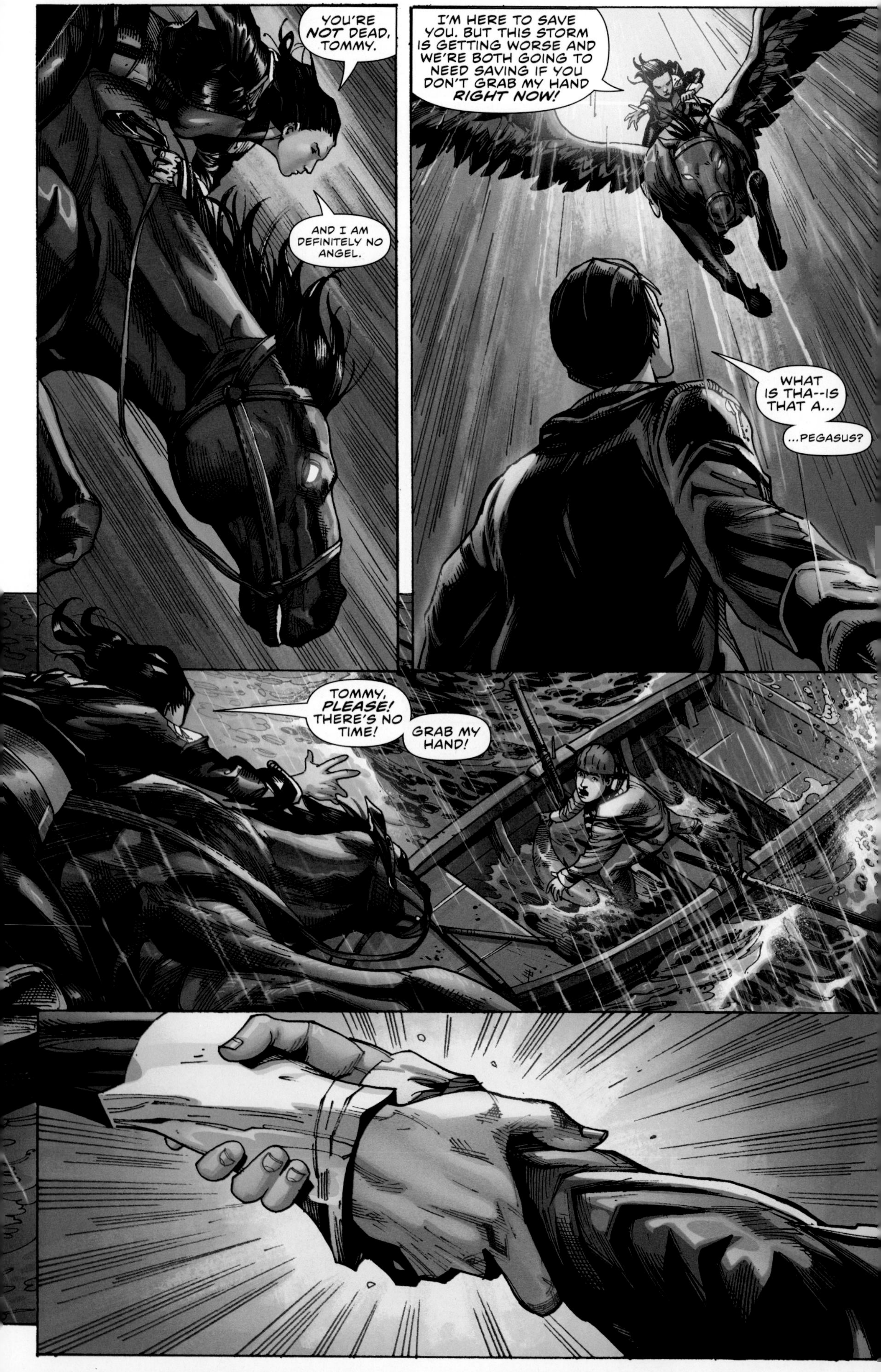
YOU'RE NOT DEAD, TOMMY.
AND I AM DEFINITELY NO ANGEL.
I'M HERE TO SAVE YOU. BUT THIS STORM IS GETTING WORSE AND WE'RE BOTH GOING TO NEED SAVING IF YOU DON'T GRAB MY HAND RIGHT NOW!
WHAT IS THA--IS THAT A...
...PEGASUS?
TOMMY, PLEASE! THERE'S NO TIME!
GRAB MY HAND!

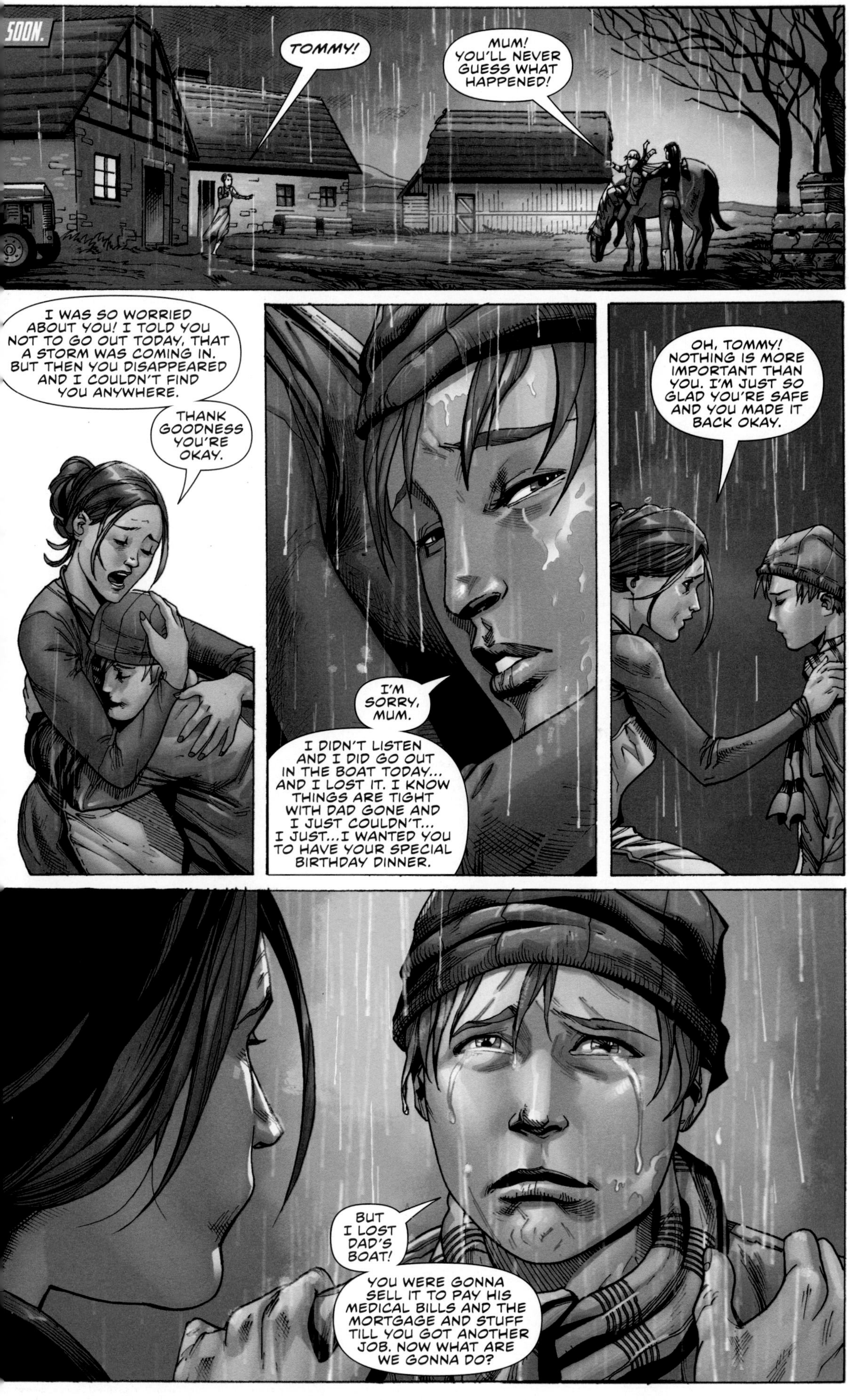
SOON.
TOMMY!
MUM! YOU'LL NEVER GUESS WHAT HAPPENED!
I WAS SO WORRIED ABOUT YOU! I TOLD YOU NOT TO GO OUT TODAY, THAT A STORM WAS COMING IN. BUT THEN YOU DISAPPEARED AND I COULDN'T FIND YOU ANYWHERE.
THANK GOODNESS YOU'RE OKAY.
I'M SORRY, MUM.
I DIDN'T LISTEN AND I DID GO OUT IN THE BOAT TODAY... AND I LOST IT. I KNOW THINGS ARE TIGHT WITH DAD GONE AND I JUST COULDN'T... I JUST...I WANTED YOU TO HAVE YOUR SPECIAL BIRTHDAY DINNER.
OH, TOMMY! NOTHING IS MORE IMPORTANT THAN YOU. I'M JUST SO GLAD YOU'RE SAFE AND YOU MADE IT BACK OKAY.
BUT I LOST DAD'S BOAT!
YOU WERE GONNA SELL IT TO PAY HIS MEDICAL BILLS AND THE MORTGAGE AND STUFF TILL YOU GOT ANOTHER JOB. NOW WHAT ARE WE GONNA DO?

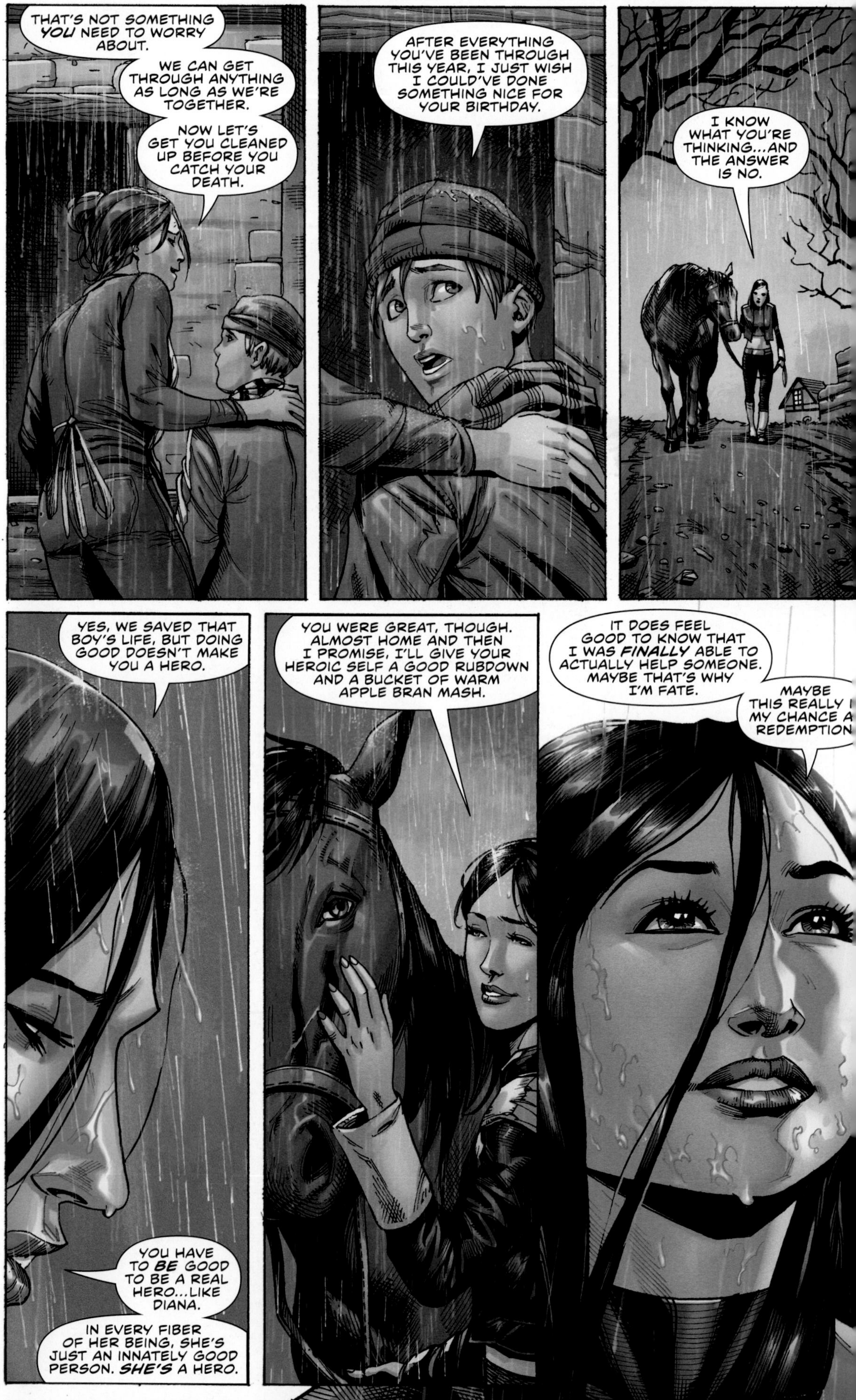
THAT'S NOT SOMETHING *YOU* NEED TO WORRY ABOUT.
WE CAN GET THROUGH ANYTHING AS LONG AS WE'RE TOGETHER.
NOW LET'S GET YOU CLEANED UP BEFORE YOU CATCH YOUR DEATH.
AFTER EVERYTHING YOU'VE BEEN THROUGH THIS YEAR, I JUST WISH I COULD'VE DONE SOMETHING NICE FOR YOUR BIRTHDAY.
I KNOW WHAT YOU'RE THINKING...AND THE ANSWER IS NO.
YES, WE SAVED THAT BOY'S LIFE, BUT DOING GOOD DOESN'T MAKE YOU A HERO.
YOU HAVE TO *BE* GOOD TO BE A REAL HERO...LIKE DIANA.
IN EVERY FIBER OF HER BEING, SHE'S JUST AN INNATELY GOOD PERSON. *SHE'S* A HERO.
YOU WERE GREAT, THOUGH. ALMOST HOME AND THEN I PROMISE, I'LL GIVE YOUR HEROIC SELF A GOOD RUBDOWN AND A BUCKET OF WARM APPLE BRAN MASH.
IT DOES FEEL GOOD TO KNOW THAT I WAS *FINALLY* ABLE TO ACTUALLY HELP SOMEONE. MAYBE THAT'S WHY I'M FATE.

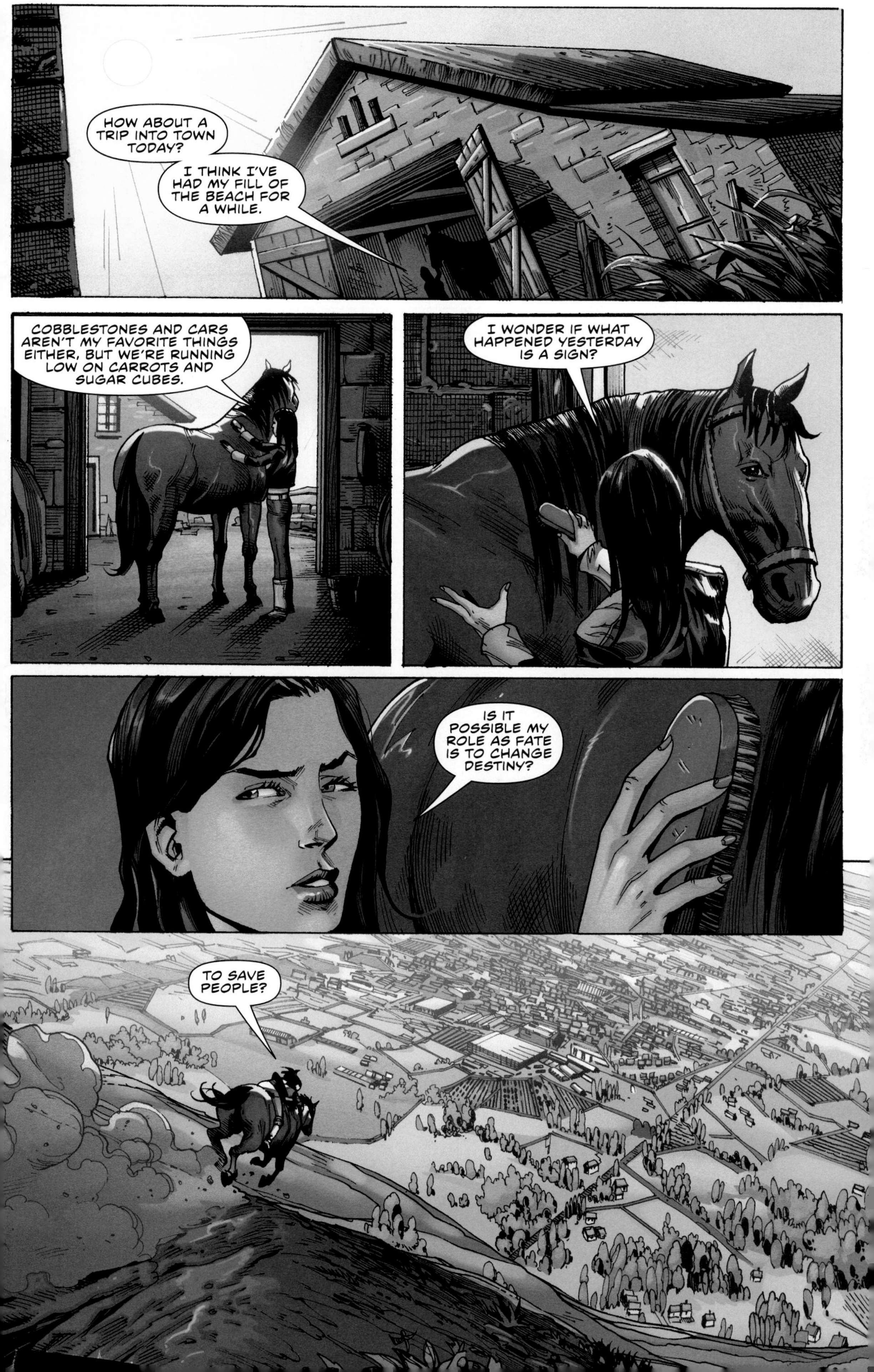
HOW ABOUT A TRIP INTO TOWN TODAY?
I THINK I'VE HAD MY FILL OF THE BEACH FOR A WHILE.
COBBLESTONES AND CARS AREN'T MY FAVORITE THINGS EITHER, BUT WE'RE RUNNING LOW ON CARROTS AND SUGAR CUBES.
I WONDER IF WHAT HAPPENED YESTERDAY IS A SIGN?
IS IT POSSIBLE MY ROLE AS FATE IS TO CHANGE DESTINY?
TO SAVE PEOPLE?

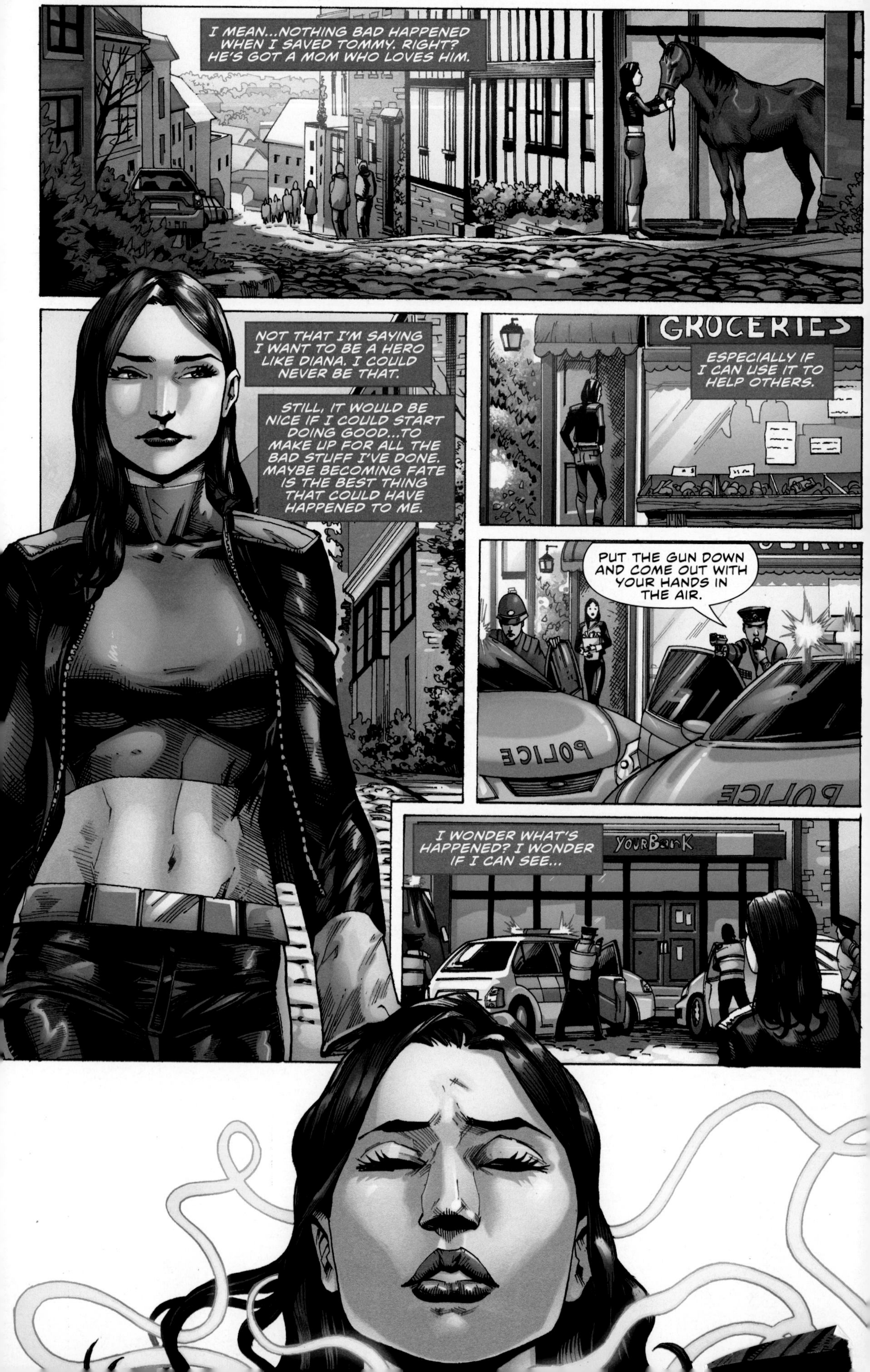
I MEAN...NOTHING BAD HAPPENED WHEN I SAVED TOMMY. RIGHT? HE'S GOT A MOM WHO LOVES HIM.
NOT THAT I'M SAYING I WANT TO BE A HERO LIKE DIANA. I COULD NEVER BE THAT.
STILL, IT WOULD BE NICE IF I COULD START DOING GOOD...TO MAKE UP FOR ALL THE BAD STUFF I'VE DONE. MAYBE BECOMING FATE IS THE BEST THING THAT COULD HAVE HAPPENED TO ME.
GROCERIES
ESPECIALLY IF I CAN USE IT TO HELP OTHERS.
PUT THE GUN DOWN AND COME OUT WITH YOUR HANDS IN THE AIR.
POLICE
POLICE
I WONDER WHAT'S HAPPENED? I WONDER IF I CAN SEE...
YOURBank

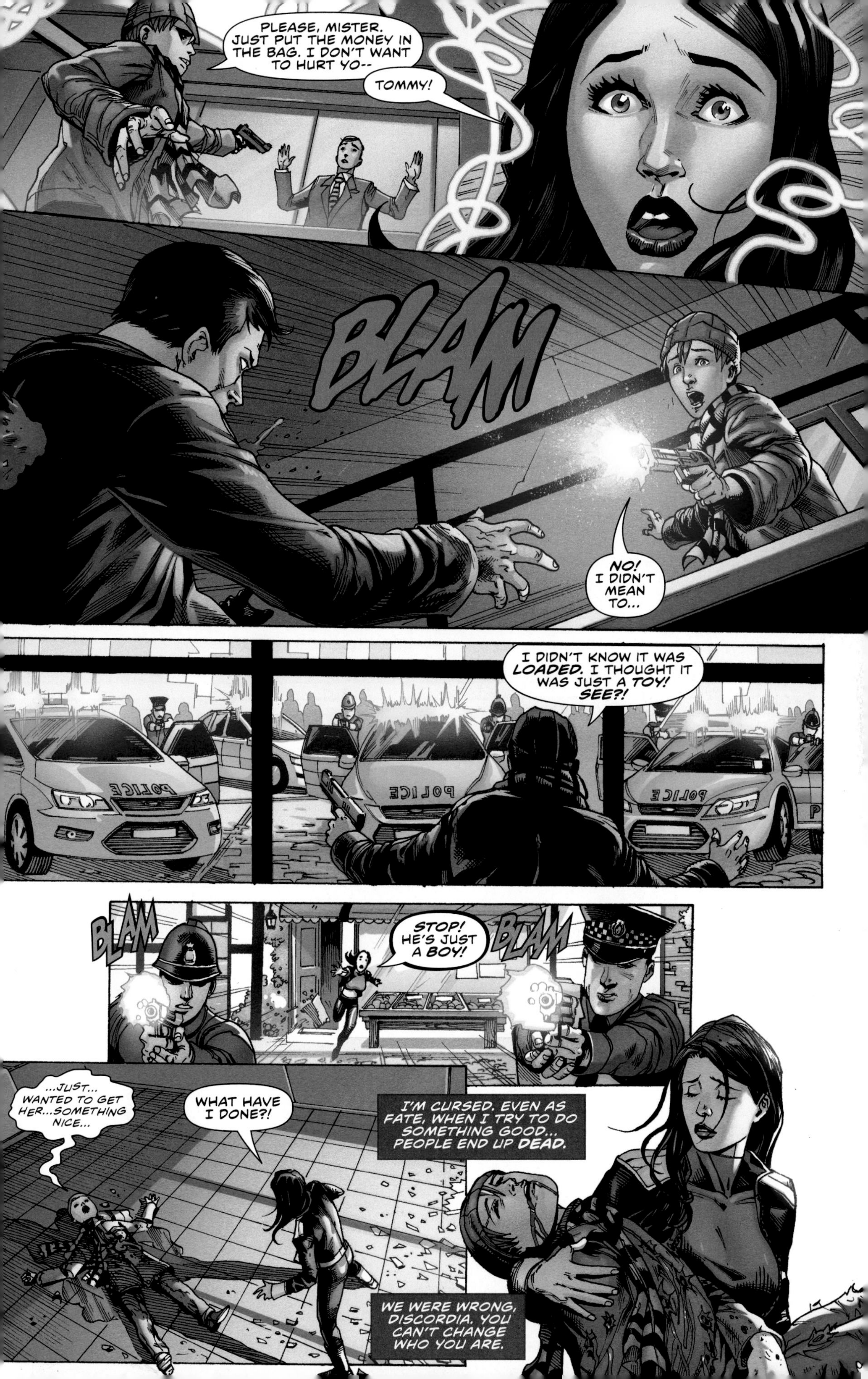
PLEASE, MISTER. JUST PUT THE MONEY IN THE BAG. I DON'T WANT TO HURT YO--
TOMMY!
BLAM
NO! I DIDN'T MEAN TO...
I DIDN'T KNOW IT WAS LOADED. I THOUGHT IT WAS JUST A TOY! SEE?!
POLICE
POLICE
POLICE
BLAM
STOP! HE'S JUST A BOY!
BLAM
...JUST... WANTED TO GET HER...SOMETHING NICE...
WHAT HAVE I DONE?!
I'M CURSED. EVEN AS FATE, WHEN I TRY TO DO SOMETHING GOOD... PEOPLE END UP DEAD.
WE WERE WRONG, DISCORDIA. YOU CAN'T CHANGE WHO YOU ARE.

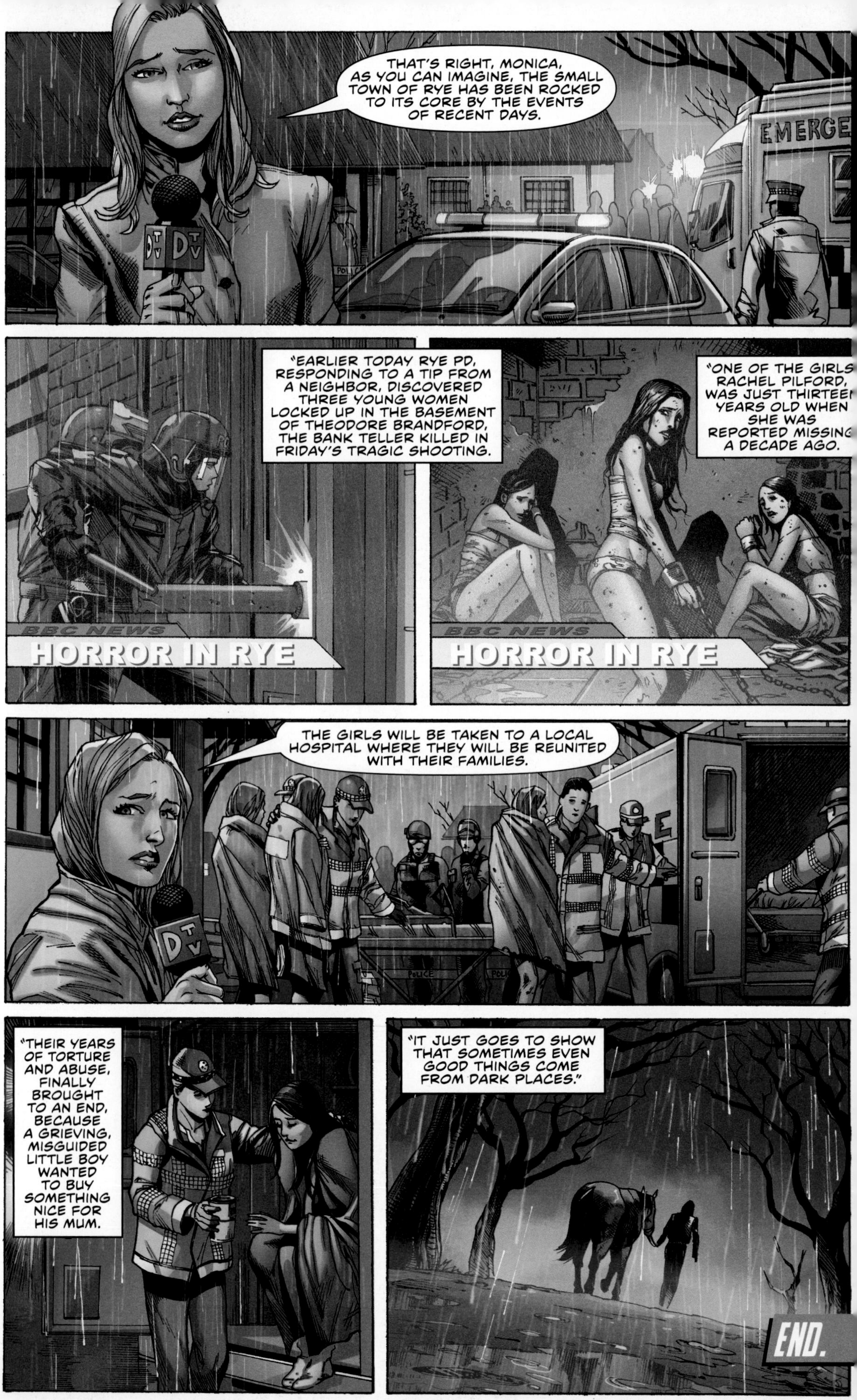
THAT'S RIGHT, MONICA, AS YOU CAN IMAGINE, THE SMALL TOWN OF RYE HAS BEEN ROCKED TO ITS CORE BY THE EVENTS OF RECENT DAYS.
EMERGE
"EARLIER TODAY RYE PD, RESPONDING TO A TIP FROM A NEIGHBOR, DISCOVERED THREE YOUNG WOMEN LOCKED UP IN THE BASEMENT OF THEODORE BRANDFORD, THE BANK TELLER KILLED IN FRIDAY'S TRAGIC SHOOTING.
BBC NEWS
HORROR IN RYE
"ONE OF THE GIRLS, RACHEL PILFORD, WAS JUST THIRTEEN YEARS OLD WHEN SHE WAS REPORTED MISSING A DECADE AGO.
BBC NEWS
HORROR IN RYE
THE GIRLS WILL BE TAKEN TO A LOCAL HOSPITAL WHERE THEY WILL BE REUNITED WITH THEIR FAMILIES.
"THEIR YEARS OF TORTURE AND ABUSE, FINALLY BROUGHT TO AN END, BECAUSE A GRIEVING, MISGUIDED LITTLE BOY WANTED TO BUY SOMETHING NICE FOR HIS MUM.
"IT JUST GOES TO SHOW THAT SOMETIMES EVEN GOOD THINGS COME FROM DARK PLACES."
END.

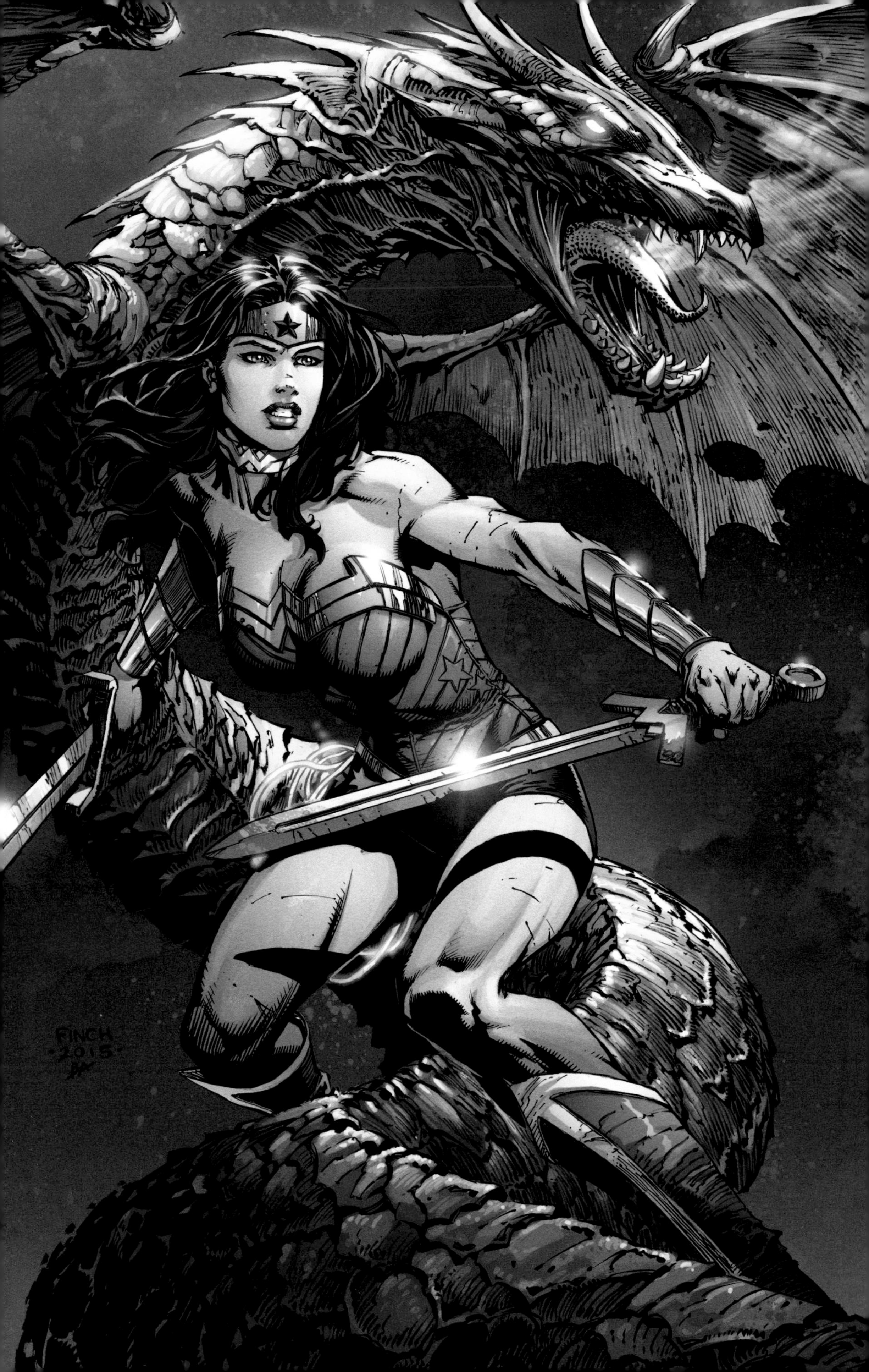
FINCH
2015

FAMILY TIES

MEREDITH FINCH writer **MIGUEL MENDONÇA** penciller **DEXTER VINES DIANA EGEA** inkers **STEPHEN DOWNER ULISES ARREOLA** colorists **ROB LEIGH** letterer
cover art by **DAVID FINCH & BRAD ANDERSON**

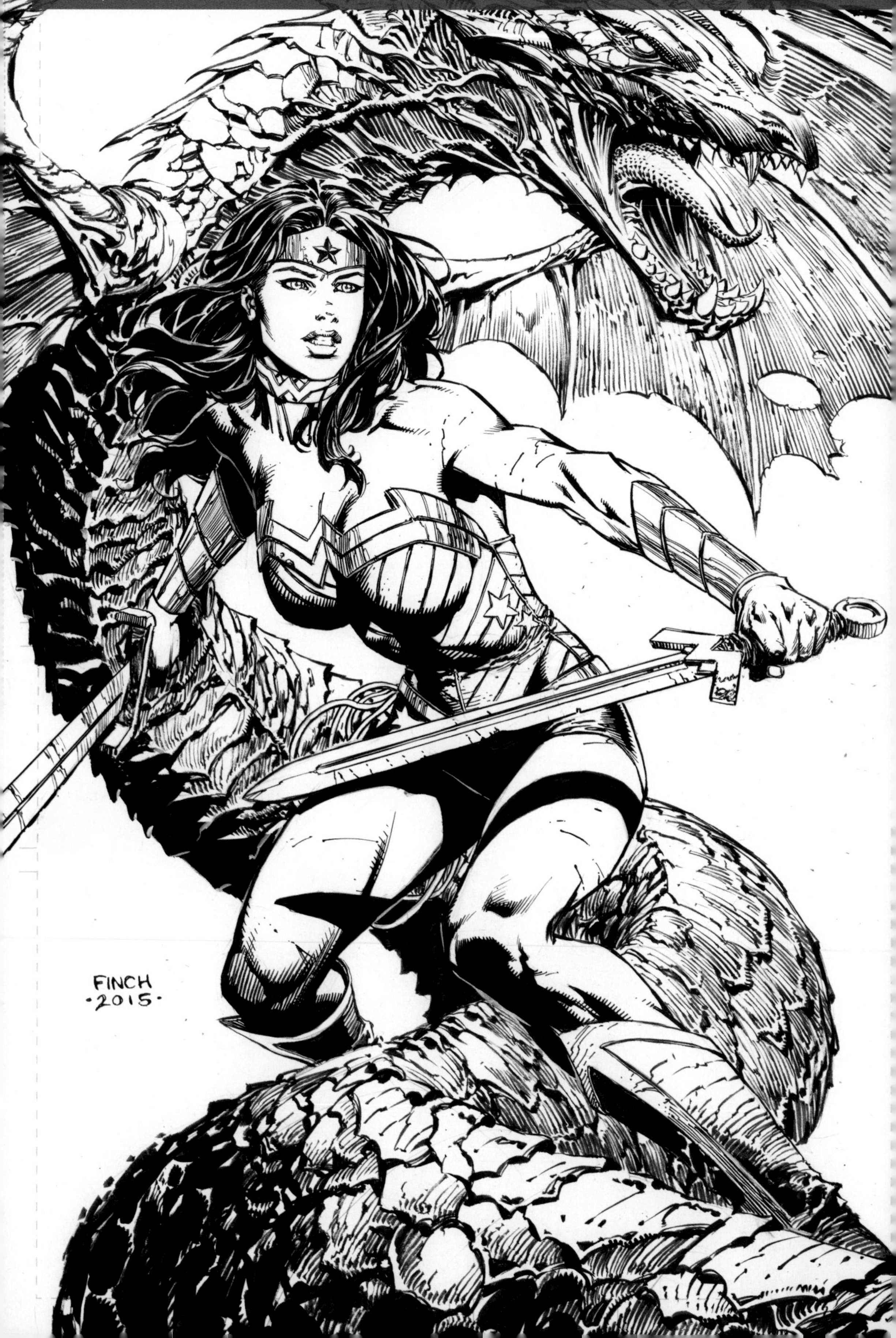
FINCH
·2015·

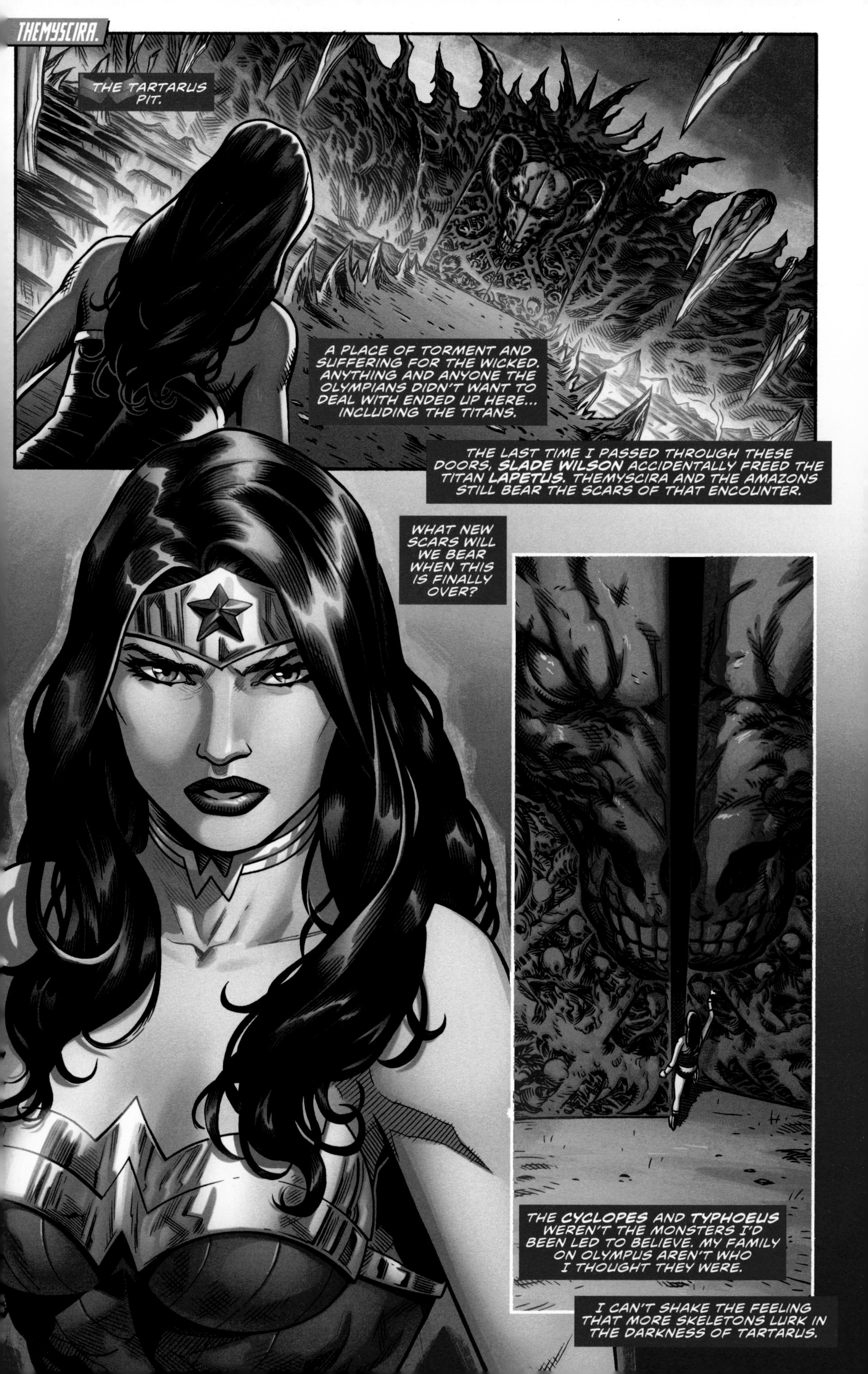
THEMYSCIRA.
THE TARTARUS PIT.
A PLACE OF TORMENT AND SUFFERING FOR THE WICKED. ANYTHING AND ANYONE THE OLYMPIANS DIDN'T WANT TO DEAL WITH ENDED UP HERE... INCLUDING THE TITANS.
THE LAST TIME I PASSED THROUGH THESE DOORS, SLADE WILSON ACCIDENTALLY FREED THE TITAN LAPETUS. THEMYSCIRA AND THE AMAZONS STILL BEAR THE SCARS OF THAT ENCOUNTER.
WHAT NEW SCARS WILL WE BEAR WHEN THIS IS FINALLY OVER?
THE CYCLOPES AND TYPHOEUS WEREN'T THE MONSTERS I'D BEEN LED TO BELIEVE. MY FAMILY ON OLYMPUS AREN'T WHO I THOUGHT THEY WERE.
I CAN'T SHAKE THE FEELING THAT MORE SKELETONS LURK IN THE DARKNESS OF TARTARUS.

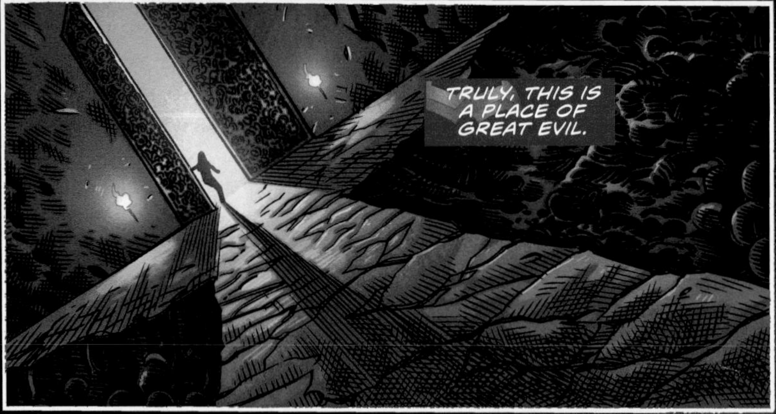
TRULY, THIS IS A PLACE OF GREAT EVIL.
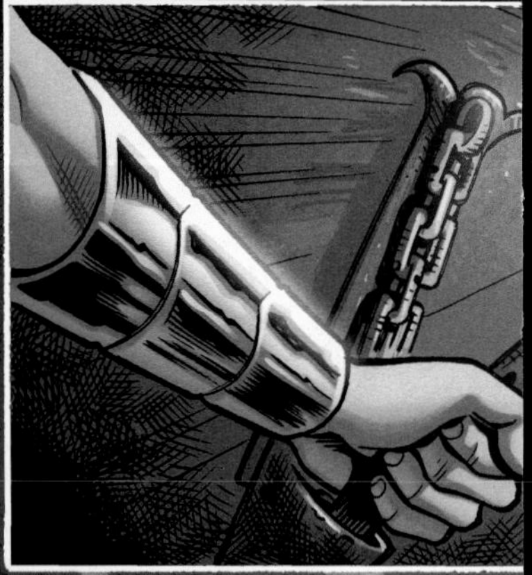
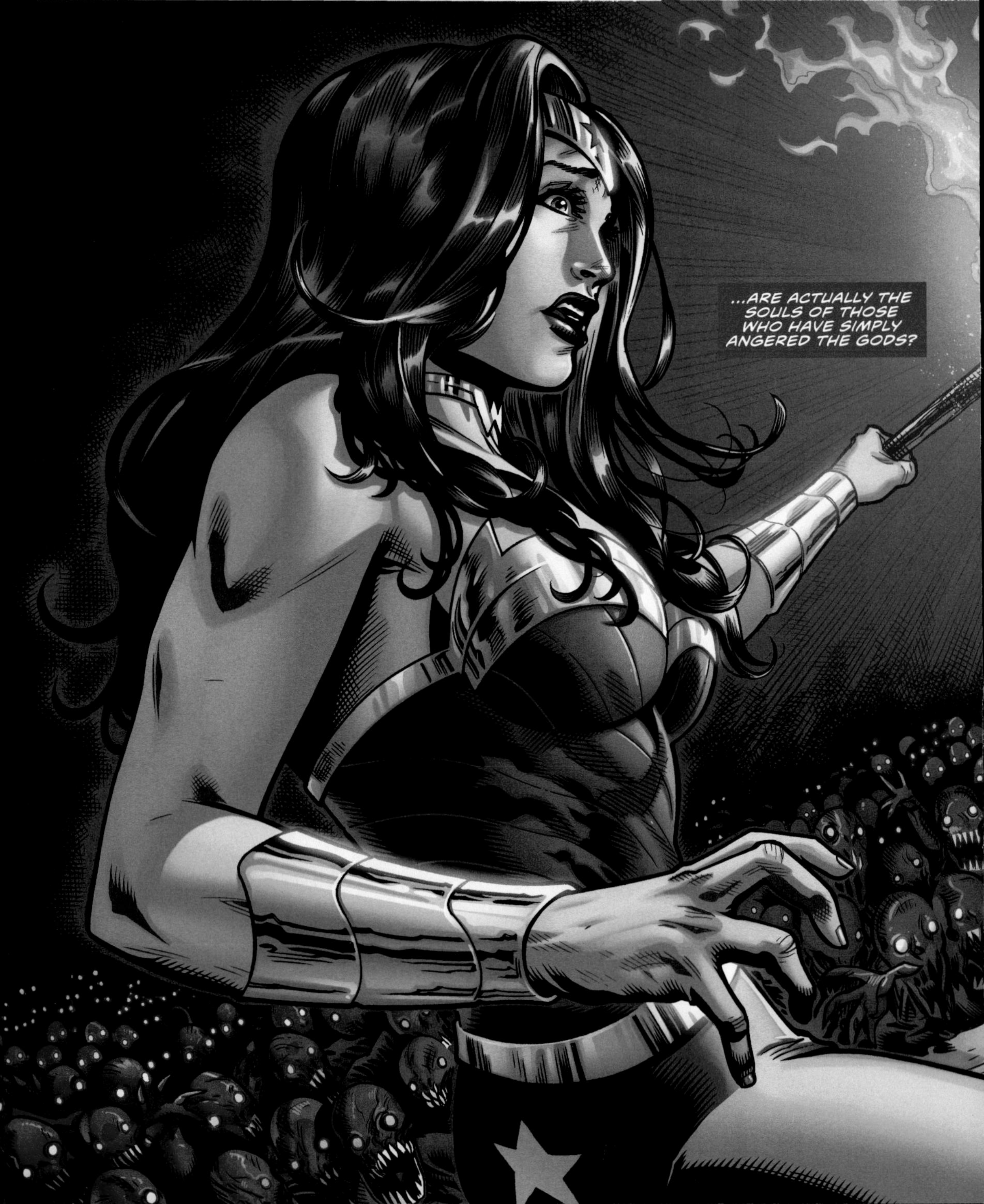
...ARE ACTUALLY THE SOULS OF THOSE WHO HAVE SIMPLY ANGERED THE GODS?

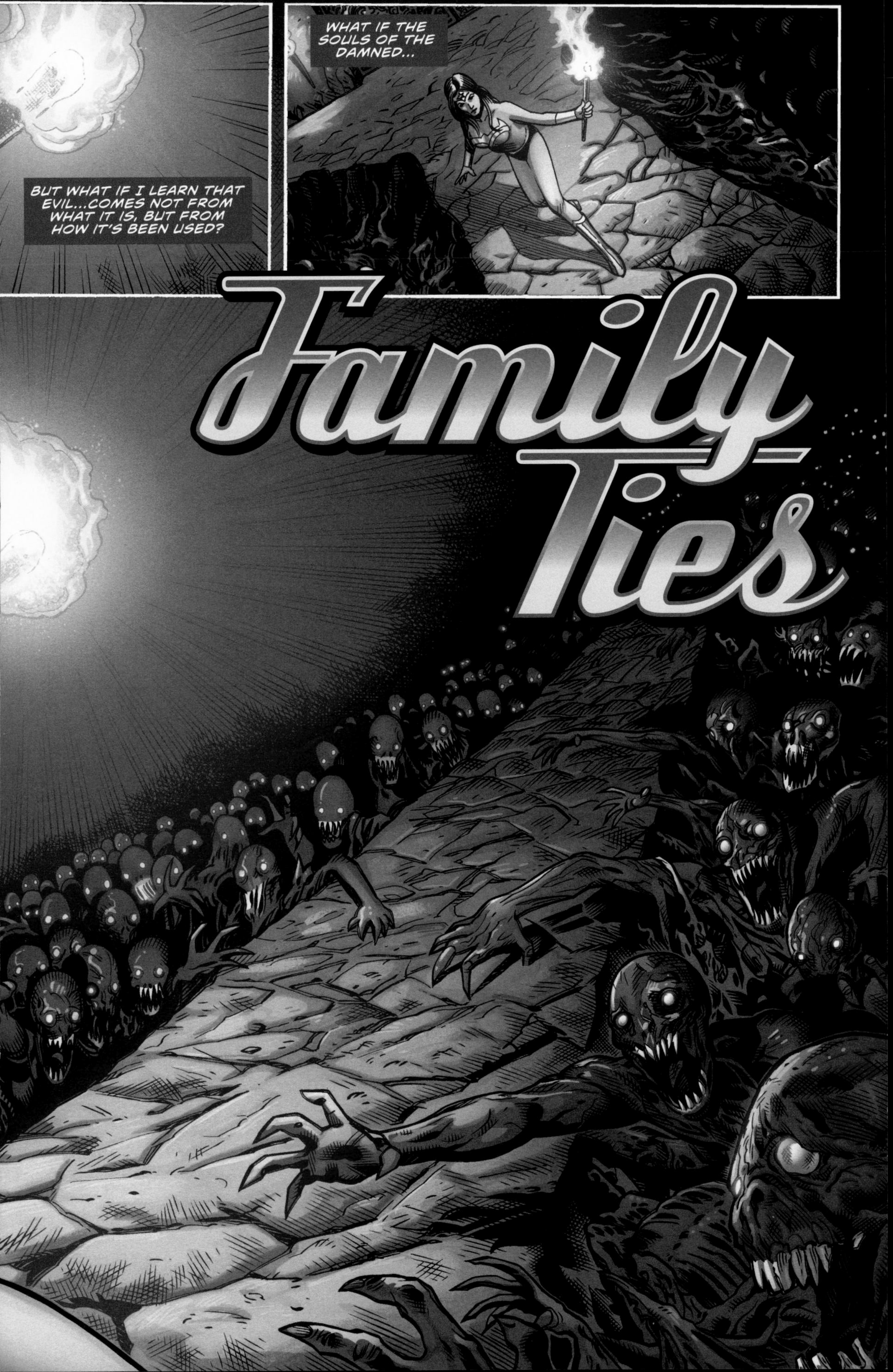
BUT WHAT IF I LEARN THAT EVIL...COMES NOT FROM WHAT IT IS, BUT FROM HOW IT'S BEEN USED?
WHAT IF THE SOULS OF THE DAMNED...
Family Ties

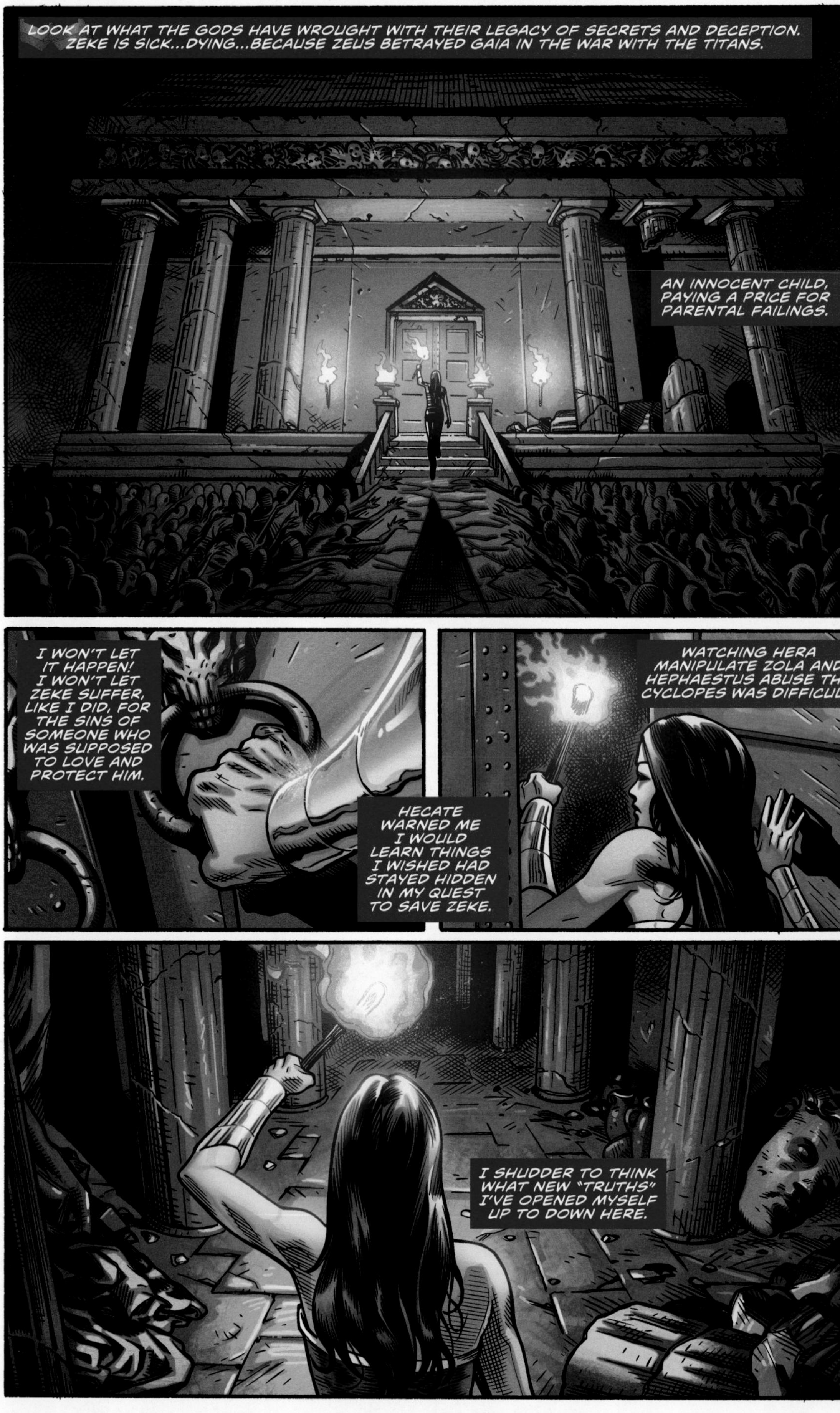
LOOK AT WHAT THE GODS HAVE WROUGHT WITH THEIR LEGACY OF SECRETS AND DECEPTION. ZEKE IS SICK...DYING...BECAUSE ZEUS BETRAYED GAIA IN THE WAR WITH THE TITANS.
AN INNOCENT CHILD, PAYING A PRICE FOR PARENTAL FAILINGS.
I WON'T LET IT HAPPEN! I WON'T LET ZEKE SUFFER, LIKE I DID, FOR THE SINS OF SOMEONE WHO WAS SUPPOSED TO LOVE AND PROTECT HIM.
HECATE WARNED ME I WOULD LEARN THINGS I WISHED HAD STAYED HIDDEN IN MY QUEST TO SAVE ZEKE.
WATCHING HERA MANIPULATE ZOLA AND HEPHAESTUS ABUSE THE CYCLOPES WAS DIFFICULT.
I SHUDDER TO THINK WHAT NEW "TRUTHS" I'VE OPENED MYSELF UP TO DOWN HERE.

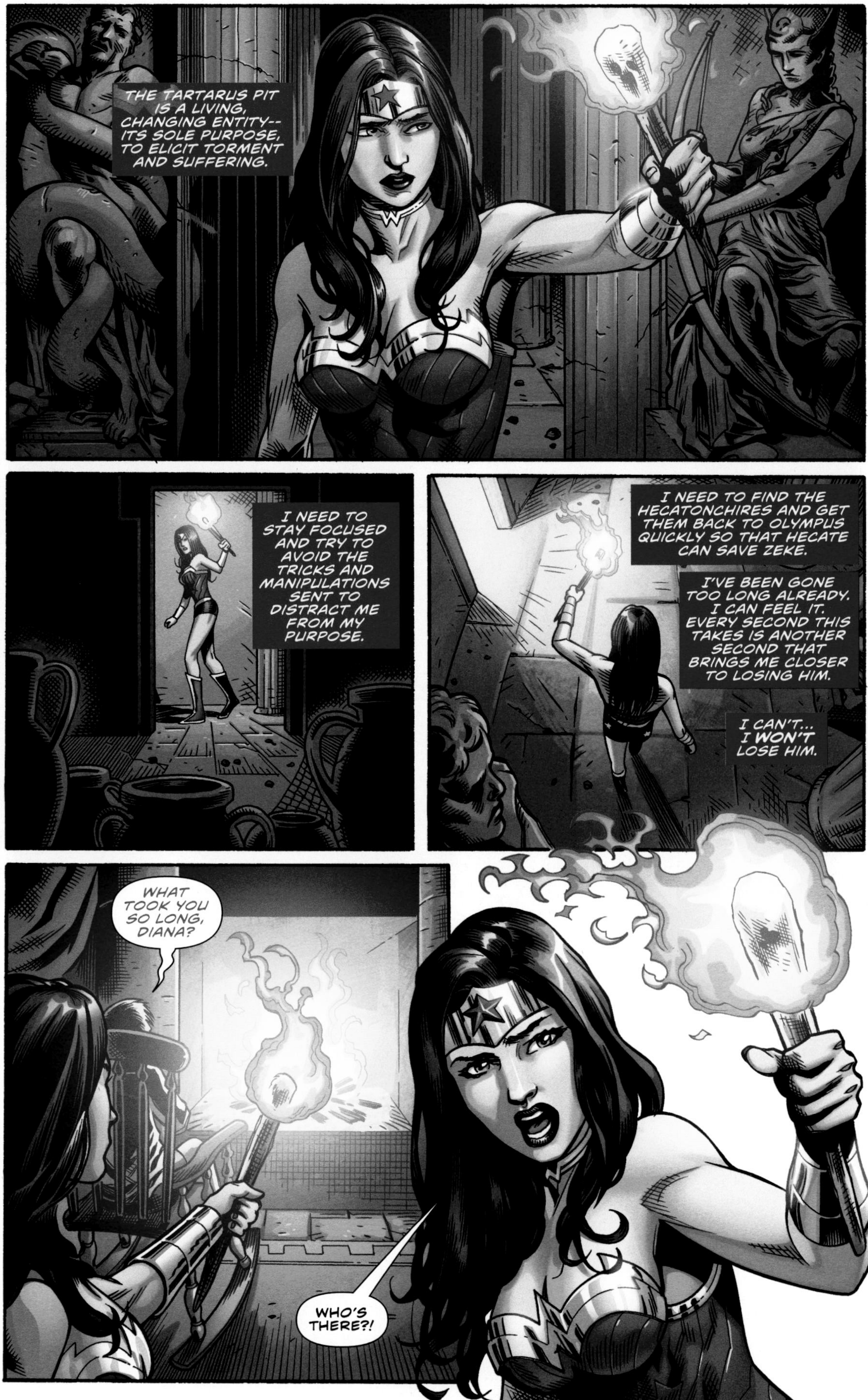
THE TARTARUS PIT IS A LIVING, CHANGING ENTITY-- ITS SOLE PURPOSE, TO ELICIT TORMENT AND SUFFERING.
I NEED TO STAY FOCUSED AND TRY TO AVOID THE TRICKS AND MANIPULATIONS SENT TO DISTRACT ME FROM MY PURPOSE.
I NEED TO FIND THE HECATONCHIRES AND GET THEM BACK TO OLYMPUS QUICKLY SO THAT HECATE CAN SAVE ZEKE.
I'VE BEEN GONE TOO LONG ALREADY. I CAN FEEL IT. EVERY SECOND THIS TAKES IS ANOTHER SECOND THAT BRINGS ME CLOSER TO LOSING HIM.
I CAN'T... I **WON'T** LOSE HIM.
WHAT TOOK YOU SO LONG, DIANA?
WHO'S THERE?!

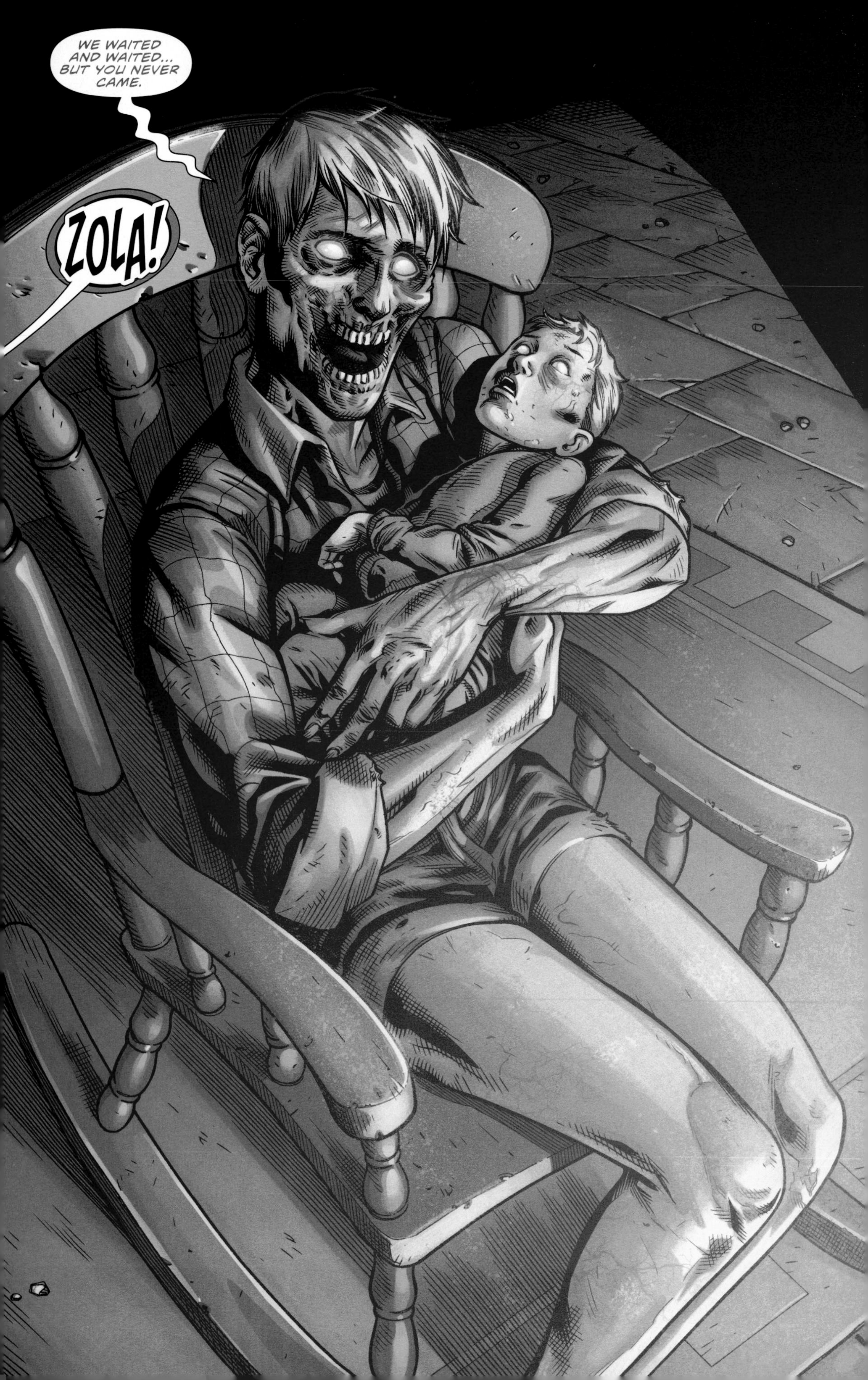
WE WAITED AND WAITED... BUT YOU NEVER CAME.
ZOLA!

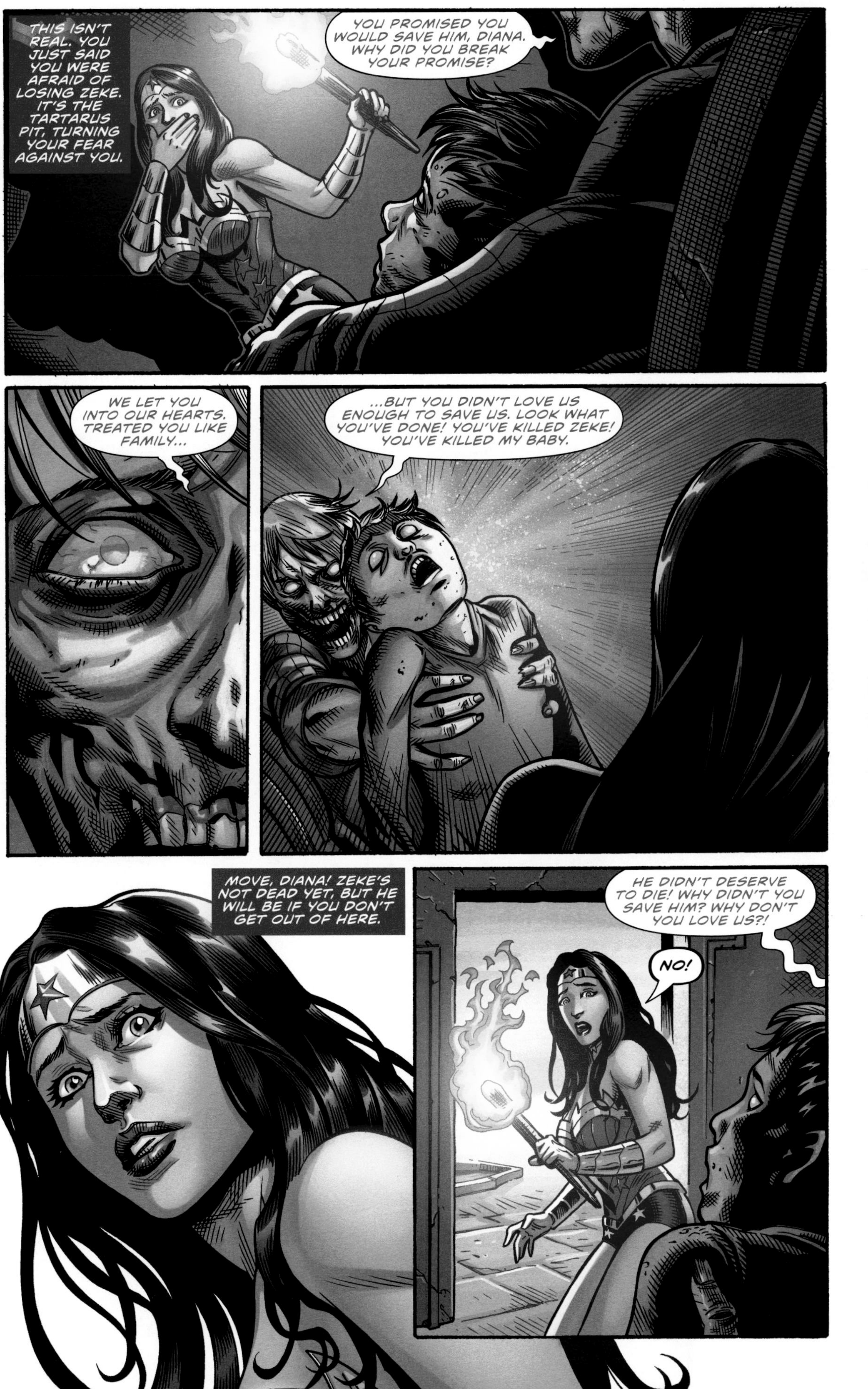
THIS ISN'T REAL. YOU JUST SAID YOU WERE AFRAID OF LOSING ZEKE. IT'S THE TARTARUS PIT, TURNING YOUR FEAR AGAINST YOU.
YOU PROMISED YOU WOULD SAVE HIM, DIANA. WHY DID YOU BREAK YOUR PROMISE?
WE LET YOU INTO OUR HEARTS. TREATED YOU LIKE FAMILY...
...BUT YOU DIDN'T LOVE US ENOUGH TO SAVE US. LOOK WHAT YOU'VE DONE! YOU'VE KILLED ZEKE! YOU'VE KILLED MY BABY.
MOVE, DIANA! ZEKE'S NOT DEAD YET, BUT HE WILL BE IF YOU DON'T GET OUT OF HERE.
HE DIDN'T DESERVE TO DIE! WHY DIDN'T YOU SAVE HIM? WHY DON'T YOU LOVE US?!
NO!

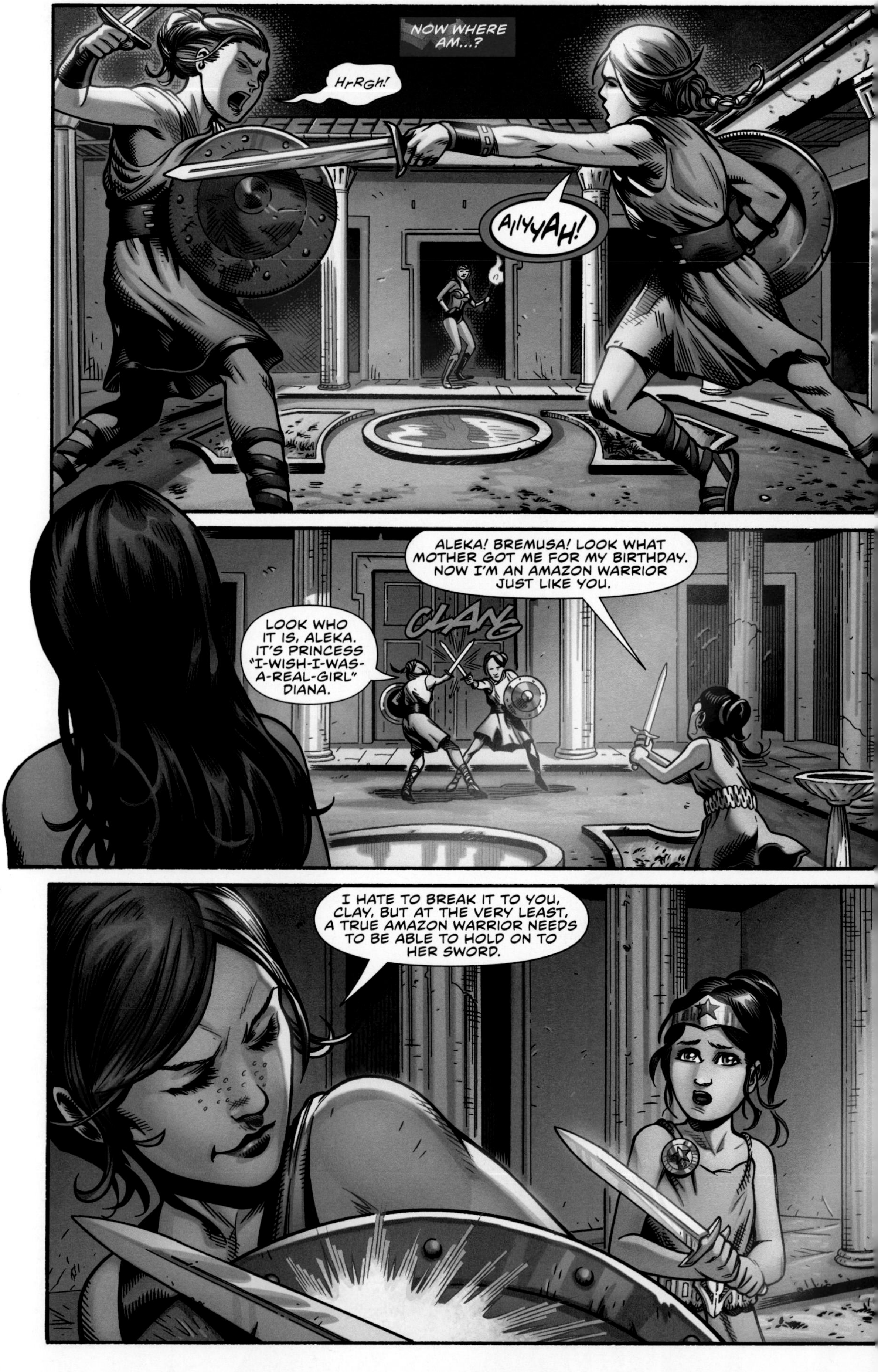
NOW WHERE AM...?
HrRgh!
AIIYYAH!
ALEKA! BREMUSA! LOOK WHAT MOTHER GOT ME FOR MY BIRTHDAY. NOW I'M AN AMAZON WARRIOR JUST LIKE YOU.
CLANG
LOOK WHO IT IS, ALEKA. IT'S PRINCESS "I-WISH-I-WAS-A-REAL-GIRL" DIANA.
I HATE TO BREAK IT TO YOU, CLAY, BUT AT THE VERY LEAST, A TRUE AMAZON WARRIOR NEEDS TO BE ABLE TO HOLD ON TO HER SWORD.

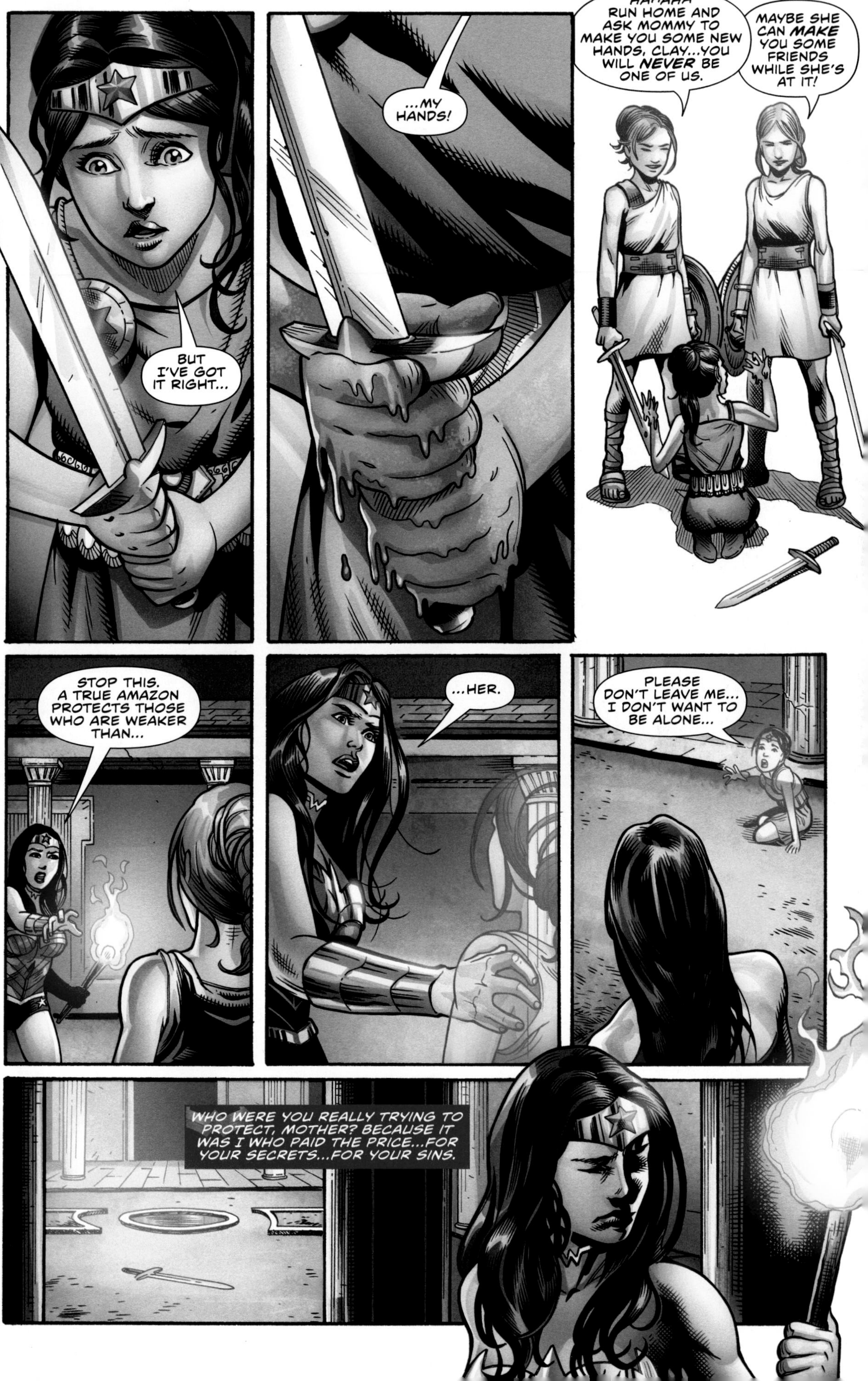
BUT I'VE GOT IT RIGHT...
...MY HANDS!
HAHAHA RUN HOME AND ASK MOMMY TO MAKE YOU SOME NEW HANDS, CLAY...YOU WILL NEVER BE ONE OF US.
MAYBE SHE CAN MAKE YOU SOME FRIENDS WHILE SHE'S AT IT!
STOP THIS. A TRUE AMAZON PROTECTS THOSE WHO ARE WEAKER THAN...
...HER.
PLEASE DON'T LEAVE ME... I DON'T WANT TO BE ALONE...
WHO WERE YOU REALLY TRYING TO PROTECT, MOTHER? BECAUSE IT WAS I WHO PAID THE PRICE...FOR YOUR SECRETS...FOR YOUR SINS.

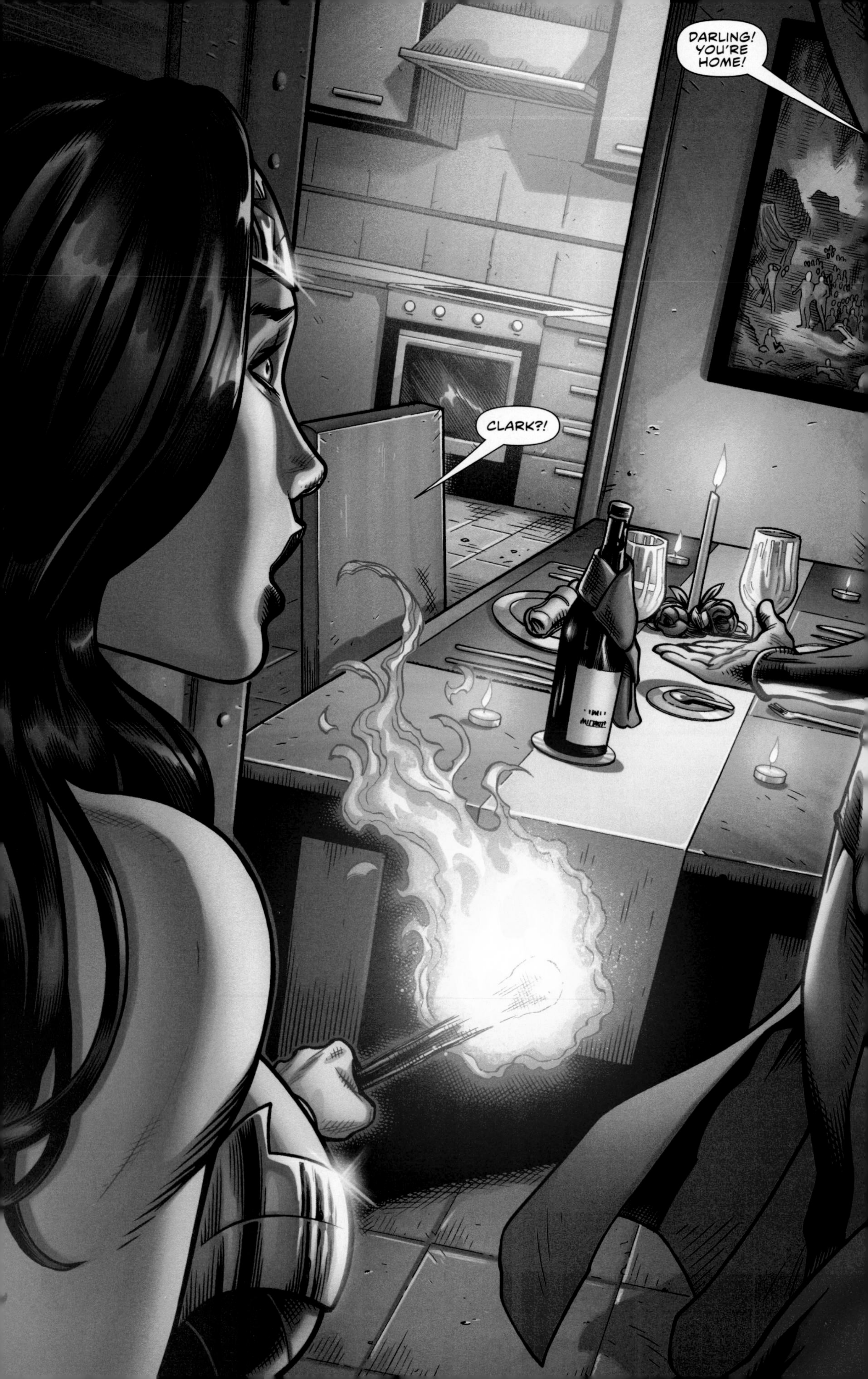
DARLING! YOU'RE HOME!
CLARK?!

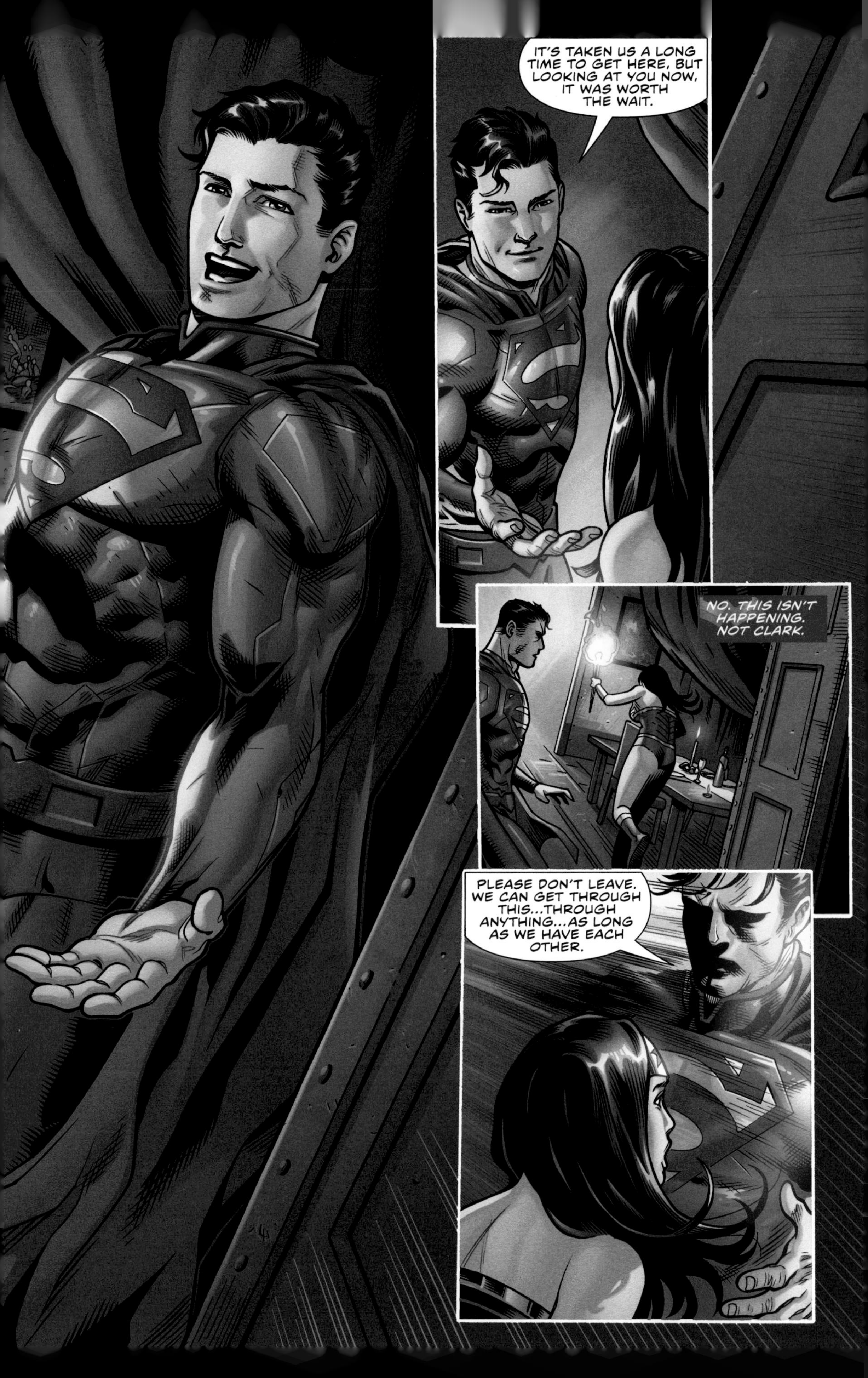
IT'S TAKEN US A LONG TIME TO GET HERE, BUT LOOKING AT YOU NOW, IT WAS WORTH THE WAIT.
NO. THIS ISN'T HAPPENING. NOT CLARK.
PLEASE DON'T LEAVE. WE CAN GET THROUGH THIS...THROUGH ANYTHING...AS LONG AS WE HAVE EACH OTHER.

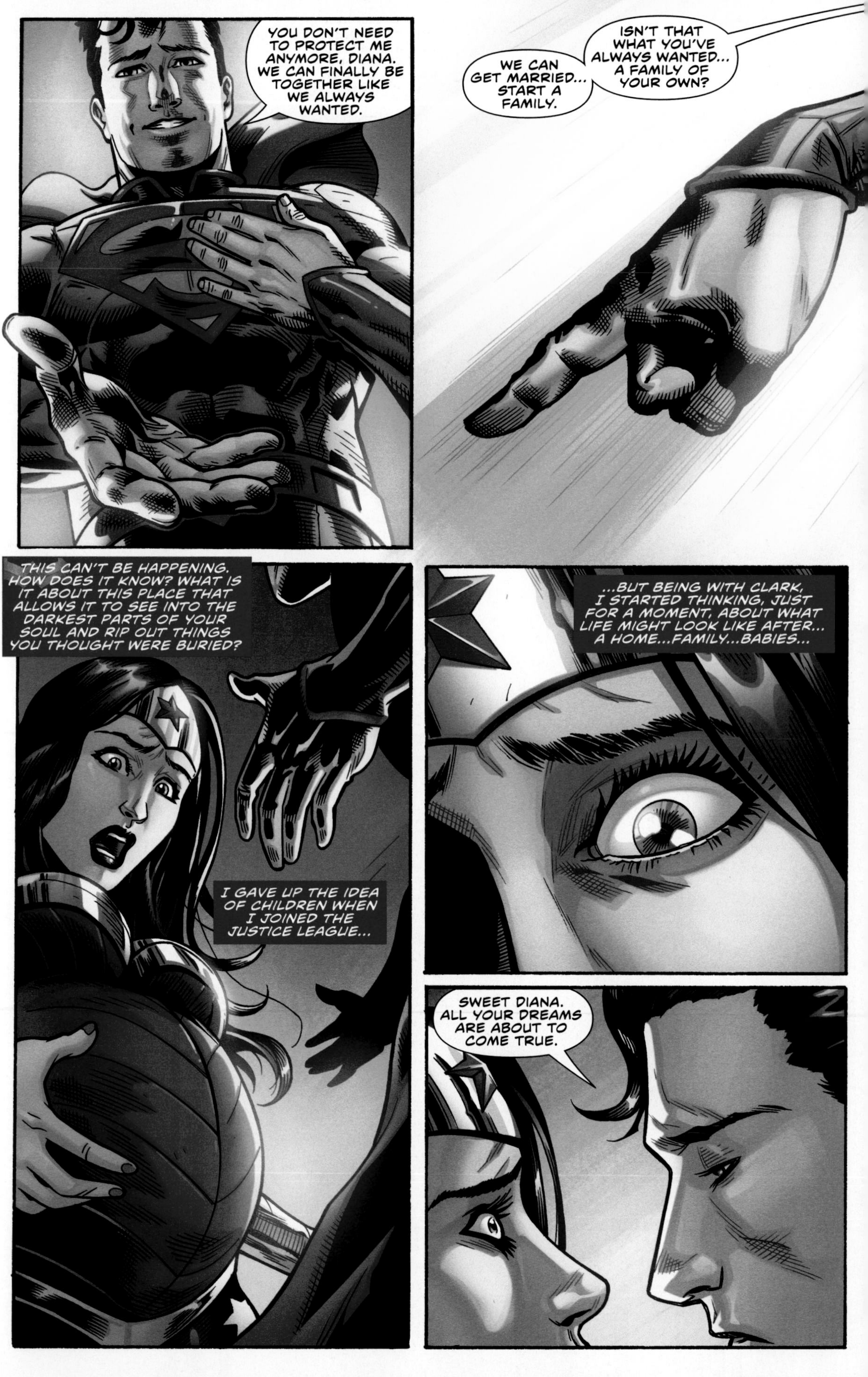
YOU DON'T NEED TO PROTECT ME ANYMORE, DIANA. WE CAN FINALLY BE TOGETHER LIKE WE ALWAYS WANTED.
WE CAN GET MARRIED... START A FAMILY.
ISN'T THAT WHAT YOU'VE ALWAYS WANTED... A FAMILY OF YOUR OWN?
THIS CAN'T BE HAPPENING. HOW DOES IT KNOW? WHAT IS IT ABOUT THIS PLACE THAT ALLOWS IT TO SEE INTO THE DARKEST PARTS OF YOUR SOUL AND RIP OUT THINGS YOU THOUGHT WERE BURIED?
I GAVE UP THE IDEA OF CHILDREN WHEN I JOINED THE JUSTICE LEAGUE...
...BUT BEING WITH CLARK, I STARTED THINKING, JUST FOR A MOMENT, ABOUT WHAT LIFE MIGHT LOOK LIKE AFTER... A HOME...FAMILY...BABIES...
SWEET DIANA. ALL YOUR DREAMS ARE ABOUT TO COME TRUE.

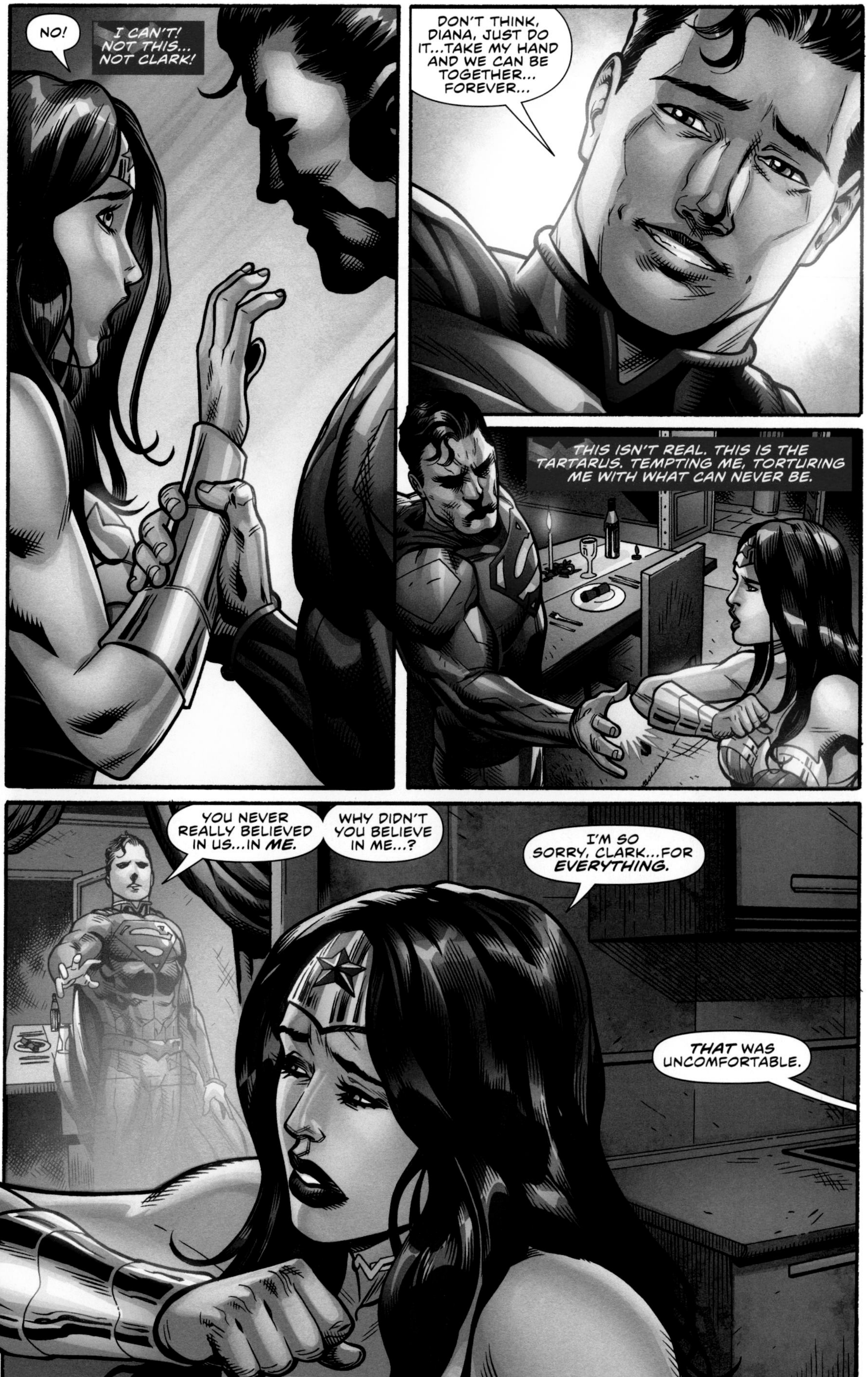
NO!
I CAN'T! NOT THIS... NOT CLARK!
DON'T THINK, DIANA, JUST DO IT...TAKE MY HAND AND WE CAN BE TOGETHER... FOREVER...
THIS ISN'T REAL. THIS IS THE TARTARUS. TEMPTING ME, TORTURING ME WITH WHAT CAN NEVER BE.
YOU NEVER REALLY BELIEVED IN US...IN ME.
WHY DIDN'T YOU BELIEVE IN ME...?
I'M SO SORRY, CLARK...FOR EVERYTHING.
THAT WAS UNCOMFORTABLE.

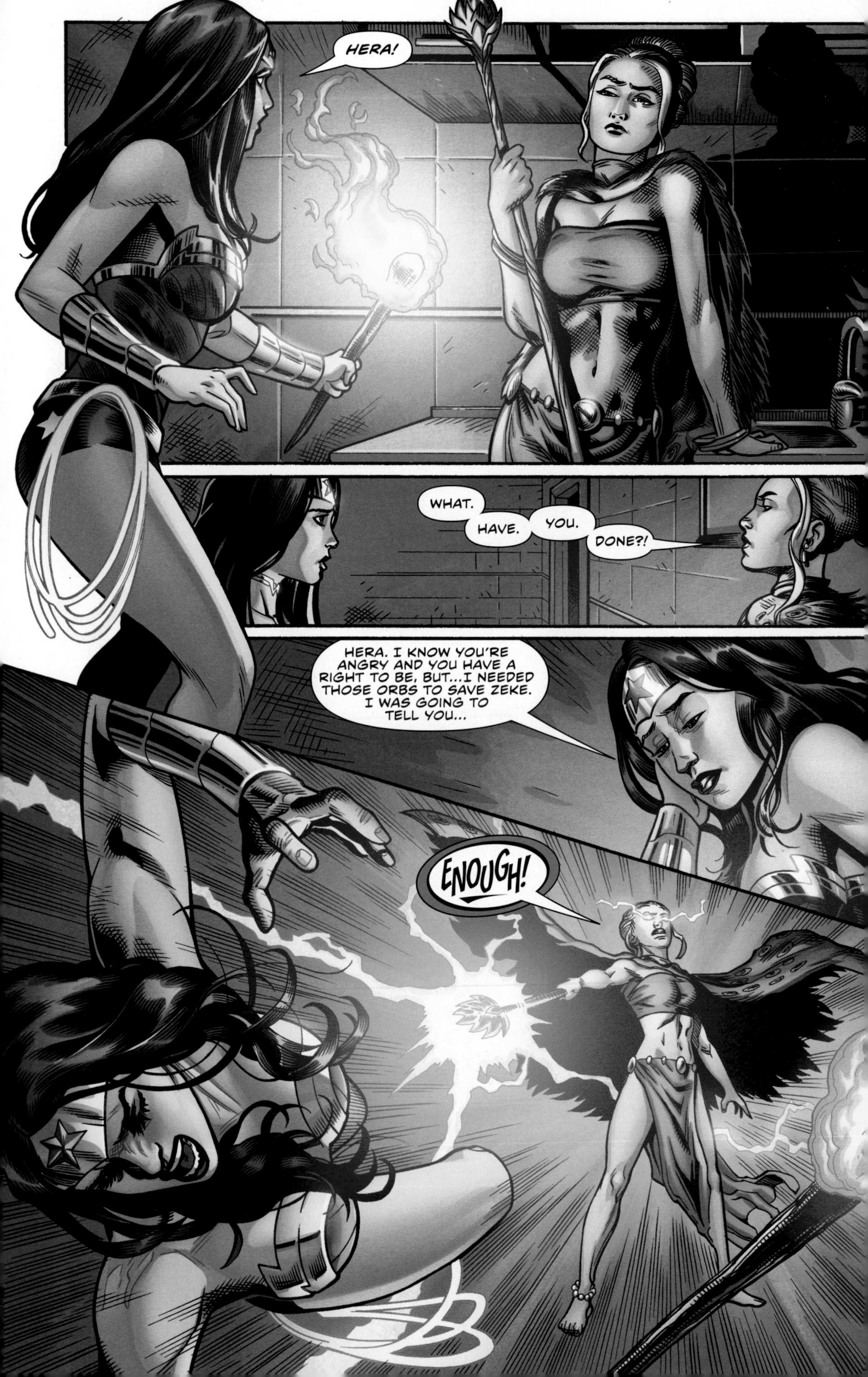
HERA!
WHAT.
HAVE.
YOU.
DONE?!
HERA. I KNOW YOU'RE ANGRY AND YOU HAVE A RIGHT TO BE, BUT...I NEEDED THOSE ORBS TO SAVE ZEKE. I WAS GOING TO TELL YOU...
ENOUGH!

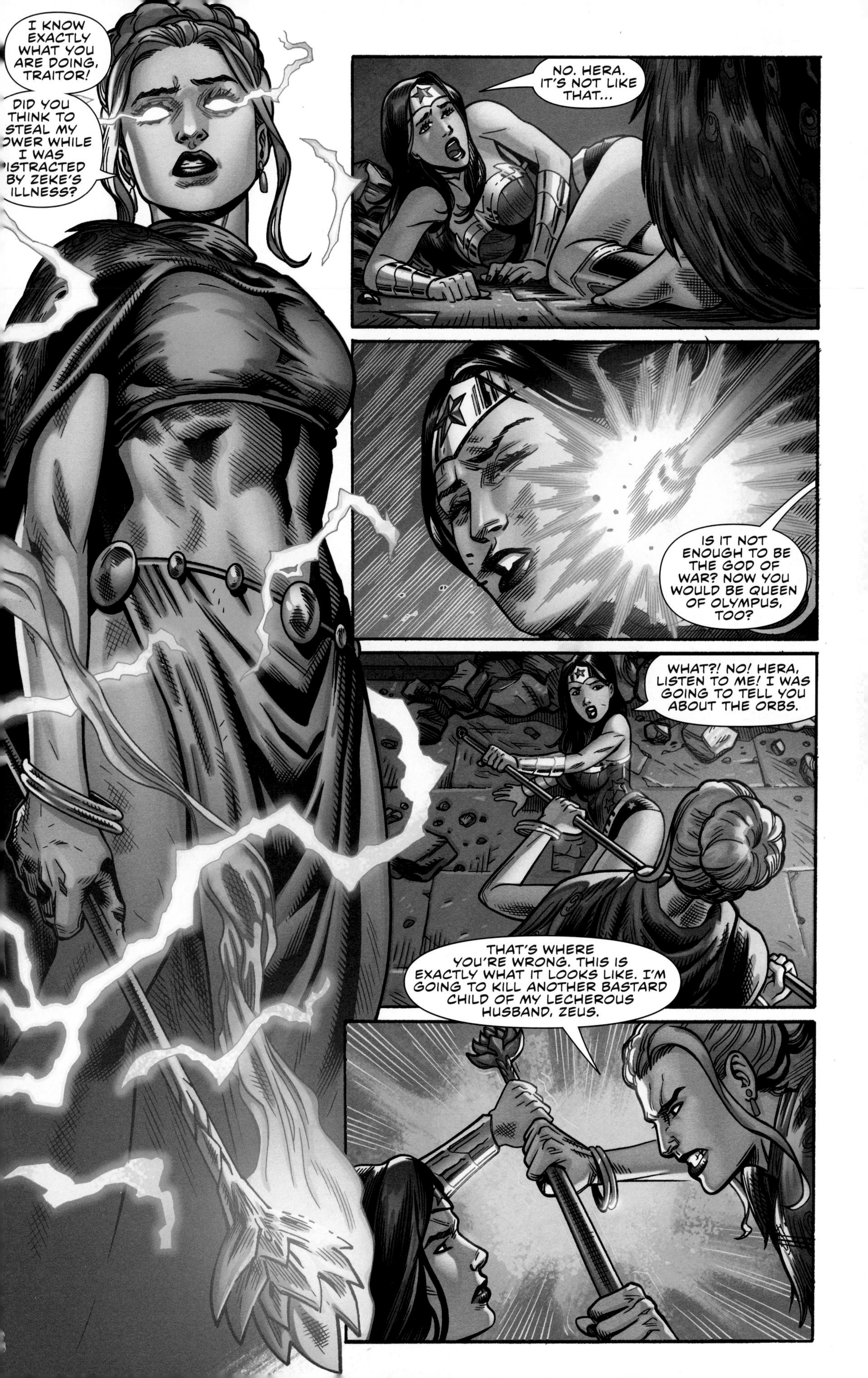
I KNOW EXACTLY WHAT YOU ARE DOING, TRAITOR!
DID YOU THINK TO STEAL MY POWER WHILE I WAS DISTRACTED BY ZEKE'S ILLNESS?
NO. HERA. IT'S NOT LIKE THAT...
IS IT NOT ENOUGH TO BE THE GOD OF WAR? NOW YOU WOULD BE QUEEN OF OLYMPUS, TOO?
WHAT?! NO! HERA, LISTEN TO ME! I WAS GOING TO TELL YOU ABOUT THE ORBS.
THAT'S WHERE YOU'RE WRONG. THIS IS EXACTLY WHAT IT LOOKS LIKE. I'M GOING TO KILL ANOTHER BASTARD CHILD OF MY LECHEROUS HUSBAND, ZEUS.

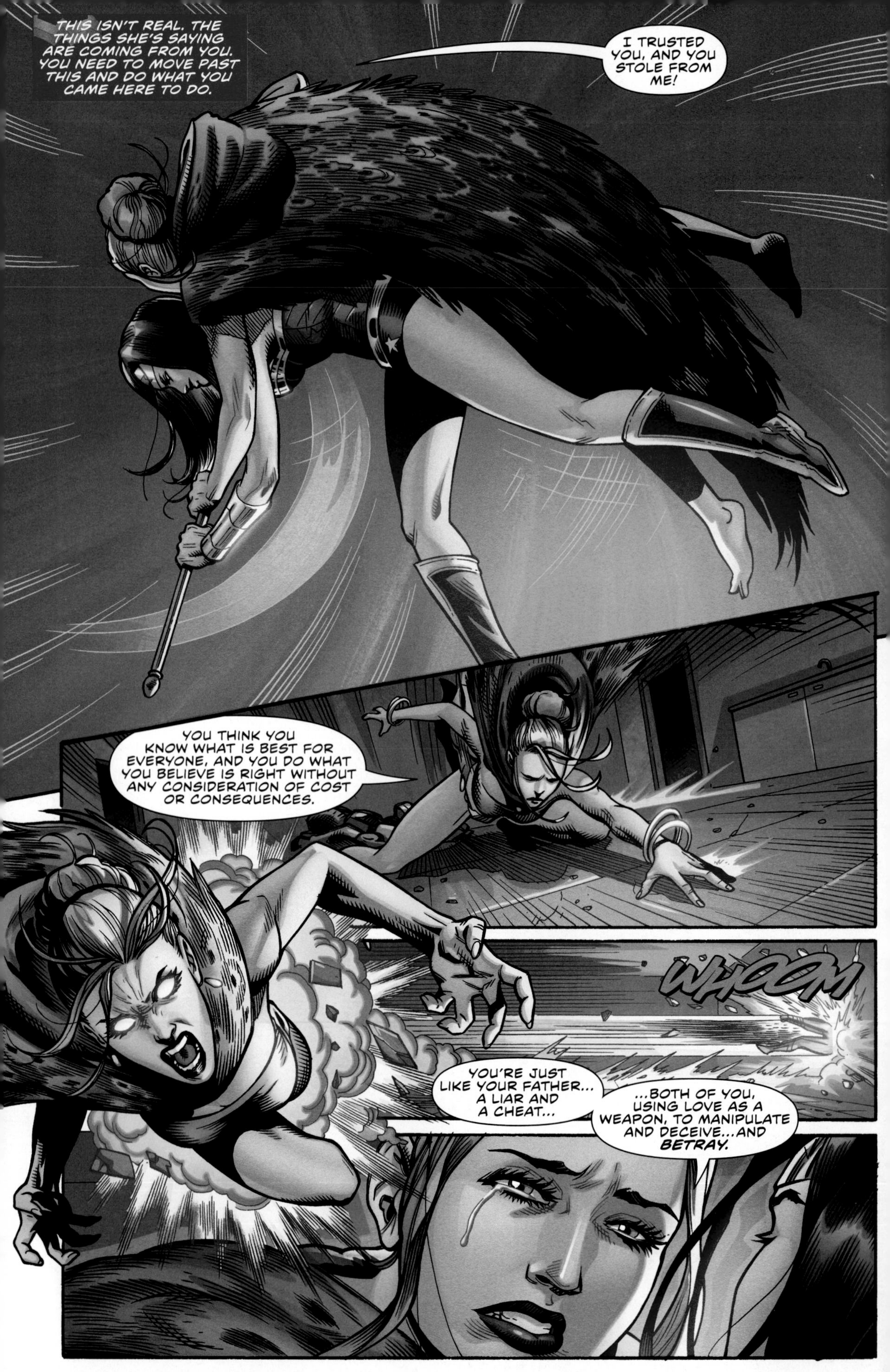
THIS ISN'T REAL. THE THINGS SHE'S SAYING ARE COMING FROM YOU. YOU NEED TO MOVE PAST THIS AND DO WHAT YOU CAME HERE TO DO.
I TRUSTED YOU, AND YOU STOLE FROM ME!
YOU THINK YOU KNOW WHAT IS BEST FOR EVERYONE, AND YOU DO WHAT YOU BELIEVE IS RIGHT WITHOUT ANY CONSIDERATION OF COST OR CONSEQUENCES.
WHOOOM
YOU'RE JUST LIKE YOUR FATHER... A LIAR AND A CHEAT...
...BOTH OF YOU, USING LOVE AS A WEAPON, TO MANIPULATE AND DECEIVE...AND *BETRAY.*

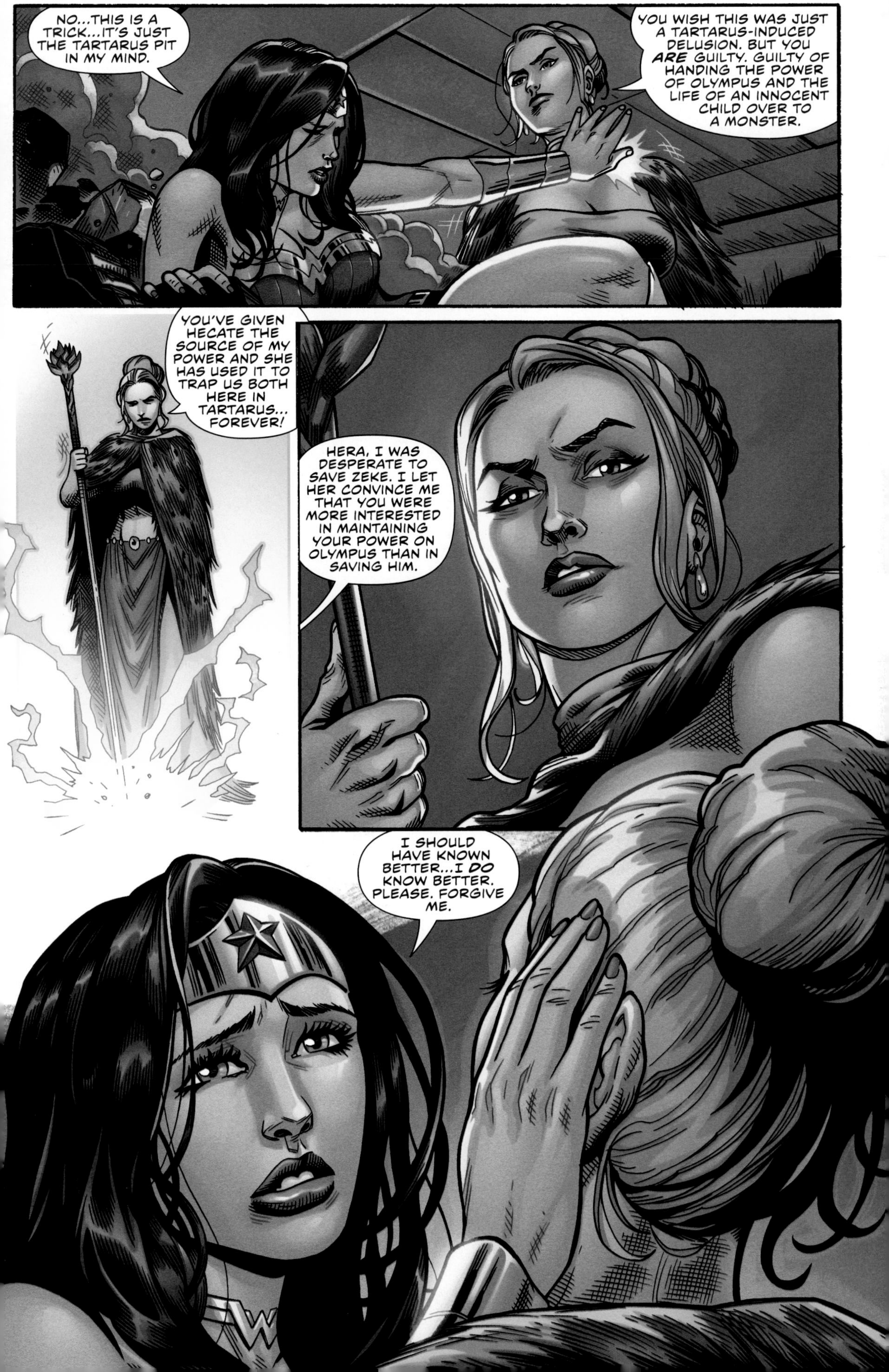
NO...THIS IS A TRICK...IT'S JUST THE TARTARUS PIT IN MY MIND.
YOU WISH THIS WAS JUST A TARTARUS-INDUCED DELUSION. BUT YOU ARE GUILTY. GUILTY OF HANDING THE POWER OF OLYMPUS AND THE LIFE OF AN INNOCENT CHILD OVER TO A MONSTER.
YOU'VE GIVEN HECATE THE SOURCE OF MY POWER AND SHE HAS USED IT TO TRAP US BOTH HERE IN TARTARUS... FOREVER!
HERA, I WAS DESPERATE TO SAVE ZEKE. I LET HER CONVINCE ME THAT YOU WERE MORE INTERESTED IN MAINTAINING YOUR POWER ON OLYMPUS THAN IN SAVING HIM.
I SHOULD HAVE KNOWN BETTER...I DO KNOW BETTER. PLEASE. FORGIVE ME.

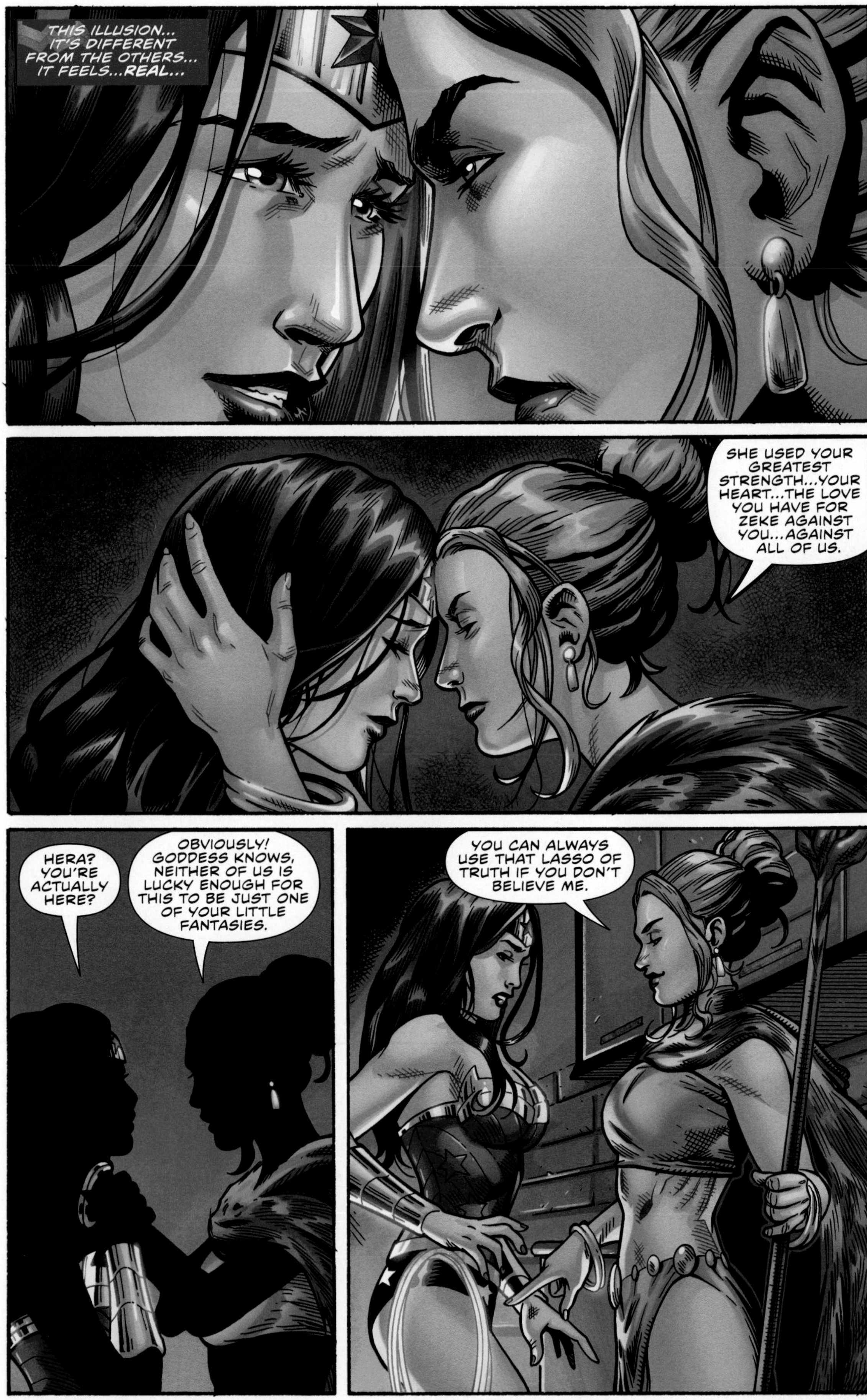
THIS ILLUSION... IT'S DIFFERENT FROM THE OTHERS... IT FEELS...REAL...
SHE USED YOUR GREATEST STRENGTH...YOUR HEART...THE LOVE YOU HAVE FOR ZEKE AGAINST YOU...AGAINST ALL OF US.
HERA? YOU'RE ACTUALLY HERE?
OBVIOUSLY! GODDESS KNOWS, NEITHER OF US IS LUCKY ENOUGH FOR THIS TO BE JUST ONE OF YOUR LITTLE FANTASIES.
YOU CAN ALWAYS USE THAT LASSO OF TRUTH IF YOU DON'T BELIEVE ME.

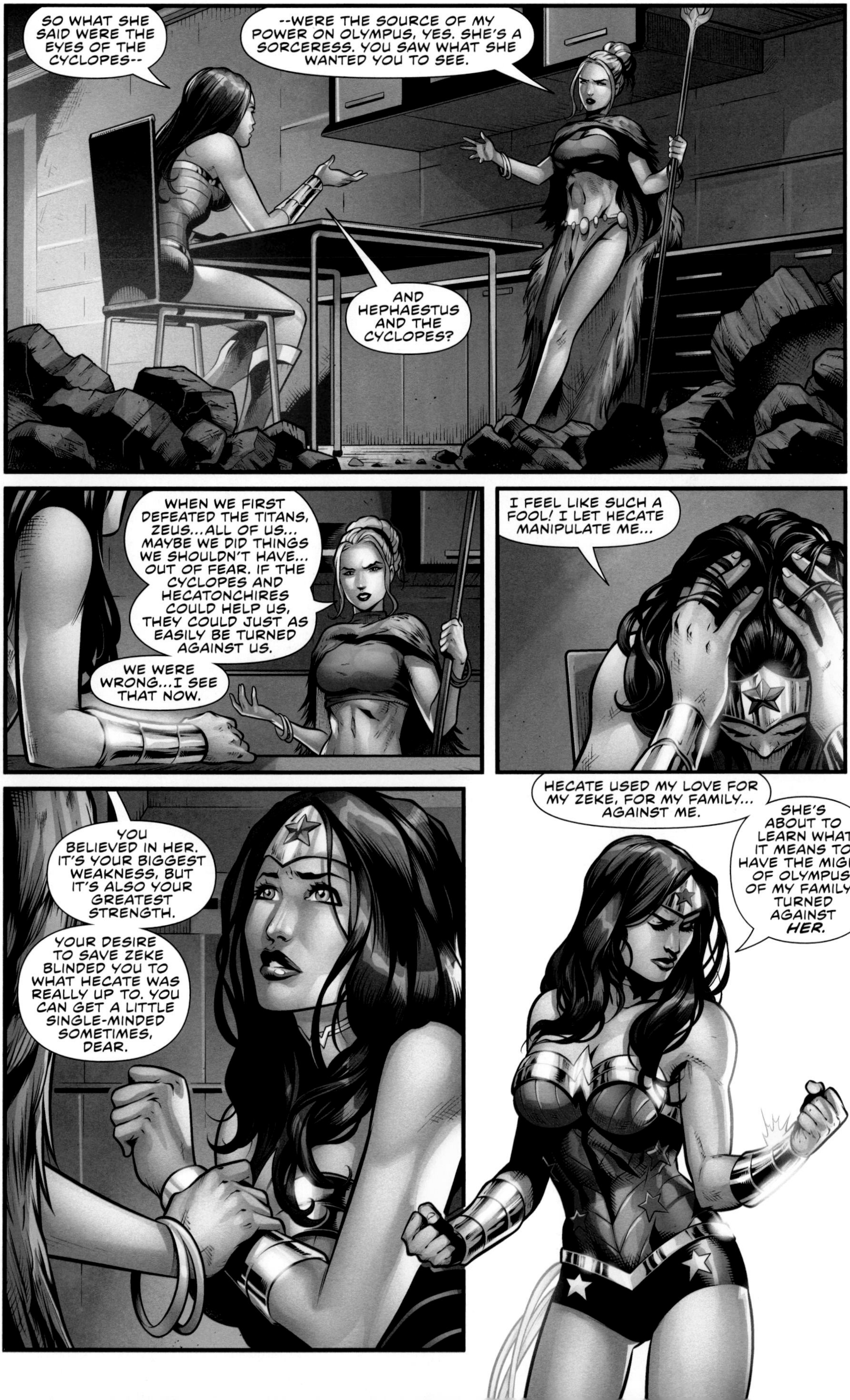
SO WHAT SHE SAID WERE THE EYES OF THE CYCLOPES--
--WERE THE SOURCE OF MY POWER ON OLYMPUS, YES. SHE'S A SORCERESS. YOU SAW WHAT SHE WANTED YOU TO SEE.
AND HEPHAESTUS AND THE CYCLOPES?
WHEN WE FIRST DEFEATED THE TITANS, ZEUS...ALL OF US... MAYBE WE DID THINGS WE SHOULDN'T HAVE... OUT OF FEAR. IF THE CYCLOPES AND HECATONCHIRES COULD HELP US, THEY COULD JUST AS EASILY BE TURNED AGAINST US.
WE WERE WRONG...I SEE THAT NOW.
I FEEL LIKE SUCH A FOOL! I LET HECATE MANIPULATE ME...
YOU BELIEVED IN HER. IT'S YOUR BIGGEST WEAKNESS, BUT IT'S ALSO YOUR GREATEST STRENGTH.
YOUR DESIRE TO SAVE ZEKE BLINDED YOU TO WHAT HECATE WAS REALLY UP TO. YOU CAN GET A LITTLE SINGLE-MINDED SOMETIMES, DEAR.
HECATE USED MY LOVE FOR MY ZEKE, FOR MY FAMILY... AGAINST ME.
SHE'S ABOUT TO LEARN WHAT IT MEANS TO HAVE THE MIGHT OF OLYMPUS, OF MY FAMILY... TURNED AGAINST HER.

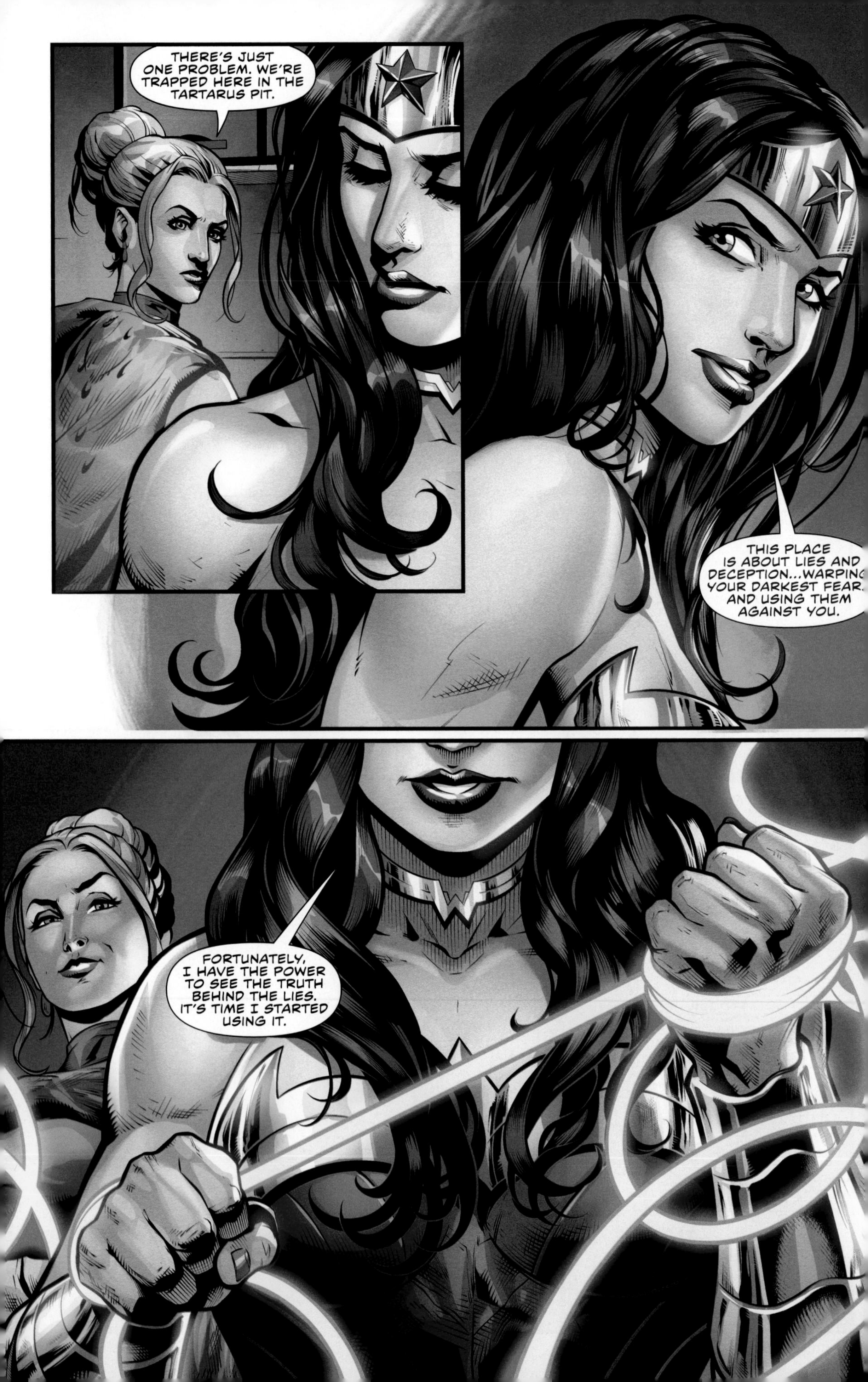
THERE'S JUST ONE PROBLEM. WE'RE TRAPPED HERE IN THE TARTARUS PIT.
THIS PLACE IS ABOUT LIES AND DECEPTION...WARPING YOUR DARKEST FEAR AND USING THEM AGAINST YOU.
FORTUNATELY, I HAVE THE POWER TO SEE THE TRUTH BEHIND THE LIES. IT'S TIME I STARTED USING IT.

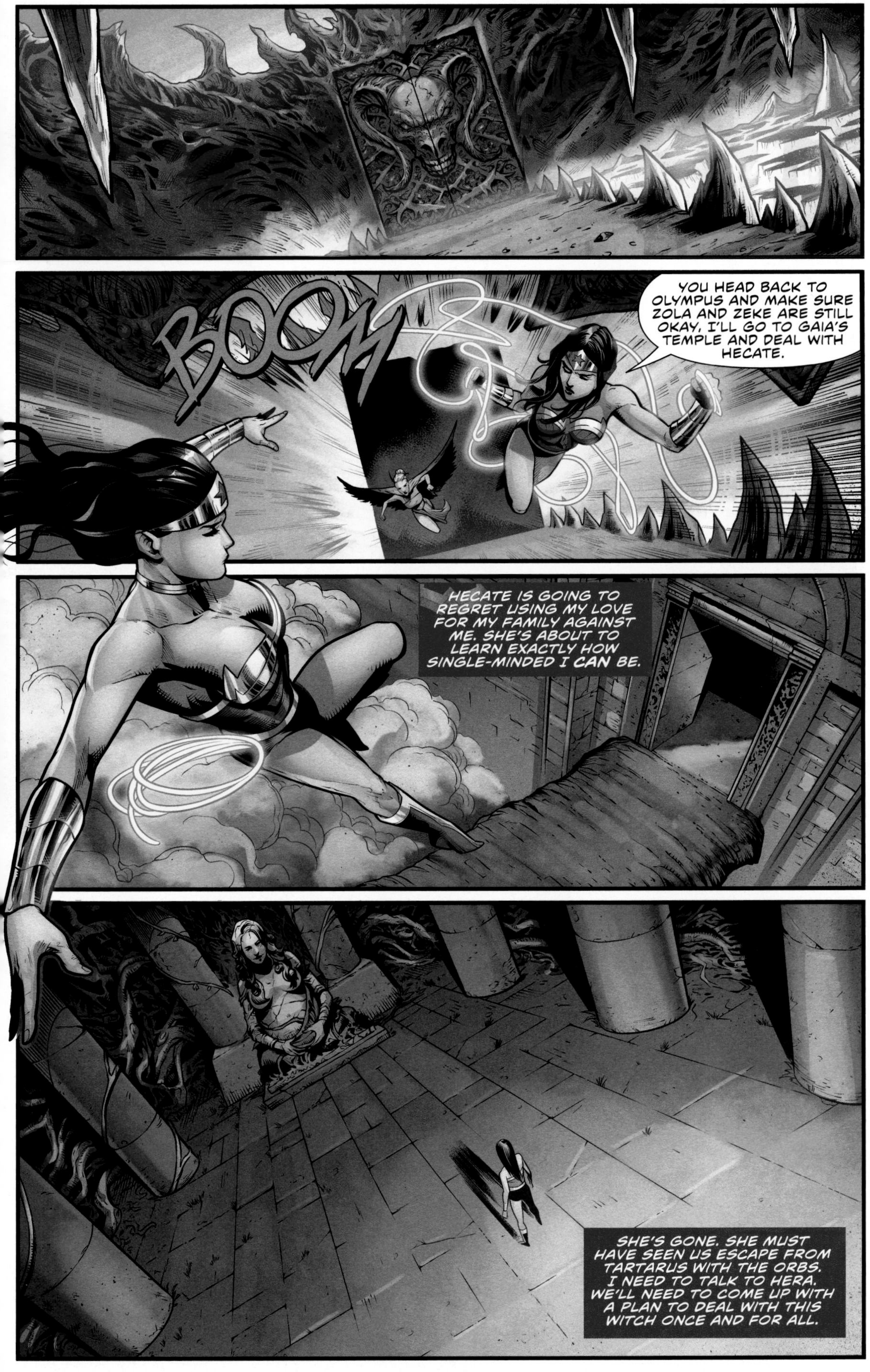
BOOM
YOU HEAD BACK TO OLYMPUS AND MAKE SURE ZOLA AND ZEKE ARE STILL OKAY, I'LL GO TO GAIA'S TEMPLE AND DEAL WITH HECATE.
HECATE IS GOING TO REGRET USING MY LOVE FOR MY FAMILY AGAINST ME. SHE'S ABOUT TO LEARN EXACTLY HOW SINGLE-MINDED I CAN BE.
SHE'S GONE. SHE MUST HAVE SEEN US ESCAPE FROM TARTARUS WITH THE ORBS. I NEED TO TALK TO HERA. WE'LL NEED TO COME UP WITH A PLAN TO DEAL WITH THIS WITCH ONCE AND FOR ALL.

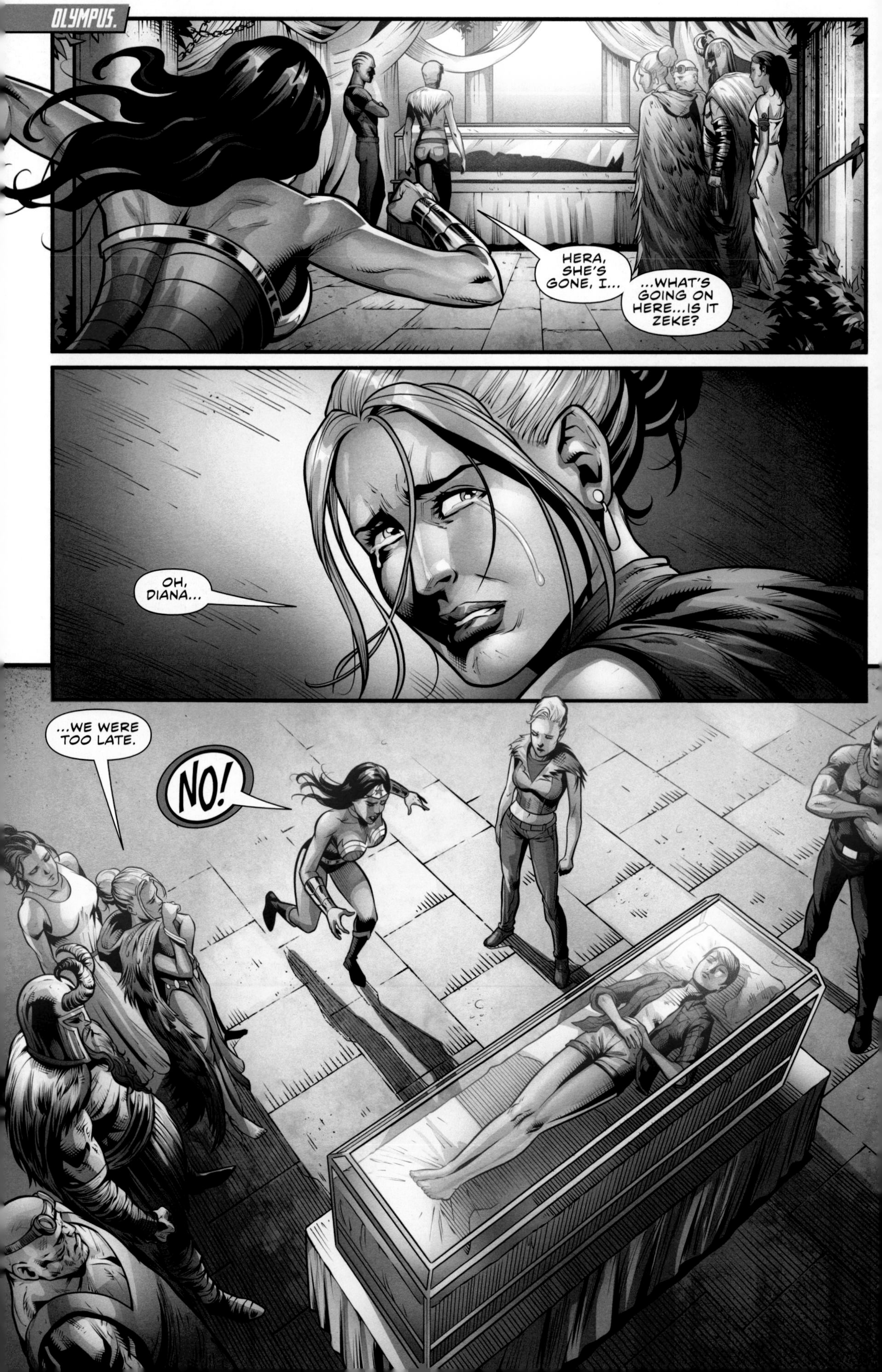
OLYMPUS.
HERA, SHE'S GONE, I...
...WHAT'S GOING ON HERE...IS IT ZEKE?
OH, DIANA...
...WE WERE TOO LATE.
NO!

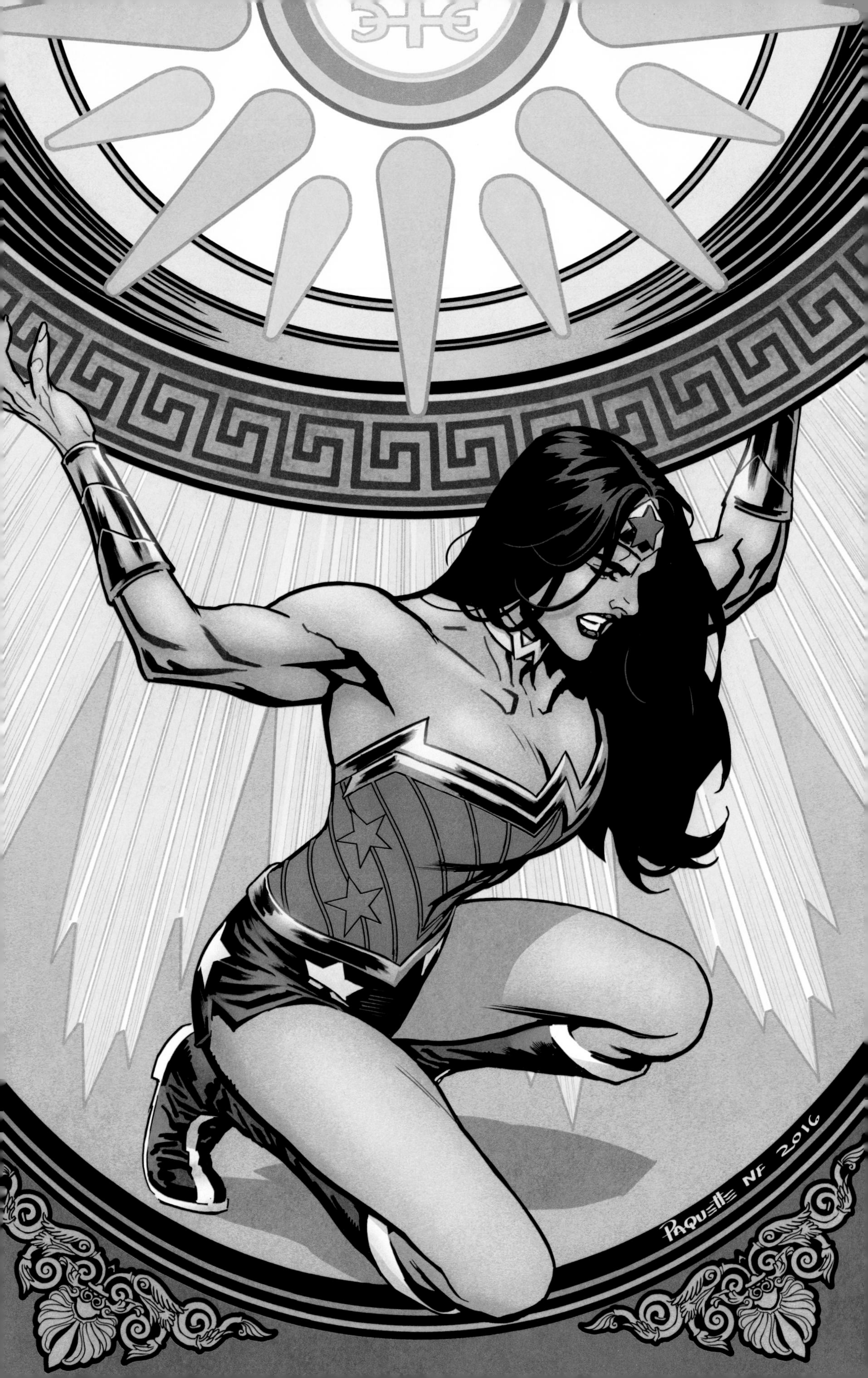
PAQUETTE NF 2016

IN THE NAME OF LOVE

MEREDITH FINCH writer **MIGUEL MENDONÇA** penciller **DIANA EGEA JUAN ALBARRAN** inkers **STEPHEN DOWNER** colorist **ROB LEIGH** letterer
cover art by **YANICK PAQUETTE & NATHAN FAIRBAIRN**

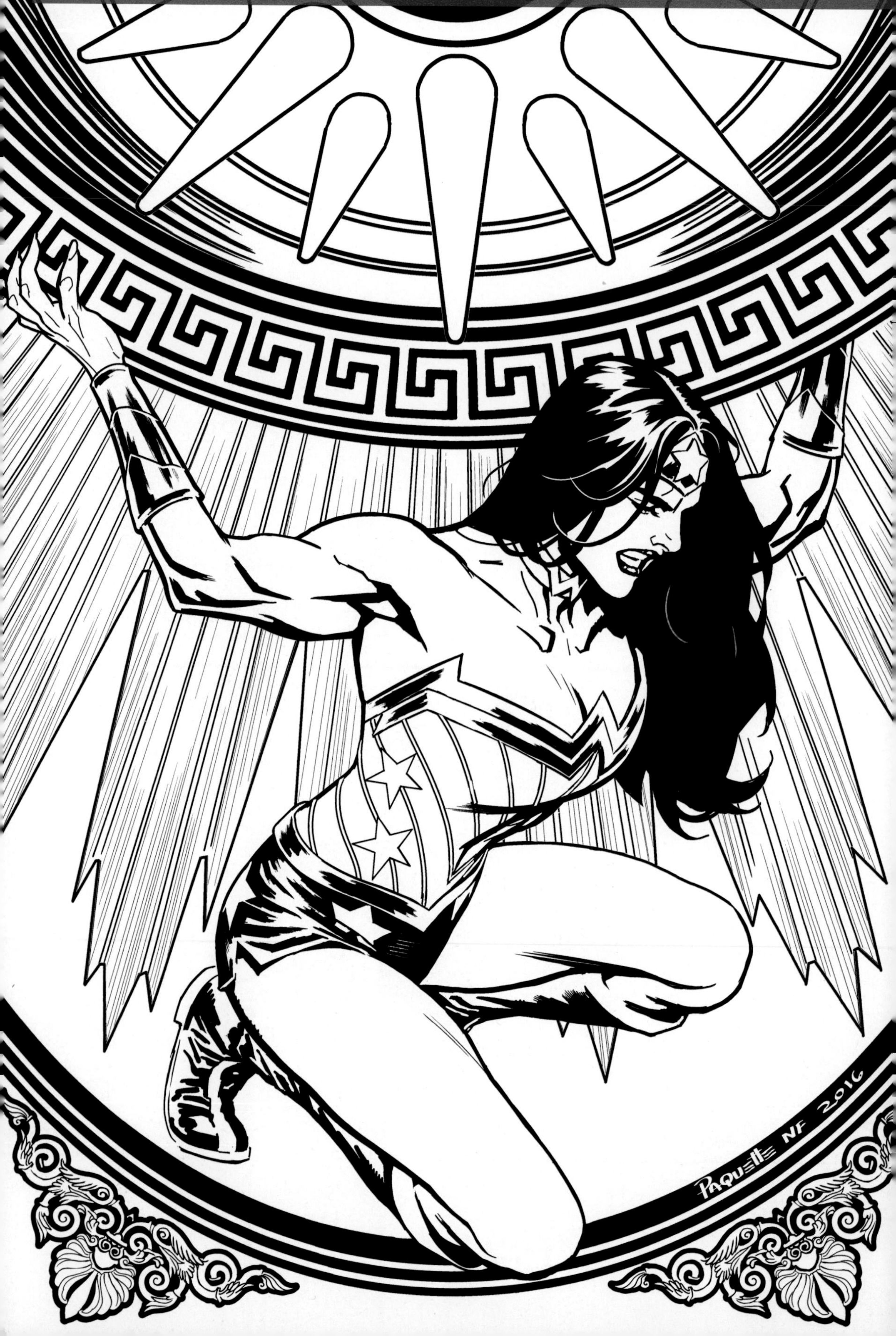
PAQUETTE NF 2016

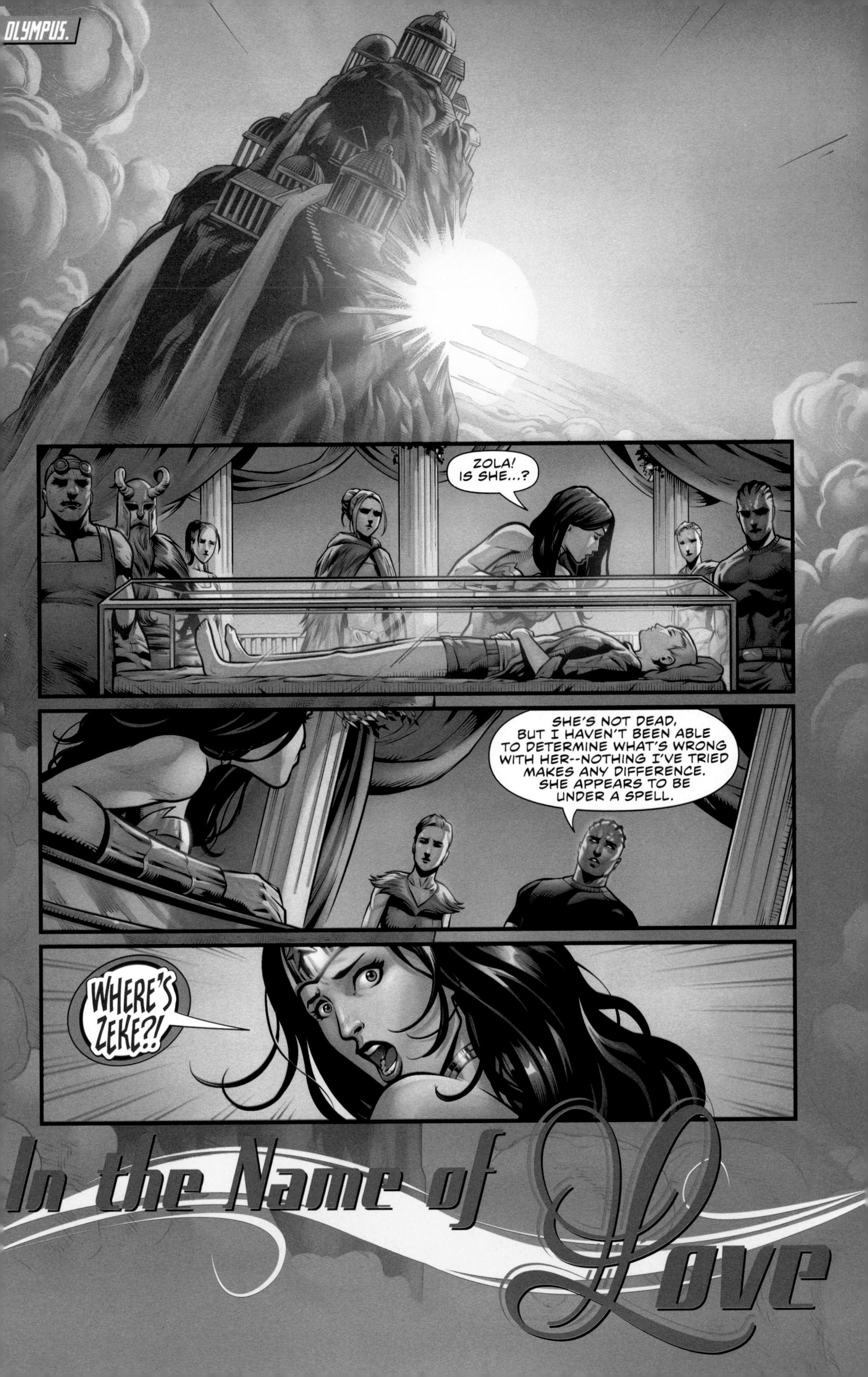

OLYMPUS.
ZOLA! IS SHE...?
SHE'S NOT DEAD, BUT I HAVEN'T BEEN ABLE TO DETERMINE WHAT'S WRONG WITH HER--NOTHING I'VE TRIED MAKES ANY DIFFERENCE. SHE APPEARS TO BE UNDER A SPELL.
WHERE'S ZEKE?!
In the Name of Love

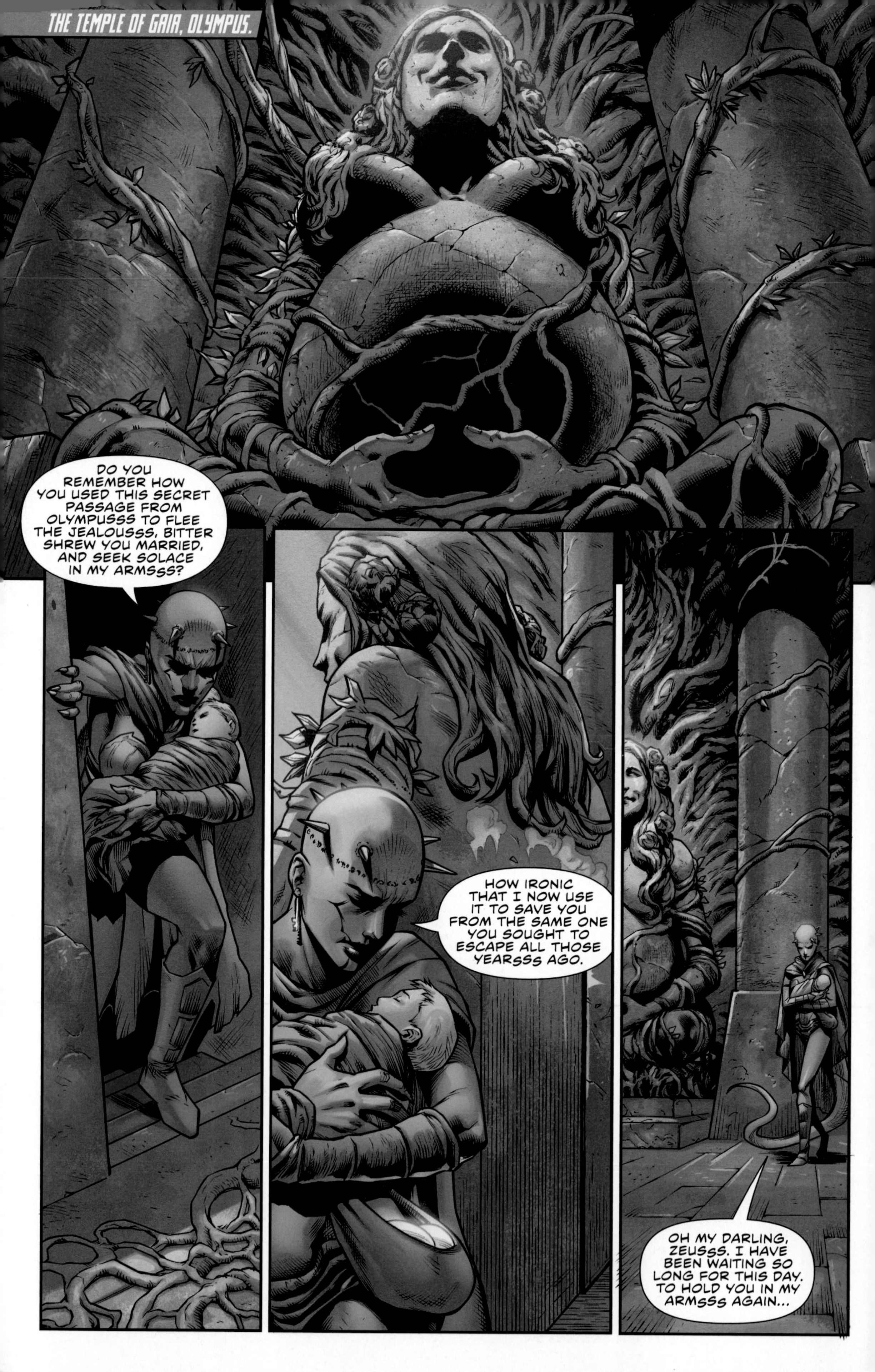
THE TEMPLE OF GAIA, OLYMPUS.
DO YOU REMEMBER HOW YOU USED THIS SECRET PASSAGE FROM OLYMPUSSS TO FLEE THE JEALOUSSS, BITTER SHREW YOU MARRIED, AND SEEK SOLACE IN MY ARMSSS?
HOW IRONIC THAT I NOW USE IT TO SAVE YOU FROM THE SAME ONE YOU SOUGHT TO ESCAPE ALL THOSE YEARSSS AGO.
OH MY DARLING, ZEUSSS. I HAVE BEEN WAITING SO LONG FOR THIS DAY. TO HOLD YOU IN MY ARMSSS AGAIN...

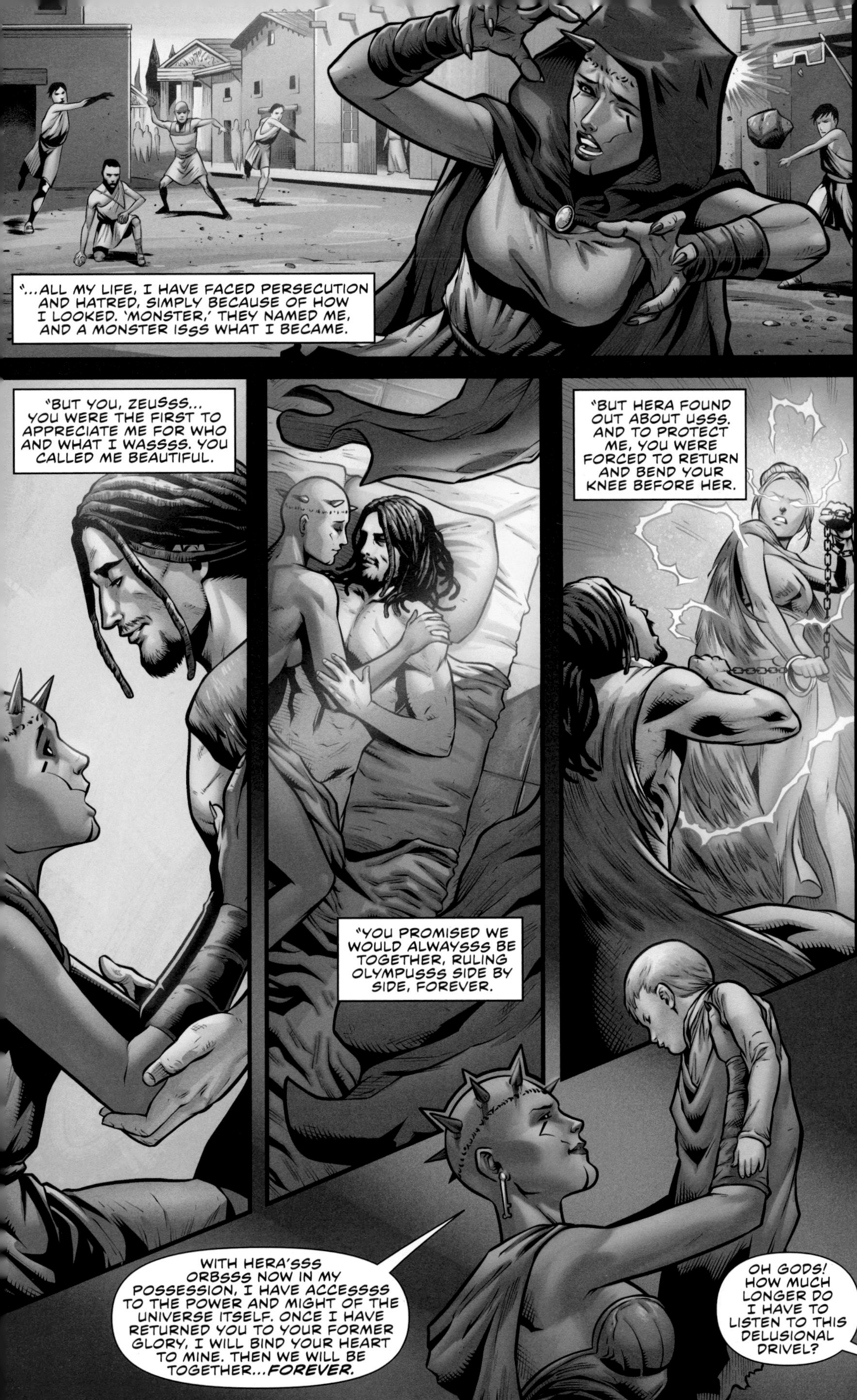
"...ALL MY LIFE, I HAVE FACED PERSECUTION AND HATRED, SIMPLY BECAUSE OF HOW I LOOKED. 'MONSTER,' THEY NAMED ME, AND A MONSTER ISSS WHAT I BECAME.
"BUT YOU, ZEUSSS... YOU WERE THE FIRST TO APPRECIATE ME FOR WHO AND WHAT I WASSSS. YOU CALLED ME BEAUTIFUL.
"BUT HERA FOUND OUT ABOUT USSS. AND TO PROTECT ME, YOU WERE FORCED TO RETURN AND BEND YOUR KNEE BEFORE HER.
"YOU PROMISED WE WOULD ALWAYSSS BE TOGETHER, RULING OLYMPUSSS SIDE BY SIDE, FOREVER.
WITH HERA'SSS ORBSSS NOW IN MY POSSESSION, I HAVE ACCESSSS TO THE POWER AND MIGHT OF THE UNIVERSE ITSELF. ONCE I HAVE RETURNED YOU TO YOUR FORMER GLORY, I WILL BIND YOUR HEART TO MINE. THEN WE WILL BE TOGETHER...*FOREVER.*
OH GODS! HOW MUCH LONGER DO I HAVE TO LISTEN TO THIS DELUSIONAL DRIVEL?

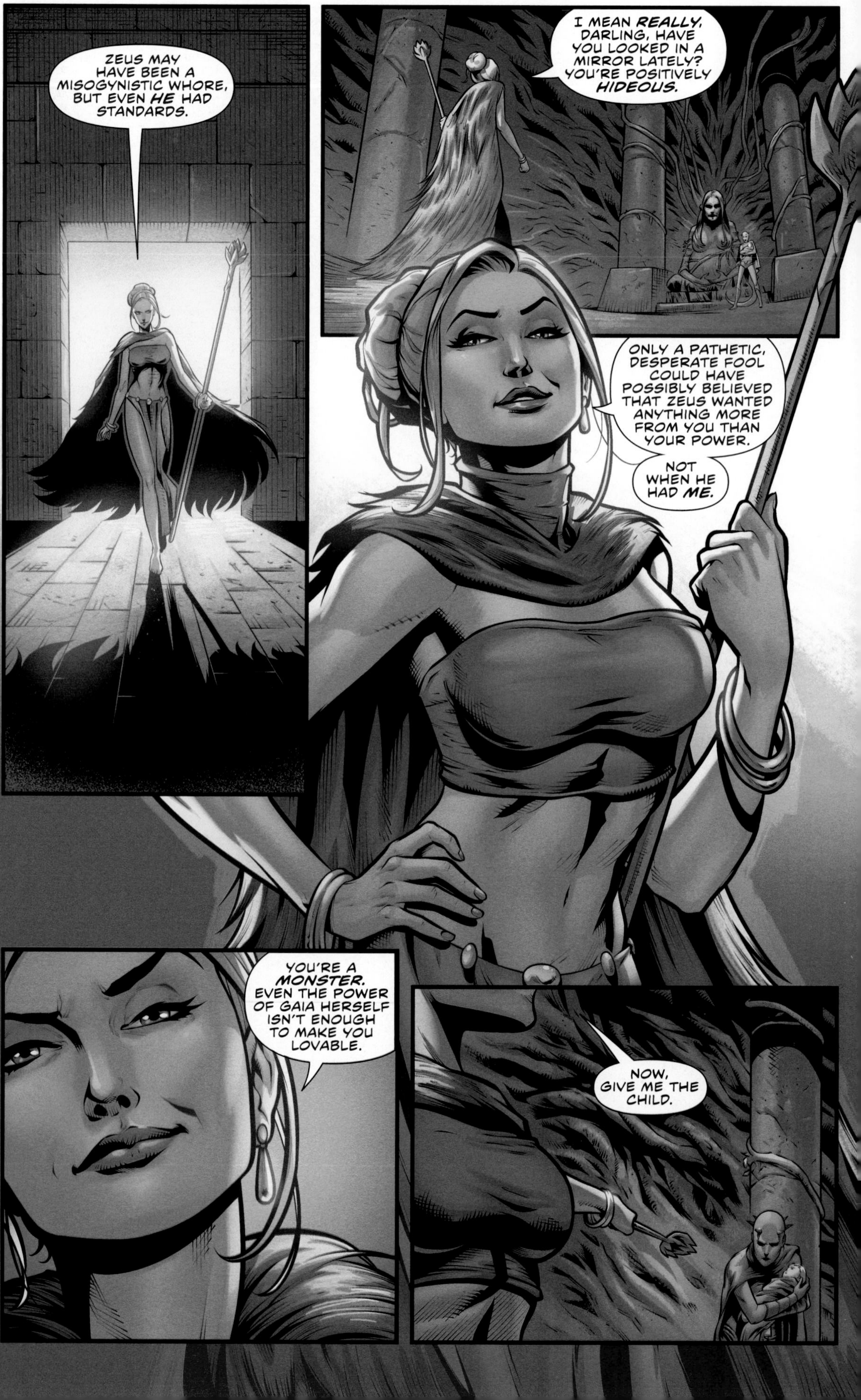
ZEUS MAY HAVE BEEN A MISOGYNISTIC WHORE, BUT EVEN HE HAD STANDARDS.
I MEAN REALLY, DARLING, HAVE YOU LOOKED IN A MIRROR LATELY? YOU'RE POSITIVELY HIDEOUS.
ONLY A PATHETIC, DESPERATE FOOL COULD HAVE POSSIBLY BELIEVED THAT ZEUS WANTED ANYTHING MORE FROM YOU THAN YOUR POWER.
NOT WHEN HE HAD ME.
YOU'RE A MONSTER. EVEN THE POWER OF GAIA HERSELF ISN'T ENOUGH TO MAKE YOU LOVABLE.
NOW, GIVE ME THE CHILD.

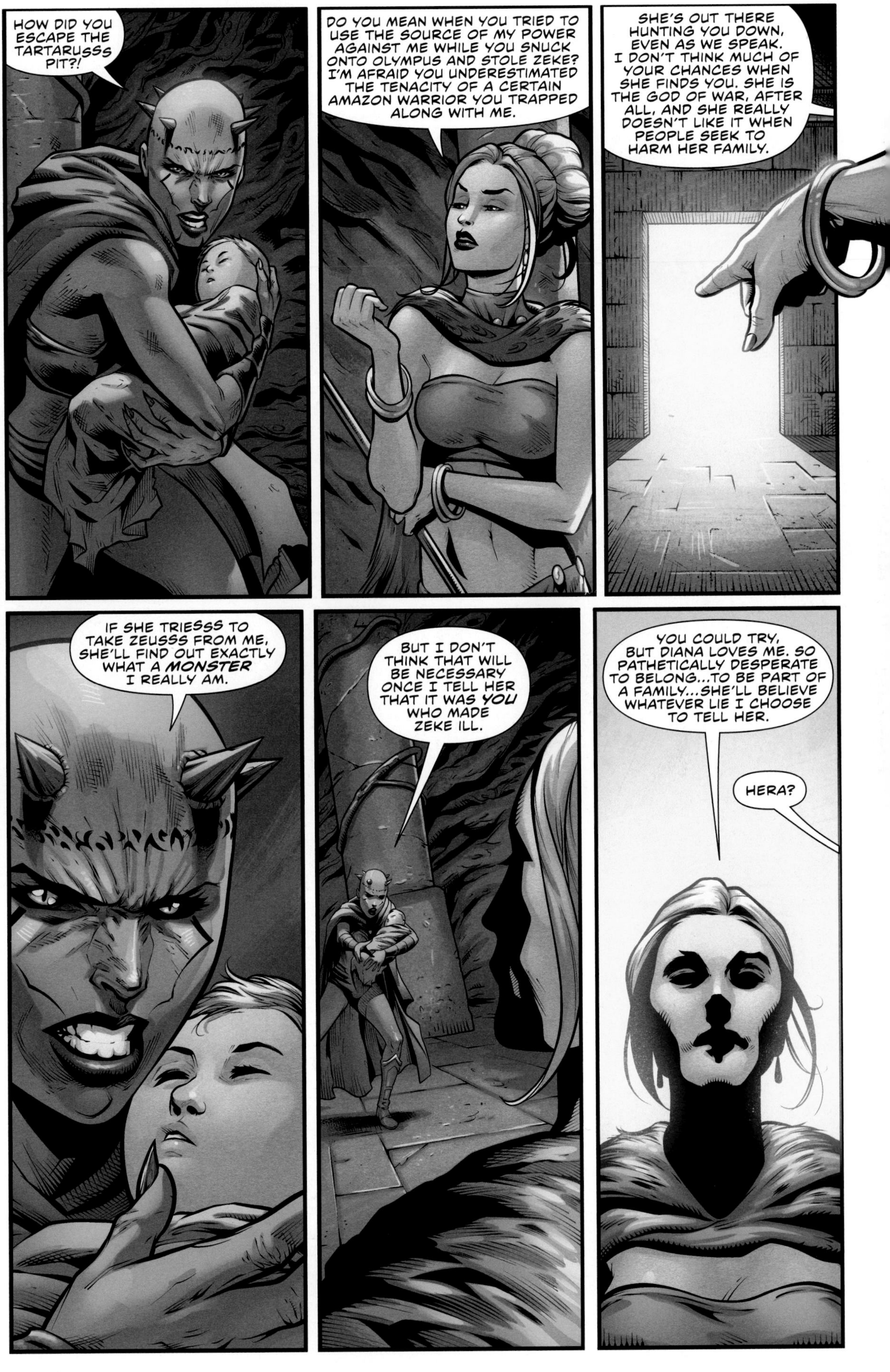
HOW DID YOU ESCAPE THE TARTARUSSS PIT?!
DO YOU MEAN WHEN YOU TRIED TO USE THE SOURCE OF MY POWER AGAINST ME WHILE YOU SNUCK ONTO OLYMPUS AND STOLE ZEKE? I'M AFRAID YOU UNDERESTIMATED THE TENACITY OF A CERTAIN AMAZON WARRIOR YOU TRAPPED ALONG WITH ME.
SHE'S OUT THERE HUNTING YOU DOWN, EVEN AS WE SPEAK. I DON'T THINK MUCH OF YOUR CHANCES WHEN SHE FINDS YOU. SHE IS THE GOD OF WAR, AFTER ALL, AND SHE REALLY DOESN'T LIKE IT WHEN PEOPLE SEEK TO HARM HER FAMILY.
IF SHE TRIESSS TO TAKE ZEUSSS FROM ME, SHE'LL FIND OUT EXACTLY WHAT A *MONSTER* I REALLY AM.
BUT I DON'T THINK THAT WILL BE NECESSARY ONCE I TELL HER THAT IT WAS *YOU* WHO MADE ZEKE ILL.
YOU COULD TRY, BUT DIANA LOVES ME. SO PATHETICALLY DESPERATE TO BELONG...TO BE PART OF A FAMILY...SHE'LL BELIEVE WHATEVER LIE I CHOOSE TO TELL HER.
HERA?

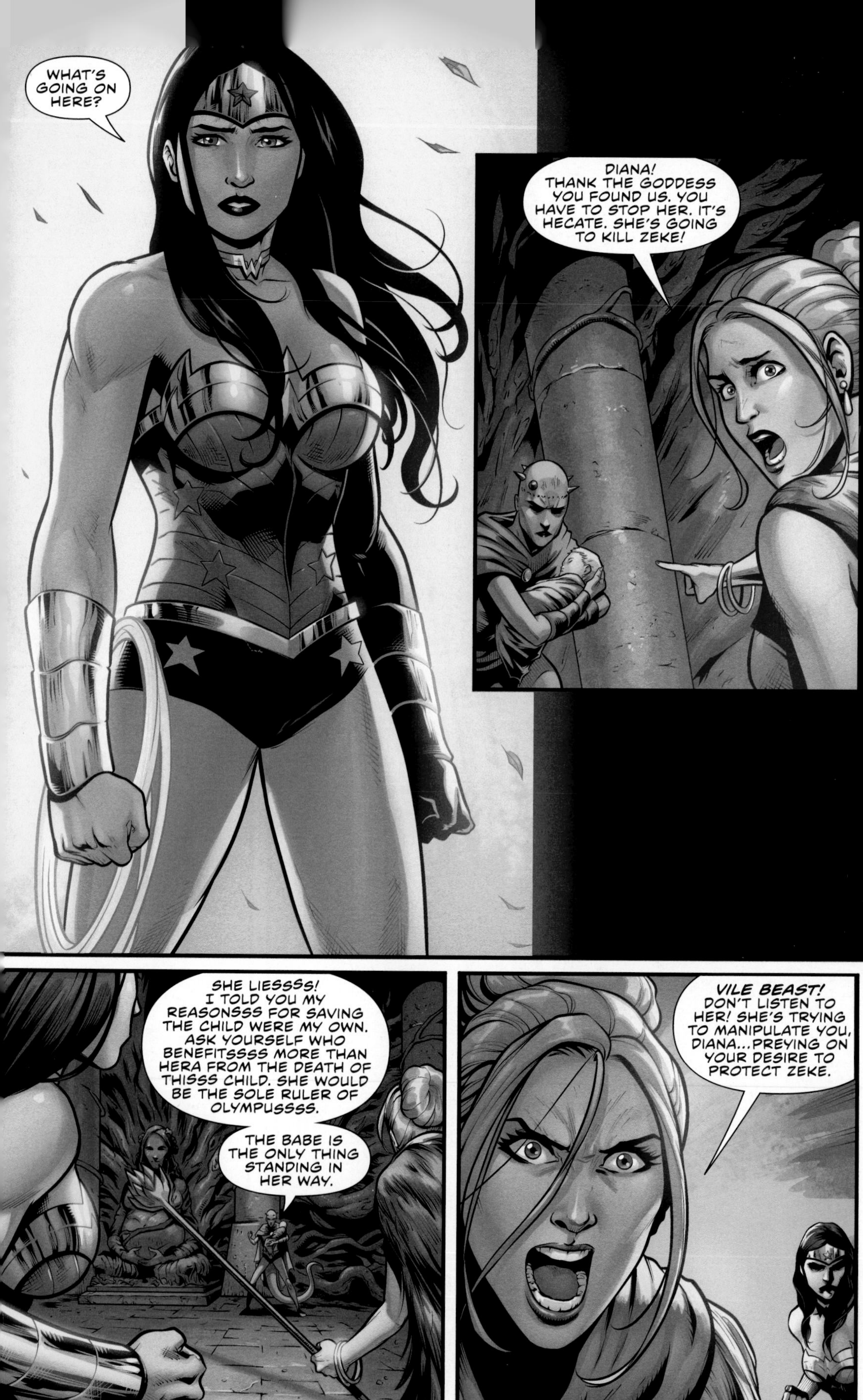
WHAT'S GOING ON HERE?
DIANA! THANK THE GODDESS YOU FOUND US. YOU HAVE TO STOP HER. IT'S HECATE. SHE'S GOING TO KILL ZEKE!
SHE LIESSSS! I TOLD YOU MY REASONSSS FOR SAVING THE CHILD WERE MY OWN. ASK YOURSELF WHO BENEFITSSSS MORE THAN HERA FROM THE DEATH OF THISSS CHILD. SHE WOULD BE THE SOLE RULER OF OLYMPUSSSS.
THE BABE IS THE ONLY THING STANDING IN HER WAY.
VILE BEAST! DON'T LISTEN TO HER! SHE'S TRYING TO MANIPULATE YOU, DIANA...PREYING ON YOUR DESIRE TO PROTECT ZEKE.

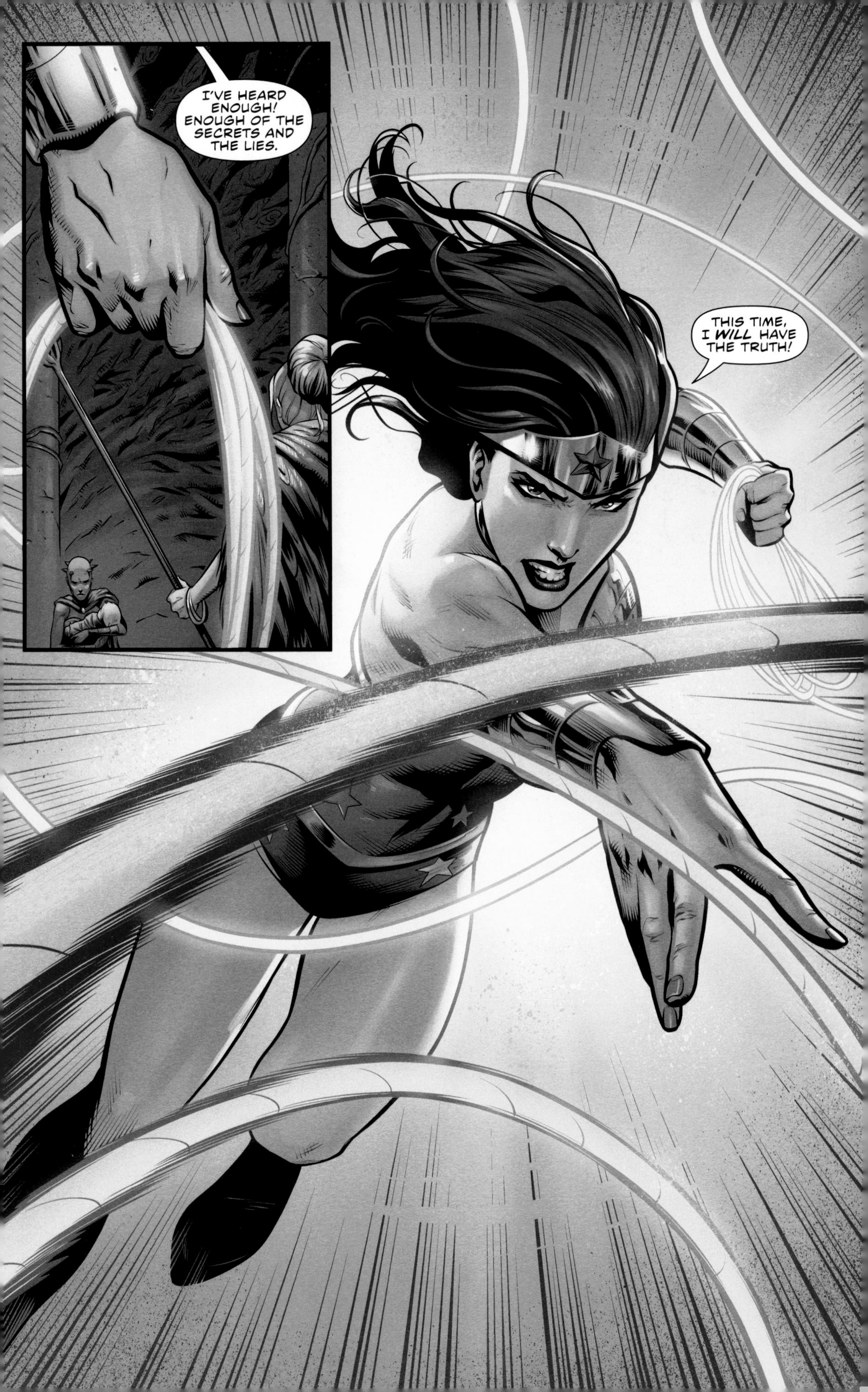
I'VE HEARD ENOUGH! ENOUGH OF THE SECRETS AND THE LIES.
THIS TIME, I WILL HAVE THE TRUTH!

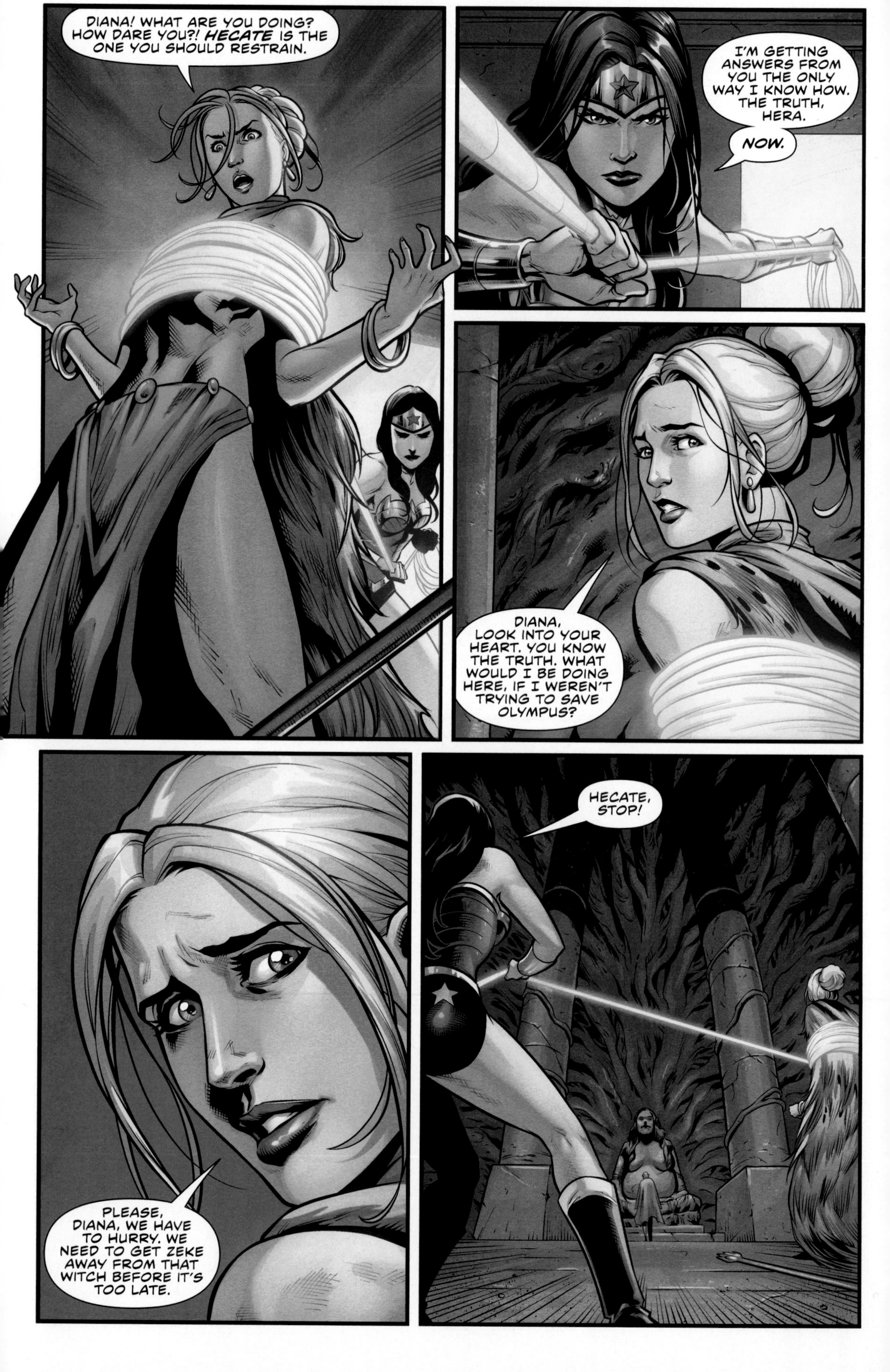
DIANA! WHAT ARE YOU DOING? HOW DARE YOU?! HECATE IS THE ONE YOU SHOULD RESTRAIN.
I'M GETTING ANSWERS FROM YOU THE ONLY WAY I KNOW HOW. THE TRUTH, HERA.
NOW.
DIANA, LOOK INTO YOUR HEART. YOU KNOW THE TRUTH. WHAT WOULD I BE DOING HERE, IF I WEREN'T TRYING TO SAVE OLYMPUS?
PLEASE, DIANA, WE HAVE TO HURRY. WE NEED TO GET ZEKE AWAY FROM THAT WITCH BEFORE IT'S TOO LATE.
HECATE, STOP!

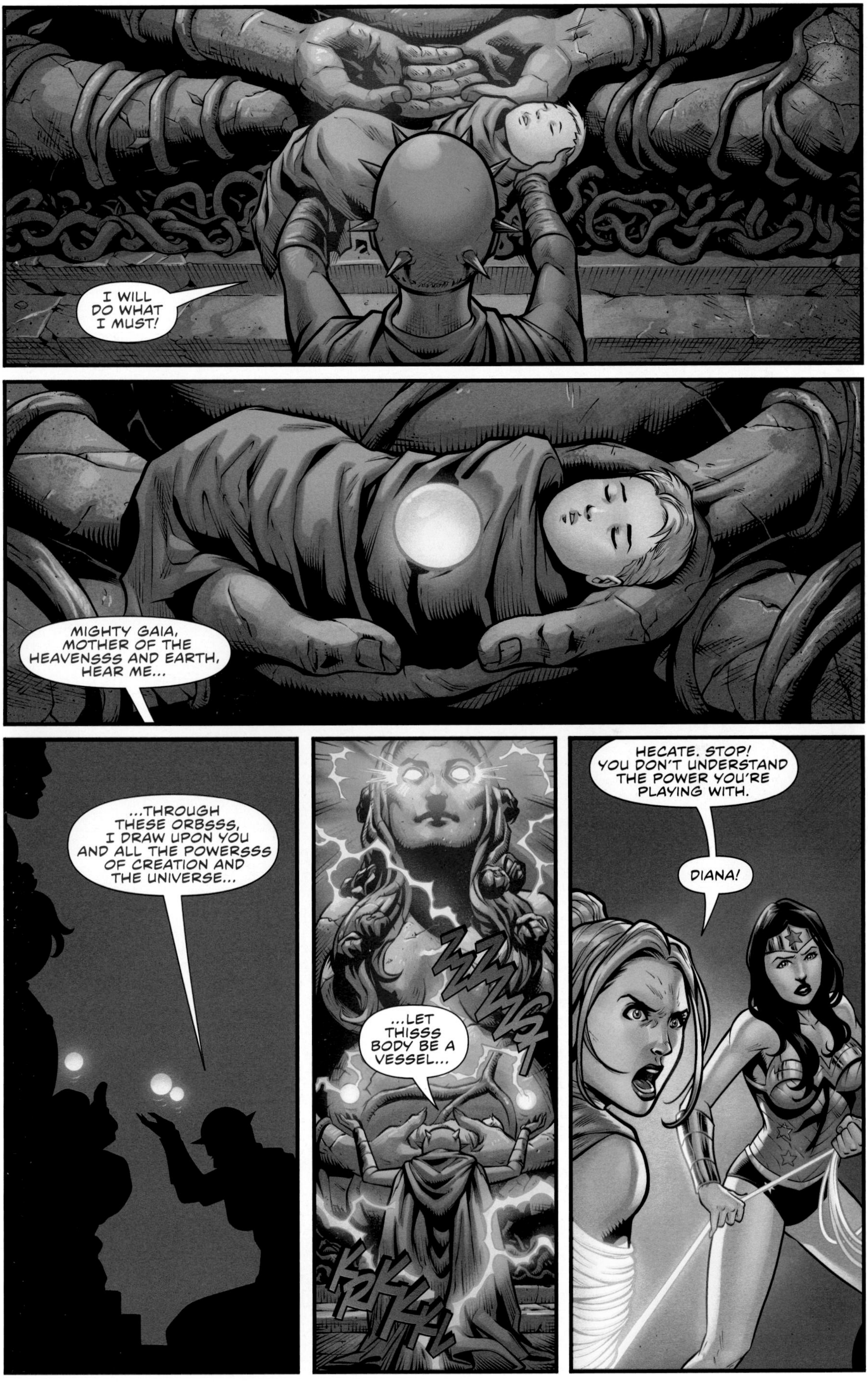
I WILL DO WHAT I MUST!
MIGHTY GAIA, MOTHER OF THE HEAVENSSS AND EARTH, HEAR ME...
...THROUGH THESE ORBSSS, I DRAW UPON YOU AND ALL THE POWERSSS OF CREATION AND THE UNIVERSE...
...LET THISSS BODY BE A VESSEL...
HECATE. STOP! YOU DON'T UNDERSTAND THE POWER YOU'RE PLAYING WITH.
DIANA!

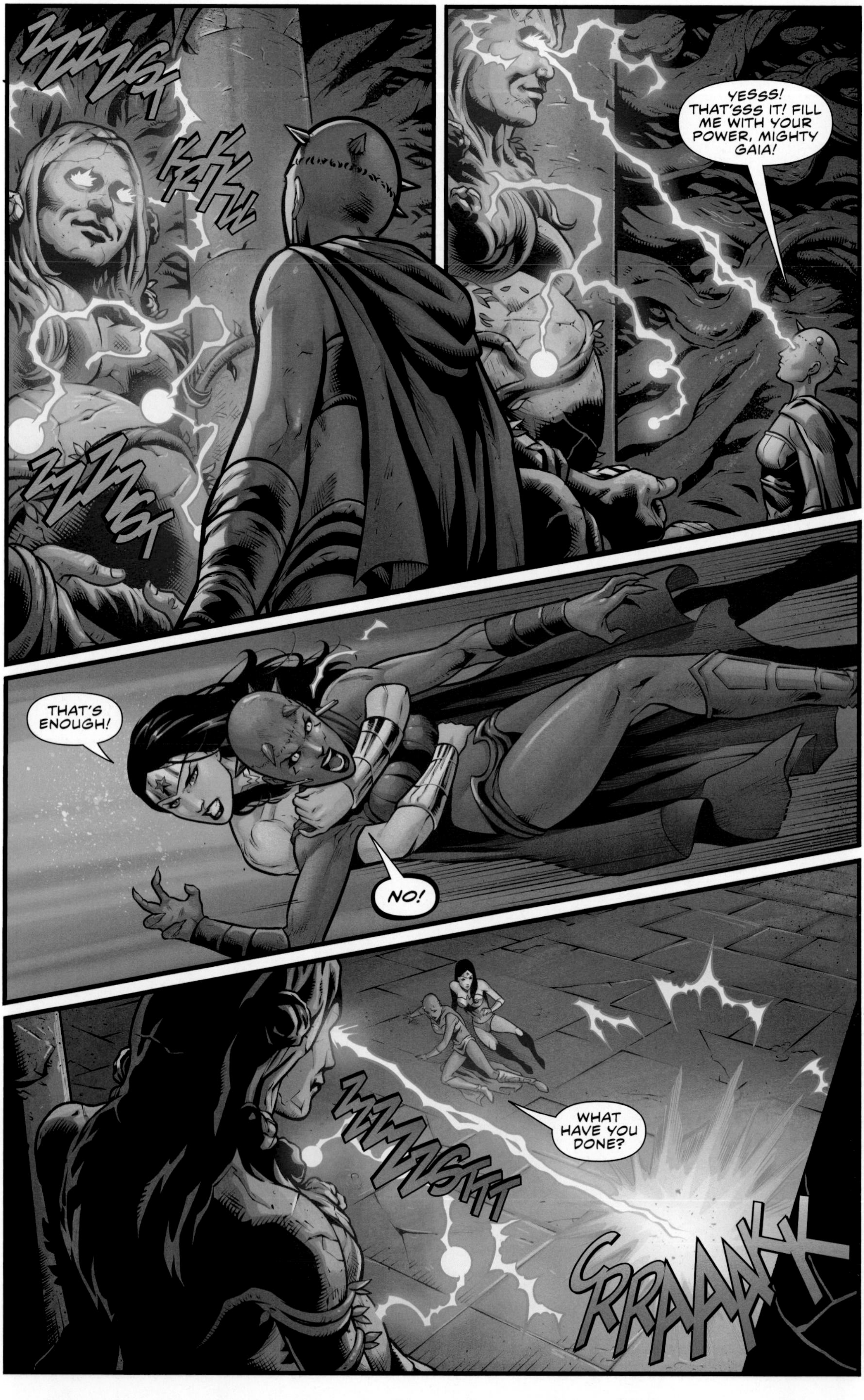
ZZZZZGK
KZKZKW
ZZZZZNGK
YESSS! THAT'SSS IT! FILL ME WITH YOUR POWER, MIGHTY GAIA!
THAT'S ENOUGH!
NO!
WHAT HAVE YOU DONE?
ZZZZNGKKK
CRRAAKK

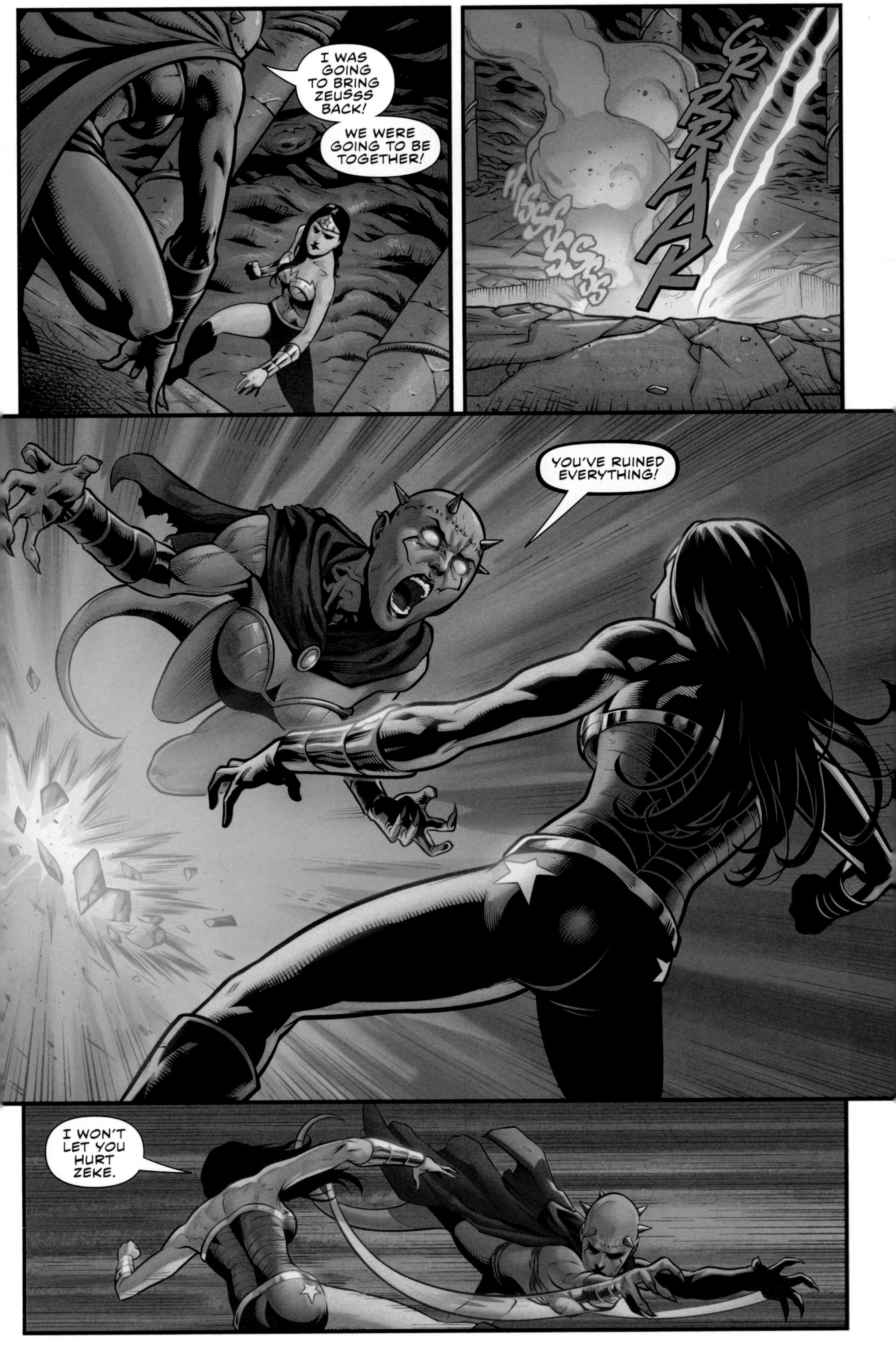
I WAS GOING TO BRING ZEUSSS BACK!
WE WERE GOING TO BE TOGETHER!
GRRRAAK
HISSSSSSS
YOU'VE RUINED EVERYTHING!
I WON'T LET YOU HURT ZEKE.

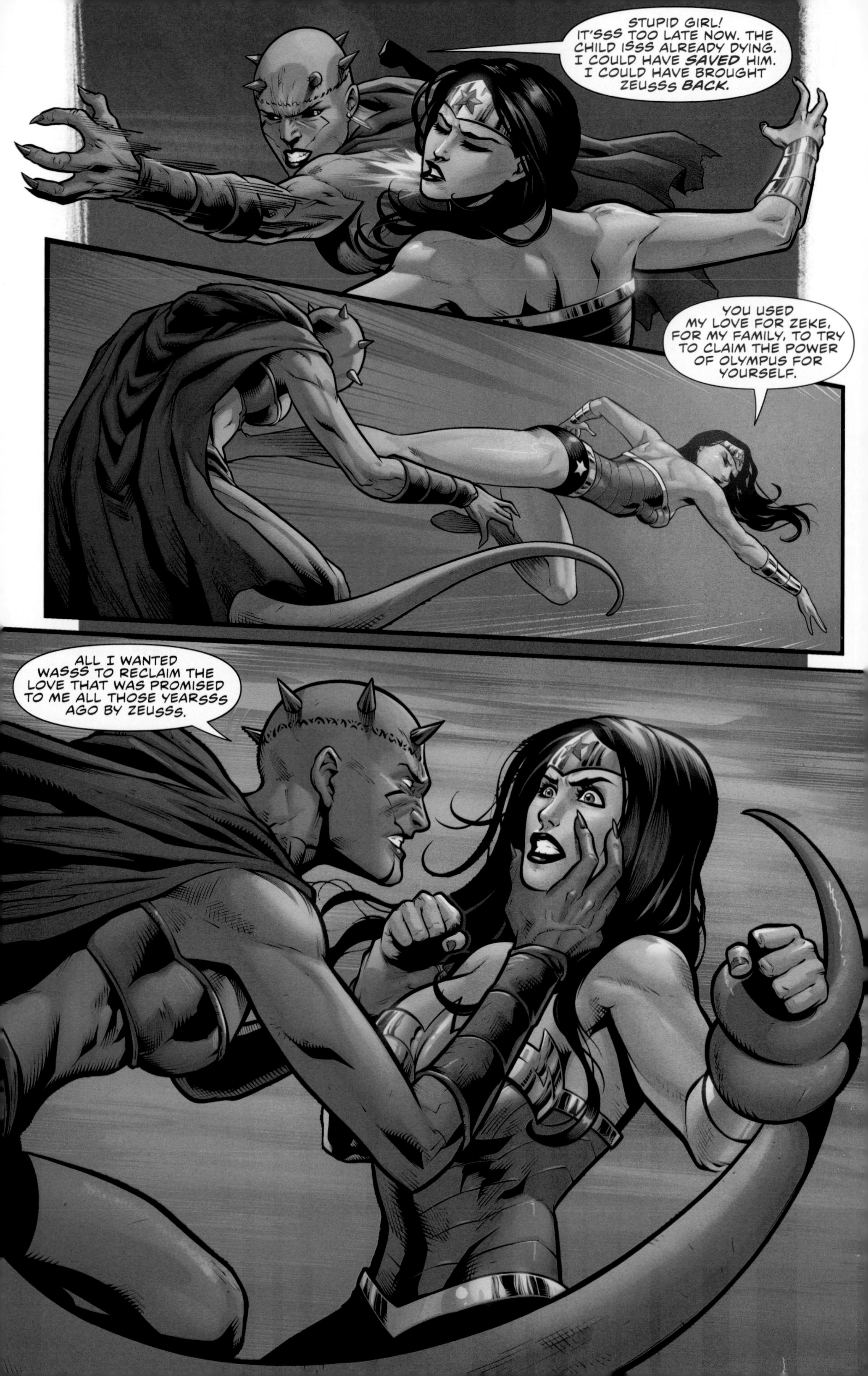
STUPID GIRL! IT'SSS TOO LATE NOW. THE CHILD ISSS ALREADY DYING. I COULD HAVE SAVED HIM. I COULD HAVE BROUGHT ZEUSSS BACK.
YOU USED MY LOVE FOR ZEKE, FOR MY FAMILY, TO TRY TO CLAIM THE POWER OF OLYMPUS FOR YOURSELF.
ALL I WANTED WASSS TO RECLAIM THE LOVE THAT WAS PROMISED TO ME ALL THOSE YEARSSS AGO BY ZEUSSS.

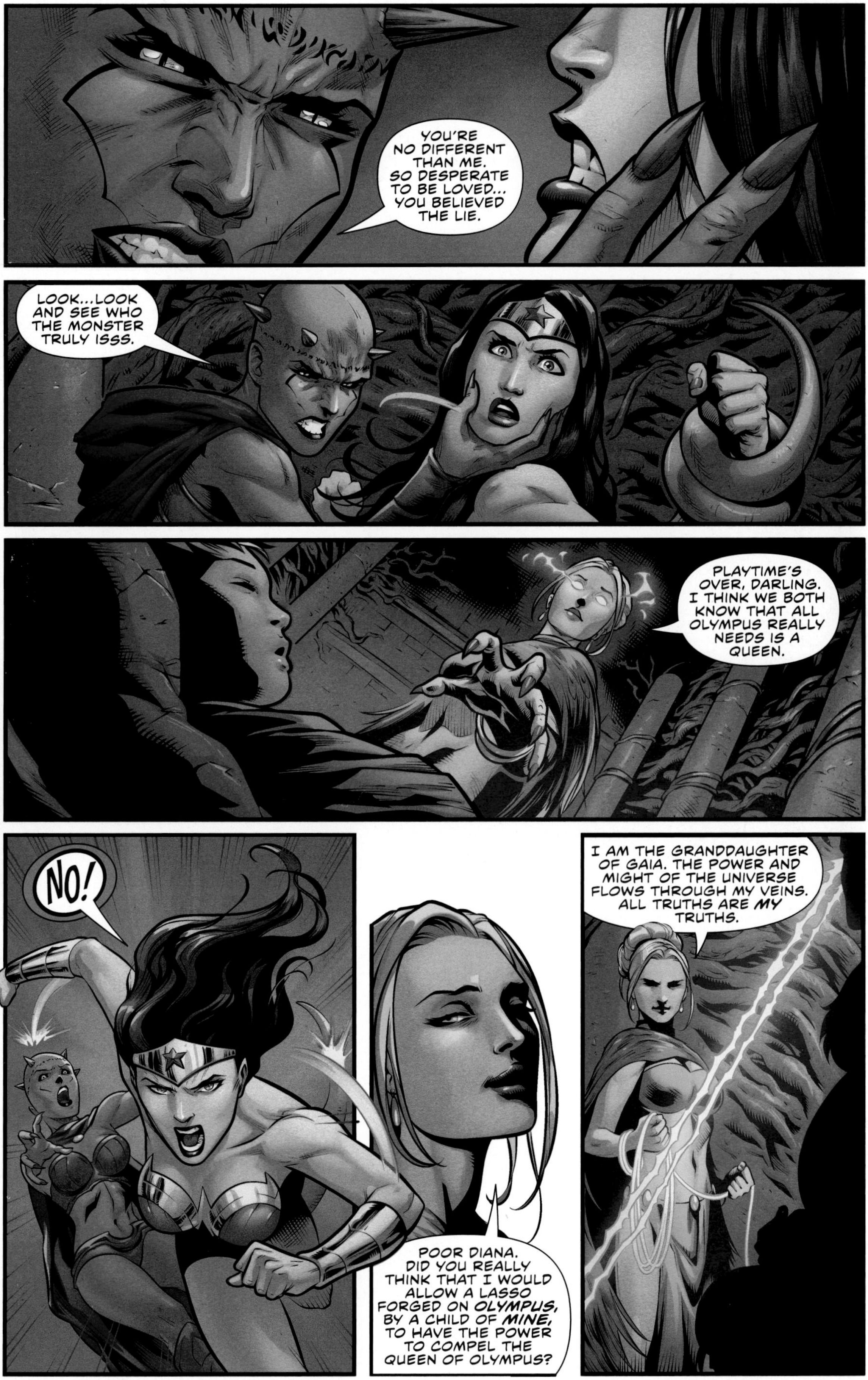
YOU'RE NO DIFFERENT THAN ME. SO DESPERATE TO BE LOVED... YOU BELIEVED THE LIE.
LOOK...LOOK AND SEE WHO THE MONSTER TRULY ISSS.
PLAYTIME'S OVER, DARLING. I THINK WE BOTH KNOW THAT ALL OLYMPUS REALLY NEEDS IS A QUEEN.
NO!
POOR DIANA. DID YOU REALLY THINK THAT I WOULD ALLOW A LASSO FORGED ON *OLYMPUS*, BY A CHILD OF *MINE*, TO HAVE THE POWER TO COMPEL THE QUEEN OF OLYMPUS?
I AM THE GRANDDAUGHTER OF GAIA. THE POWER AND MIGHT OF THE UNIVERSE FLOWS THROUGH MY VEINS. ALL TRUTHS ARE *MY* TRUTHS.

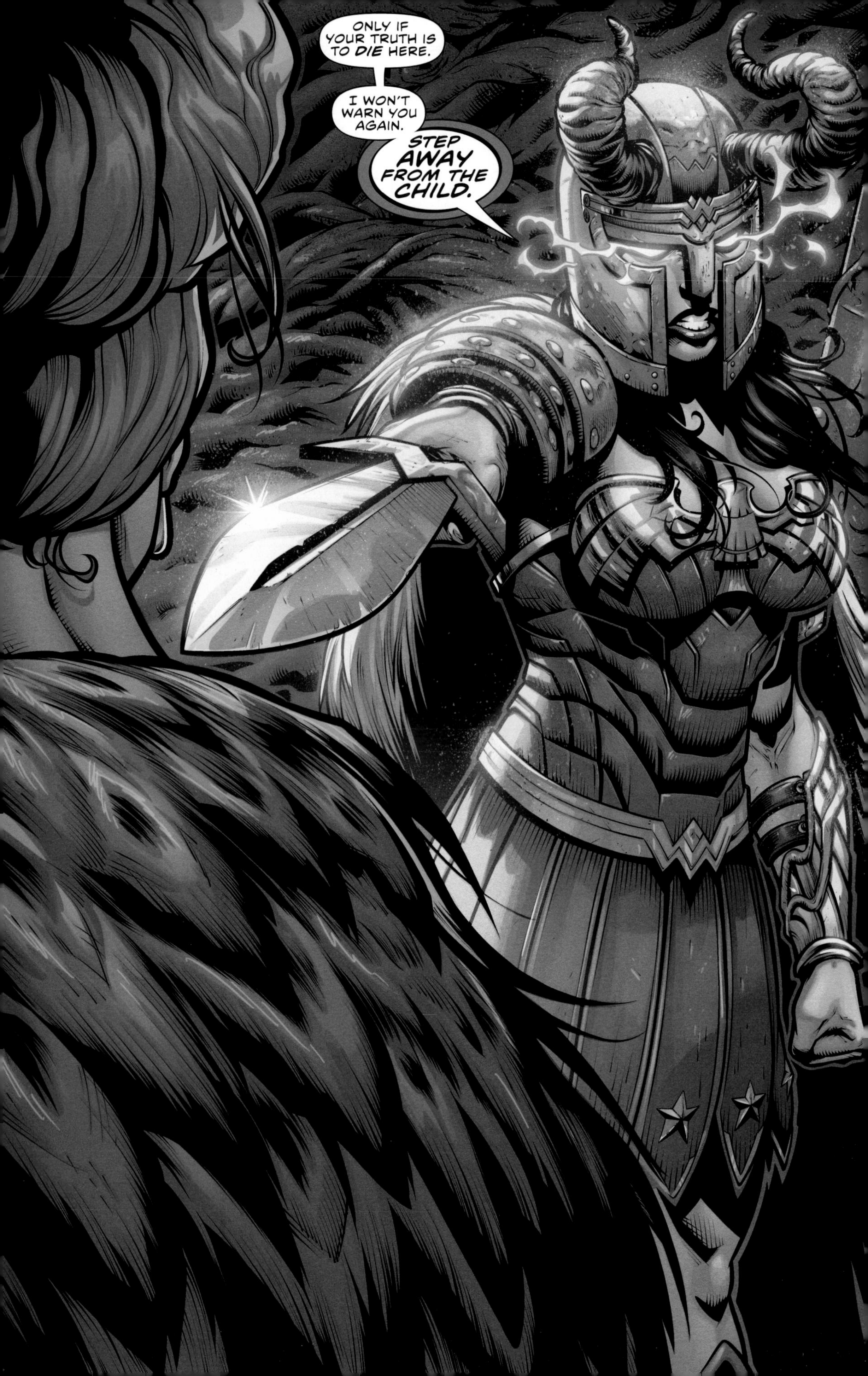
ONLY IF YOUR TRUTH IS TO DIE HERE.
I WON'T WARN YOU AGAIN.
STEP AWAY FROM THE CHILD.

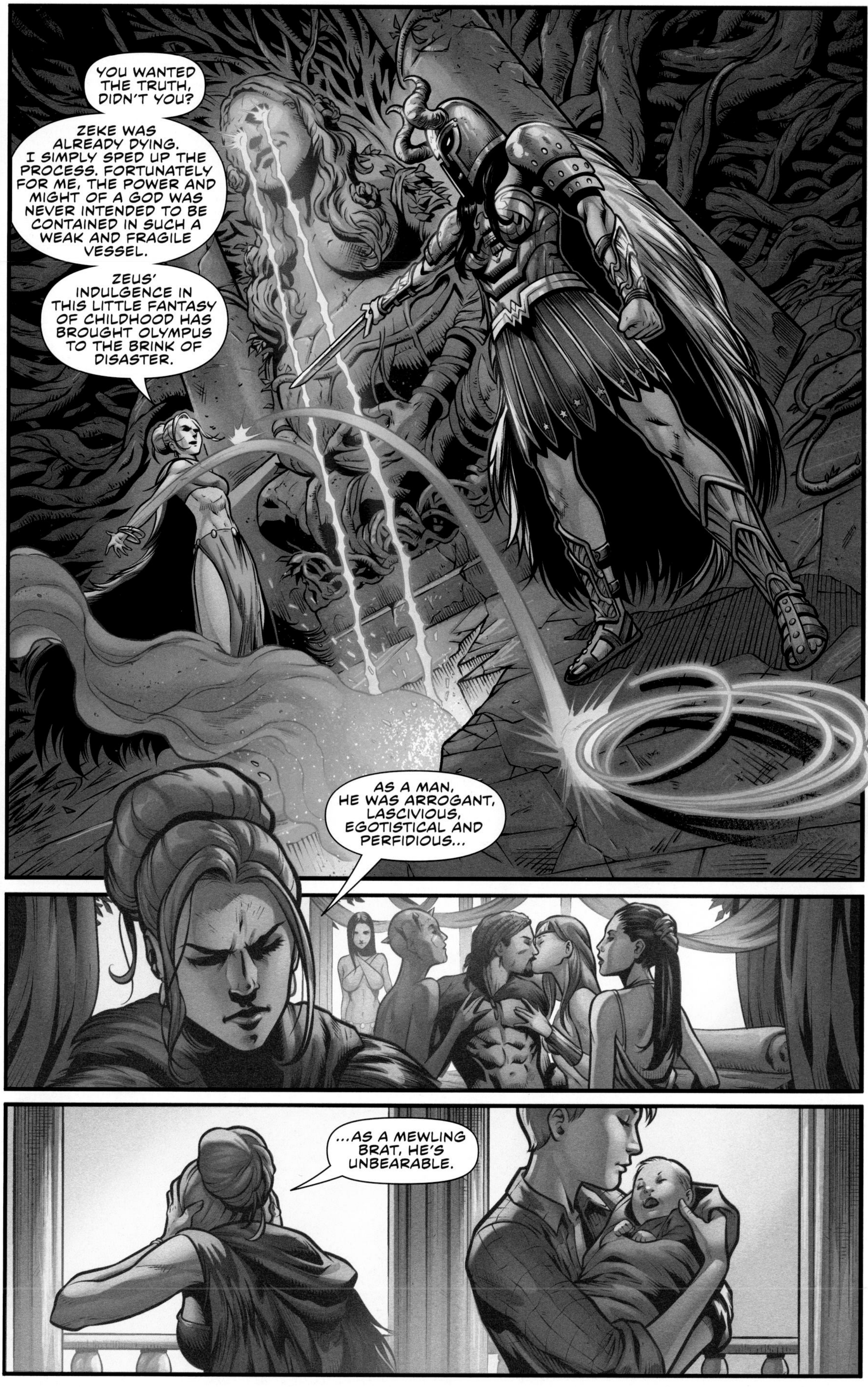
YOU WANTED THE TRUTH, DIDN'T YOU?
ZEKE WAS ALREADY DYING. I SIMPLY SPED UP THE PROCESS. FORTUNATELY FOR ME, THE POWER AND MIGHT OF A GOD WAS NEVER INTENDED TO BE CONTAINED IN SUCH A WEAK AND FRAGILE VESSEL.
ZEUS' INDULGENCE IN THIS LITTLE FANTASY OF CHILDHOOD HAS BROUGHT OLYMPUS TO THE BRINK OF DISASTER.
AS A MAN, HE WAS ARROGANT, LASCIVIOUS, EGOTISTICAL AND PERFIDIOUS...
...AS A MEWLING BRAT, HE'S UNBEARABLE.

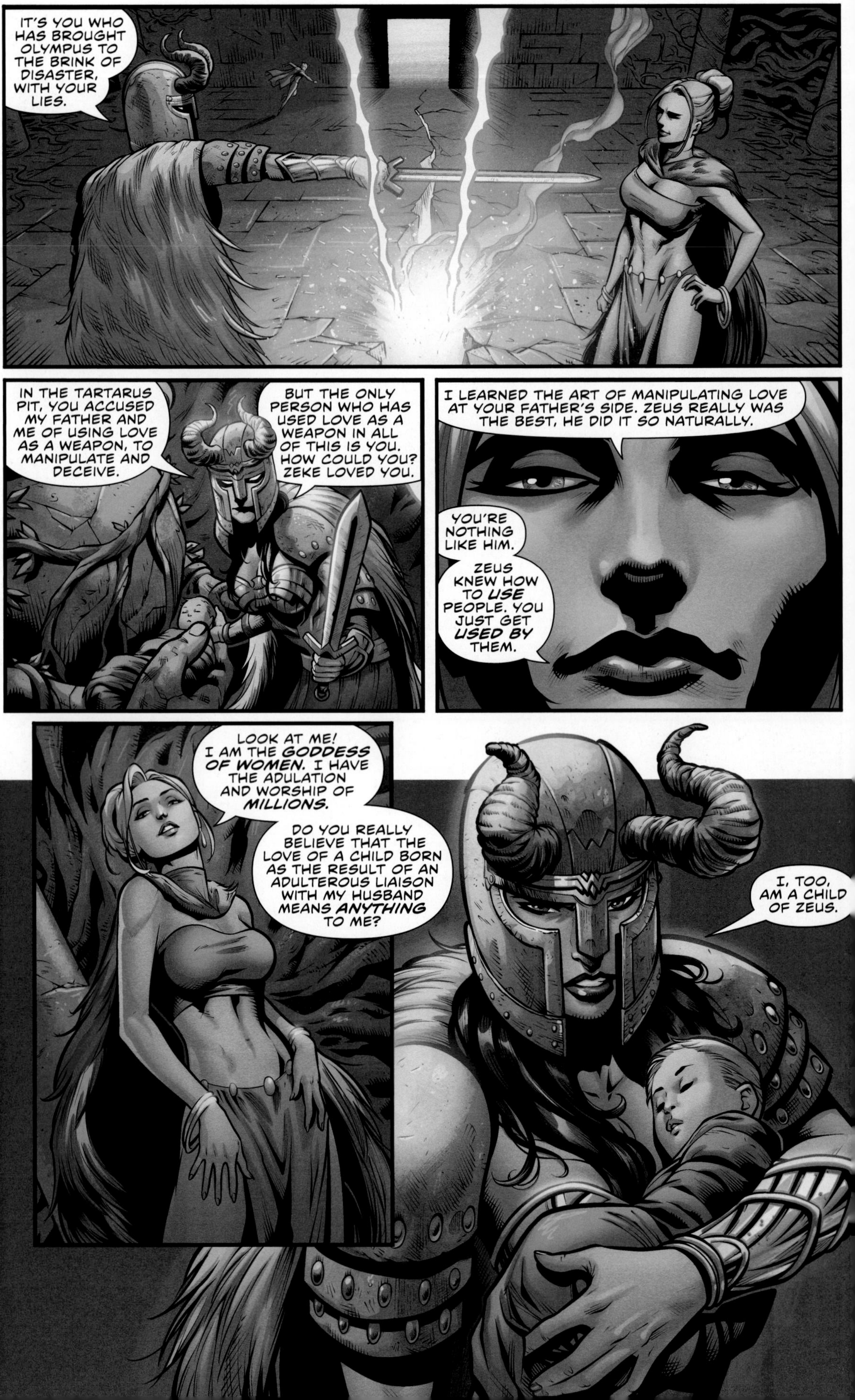
IT'S YOU WHO HAS BROUGHT OLYMPUS TO THE BRINK OF DISASTER, WITH YOUR LIES.
IN THE TARTARUS PIT, YOU ACCUSED MY FATHER AND ME OF USING LOVE AS A WEAPON, TO MANIPULATE AND DECEIVE.
BUT THE ONLY PERSON WHO HAS USED LOVE AS A WEAPON IN ALL OF THIS IS YOU. HOW COULD YOU? ZEKE LOVED YOU.
I LEARNED THE ART OF MANIPULATING LOVE AT YOUR FATHER'S SIDE. ZEUS REALLY WAS THE BEST, HE DID IT SO NATURALLY.
YOU'RE NOTHING LIKE HIM.
ZEUS KNEW HOW TO *USE* PEOPLE. YOU JUST GET *USED BY* THEM.
LOOK AT ME! I AM THE *GODDESS OF WOMEN.* I HAVE THE ADULATION AND WORSHIP OF *MILLIONS.*
DO YOU REALLY BELIEVE THAT THE LOVE OF A CHILD BORN AS THE RESULT OF AN ADULTEROUS LIAISON WITH MY HUSBAND MEANS *ANYTHING* TO ME?
I, TOO, AM A CHILD OF ZEUS.

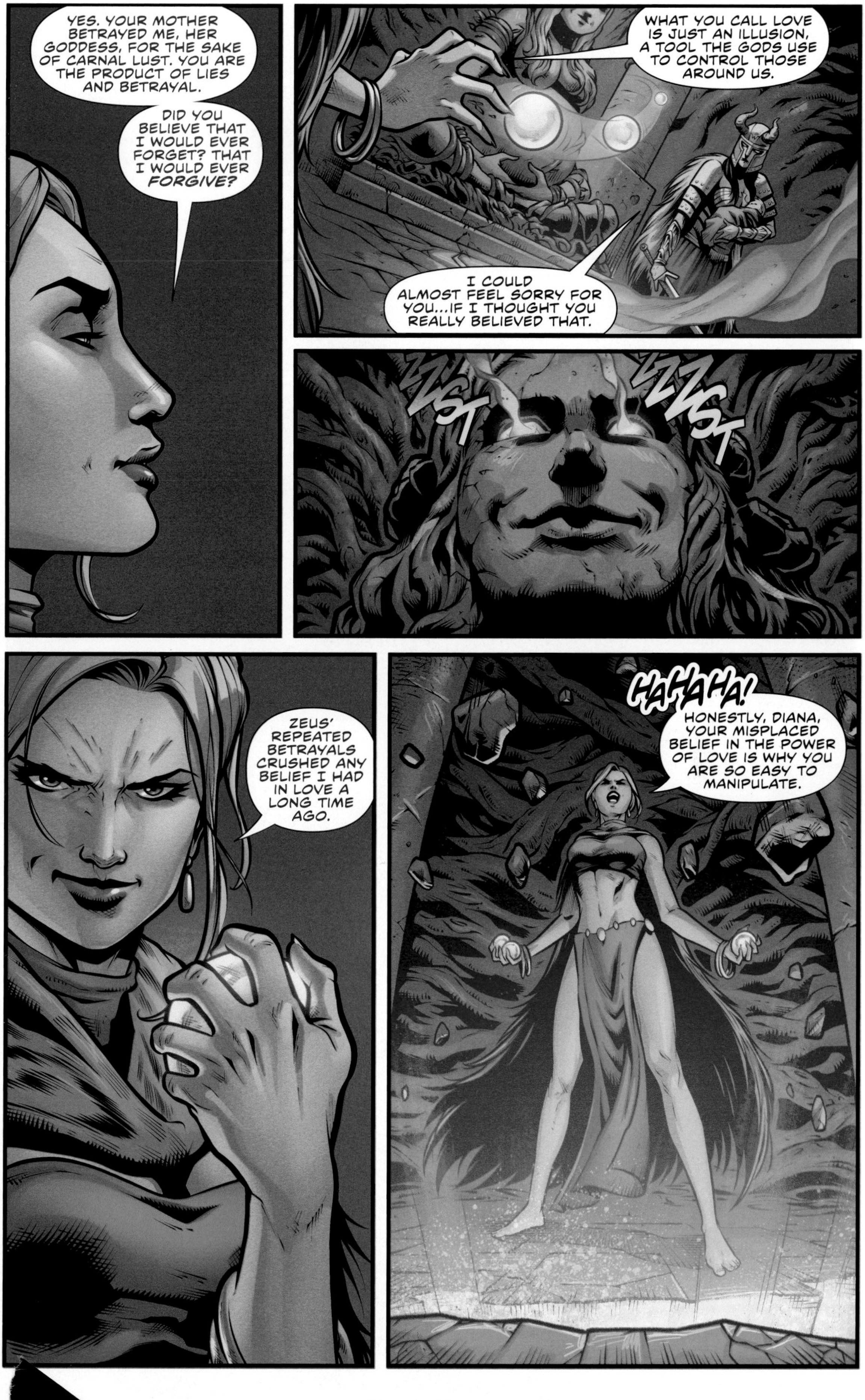
YES. YOUR MOTHER BETRAYED ME, HER GODDESS, FOR THE SAKE OF CARNAL LUST. YOU ARE THE PRODUCT OF LIES AND BETRAYAL.
DID YOU BELIEVE THAT I WOULD EVER FORGET? THAT I WOULD EVER *FORGIVE?*
WHAT YOU CALL LOVE IS JUST AN ILLUSION, A TOOL THE GODS USE TO CONTROL THOSE AROUND US.
I COULD ALMOST FEEL SORRY FOR YOU...IF I THOUGHT YOU REALLY BELIEVED THAT.
ZZZSST
ZZZSSST
ZEUS' REPEATED BETRAYALS CRUSHED ANY BELIEF I HAD IN LOVE A LONG TIME AGO.
HAHAHA!
HONESTLY, DIANA, YOUR MISPLACED BELIEF IN THE POWER OF LOVE IS WHY YOU ARE SO EASY TO MANIPULATE.

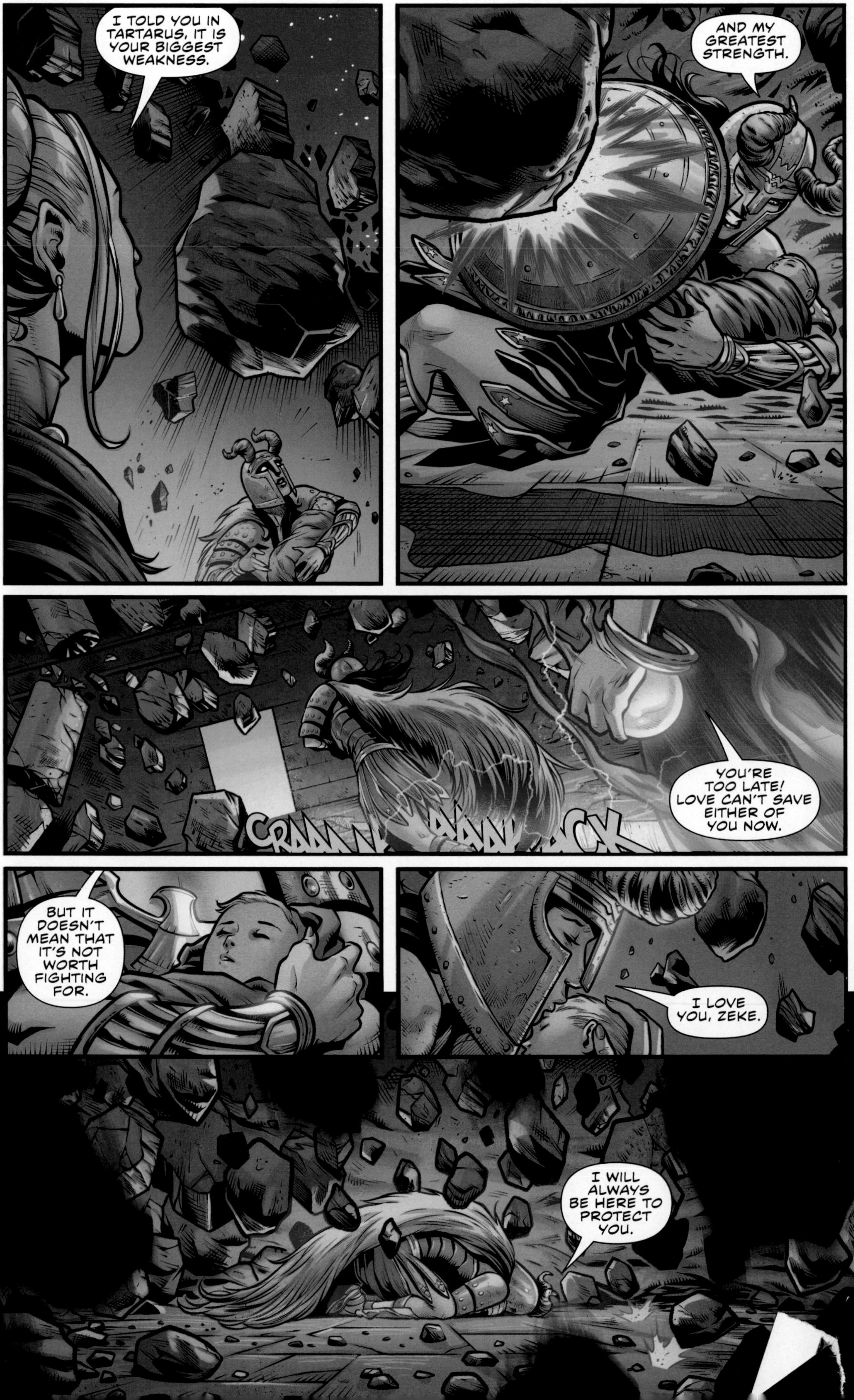
I TOLD YOU IN TARTARUS, IT IS YOUR BIGGEST WEAKNESS.
AND MY GREATEST STRENGTH.
YOU'RE TOO LATE! LOVE CAN'T SAVE EITHER OF YOU NOW.
BUT IT DOESN'T MEAN THAT IT'S NOT WORTH FIGHTING FOR.
I LOVE YOU, ZEKE.
I WILL ALWAYS BE HERE TO PROTECT YOU.

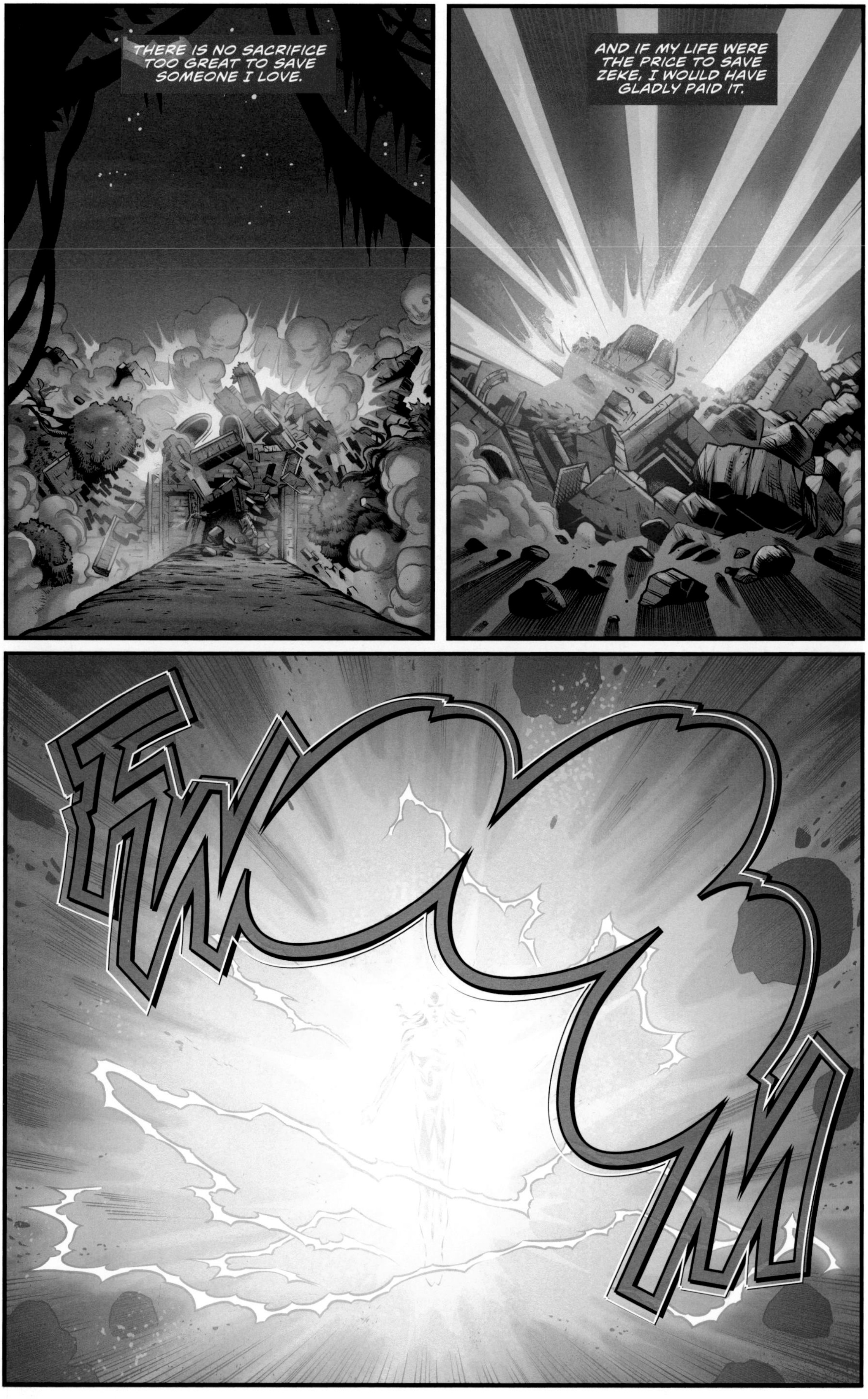
THERE IS NO SACRIFICE TOO GREAT TO SAVE SOMEONE I LOVE.
AND IF MY LIFE WERE THE PRICE TO SAVE ZEKE, I WOULD HAVE GLADLY PAID IT.
FWOOOM

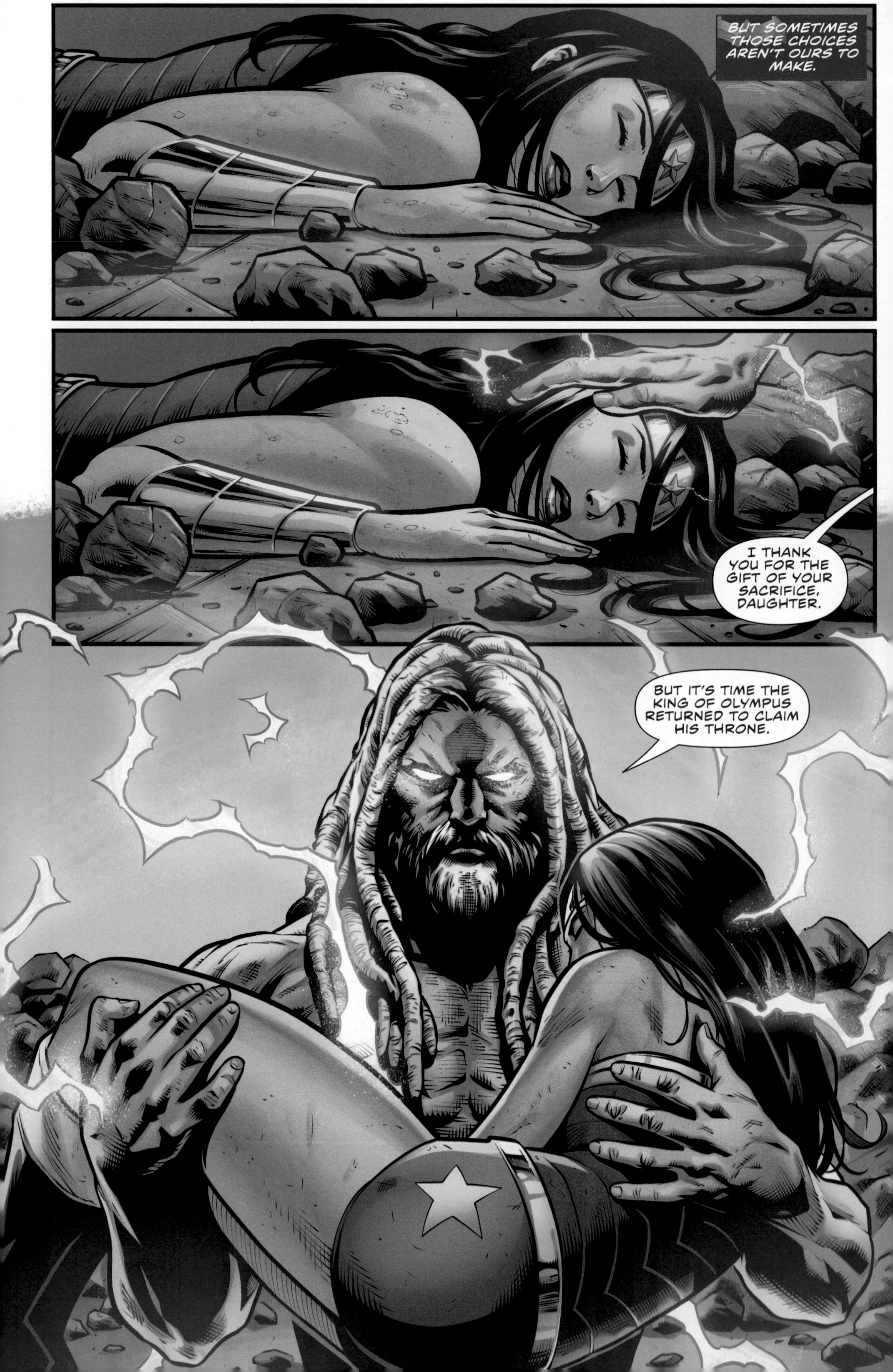
BUT SOMETIMES THOSE CHOICES AREN'T OURS TO MAKE.
I THANK YOU FOR THE GIFT OF YOUR SACRIFICE, DAUGHTER.
BUT IT'S TIME THE KING OF OLYMPUS RETURNED TO CLAIM HIS THRONE.

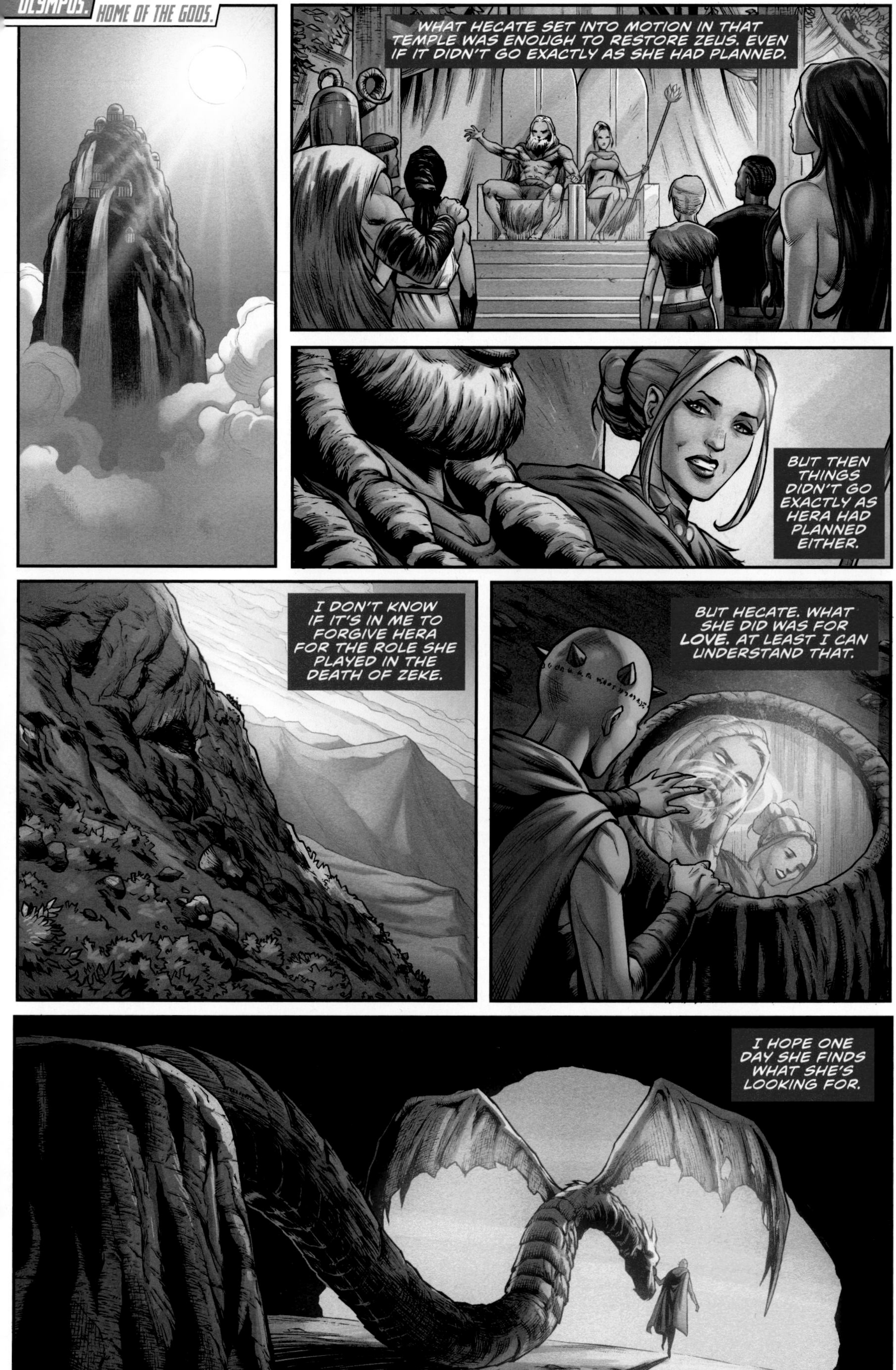
OLYMPUS. HOME OF THE GODS.
WHAT HECATE SET INTO MOTION IN THAT TEMPLE WAS ENOUGH TO RESTORE ZEUS. EVEN IF IT DIDN'T GO EXACTLY AS SHE HAD PLANNED.
BUT THEN THINGS DIDN'T GO EXACTLY AS HERA HAD PLANNED EITHER.
I DON'T KNOW IF IT'S IN ME TO FORGIVE HERA FOR THE ROLE SHE PLAYED IN THE DEATH OF ZEKE.
BUT HECATE. WHAT SHE DID WAS FOR LOVE. AT LEAST I CAN UNDERSTAND THAT.
I HOPE ONE DAY SHE FINDS WHAT SHE'S LOOKING FOR.

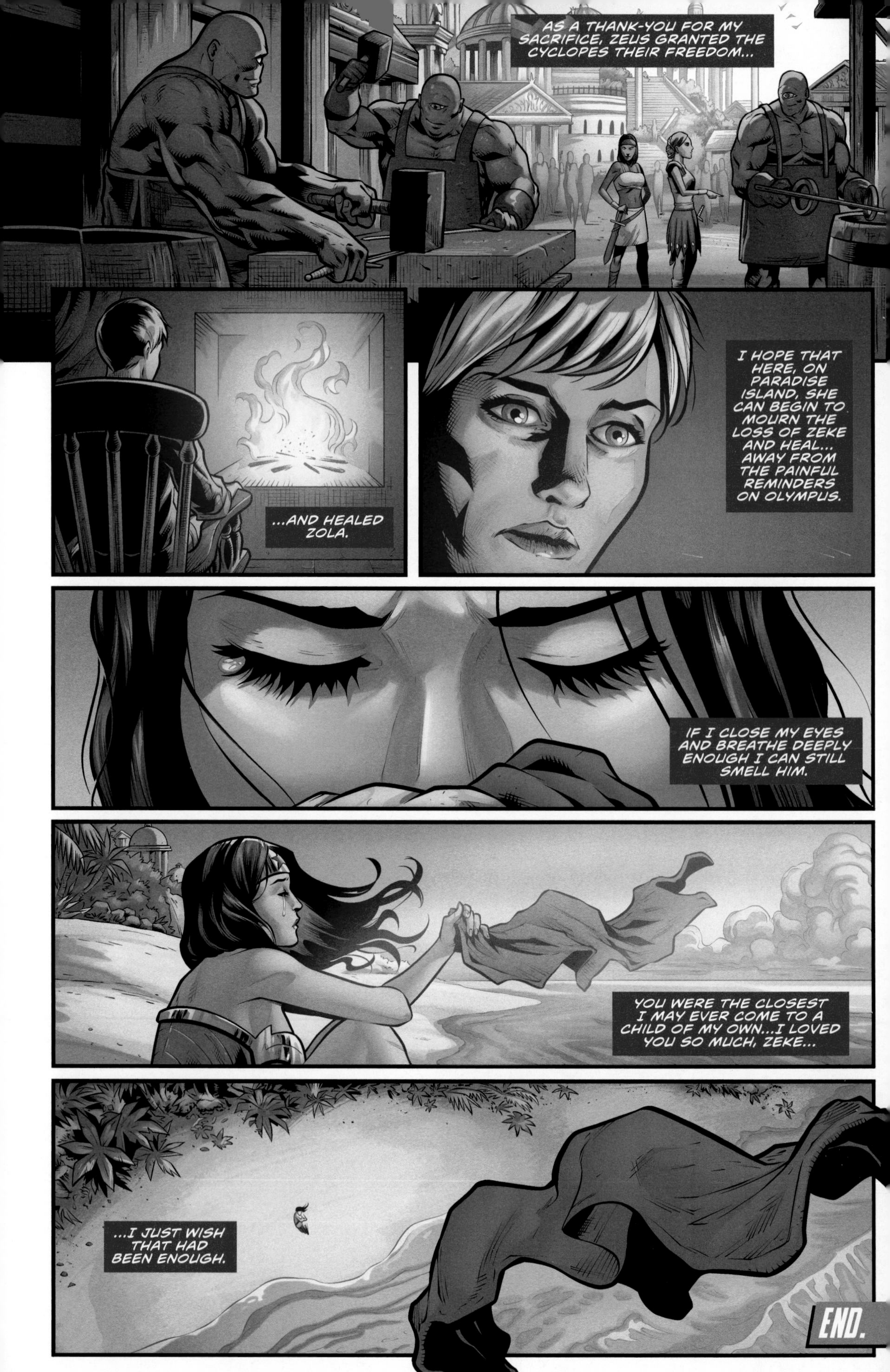
AS A THANK-YOU FOR MY SACRIFICE, ZEUS GRANTED THE CYCLOPES THEIR FREEDOM...
...AND HEALED ZOLA.
I HOPE THAT HERE, ON PARADISE ISLAND, SHE CAN BEGIN TO MOURN THE LOSS OF ZEKE AND HEAL... AWAY FROM THE PAINFUL REMINDERS ON OLYMPUS.
IF I CLOSE MY EYES AND BREATHE DEEPLY ENOUGH I CAN STILL SMELL HIM.
YOU WERE THE CLOSEST I MAY EVER COME TO A CHILD OF MY OWN...I LOVED YOU SO MUCH, ZEKE...
...I JUST WISH THAT HAD BEEN ENOUGH.
END.

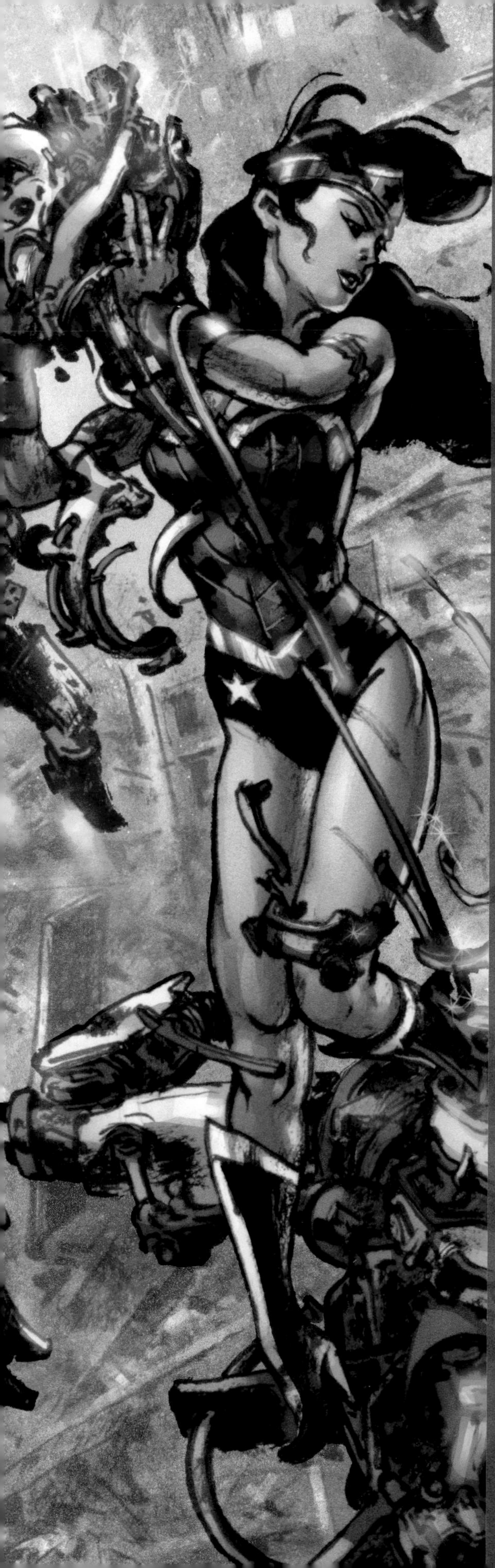

VARIANT COVER GALLERY

WONDER WOMAN #48
ADULT COLORING BOOK VARIANT COVER
BY EMANUELA LUPACCHINO

WONDER WOMAN #49
VARIANT COVER BY NEAL ADAMS AND
TERRY DODSON WITH ALEX SINCLAIR
TRIPTYCH VARIANT COVER
BY KIM JUNG GI

WONDER WOMAN #50
BATMAN V SUPERMAN VARIANT COVER
BY MASSIMO CARNEVALE

WONDER WOMAN #51
VARIANT COVER BY JOHN ROMITA JR.
AND SCOTT HANNA WITH DEAN WHITE

WONDER WOMAN #52
VARIANT COVER BY DAVID FINCH
AND MATT BANNING

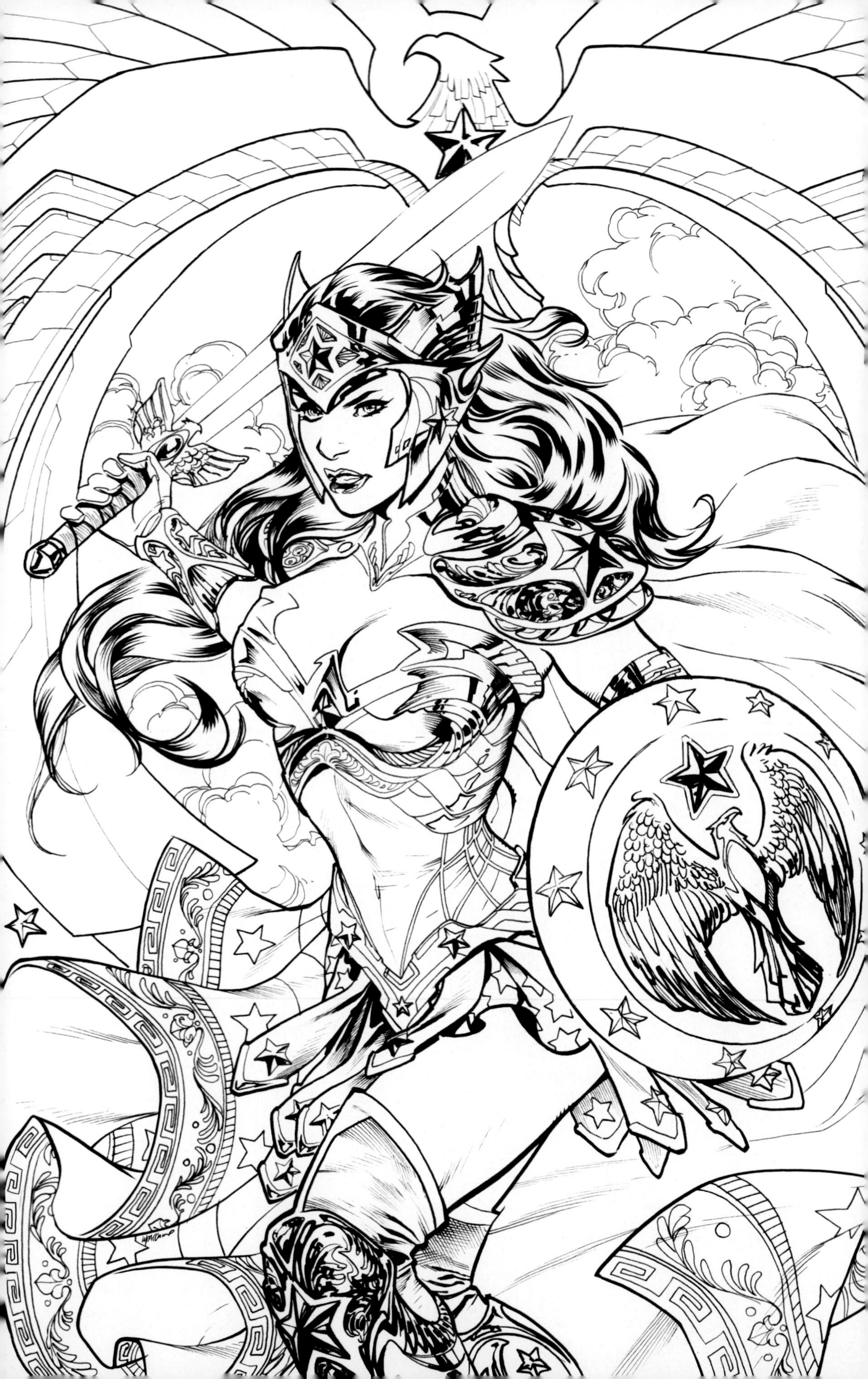

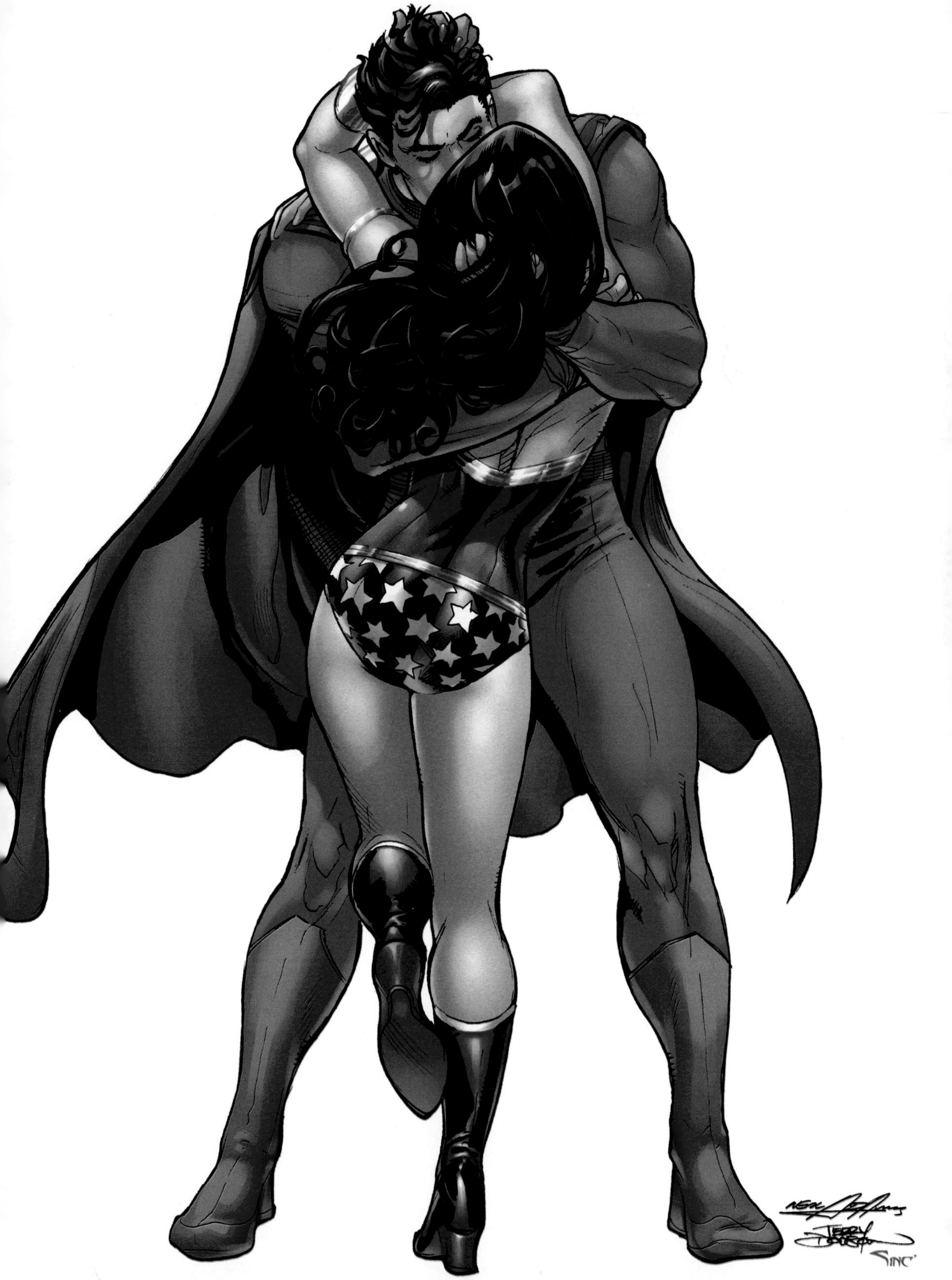

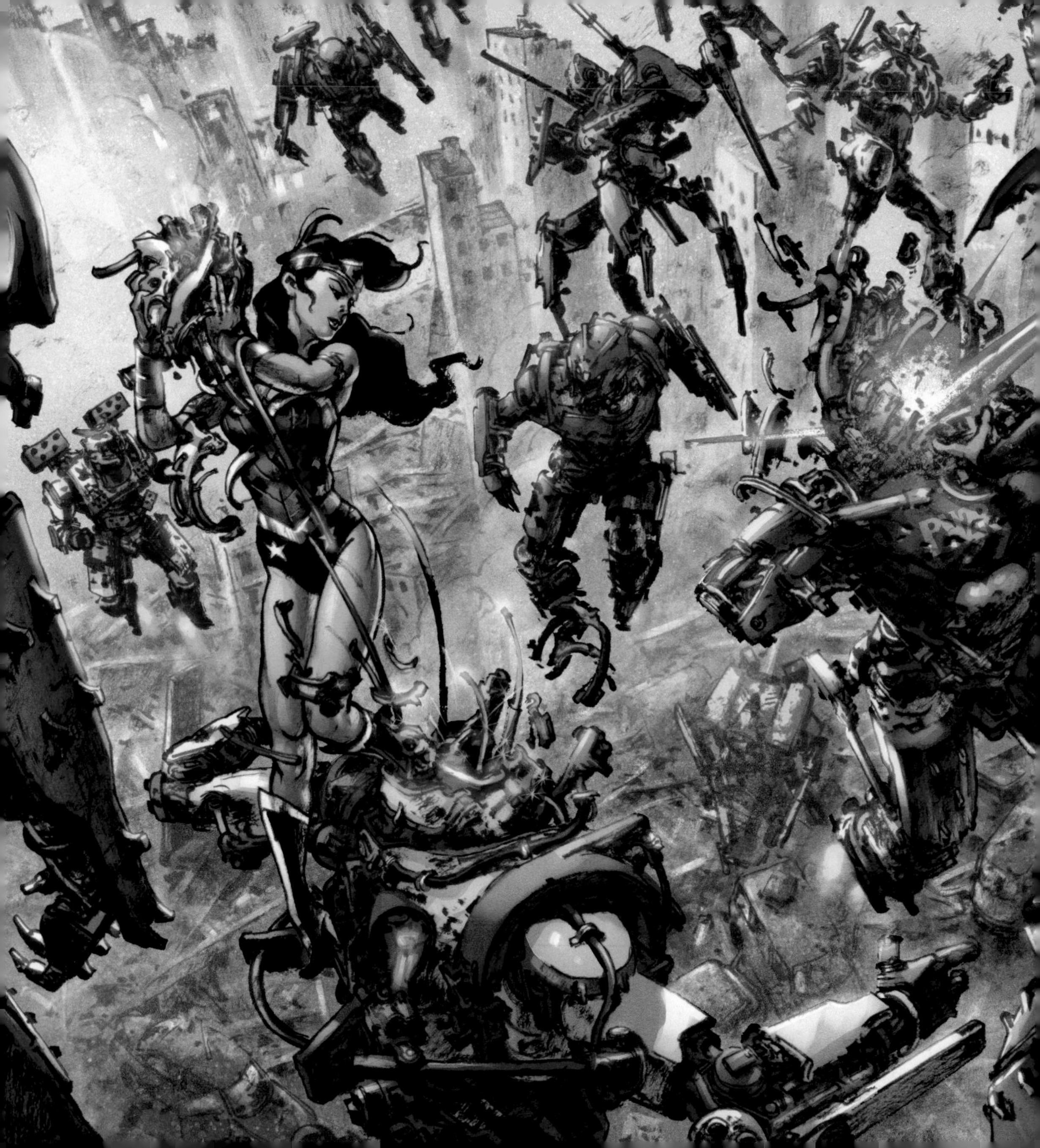

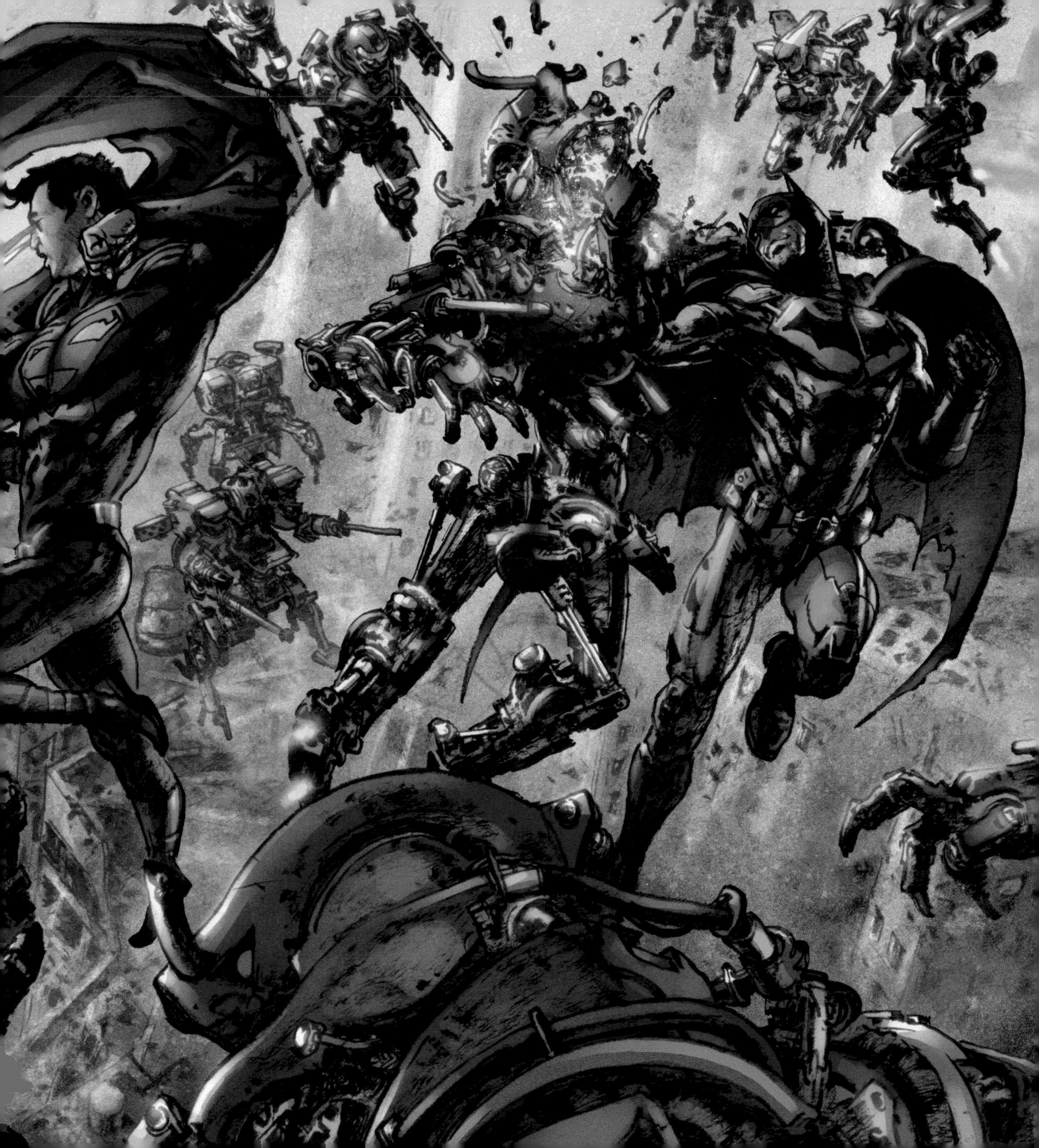

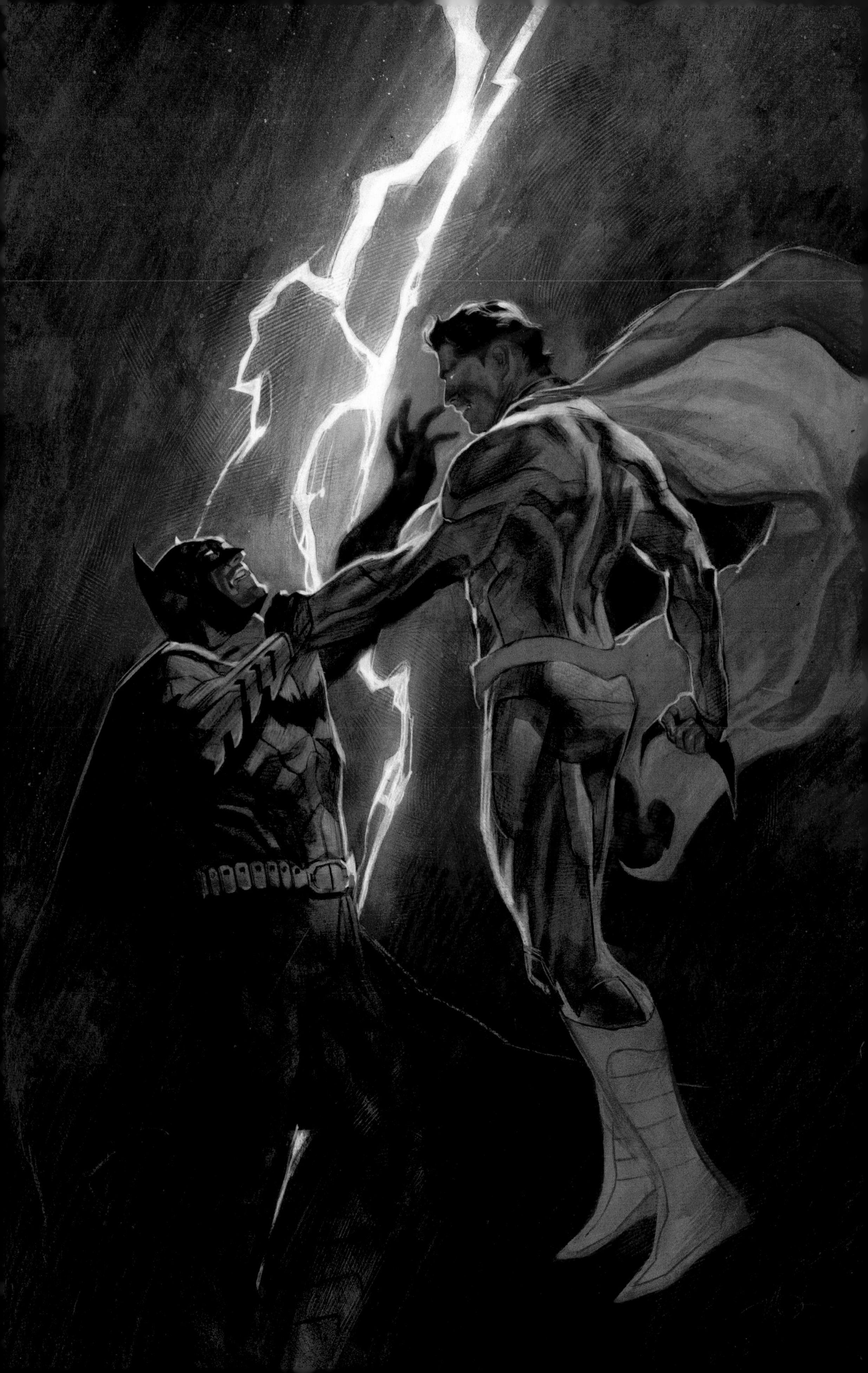

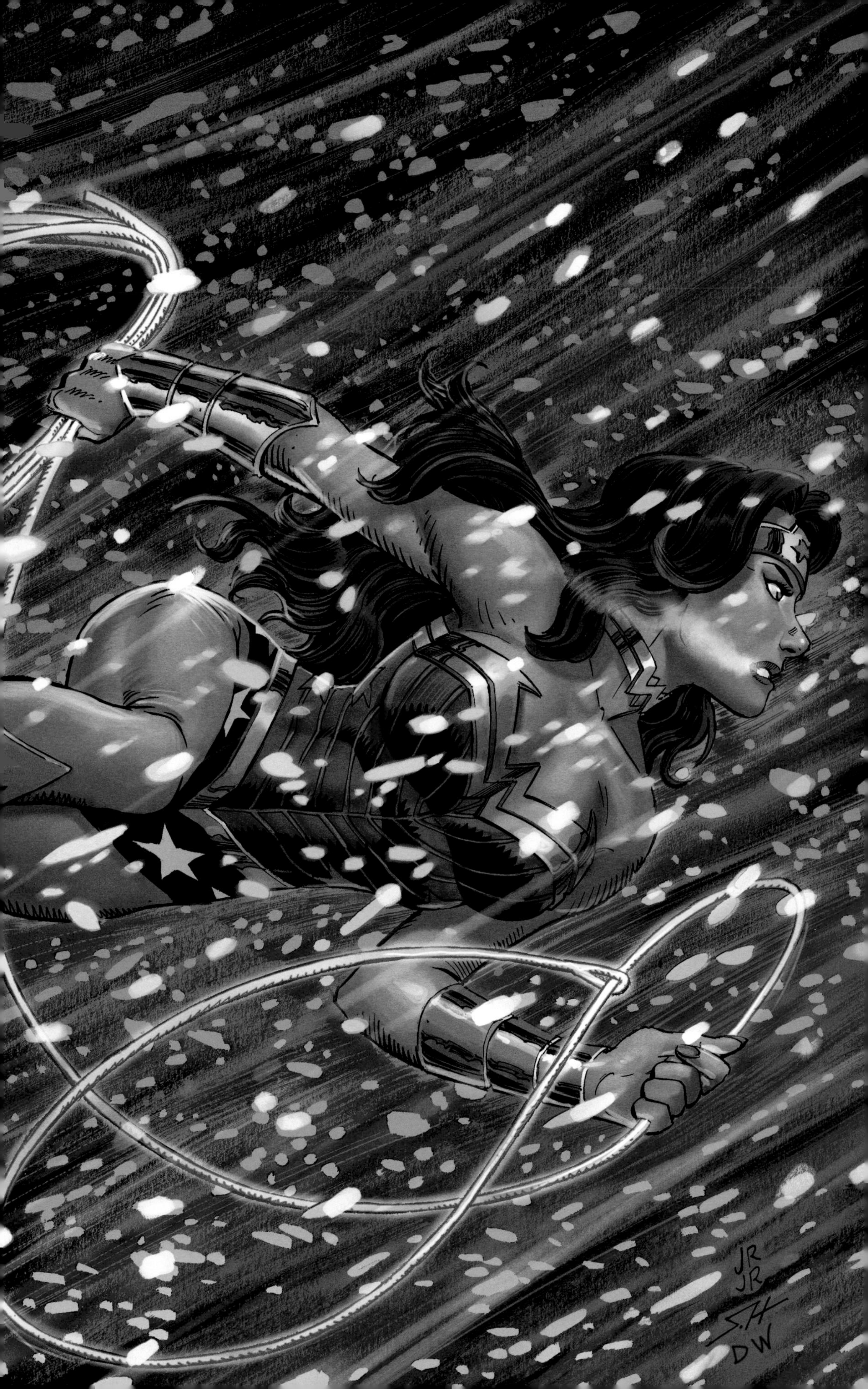
JR
JR
DW

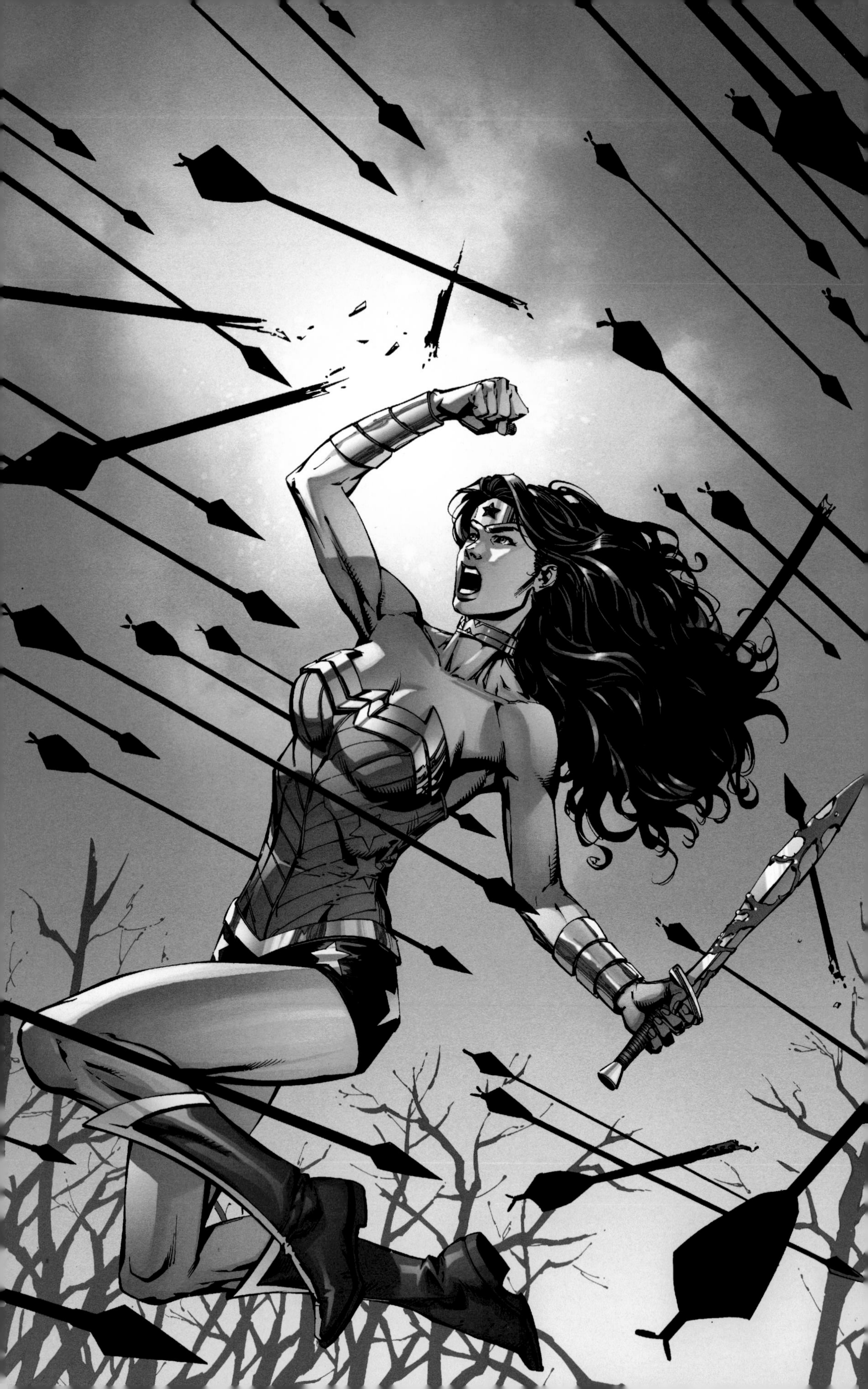

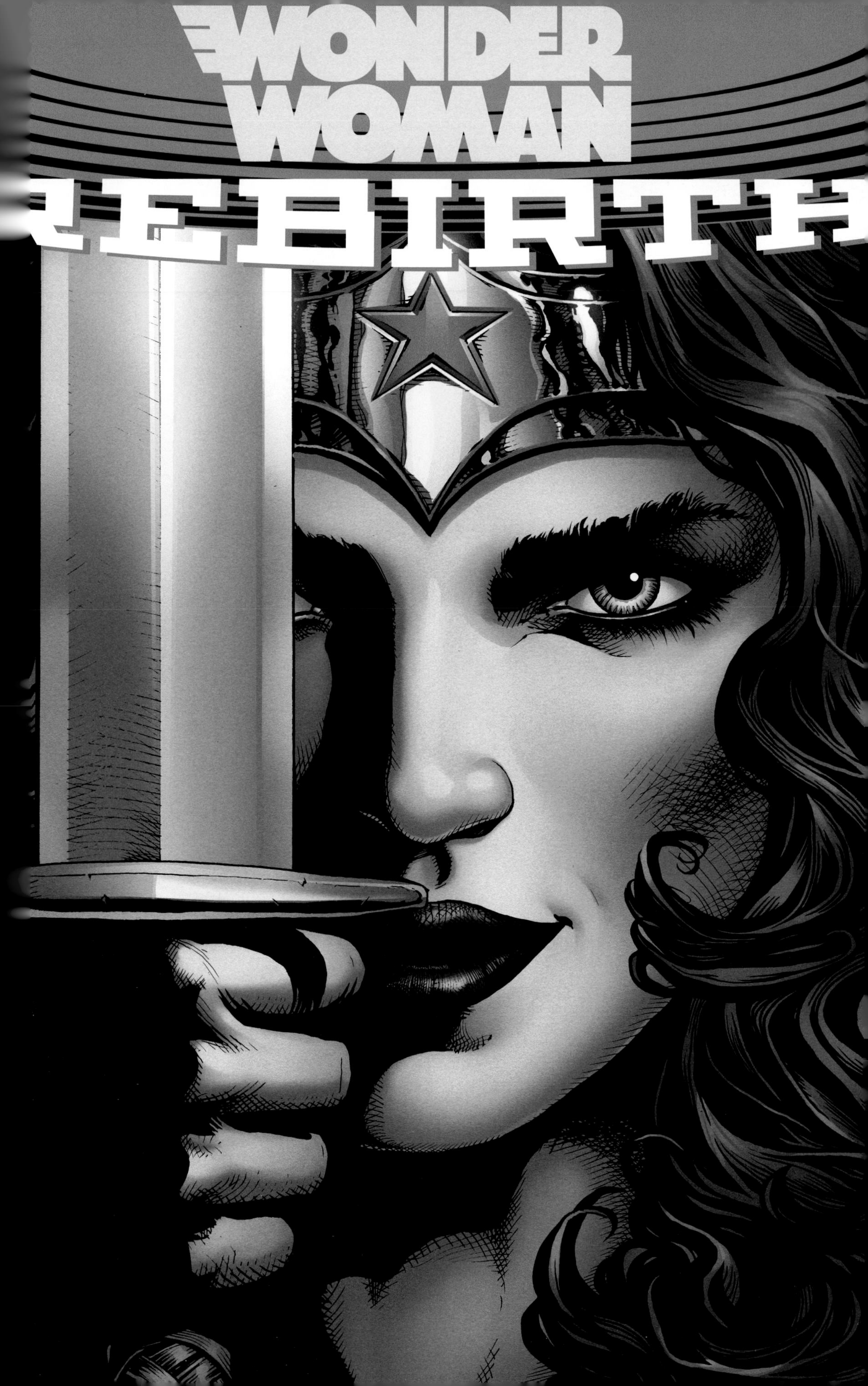
WONDER
WOMAN
REBIRTH

The future (and past) of the DC Universe starts with DC UNIVERSE: REBIRTH!

Explore the changing world of Wonder Woman in this special bonus preview of **WONDER WOMAN: REBIRTH #1!**

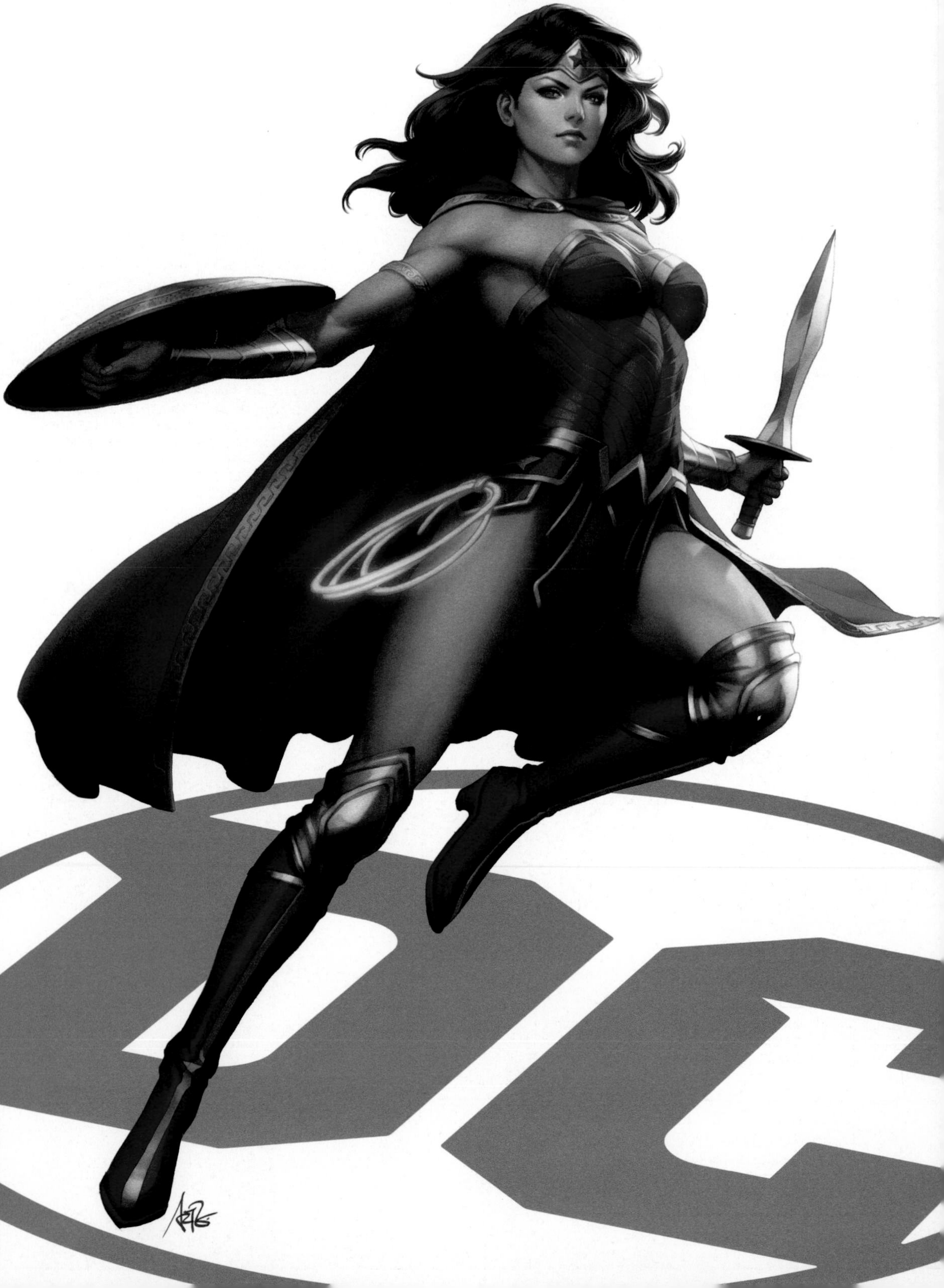

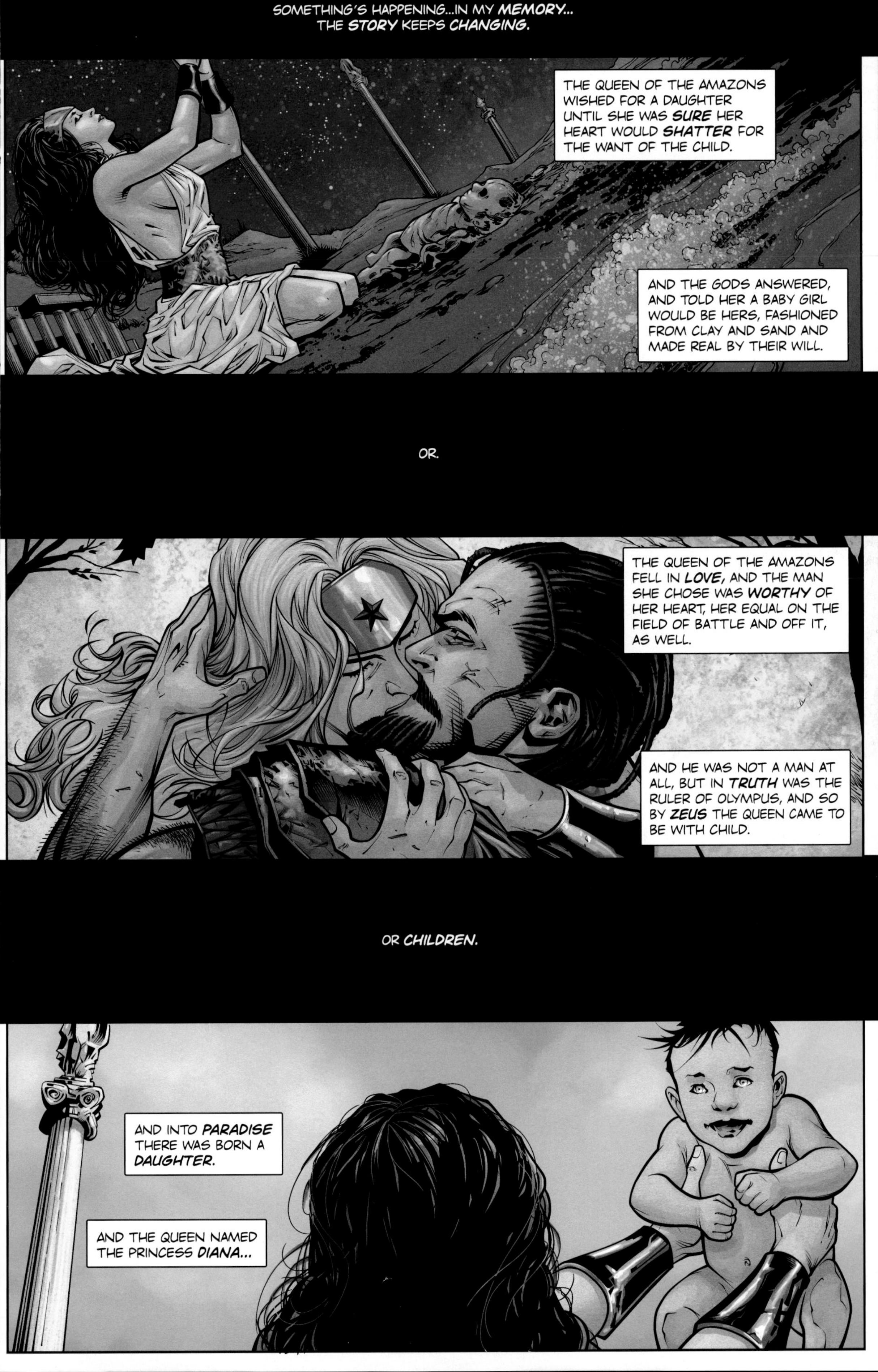
SOMETHING'S HAPPENING...IN MY MEMORY... THE STORY KEEPS CHANGING.
THE QUEEN OF THE AMAZONS WISHED FOR A DAUGHTER UNTIL SHE WAS SURE HER HEART WOULD SHATTER FOR THE WANT OF THE CHILD.
AND THE GODS ANSWERED, AND TOLD HER A BABY GIRL WOULD BE HERS, FASHIONED FROM CLAY AND SAND AND MADE REAL BY THEIR WILL.
OR.
THE QUEEN OF THE AMAZONS FELL IN LOVE, AND THE MAN SHE CHOSE WAS WORTHY OF HER HEART, HER EQUAL ON THE FIELD OF BATTLE AND OFF IT, AS WELL.
AND HE WAS NOT A MAN AT ALL, BUT IN TRUTH WAS THE RULER OF OLYMPUS, AND SO BY ZEUS THE QUEEN CAME TO BE WITH CHILD.
OR CHILDREN.
AND INTO PARADISE THERE WAS BORN A DAUGHTER.
AND THE QUEEN NAMED THE PRINCESS DIANA...

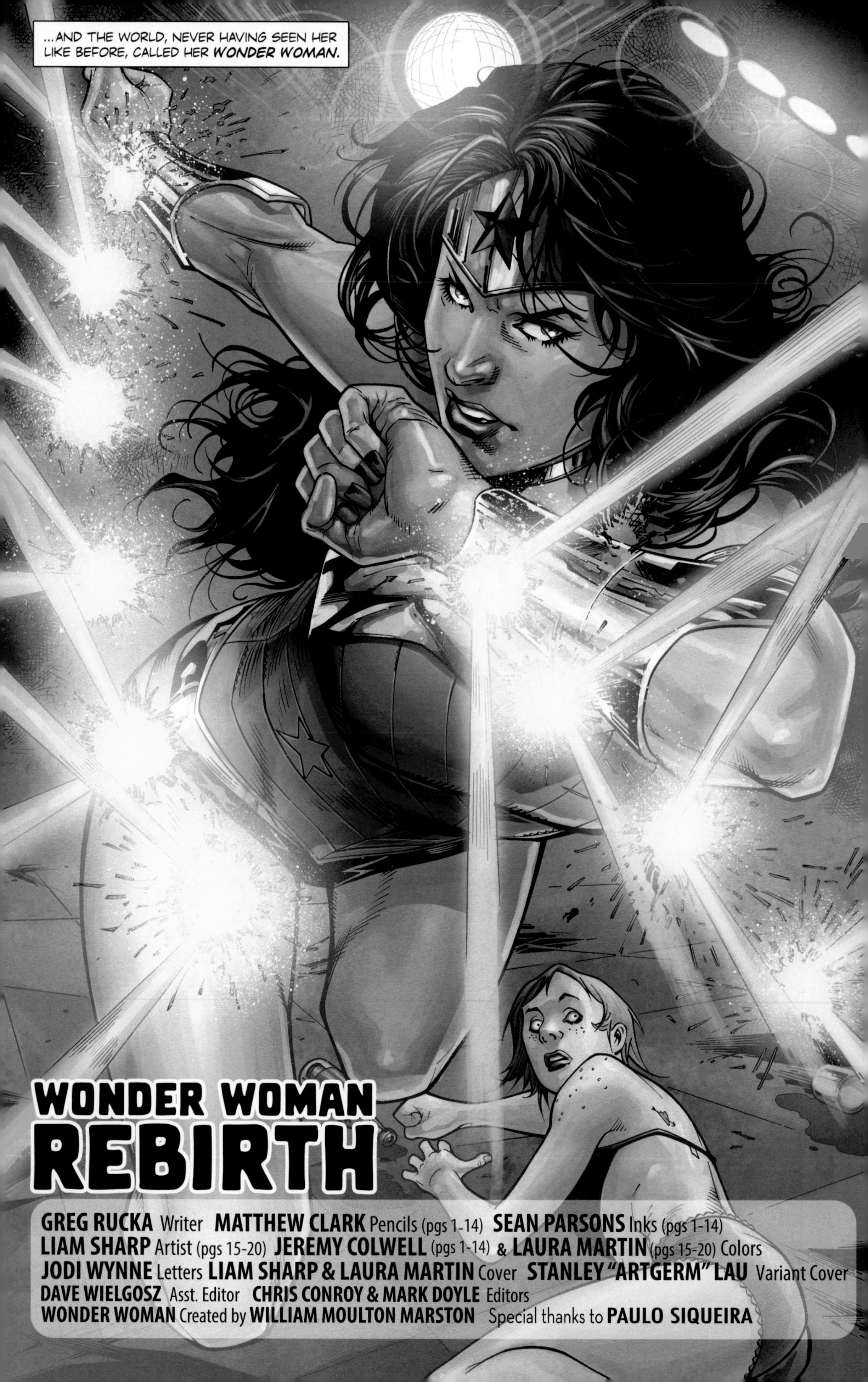

...AND THE WORLD, NEVER HAVING SEEN HER LIKE BEFORE, CALLED HER WONDER WOMAN.
WONDER WOMAN REBIRTH
GREG RUCKA Writer MATTHEW CLARK Pencils (pgs 1-14) SEAN PARSONS Inks (pgs 1-14)
LIAM SHARP Artist (pgs 15-20) JEREMY COLWELL (pgs 1-14) & LAURA MARTIN (pgs 15-20) Colors
JODI WYNNE Letters LIAM SHARP & LAURA MARTIN Cover STANLEY "ARTGERM" LAU Variant Cover
DAVE WIELGOSZ Asst. Editor CHRIS CONROY & MARK DOYLE Editors
WONDER WOMAN Created by WILLIAM MOULTON MARSTON Special thanks to PAULO SIQUEIRA

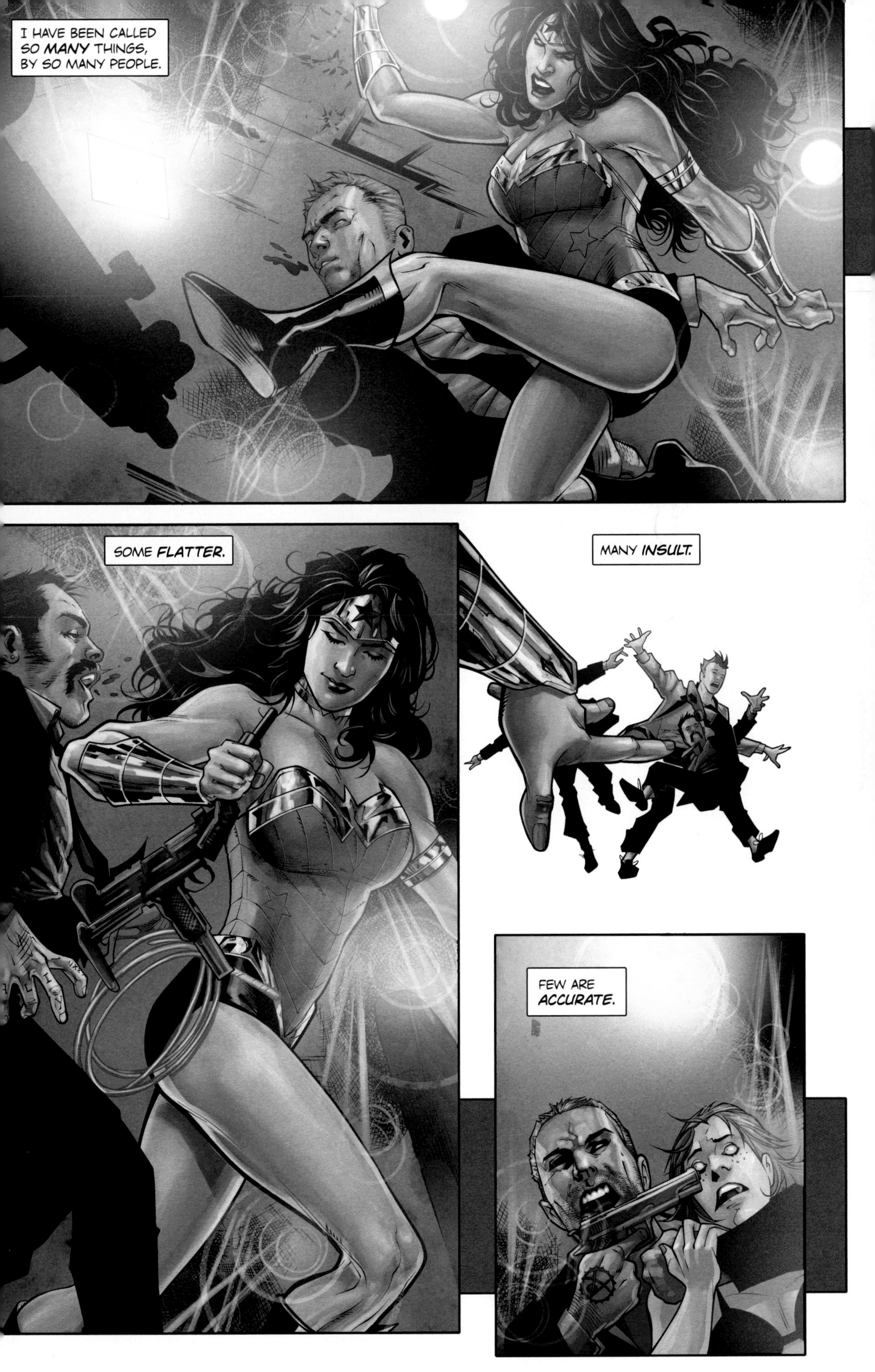
I HAVE BEEN CALLED SO MANY THINGS, BY SO MANY PEOPLE.
SOME FLATTER.
MANY INSULT.
FEW ARE ACCURATE.

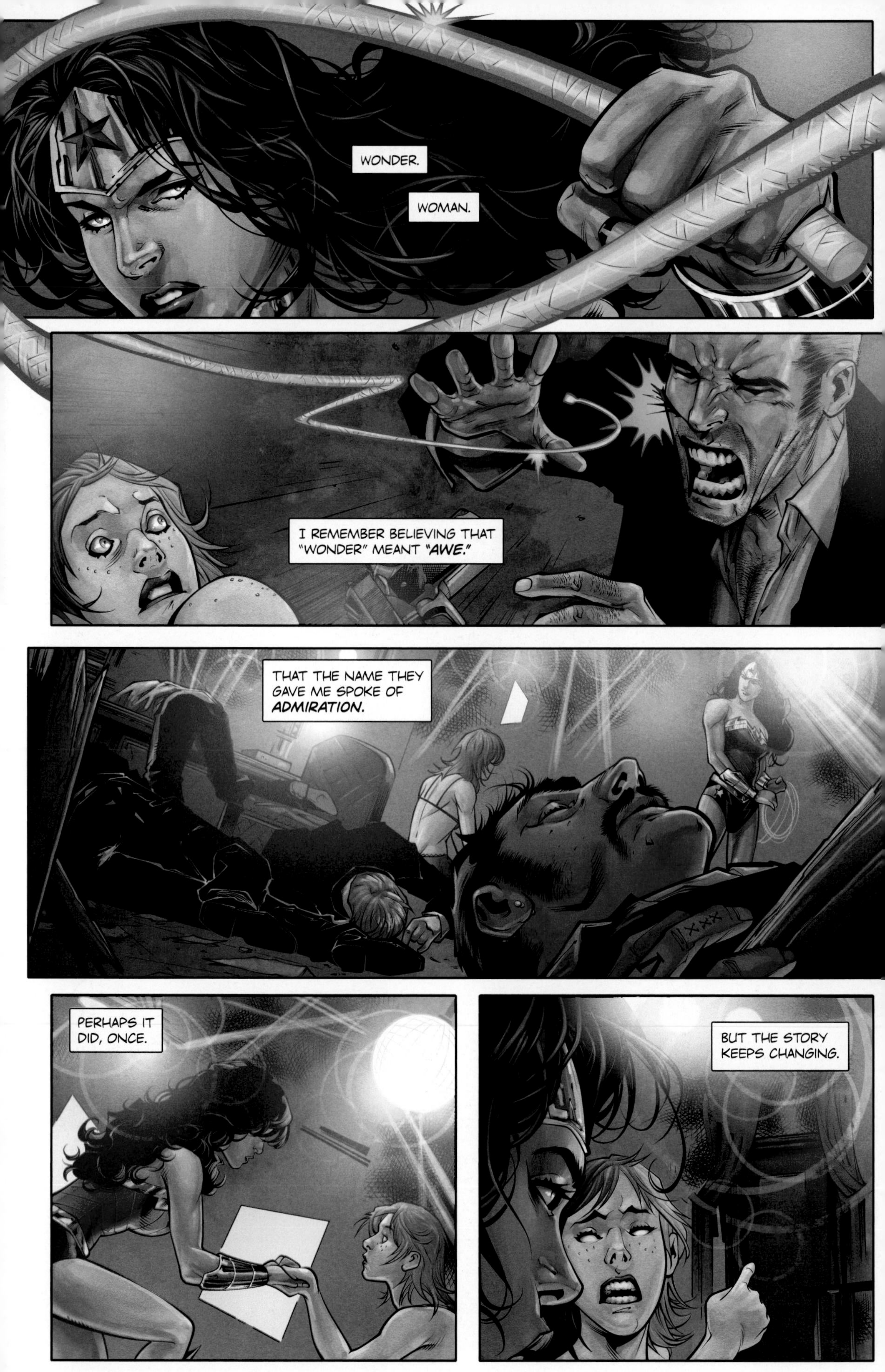
WONDER.
WOMAN.
I REMEMBER BELIEVING THAT "WONDER" MEANT ***"AWE."***
THAT THE NAME THEY GAVE ME SPOKE OF ***ADMIRATION.***
PERHAPS IT DID, ONCE.
BUT THE STORY KEEPS CHANGING.

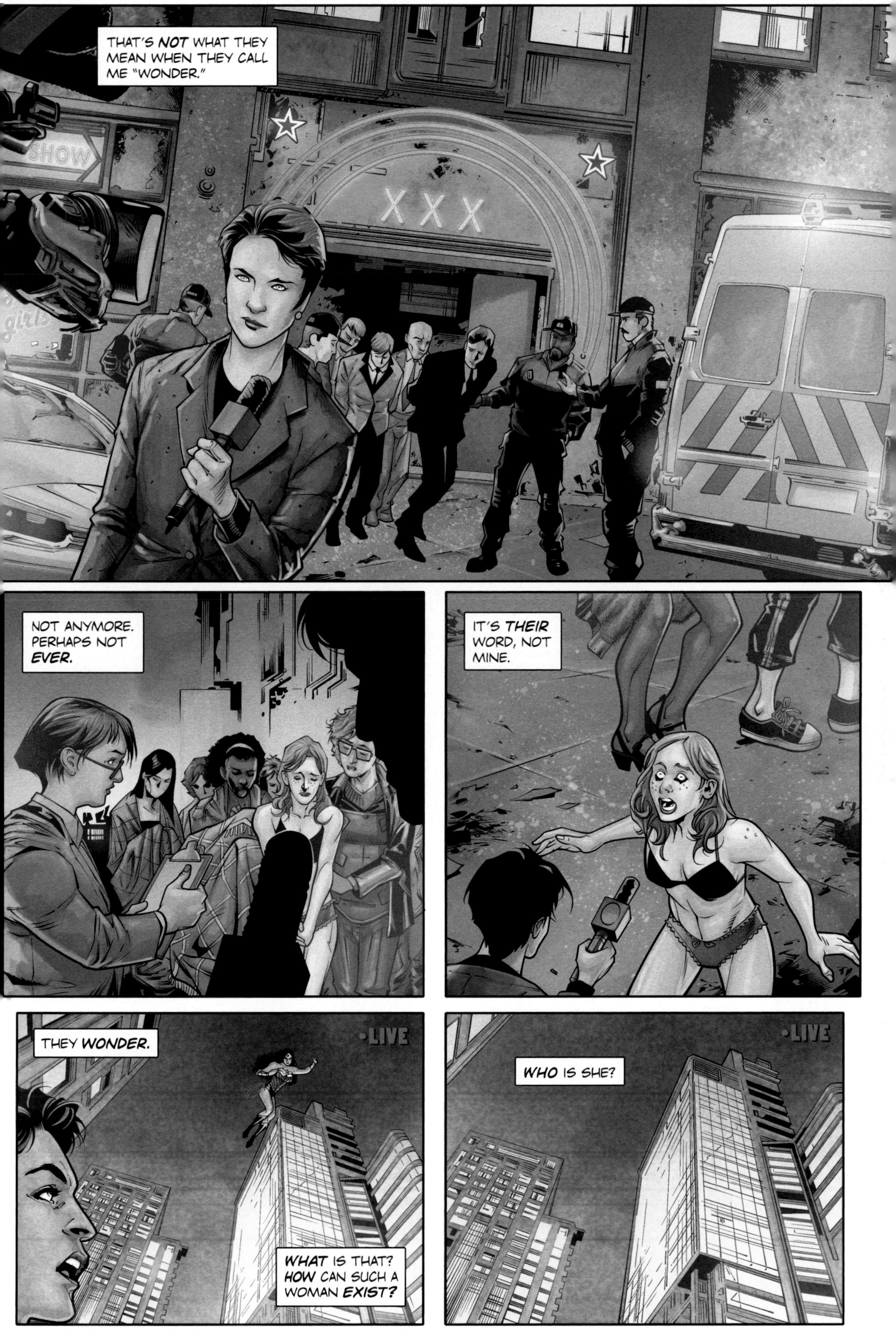
THAT'S NOT WHAT THEY MEAN WHEN THEY CALL ME "WONDER."
SHOW
XXX
NOT ANYMORE. PERHAPS NOT EVER.
IT'S THEIR WORD, NOT MINE.
THEY WONDER.
•LIVE
WHAT IS THAT? HOW CAN SUCH A WOMAN EXIST?
•LIVE
WHO IS SHE?

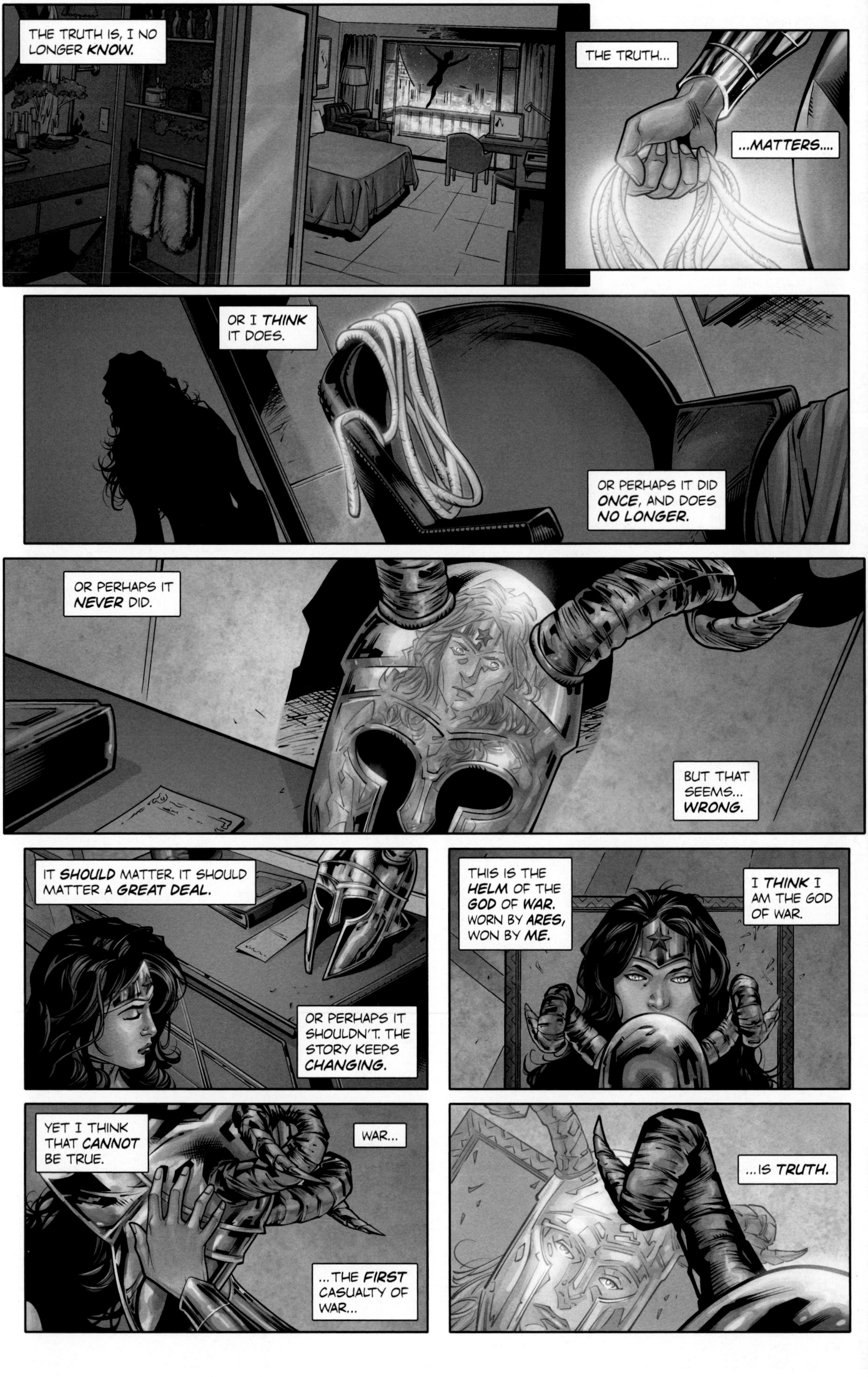

THE TRUTH IS, I NO LONGER KNOW.
THE TRUTH...
...MATTERS....
OR I THINK IT DOES.
OR PERHAPS IT DID ONCE, AND DOES NO LONGER.
OR PERHAPS IT NEVER DID.
BUT THAT SEEMS... WRONG.
IT SHOULD MATTER. IT SHOULD MATTER A GREAT DEAL.
OR PERHAPS IT SHOULDN'T. THE STORY KEEPS CHANGING.
THIS IS THE HELM OF THE GOD OF WAR. WORN BY ARES, WON BY ME.
I THINK I AM THE GOD OF WAR.
YET I THINK THAT CANNOT BE TRUE.
WAR...
...THE FIRST CASUALTY OF WAR...
...IS TRUTH.

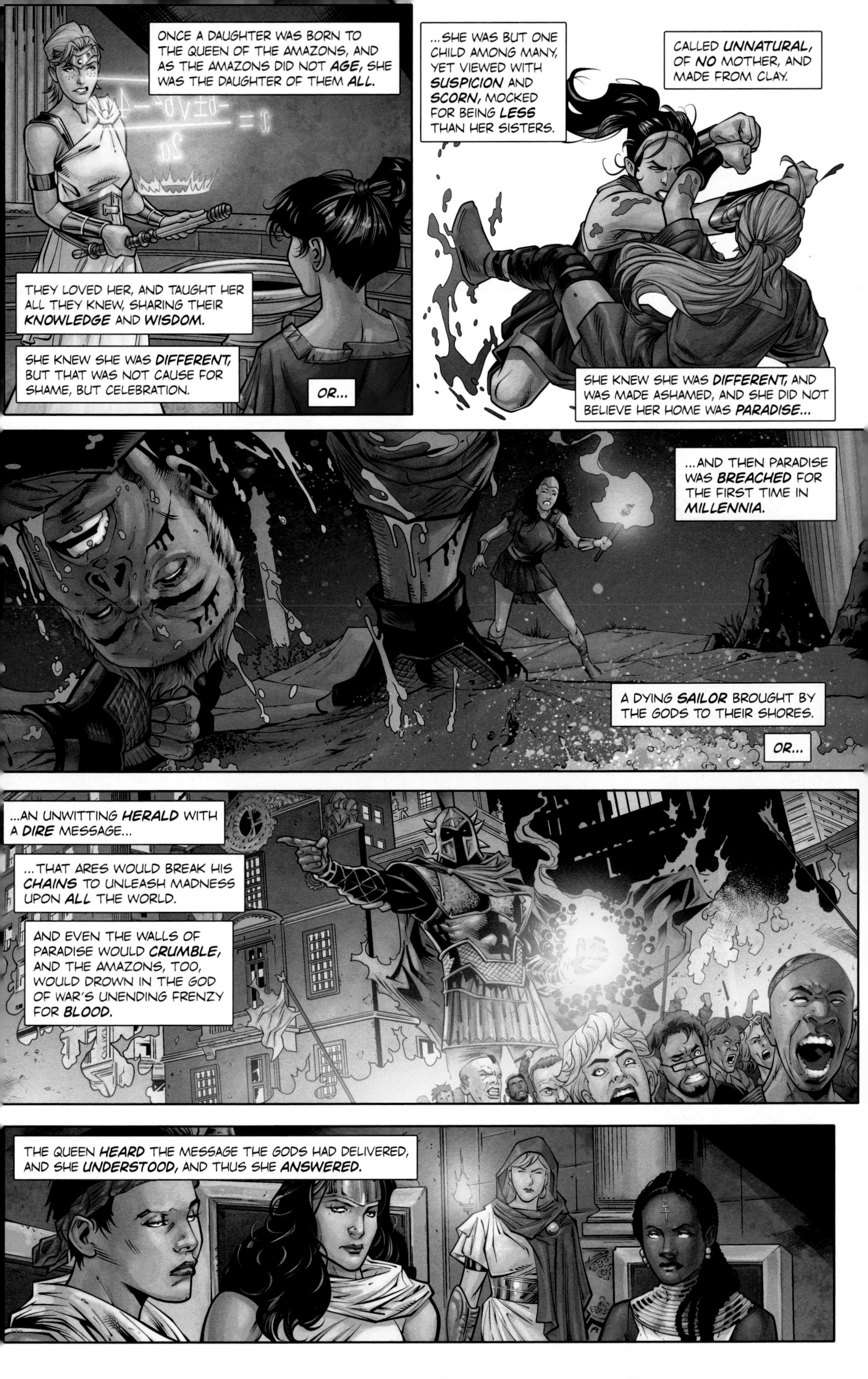

ONCE A DAUGHTER WAS BORN TO THE QUEEN OF THE AMAZONS, AND AS THE AMAZONS DID NOT AGE, SHE WAS THE DAUGHTER OF THEM ALL.
THEY LOVED HER, AND TAUGHT HER ALL THEY KNEW, SHARING THEIR KNOWLEDGE AND WISDOM.
SHE KNEW SHE WAS DIFFERENT, BUT THAT WAS NOT CAUSE FOR SHAME, BUT CELEBRATION.
OR...
...SHE WAS BUT ONE CHILD AMONG MANY, YET VIEWED WITH SUSPICION AND SCORN, MOCKED FOR BEING LESS THAN HER SISTERS.
CALLED UNNATURAL, OF NO MOTHER, AND MADE FROM CLAY.
SHE KNEW SHE WAS DIFFERENT, AND WAS MADE ASHAMED, AND SHE DID NOT BELIEVE HER HOME WAS PARADISE...
...AND THEN PARADISE WAS BREACHED FOR THE FIRST TIME IN MILLENNIA.
A DYING SAILOR BROUGHT BY THE GODS TO THEIR SHORES.
OR...
...AN UNWITTING HERALD WITH A DIRE MESSAGE...
...THAT ARES WOULD BREAK HIS CHAINS TO UNLEASH MADNESS UPON ALL THE WORLD.
AND EVEN THE WALLS OF PARADISE WOULD CRUMBLE, AND THE AMAZONS, TOO, WOULD DROWN IN THE GOD OF WAR'S UNENDING FRENZY FOR BLOOD.
THE QUEEN HEARD THE MESSAGE THE GODS HAD DELIVERED, AND SHE UNDERSTOOD, AND THUS SHE ANSWERED.

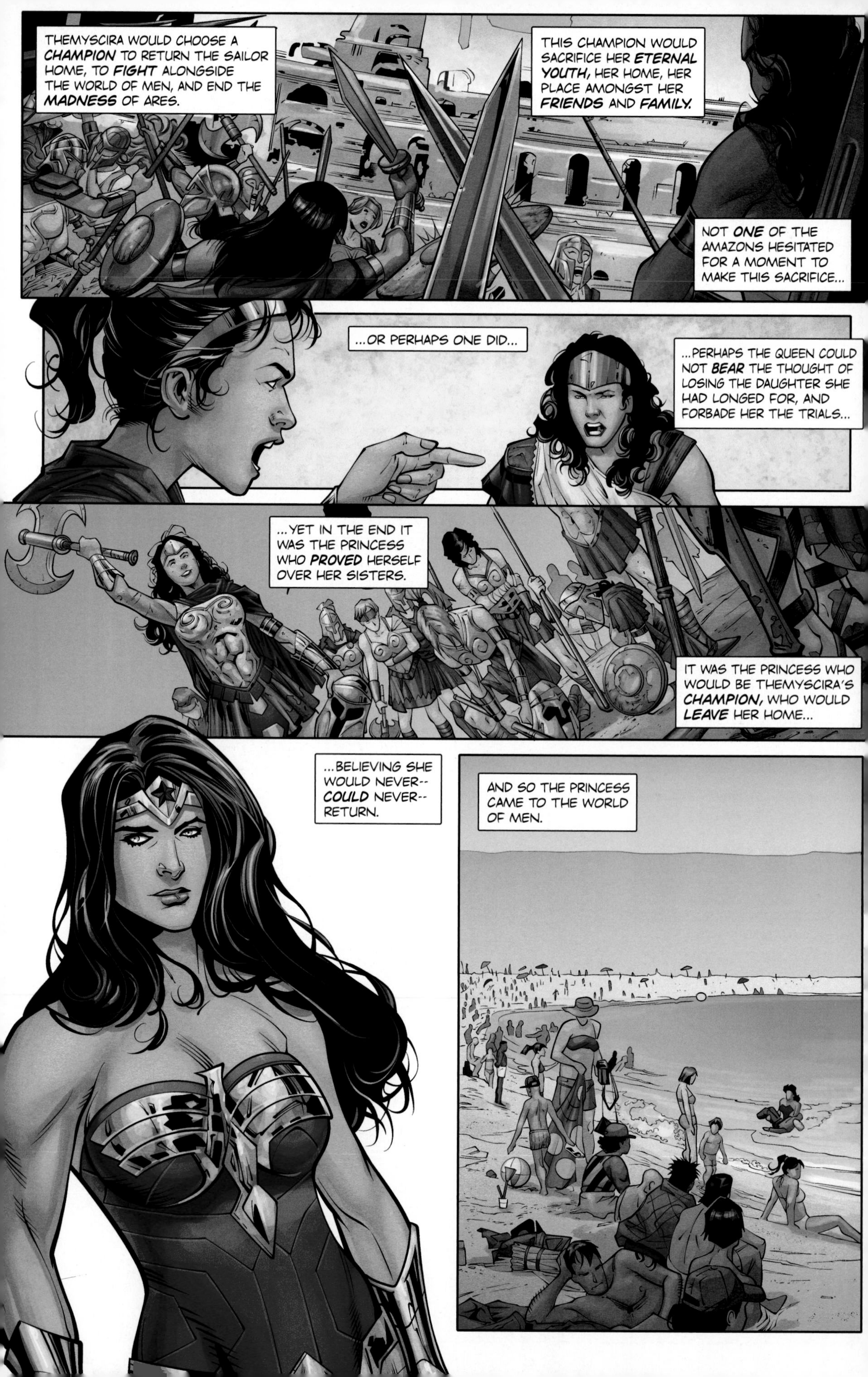
THEMYSCIRA WOULD CHOOSE A CHAMPION TO RETURN THE SAILOR HOME, TO FIGHT ALONGSIDE THE WORLD OF MEN, AND END THE MADNESS OF ARES.
THIS CHAMPION WOULD SACRIFICE HER ETERNAL YOUTH, HER HOME, HER PLACE AMONGST HER FRIENDS AND FAMILY.
NOT ONE OF THE AMAZONS HESITATED FOR A MOMENT TO MAKE THIS SACRIFICE...
...OR PERHAPS ONE DID...
...PERHAPS THE QUEEN COULD NOT BEAR THE THOUGHT OF LOSING THE DAUGHTER SHE HAD LONGED FOR, AND FORBADE HER THE TRIALS...
...YET IN THE END IT WAS THE PRINCESS WHO PROVED HERSELF OVER HER SISTERS.
IT WAS THE PRINCESS WHO WOULD BE THEMYSCIRA'S CHAMPION, WHO WOULD LEAVE HER HOME...
...BELIEVING SHE WOULD NEVER-- COULD NEVER-- RETURN.
AND SO THE PRINCESS CAME TO THE WORLD OF MEN.

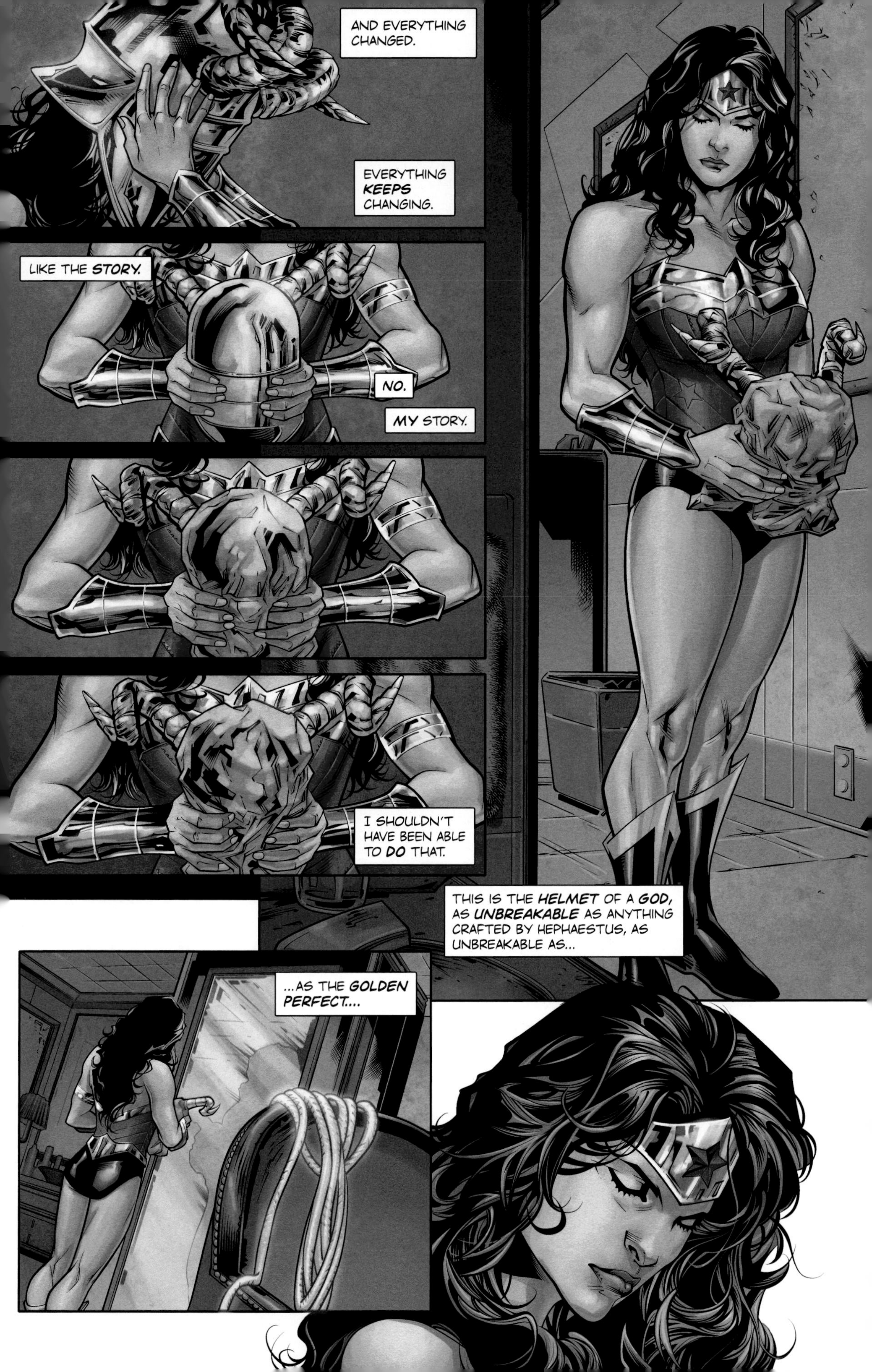
AND EVERYTHING CHANGED.
EVERYTHING KEEPS CHANGING.
LIKE THE STORY.
NO.
MY STORY.
I SHOULDN'T HAVE BEEN ABLE TO DO THAT.
THIS IS THE HELMET OF A GOD, AS UNBREAKABLE AS ANYTHING CRAFTED BY HEPHAESTUS, AS UNBREAKABLE AS...
...AS THE GOLDEN PERFECT....

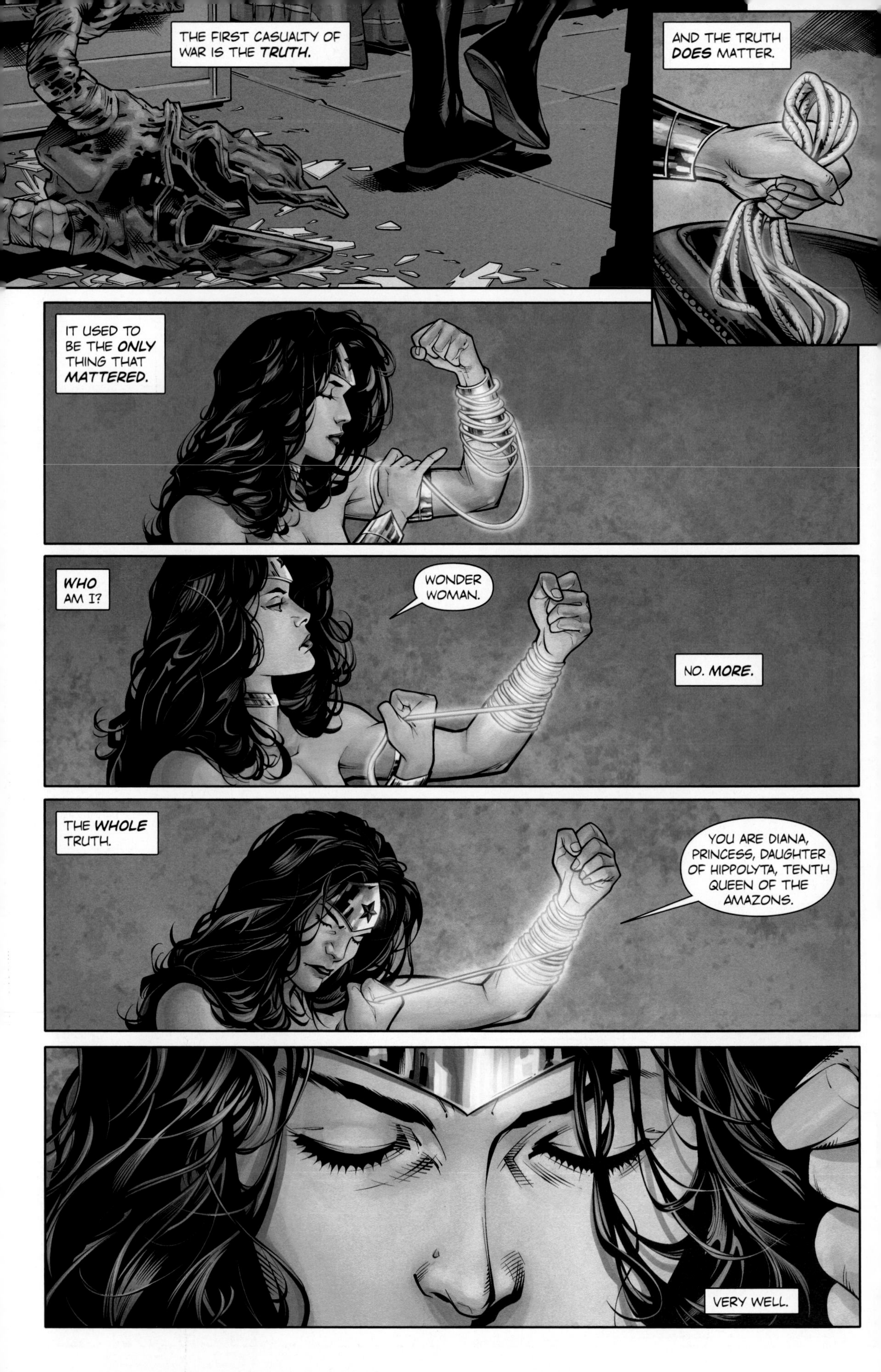
THE FIRST CASUALTY OF WAR IS THE TRUTH.
AND THE TRUTH DOES MATTER.
IT USED TO BE THE ONLY THING THAT MATTERED.
WHO AM I?
WONDER WOMAN.
NO. MORE.
THE WHOLE TRUTH.
YOU ARE DIANA, PRINCESS, DAUGHTER OF HIPPOLYTA, TENTH QUEEN OF THE AMAZONS.
VERY WELL.

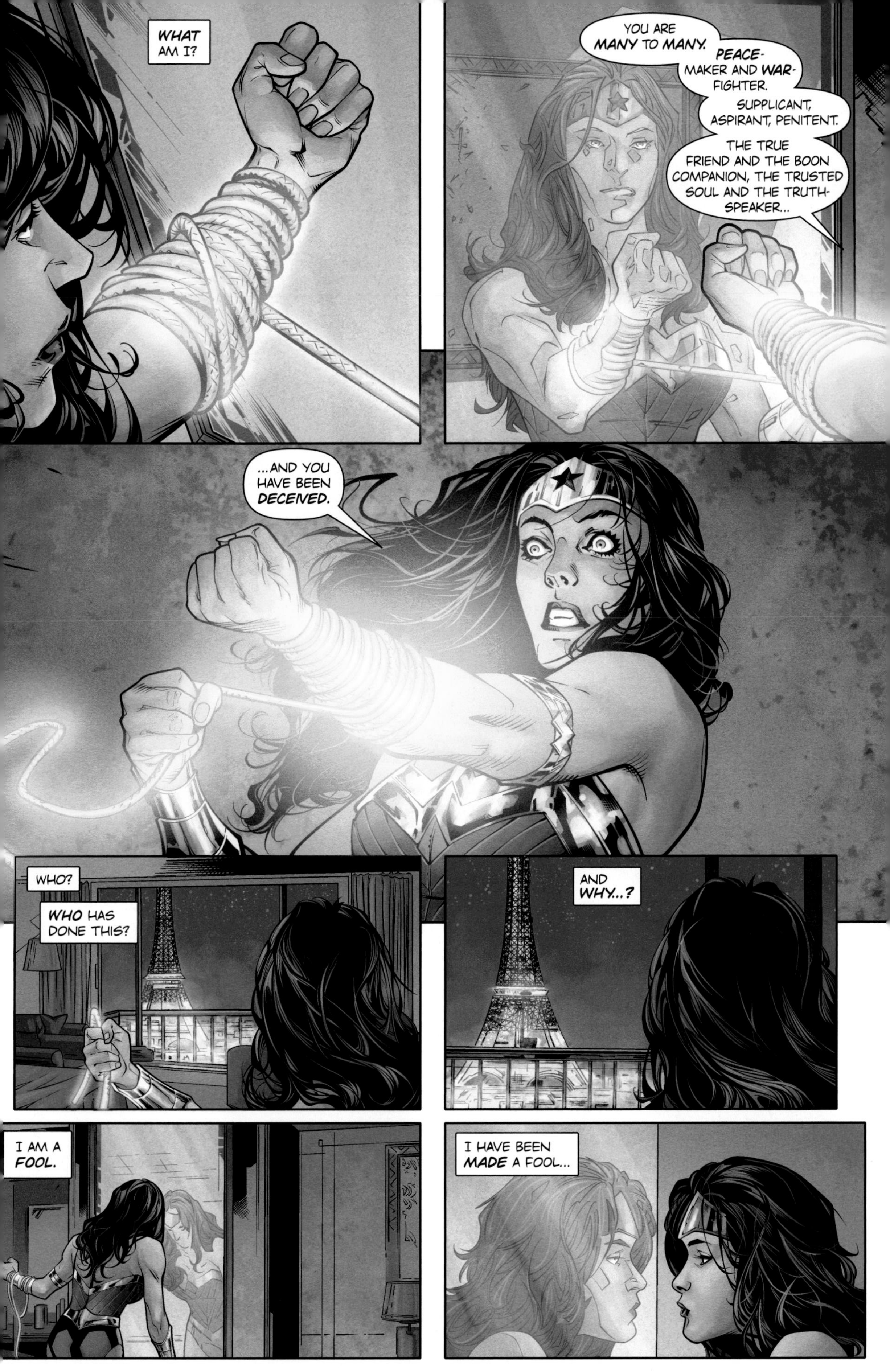
WHAT AM I?
YOU ARE MANY TO MANY.
PEACE-MAKER AND WAR-FIGHTER.
SUPPLICANT, ASPIRANT, PENITENT.
THE TRUE FRIEND AND THE BOON COMPANION, THE TRUSTED SOUL AND THE TRUTH-SPEAKER...
...AND YOU HAVE BEEN DECEIVED.
WHO?
WHO HAS DONE THIS?
AND WHY...?
I AM A FOOL.
I HAVE BEEN MADE A FOOL...

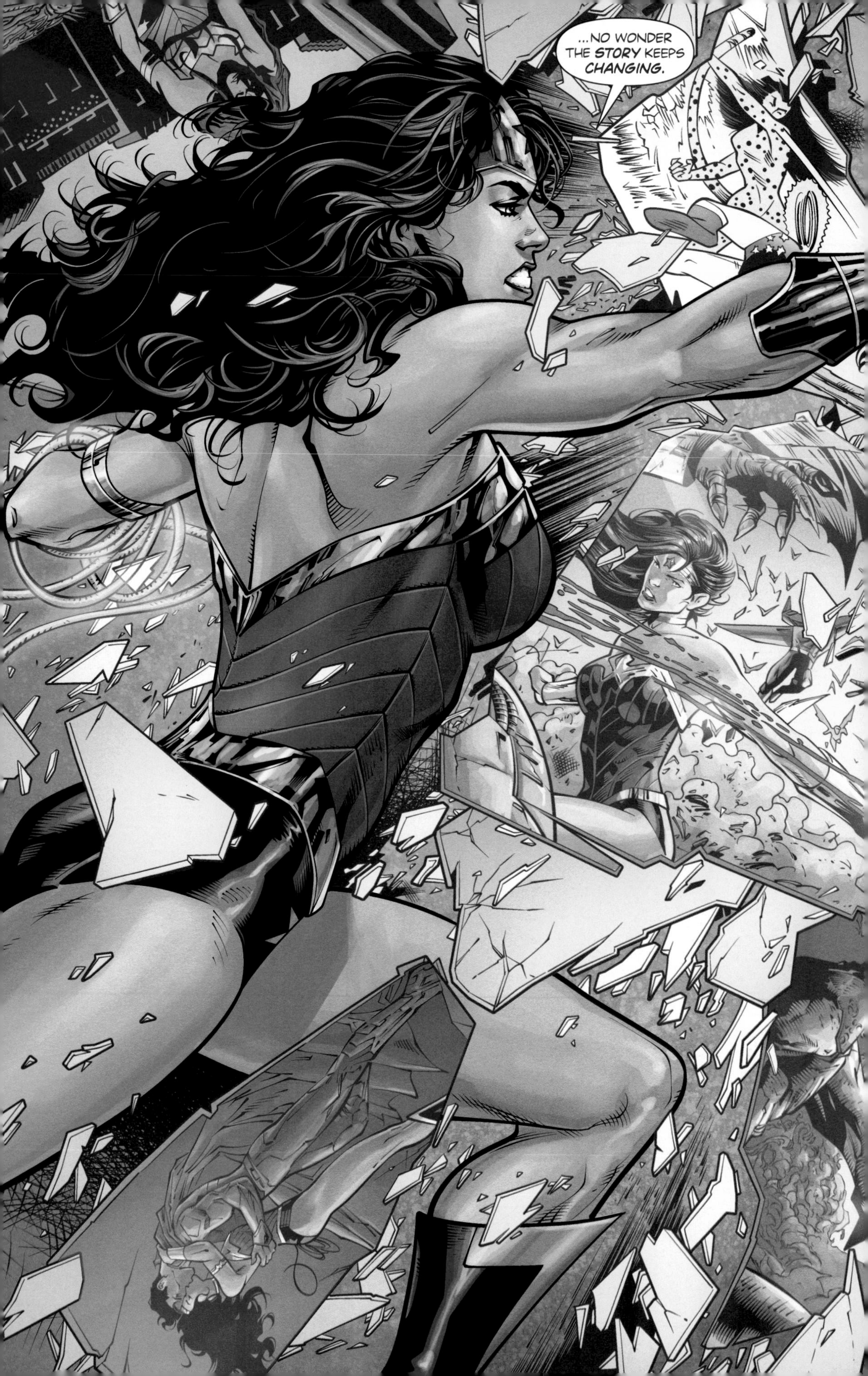
...NO WONDER THE STORY KEEPS CHANGING.

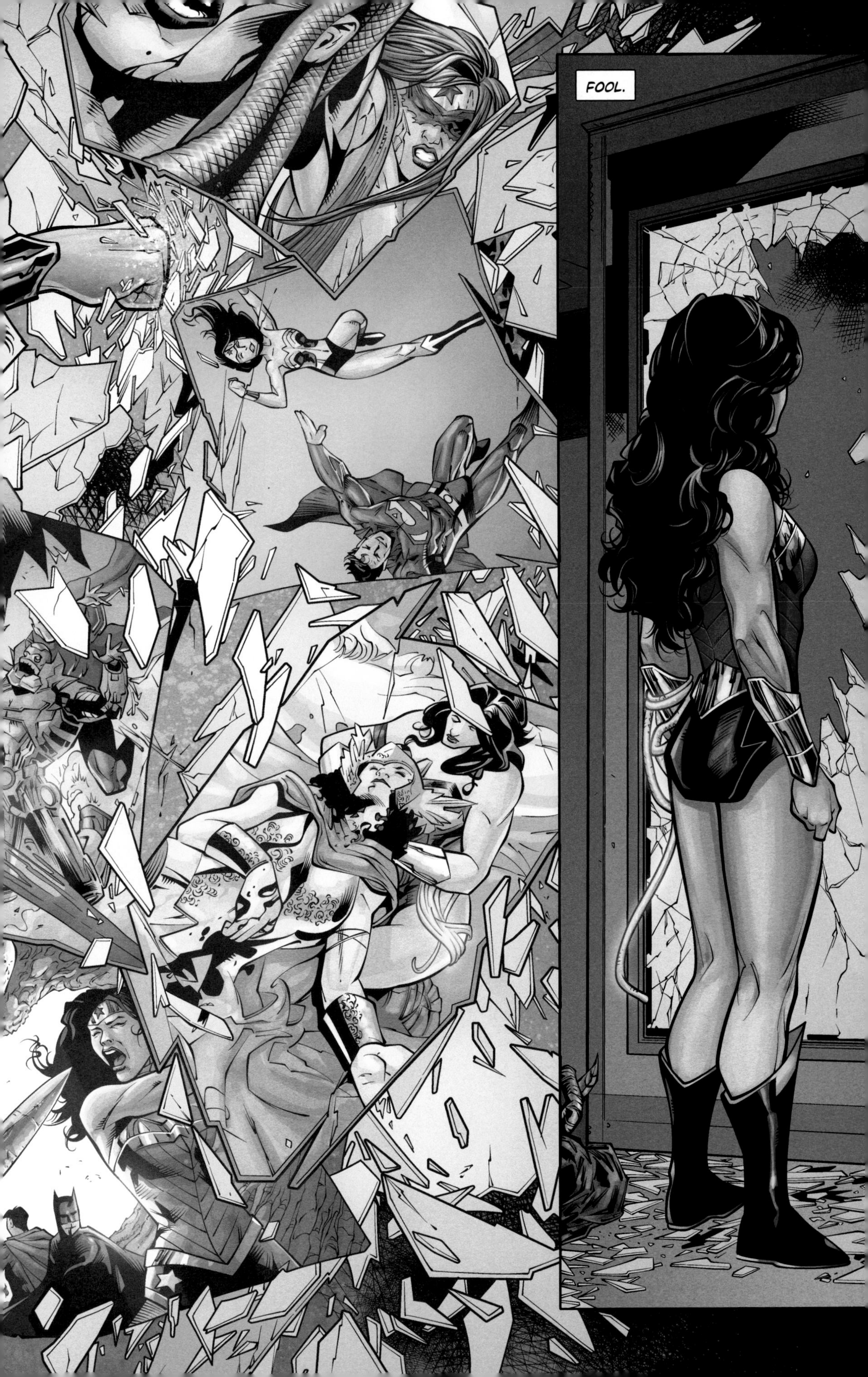
FOOL.

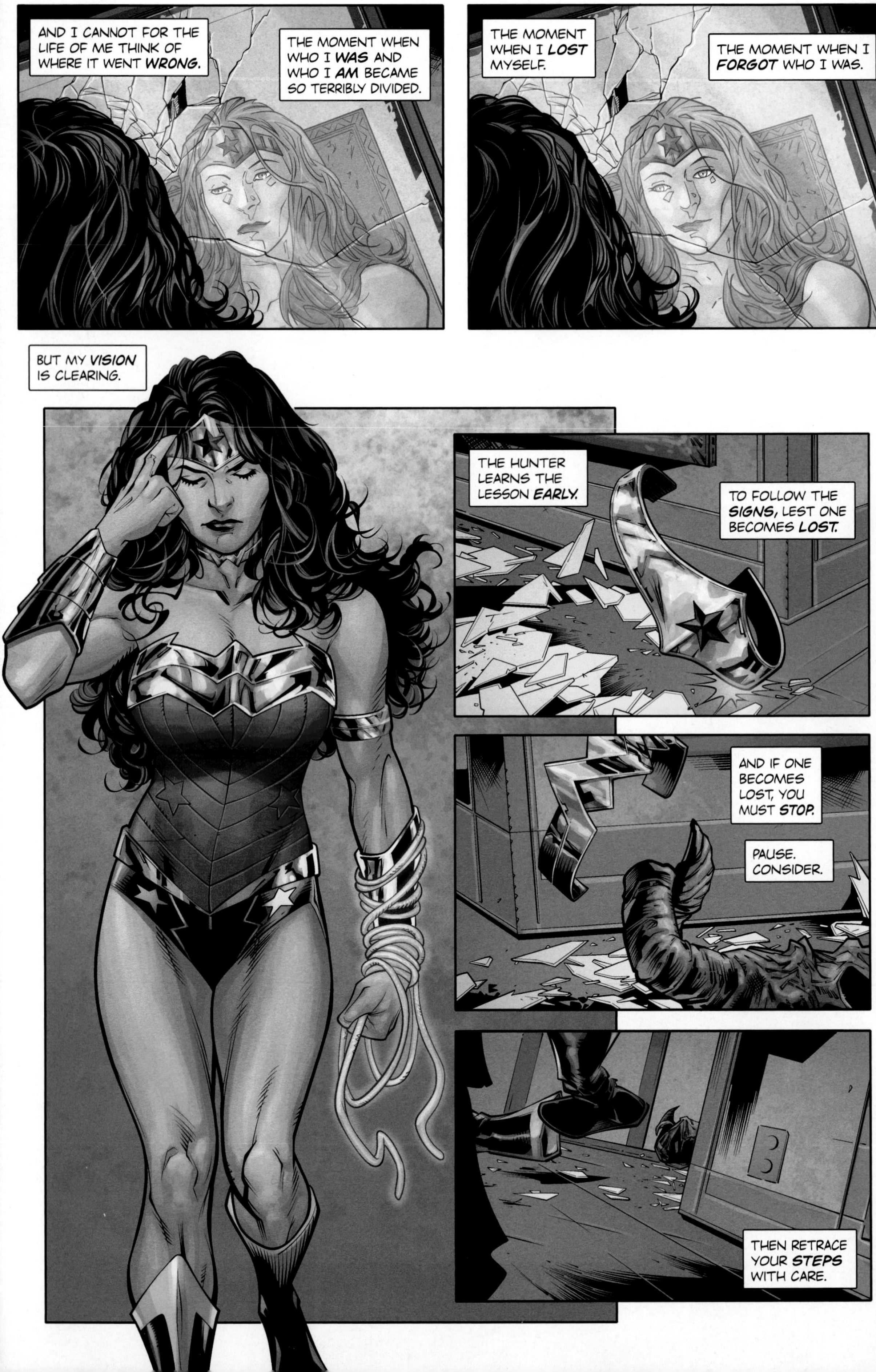

AND I CANNOT FOR THE LIFE OF ME THINK OF WHERE IT WENT WRONG.
THE MOMENT WHEN WHO I WAS AND WHO I AM BECAME SO TERRIBLY DIVIDED.
THE MOMENT WHEN I LOST MYSELF.
THE MOMENT WHEN I FORGOT WHO I WAS.
BUT MY VISION IS CLEARING.
THE HUNTER LEARNS THE LESSON EARLY.
TO FOLLOW THE SIGNS, LEST ONE BECOMES LOST.
AND IF ONE BECOMES LOST, YOU MUST STOP.
PAUSE. CONSIDER.
THEN RETRACE YOUR STEPS WITH CARE.

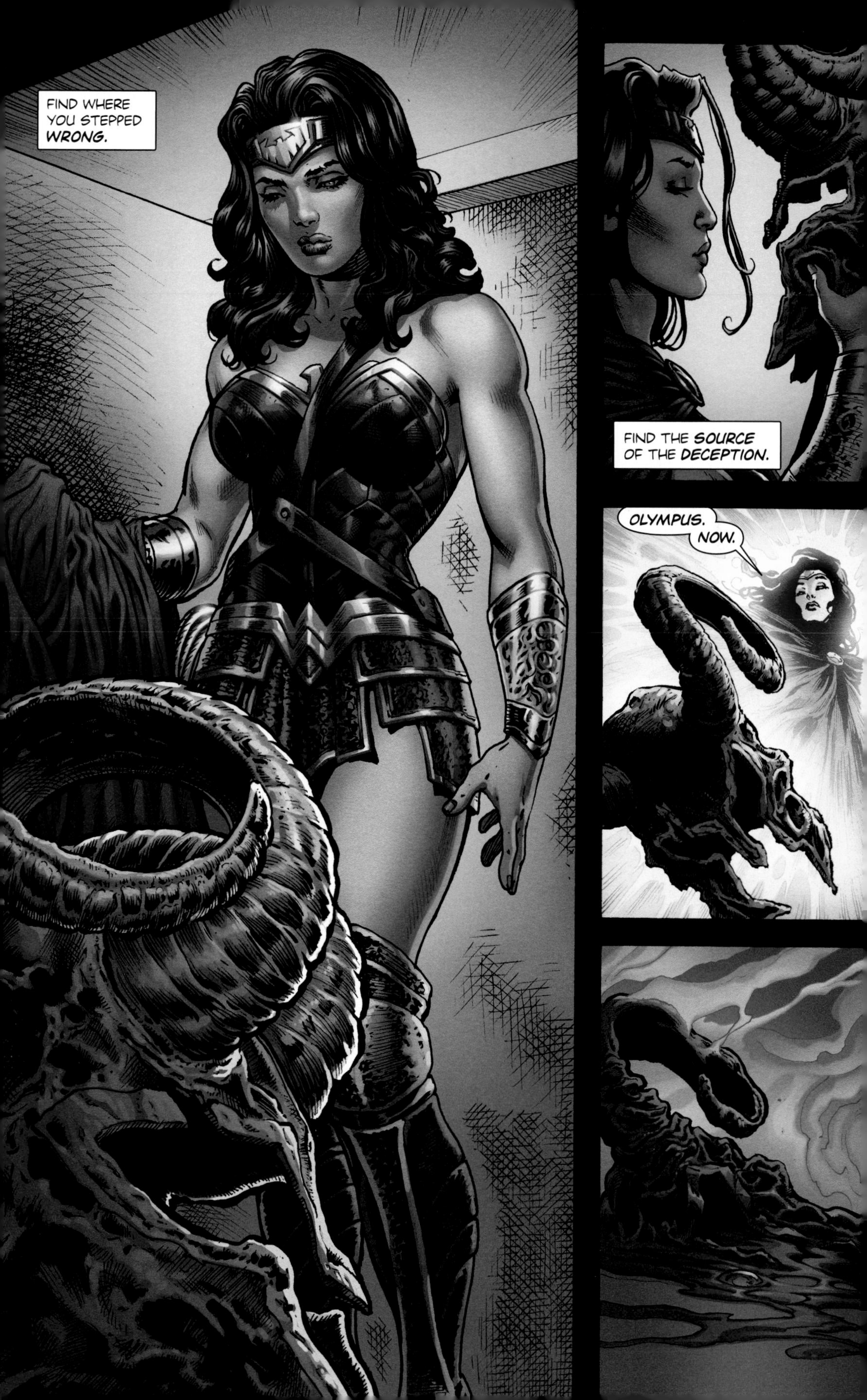
FIND WHERE YOU STEPPED WRONG.
FIND THE SOURCE OF THE DECEPTION.
OLYMPUS.
NOW.

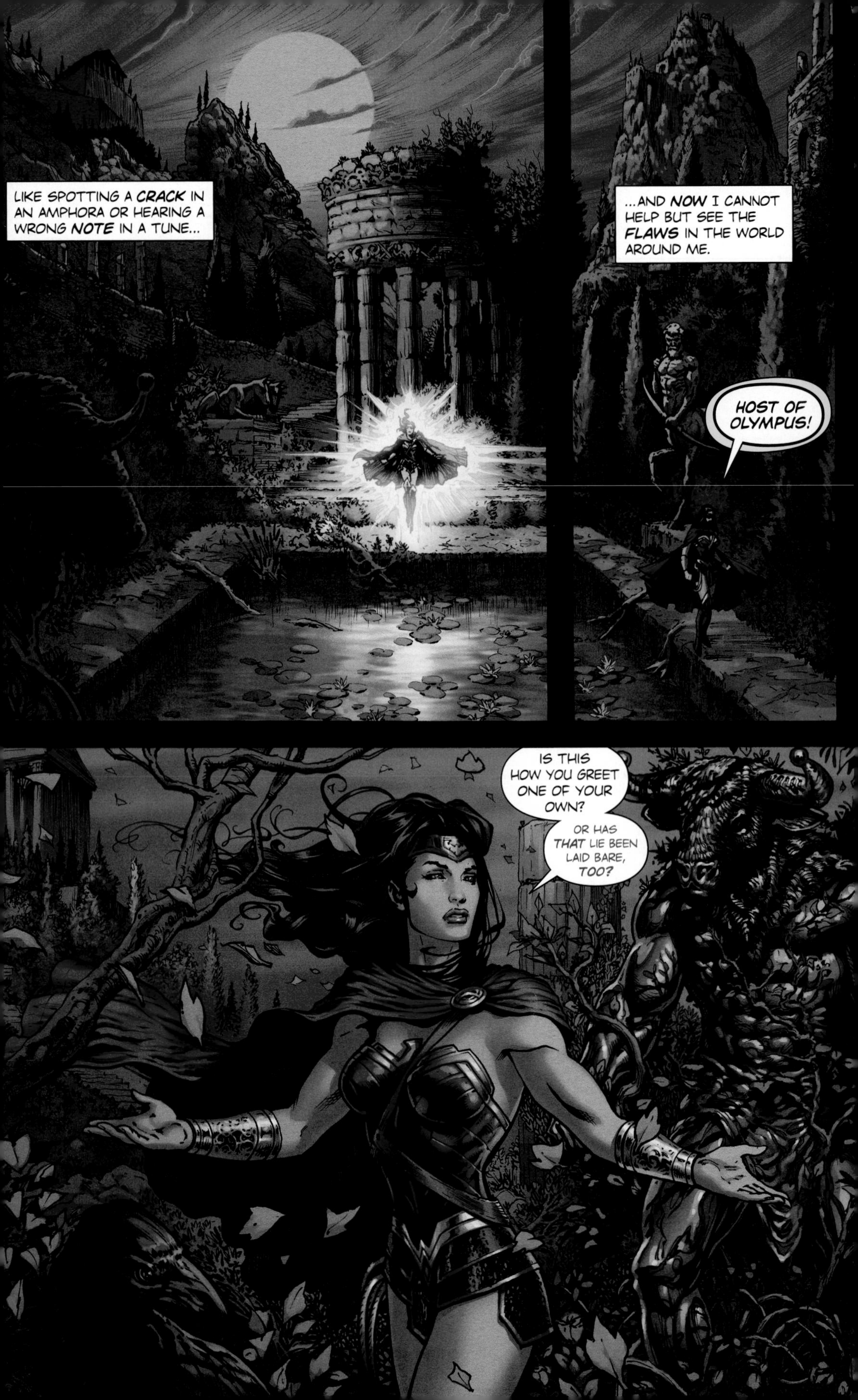

LIKE SPOTTING A CRACK IN AN AMPHORA OR HEARING A WRONG NOTE IN A TUNE...
...AND NOW I CANNOT HELP BUT SEE THE FLAWS IN THE WORLD AROUND ME.
HOST OF OLYMPUS!
IS THIS HOW YOU GREET ONE OF YOUR OWN?
OR HAS THAT LIE BEEN LAID BARE, TOO?

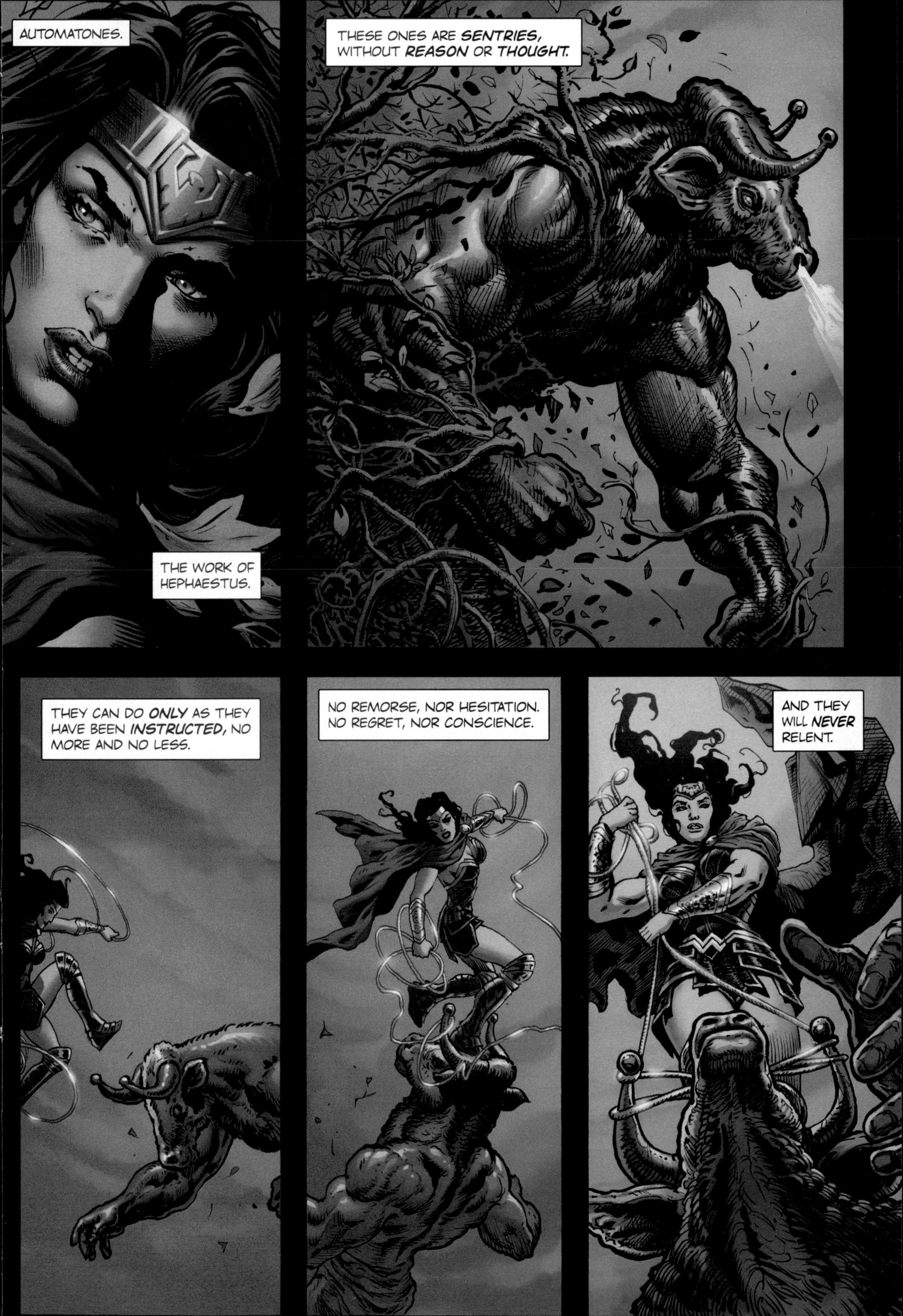
AUTOMATONES.
THE WORK OF HEPHAESTUS.
THESE ONES ARE SENTRIES, WITHOUT REASON OR THOUGHT.
THEY CAN DO ONLY AS THEY HAVE BEEN INSTRUCTED, NO MORE AND NO LESS.
NO REMORSE, NOR HESITATION. NO REGRET, NOR CONSCIENCE.
AND THEY WILL NEVER RELENT.

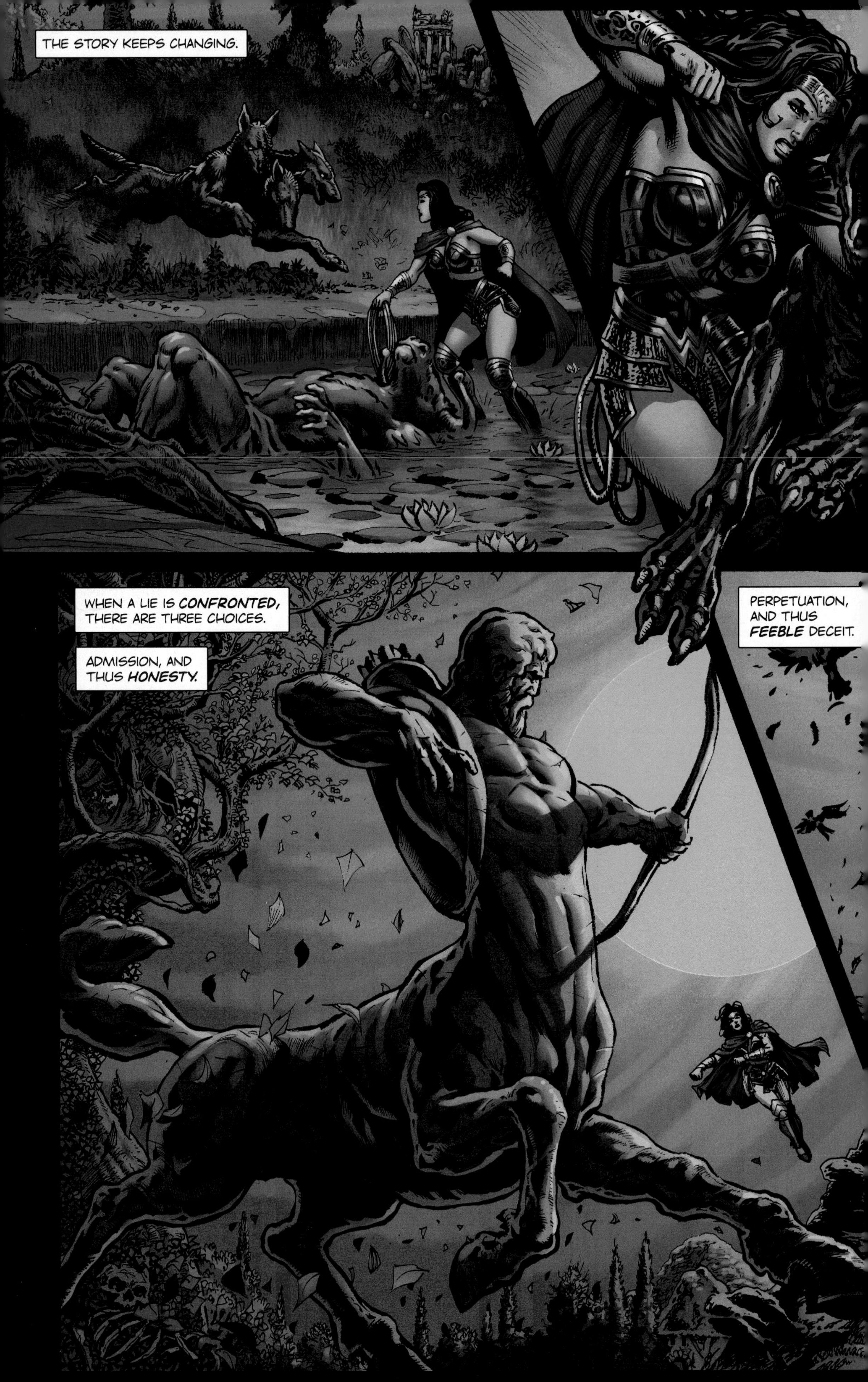
THE STORY KEEPS CHANGING.
WHEN A LIE IS **CONFRONTED,** THERE ARE THREE CHOICES.
ADMISSION, AND THUS **HONESTY.**
PERPETUATION, AND THUS **FEEBLE** DECEIT.

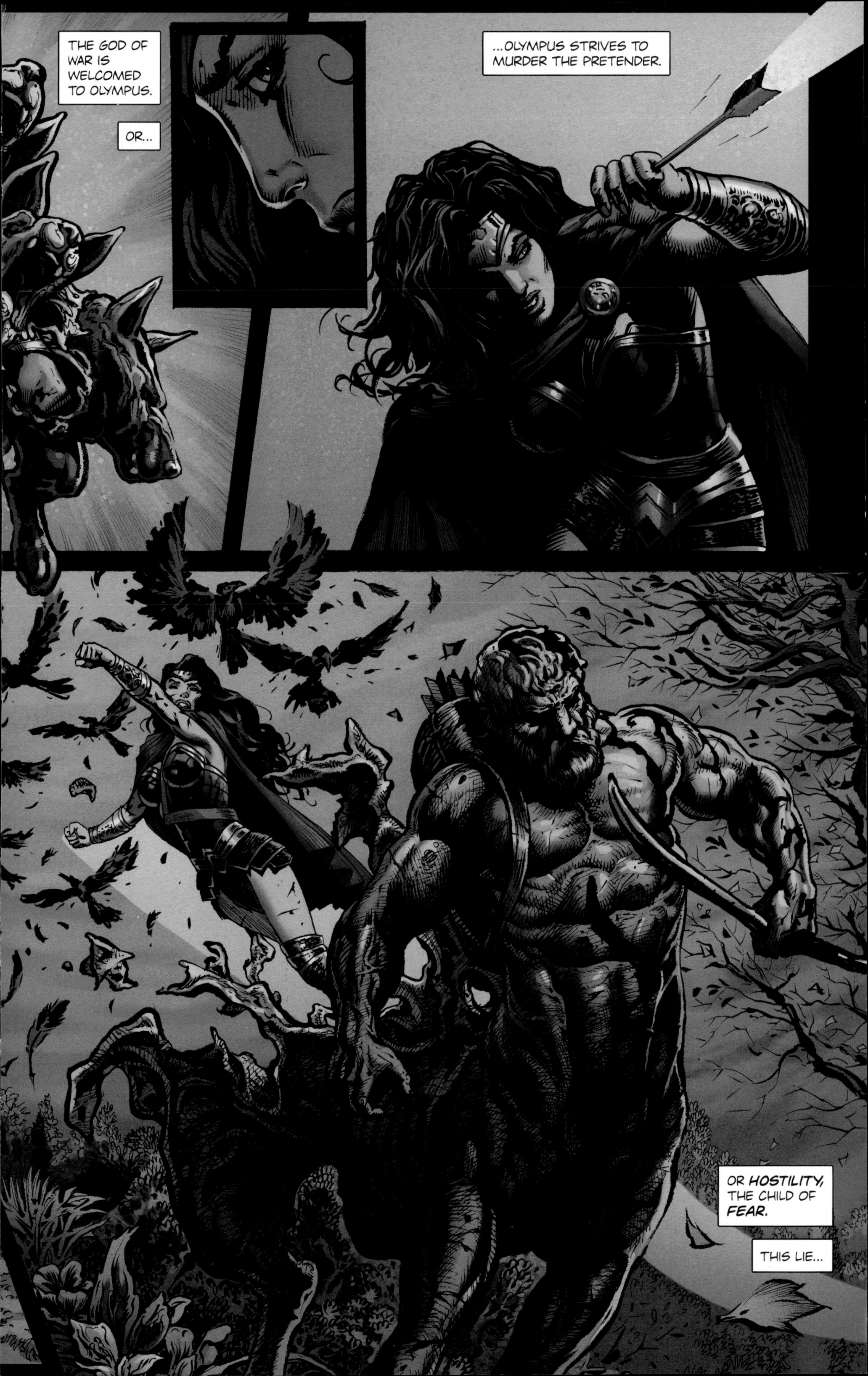
THE GOD OF WAR IS WELCOMED TO OLYMPUS.
OR...
...OLYMPUS STRIVES TO MURDER THE PRETENDER.
OR **HOSTILITY,** THE CHILD OF **FEAR.**
THIS LIE...

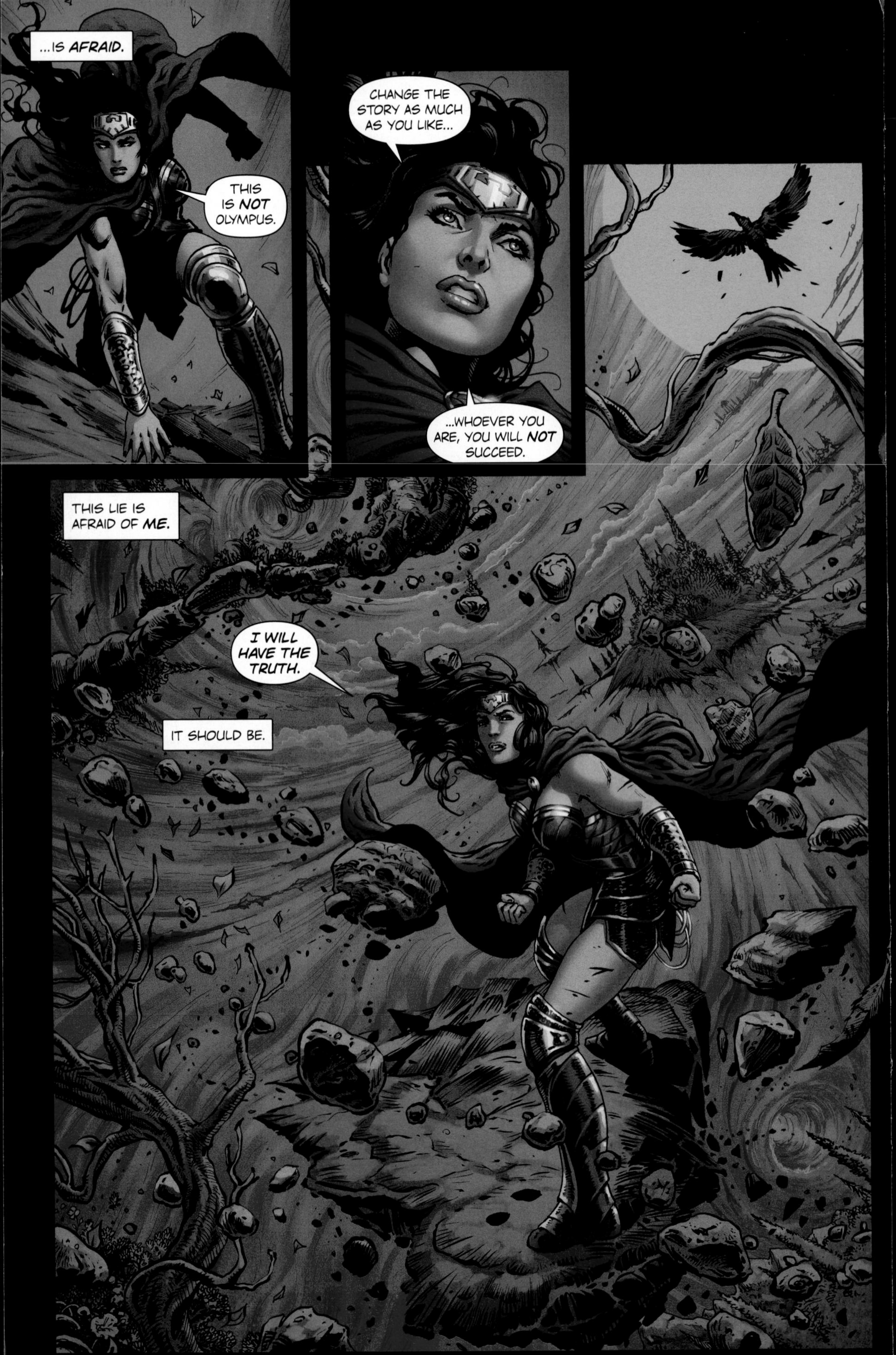
...IS **AFRAID.**
THIS IS **NOT** OLYMPUS.
CHANGE THE STORY AS MUCH AS YOU LIKE...
...WHOEVER YOU ARE, YOU WILL **NOT** SUCCEED.
THIS LIE IS AFRAID OF **ME.**
I WILL HAVE THE TRUTH.
IT SHOULD BE.

DC COMICS™

"Clear storytelling at its best. It's an intriguing concept and easy to grasp."—THE NEW YORK TIMES

"Azzarello is rebuilding the mythology of Wonder Woman."
—CRAVE ONLINE

START AT THE BEGINNING!

WONDER WOMAN VOLUME 1: BLOOD

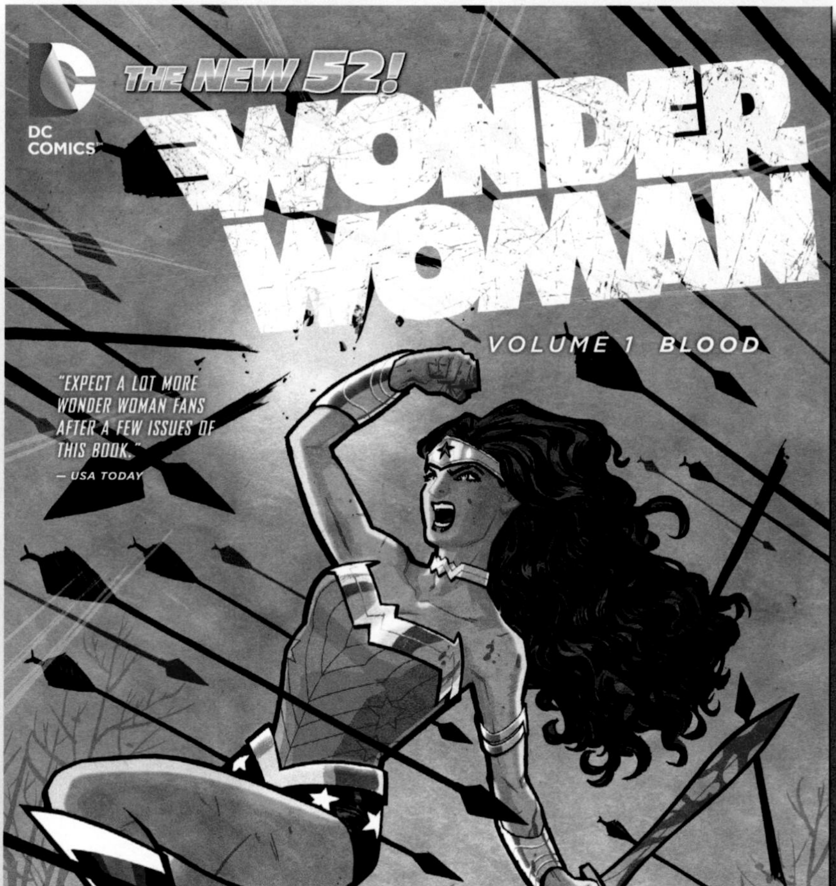
DC COMICS
THE NEW 52!
WONDER WOMAN
VOLUME 1 BLOOD
"EXPECT A LOT MORE WONDER WOMAN FANS AFTER A FEW ISSUES OF THIS BOOK."
— USA TODAY
BRIAN AZZARELLO CLIFF CHIANG TONY AKINS

WONDER WOMAN
VOL. 2: GUTS

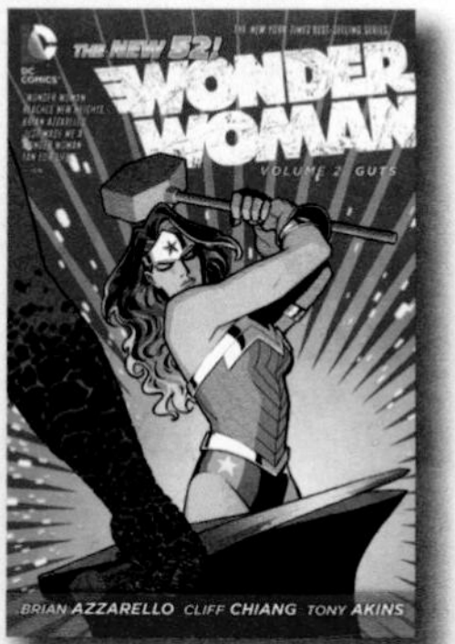
THE NEW 52!
WONDER WOMAN
VOLUME 2 GUTS
BRIAN AZZARELLO CLIFF CHIANG TONY AKINS

by BRIAN AZZARELLO and CLIFF CHIANG

WONDER WOMAN
VOL. 3: IRON

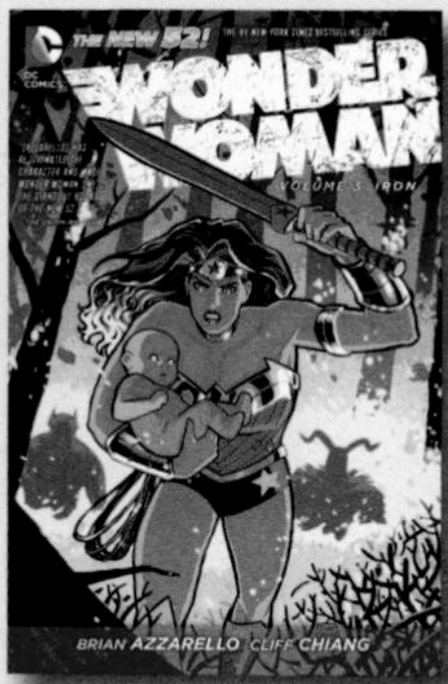
THE NEW 52!
WONDER WOMAN
BRIAN AZZARELLO CLIFF CHIANG

by BRIAN AZZARELLO and CLIFF CHIANG

SUPERGIRL VOL. 1:
LAST DAUGHTER OF KRYPTON

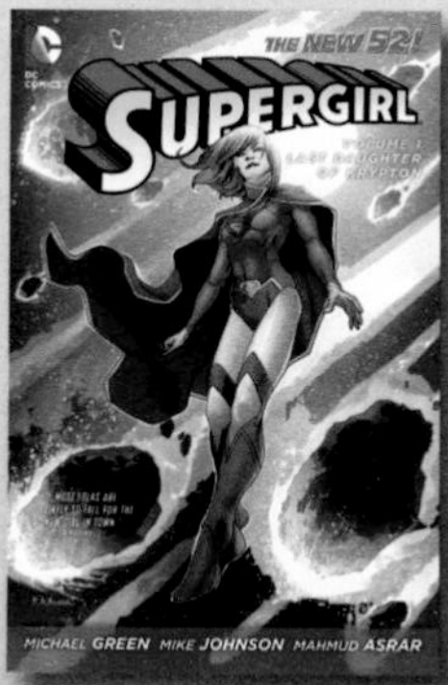
THE NEW 52!
SUPERGIRL
MICHAEL GREEN MIKE JOHNSON MAHMUD ASRAR

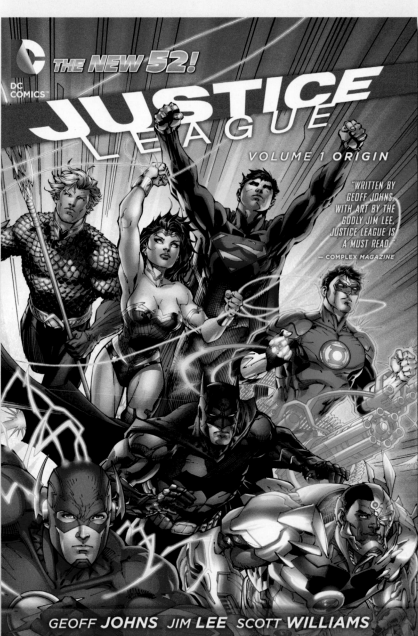